Bruce Canfield's Complete Guide to

The M1 Garand

AND

The M1 Carbine

Bruce N. Canfield

Bruce Canfield's Complete Guide to

The M1 Garand

AND

The M1 Carbine

Bruce N. Canfield

ANDREW MOWBRAY PUBLISHERS • P.O. BOX 460 • LINCOLN, RI 02865 USA

LIBRARY OF CONGRESS
CATALOG CARD NO: 98-066754
        Bruce N. Canfield
Lincoln, R.I.: ANDREW MOWBRAY INCORPORATED — *PUBLISHERS*
        pp. 296

ISBN: 0-917218-83-3

To receive our free catalog of books about arms collecting, or to order more copies of this book, call toll-free 1-800-999-4697.

This book was designed and set in type by Jo-Ann Langlois.

Printed in the United States of America.

10   9   8   7   6   5   4   3   2   1

This book is dedicated to my father, Charles K. Canfield,
who passed away on January 20, 1998.

Dad was a decorated combat veteran of World War II
who died exactly fifty-three years to the day after he was severely
wounded in the Rhineland Campaign in Southern Germany.
He was an inspiration to all who knew him.

Table of Contents

SECTION ONE: The M1 Garand

Table of Contents

Table of Contents

Preface

In the past decade or so since my first book, *A Collector's Guide to the M1 Garand and the M1 Carbine* was written, the interest in both weapons has increased by a phenomenal degree. Prior to the mid-1980s, the Garand and carbine were marginally popular as collector's items, and there was almost a feeling of "you've seen one, you've seen them all." However, as more information became available and as other more "traditional" collector's arms, such as Colts and Winchesters, began to be priced beyond the reach of the average collector, Second World War vintage weapons became increasingly popular. My book, as well as others, helped to fuel the growing interest in M1 rifles and carbines. Collector-oriented organizations like the Garand Collectors Association have come into existence in the past ten years. These organizations help disseminate information to collectors and those persons with an interest in the subject.

When I first began to write my original M1 book in 1986, it was my intent to give general information that would be helpful to the beginning collector as well as those who had been at it for a while. Since the body of knowledge about Garands and carbines has steadily increased over the years, I believe it is now time to revise and expand my original book. This affords me the opportunity to correct the errors contained in the first work and to elaborate and expand on areas only touched on previously. However, my original intent still has not changed. As experienced collectors are well aware, there is an extraordinary amount of data still unknown regarding the carbine and the Garand. As was the case with my original book, this work is intended to be a reasonably comprehensive guide aimed at the collector, or potential collector, who is interested in learning the basic aspects of the Garand and carbine.

There are some advanced collectors who may already possess all of the information (and more) contained in these pages. However, only a small fraction of collectors fall into this category. The complexity of the subject matter makes a 100 percent inclusive reference work on the subject unlikely to ever be published. Therefore, it is wise to acquire as many good reference sources on the subject as can be found. Unfortunately, there are several books and pamphlets currently on the market that provide rather questionable information. So especially recommended are *The M1 Garand: World War II* by Scott Duff and *War Baby* and *War Baby Returns Home* by Larry Ruth. Additionally, a book on the early Garand rifles is also being finalized by Garand authority Billy Pyle as this is written. These and other good books on the subject are listed in the bibliography.

Even with these good books currently available, I believe that my single volume containing information on the collecting aspects of both the Garand and carbine will prove of value to many collectors. Basic information is presented along with more detailed data. It is always difficult to strike a proper balance between presenting sufficient information and data to make a book of this sort worthwhile without delving into the most extreme minutiae of interest to only a small fraction of potential readers. As readers of my first book can readily see, this work goes into much greater detail. However, I have attempted to achieve a balance between giving more data and still presenting an interesting and readable book for even the casual collector or arms fancier. I am very pleased with the enormously positive response received by my first book and sincerely thank those who found it to be of interest. I hope those who enjoyed that book will, likewise, find this work useful and entertaining.

Bruce N. Canfield
Shreveport, LA
1997

Acknowledgments

As is always the case with projects such as this, many people have contributed to this book. Special thanks go to Billy Pyle, Konrad F. Schreier, Jr., Frank Mallory, Scott Duff, Bob Seijas, Larry Ruth, Dave McClain, Richard Deane, Dave Clark, John McCabe, Dru Bronson-Geoffroy, Mark A. Keefe, IV and my photographer, Scot Smith.

I would also like to thank my wife Betty for her patience and my son Andrew for his assistance and encouragement.

Another great debt of gratitude goes to Stuart Mowbray and the staff of Andrew Mowbray Publishers, Inc. for their professionalism and courtesy. Any author would be grateful for a publisher of this caliber, and I value our working relationship.

All items pictured not otherwise credited are from the author's collection.

E.E. Scherer, superintendent of firearms production, holding the Garand Rifle and Captain J.A. Gellatly, chief ordnance inspector at the Winchester Repeating Arms plant in New Haven, Connecticut, holding the new Winchester Carbine, are comparing these two famous gas-operated military weapons. The new Winchester Carbine is seven and one-half inches shorter and almost four and one-half pounds lighter than the Garand Rifle. Though gas operated like the Garand, the Winchester Carbine works on a new principle that takes the gas off much closer to the chamber before it cools. This prevents carbonizing of the piston. The Winchester Repeating Arms Company developed this carbine for the Army. It was chosen after exhaustive tests were given to five other types of short, light rifles. Note that the carbine depicted in the photo is a pre-production prototype with a 20-round magazine.

(Credit: Winchester Repeating Arms Company)

➤ ➤ ➤ ➤ ➤ ➤ ➤ ➤ ➤ ➤ ➤ Section One

The
M1
Garand

This photo speaks volumes about the day-to-day drudgery of the average GI during WWII. Even while taking a break, this soldier has his M1 rifle close at hand. Note the "locking bar" rear sight and the stamped triggerguard.

(Courtesy U.S. Army)

Introduction

As stated in the preface, the field of M1 rifle collecting has undergone a tremendous increase in interest and popularity. The resulting increase in demand has had the inevitable result of ever higher prices for collector-grade specimens of Garands as the available supply decreases. Another unfortunate, but probably unavoidable, consequence is the extreme number of bogus weapons now on the market. As the price of M1 rifles escalates, it becomes profitable for con artists to invest the time and money necessary to make fake weapons and/or parts. With collector-grade Garands now worth, in many cases, several thousand dollars each, the ability to detect bogus pieces is more important than ever. As always, the best defense available to the collector is knowledge. Until the mid-1980s, a collector's major concern was that the receiver of his M1 rifle was one of the "demilled" receivers that was salvaged by welding. Today, a collector is faced with myriad of potential problems, including the "imports," questionable restorations, "enhanced" stock cartouches and outright fake rifles. Most of these were not major concerns to the average collector a decade ago but are now serious issues that must be addressed before an informed decision on the legitimacy of a Garand can be ascertained with any degree of certainty.

Generally speaking, there are four major categories of M1s available to today's collectors:

(1) Original and unaltered M1s remaining in their factory "as issued" configuration

M1 Garand rifles of all vintages, particularly WWII and earlier, remaining in their original factory configuration, are surprisingly hard to find today and are highly sought after by collectors. Such rifles are, of course, the most desirable and valuable M1s on the collector market today.

(2) M1 rifles rebuilt (overhauled) by the U.S. government.

The primary reason for the scarcity of factory original M1 rifles is the fact that the vast majority of M1 rifles were (rebuilt) overhauled by a number of ordnance facilities from at least early 1941 and continuing at varying levels into the early 1970s. The purpose of the overhaul procedure was primarily to refurbish used rifles. Generally, the rifles were torn down and any worn, defective or superseded parts were replaced. In many cases, the weapons were reparkerized. A typical rebuilt M1 is a hodgepodge of miscellaneous parts of various manufacturers and vintages. The rifles were refurbished to "as new" specifications and hundreds of thousands were stored for subsequent use. Relatively large numbers of these weapons have been sold thorough the auspices of the Director of Civilian Marksmanship (DCM) which was subsequently renamed the Civilian Marksmanship Program (CMP). While most government rebuilt M1s are excellent shooters, relatively few have any substantive collector value. However, as we will discuss, some rifles of this type are legitimate collectible variants and have varying degrees of intrinsic collector value in their own right.

(3) M1 rifles that have been restored to approximate their original "as issued" configuration

Since the majority of M1 rifles seen today have been altered from their "as issued" configuration, it is logical that some collectors desire to "restore" such weapons back to their original factory configuration. This practice has gained a great amount of popularity in the past few years due to the rapidly increased demand for collectible specimens and the shortage of original condition Garands. However, as popular as the practice of restoration has become, it is fraught with misunderstanding and thorny ethical questions. We will discuss such questions like "when does restoration end and faking begin?" and "how should a restored rifle be judged?" The degree and quality of the restoration are paramount in determining the value and desirability of a restored rifle. Many rifles have been restored with no larceny in mind. However, the fact that a rifle has been restored may not be passed on to subsequent purchasers and one may be duped into acquiring a misrepresented rifle at an inflated price.

(4) The so-called "imports"

These are the weapons that were supplied to a number of foreign countries since WWII and were later acquired by commercial dealers and shipped back into the United States. Almost without exception, these weapons are in poor condition and are seldom suitable for collecting purposes "as is." A number of these weapons can be restored to some degree, and many others are valuable as sources of parts with which to restore other rifles. "Imports" have introduced many people on a limited budget to the field of Garand collecting and are gaining more and more acceptance as the supply of better conditioned M1s continues to decrease. An "import" is certainly better than no Garand at all.

The different variants of the M1 rifle will be examined in this book with particular emphasis on the aspects of interest to collectors, or potential collectors, of these arms.

➤ ➤ ➤ ➤ ➤ ➤ ➤ ➤ Historical Background ◄ ◄ ◄ ◄ ◄ ◄ ◄ ◄ ◄

Without question, the most widely used and one of the most effective semiautomatic military rifles of all time is the "U.S. Rifle, Caliber .30, M1". Popularly known as the "Garand" after its inventor, the M1 was widely used in World War II and Korea and remained the mainstay of the United States military until the early 1960s. During the Second World War, our allies and adversaries alike armed their infantrymen primarily with bolt action rifles little different than those fielded on the Western Front a quarter of a century earlier. Two belligerents did field a relatively small number of semiautomatic rifles during WWII. The German G41 and G43 and the Soviet Tokarev were produced and issued in limited numbers. Neither weapon was in the class of the M1. The Garand rifle provided the American GIs of WWII with a decided edge on the battlefield, and the weapon was universally popular with combat troops. Even when officially superseded by the M14 rifle in 1957, the M1 remained in service well into the 1970s. Its place as one of the best and most significant U.S. military weapons of all time is secure.

No discussion of the M1 rifle can be complete without a brief biographical study of the man behind the weapon. The story of the M1 rifle began with the birth of its inventor in January 1888. Jean (later anglicized to John) Cantius Garand was born on a small farm near St. Remi, Quebec (about twenty miles from Quebec City),

as the seventh of fourteen children. Young Garand's mother died when he was eight years old, and his family immigrated to the United States some three years later. The family eventually located in Jewett City, Connecticut, where John's father and several other family members found employment at Slater Textile Mill. John began working at the mill as a bobbin boy and floor sweeper but was quickly drawn to less mundane pursuits. He convinced a foreman to teach him the intricacies of the mill's machines. The lad demonstrated an interest in, and an aptitude for, mechanical objects and, by the age of fourteen, had designed an improved jackscrew. Other inventions flowed from his fertile mind including a novel bullet target backstop.

In addition to his love of machines, John Garand developed other passions as well. He reportedly spent a great deal of his spare time (in addition to a large portion of his disposable income) at shooting galleries. It has been reported that Garand spent over one hundred dollars at a Coney Island shooting arcade one Saturday afternoon while attracting a large crowd, which witnessed his amazing shooting ability. Garand also developed a love for ice-skating. In order to pursue this hobby, he once flooded his living room and allowed the water to freeze in order to have an indoor ice rink!

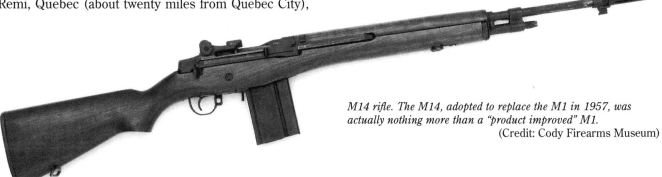

M14 rifle. The M14, adopted to replace the M1 in 1957, was actually nothing more than a "product improved" M1.
(Credit: Cody Firearms Museum)

John C. Garand.

(Credit: National Park Service,
Springfield Armory NHS, Springfield, Massachusetts)

John Garand eventually departed Slater Mill to take employment in Providence, Rhode Island. While in Rhode Island, Garand became fascinated with motorcycles and became an accomplished racer. John's mechanical ability enabled him to modify the engines for more power. Garand moved to New York City when his former employer experienced business difficulties due to a labor strike. While in New York, Garand noticed a newspaper article regarding the government's desire for an effective semiautomatic military rifle. He soon became intrigued with the idea of creating such a rifle. Garand procured a surplus M1903 rifle and tinkered with converting the bolt action arm into a self-loading weapon. Garand joined the National Guard on April 1, 1918, and was assigned to the First Field Artillery. He served in the Guard until discharged on May 20, 1919.

John Garand's ability attracted the attention of the government, and he accepted a job offer with the Bureau of Standards in Washington, D.C. The government was interested in an improved machine gun, and Garand was tasked with the project. However, the proven success during the First World War of John

Browning's machine gun design resulted in the focus of Garand's work being shifted to the development of a self-loading rifle. While working at the Bureau of Standards, Garand's efforts were observed by Douglas MacArthur. Garand was temporarily assigned to the National Armory at Springfield, Massachusetts, on November 4, 1919. Garand's temporary assignment was changed to permanent status on August 21, 1921.

Garand chose to utilize a rather novel primer actuated mechanism instead of the more conventional gas or recoil operated designs for his semiautomatic rifle. The first prototype rifle Garand designed at Springfield was tested in May of 1920. The design, which utilized either a 20- or 30-round detachable box magazine, showed much promise but further refinement was needed. Garand's second rifle showed substantial changes from his first prototype but the primer actuated mechanism was retained. The rifle had an internal magazine rather than the detachable type and was lighter and more compact. Garand's second design greatly impressed the Ordnance Department, and twenty-four were fabricated by Springfield Armory in March of 1922 for field testing by the infantry and cavalry.

While John Garand was perfecting his designs, another noted arms designer, John D. Pedersen, was also working at Springfield on the quest for a semiautomatic service rifle. Pedersen and Garand were working concurrently on the same project but tackled the job using substantially different designs. The two were friendly (or by some accounts not so friendly) rivals and each undoubtedly pushed the other to strive for perfection.

While Garand's experimental rifles were chambered for the standard U.S. .30 caliber cartridge, Pedersen focused on the use of a ballistically improved (in the eyes of some) .276 caliber cartridge. Pedersen's rifle had the handicap of requiring lubricated ammunition.

In 1926, ten of Garand's newest model rifle and ten of the Pedersen-designed rifles were tested at Ft. Benning in Georgia. Garand's design was very similar to the type tested in 1922 but had improved sights. Although further development work was needed on both weapons, the Garand and Pedersen rifles fared well in the tests.

However, soon after the 1926 tests, Garand was forced to abandon his primer actuated mechanism due to a change from the M1906 to the M1 cartridge by the government. Garand went back to the drawing board, literally, and designed a gas operated rifle that utilized a muzzle cap to trap the gas needed to operate the mechanism. This concept was similar to the Danish Bang rifle previously tested by the U.S. government. Garand's new gas operated rifle was given the designation "T3" by the Ordnance Department.

The T3 Garand rifle proved to be a sound design and performed well in preliminary tests. In December of 1927, however, the government once again forced John Garand to alter his design by directing him to modify his rifle to the same .276 cartridge utilized with the Pedersen rifle. Garand rather reluctantly rechambered his rifle for the new cartridge, and the modified design was designated as the "T3E2."

In spring of 1931, twenty .276 caliber T3E2 Garand rifles were made at Springfield Armory and sent for field testing along with a like number of .276 Pedersen rifles. After exhaustive tests, the Garand design won out over the Pedersen, and the way seemed clear for adoption of the .276 Garand rifle.

Once again, Garand was forced to make a change in his design. General Douglas MacArthur disapproved adoption of the .276 caliber cartridge due to questions about its overall effectiveness and the vast stocks of .30 caliber ammunition still in the government's inventory. Garand probably wasn't too displeased with the turn of events as he felt the .30 caliber round was superior to the .276. It was a relatively simple matter for Garand to reconfigure his rifle for the .30 caliber (".30-06") cartridge.

The modified rifle was designated as the "T1E2," and in March of 1932, Springfield Armory was directed to produce eighty rifles of this pattern for thorough testing and evaluation. These eighty rifles were fabricated under John Garand's personal direction in Springfield's model shop. For obvious reasons, these rifles are colloquially known today as "Model Shop" rifles.

On August 3, 1933, the rifle's "T1E2" designation was formally changed to "U.S. Semiautomatic Rifle, Caliber .30, M1." This official nomenclature change reflected the War Department's recently adopted policy of using the "Model" ("M") designation for a weapon rather than the year of adoption as had been the previous practice. The first rifle adopted (or considered for adoption) under the new system was given the designation of "M1" (**Model** Number 1"). It should be noted that there is not a dash between M and 1. References to the "M-1" rifle are technically incorrect; the proper designation is M1.

The M1 rifle utilized an "en bloc" loading system. A sheet metal clip holding eight rounds was inserted into the rifle. After the last round was fired, the empty clip was ejected from the rifle, and the bolt remained open

and ready to be reloaded. As will be discussed later, this method of operation had some drawbacks, but it allowed a relatively streamlined rifle without a magazine protruding from the bottom.

The eighty Model Shop rifles were completed in May of 1934, and 50 were sent to the infantry and 25 to the cavalry for field testing. After these preliminary field tests, the rifles were returned to Springfield for modification and overhaul. In May of 1935, the Model Shop rifles were again issued for further tests, which were completed in October of the same year. The results of the tests were overwhelmingly positive, and the rifle was recommended for formal adoption by the U.S. Army. This recommendation was officially approved on January 9, 1936. By the time of the official adoption, however, the nomenclature of the weapon was changed to "U.S. Rifle, Caliber .30, M1." Although never an official term, the M1 rifle became universally known, in and out of the service, as the Garand. This was a fitting honor to the man who labored so long and diligently to give his adopted country the finest service rifle available.

When the M1 rifle was adopted, each part was assigned a "drawing number" which had a letter prefix ("A" through "F") that denoted the size of the part and a number that identified the specific part. When a part was revised, a revision number was generally added to the drawing number. These drawing numbers are very important when determining the originality of a rifle and will be examined in detail later.

Despite the tremendous success of his rifle, Mr. Garand did not become a wealthy man, and lived on his $5,500 annual government salary. Shortly after WWII, a bill was introduced in Congress to award John Garand $100,000 in recognition of his efforts. However, the bill did not pass, and Garand received no monetary benefits for the invention of his rifle beyond his modest salary. John Garand continued his employment at Springfield Armory until his well-deserved retirement on April 30, 1953. Following his retirement, Garand lived in Springfield, Massachusetts, tending his blueberry patch and enjoying a regular game of checkers. He passed away on February 16, 1974, at the age of 86.

Always the perfectionist, John Garand was never totally satisfied with his rifle. Throughout the M1's WWII production run (and afterward), Garand continued his efforts to improve his original invention. Virtually every part of the M1 was modified to some extent in order to improve performance or speed production time. Many of these changes, such as the incorporation of a new type of

An interestingly posed photo depicting M1 rifles with fixed M1905 bayonets. Close examination will reveal that the rifles are the early gas trap type.
(Credit: U.S. Army)

gas system (to be discussed later), were quite noteworthy, while others were rather subtle in nature. Each of these changes, to some extent, made a good weapon better.

In 1939, the Winchester Repeating Arms Company was given a contract to produce the M1 rifle, and the firm produced over a half million Garands before termination of its contract in 1945.

At the end of WWII, the M1 was firmly established as the standard by which all other military service rifles of the time were measured. Production of the M1 rifle ceased with the conclusion of the Second World War. During the late 1940s, the Springfield Armory concentrated primarily on overhauling and refurbishing many of the four million Garand rifles in the government's inventory. However, with the onset of the Korean War in 1950, Springfield again tooled up for new production of the M1. A couple of years later, two other firms, Harrington & Richardson and International Harvester, began production of the M1 rifle as well.

In addition to the service rifles, several other variants of the M1 were produced, including telescopic-sighted sniper rifles and specially crafted National Match versions.

All of the subsequent variants of the M1 rifle were a tribute to the genius of John Garand's original design. Even the Garand's successor, the M14, was essentially nothing more than a product improved M1.

From the time of the M1's adoption until production ceased in 1957, there were innumerable changes, both large and small, made to the weapon. As stated, these changes were generally done to improve the rifle's effectiveness or to make production faster and/or cheaper. Some of the changes were significant enough to warrant classification as an identifiable variant of the M1 rifle, while other changes were extremely minor in nature. Even the most esoteric of these changes are of interest to today's collectors especially in determining if a particular rifle remains in its original configuration or has been altered. In some cases, the difference between an original M1 and one that has been altered (even if subsequently restored) can be thousands of dollars. Since most of the nearly six million M1 rifles made have been overhauled ("rebuilt") by the government since their manufacture, it is extremely important for a collector, or potential collector, to be able to ascertain the originality (or lack thereof) of any particular M1 that may be encountered.

> > > > > **Components** < < < < < < < < < <

Before the specific variations of the M1 can be discussed, some information on the various components of the rifle is needed. This section will detail the major changes and the approximate time period or serial number range in which they were introduced. It must be stressed that these are usually estimates and some overlap in the use of early and later parts almost invariably occurred. Close attention should be paid to the configuration of the various parts as this information is vital when determining the originality or correctness of a particular M1. It should also be noted that not every single component of the M1 is profiled. The parts examined are primarily those that are most important when evaluating a particular rifle. As we will discuss, there were differences in the configuration of the parts as well as the markings. Seemingly minor details can easily spell the difference between an incorrect and an original rifle. The various parts examined are grouped into Receiver Group (including barrel, gas system, etc.), Trigger Housing Group and Stock Group (including handguards). For the sake of continuity, these parts are not necessarily grouped in accordance with the official categories as found in the government technical manuals.

WWII M1 Garand rifle fitted with M7 grenade launcher and M1907 sling.

Receiver/Barrel Group

Receiver

Actually, the receiver underwent fewer readily observable changes than most of the major components of the M1. The original "Model Shop" rifles are characterized by an angular "V"-shaped area between the receiver legs. By the time the first production M1 rifles were made, the legs were changed to the now familiar square configuration.

The shape of the rear portion of the bolt recess differed in early and later production Springfield Armory M1s. Prior to approximately serial number 50,000, the receivers were square in this area then changed to a rounded shape. Winchester used the square-shaped bolt recess much longer than Springfield, not changing until circa early 1944. The post-WWII receivers (manufactured by Springfield, International Harvester and Harrington & Richardson) were all of the rounded variety.

There were also differences found in the area of the receiver behind the rear sight. These will be discussed primarily in the section covering the Winchester M1.

As we will subsequently discuss regarding the "gas trap" rifles, early receivers had a bevel on the front guide rib, inside the receiver, which caused some functioning problems. This was corrected at about the same time that the bolt recess shape was changed. The early receivers were then modified during overhaul by adding a spot of welding to the beveled guide rib to build it up to the proper contour.

The receivers were stamped with the name of the manufacturer and serial number behind the rear sight. The drawing number, manufacturer's initials and (generally) the heat lot number were stamped on the right front leg of the receiver. Some variances in the format of the receiver markings will be found. These will be discussed in the sections under the individual variations.

One fairly common feature seen on some WWII (and earlier) vintage M1 receivers is a noticeable "two tone" appearance at the rear. During the war, it was found that the bolt could crack the rear of the receiver, particularly when firing rifle grenades. In order to strengthen the receiver in this area it was dipped in molten lead. This procedure was done at the factory for a brief period of time until the metallurgy specifications were changed to reduce this problem. Many of the earlier receivers were annealed in this manner, thus producing the two tone effect. Except for the relatively few receivers done at Springfield circa 1943, this feature is a sign that the receiver has gone through a modification process.

From a collecting viewpoint, the receiver should be closely examined to be certain that it is not one of the receivers that was "demilled" and subsequently welded back together. These are often referred to as "re-welds" but, as one student of the subject put it, "How it be a 're-weld' when it wasn't welded to begin with" Good point. Anyway, a discolored line or area on the receiver should be cause for concern as the welded portion will not show the same tint of parkerizing as the rest of the receiver.

Bolt

Early production (up to early 1940) Springfield bolts did not have a hole on the bottom as found on all later production rifles, including those made by IHC and H&R. Early Winchester bolts also lacked this hole until around mid-1941.

Bolts were stamped on top with the drawing number and, normally, the heat lot number. Except for very early Springfields, the initials of the manufacturers were also stamped on the bolt.

Firing Pin

When originally adopted, the M1's firing pin had a fully rounded profile. In very late 1941, Springfield changed to an improved firing pin with half of the body milled out ("flat body" configuration). Some early firing pins were modified to the later configuration. Winchester also changed to the later type of firing pin several months after Springfield. Winchester firing pins will often have a roughly machined finish and exhibit a punch mark. All post-WWII firing pins were of the flat body variety. Some very late production firing pins were made with a chromed plated tip to help reduce corrosion. Early firing pins were blued but the majority were parkerized. Interestingly, some early round firing pins show up from time to time in rifles long after the change in configuration took place. This is undoubtedly due to the practice of using up superseded, but still functional, parts on hand.

Rear Sight

There were three basic variants of rear sights used with the M1 rifle. As originally adopted, the rear sight utilized a spanner nut (a.k.a. "flush nut") that held the adjustment of the sight. These sights were found not to always hold this adjustment well, and the spanner nut was replaced by a "locking bar," which could be securely tightened by hand. This modification came into use circa very late 1942. After a short period, the rear sight's pinion was lengthened. A slightly modified locking bar

Text continued on page 25

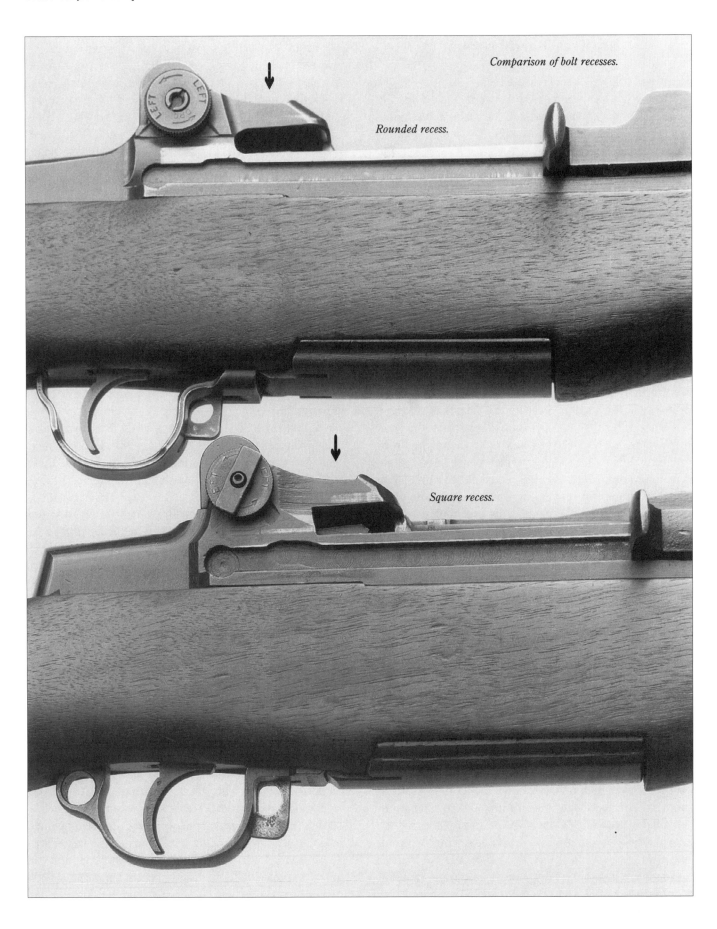

Comparison of bolt recesses.

Rounded recess.

Square recess.

(Above, left) Receiver markings on Springfield Armory M1 as manufactured circa November 1943. (Above, right) Receiver markings on Winchester M1 rifle as manufactured circa July 1942.

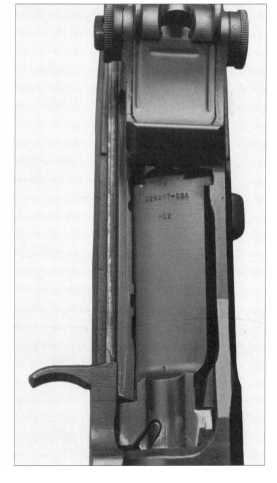

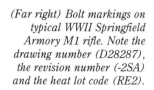

(Right) Bolt markings on Winchester M1 rifle. Note the lack of heat lot codes.

(Far right) Bolt markings on typical WWII Springfield Armory M1 rifle. Note the drawing number (D28287), the revision number (-2SA) and the heat lot code (RE2).

M1 Rifle rear sights.
(Top) Post-WWII T105E1 sight.
(Middle) WWII "locking bar" sight.
(Bottom) Early sight with spanner nut.

Soldier in WWII talking on a field telephone with his M1 rifle close at hand. Note the milled triggerguard and "locking bar" rear sight.

(Credit: U.S. Army)

Text continued from page 21

remained in use with the longer pinion. Winchester used the early sights with the spanner nut into early 1943.

Near the end of WWII, the "T105E1" rear sight was introduced. This sight had an improved locking mechanism that eliminated the need for the manual locking bar. Very few, if any, of these sights were used before the end of WWII on production M1s, although the rifles subsequently overhauled were fitted with T105E1 sights. The post-WWII manufacturers used this type of sight exclusively. There were differences in the type of checkering or grooves used on the sight knobs. These variances and marking formats will be explored later. There were also differences between Springfield and Winchester rifles in the configuration of the rear sight aperture.

The rear sight base on early production rifles had three distinct radius cuts and rings by the pinion hole. These early bases were stamped with drawing numbers. The radius cuts and rings were eliminated by Springfield

fairly early in production. Winchester rear sight bases had the radius area but did not have the rings. Post-WWII rifles utilized the same type of rear sight base as used on the later Second World War rifles.

Several variants of the sheet metal rear sight cover exist. The earliest were flat with no indentions and stamped with drawing numbers. An indented rib was added circa late 1940, although there was overlap between the two types. Winchester covers were not marked with drawing numbers, and the company changed to the indented rib type several months after Springfield (circa mid-1941). The post-Second World War covers were all of the indented rib variety.

Barrel

There were two basic types of M1 barrels. As originally adopted, the M1 was fitted with a 22" barrel with no gas port hole. This barrel was used with the "gas trap" system (discussed at length later), which took off the necessary gas at the muzzle to work the action. By early 1940, the gas system was changed to the "gas port" type. This necessitated a change to a 24" barrel with a gas port drilled in the bottom. Only Springfield used the 22" gas trap barrel. The gas trap barrels were stamped with drawing numbers and, often, the heat lot, but unlike later barrels, they were not marked with the date of production.

Both Winchester and Springfield Armory made their own M1 barrels during WWII. Some barrels were produced by Marlin during the war, but extremely few, if any, were used on production rifles due to manufacturing defects. However, some of the World War II Marlin barrels were used during the postwar rebuild programs. Some barrels were also believed to have been made by Buffalo Arms, but there is no evidence any were used on new production rifles. Their use was presumably restricted to overhaul purposes.

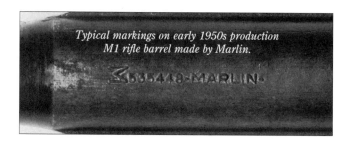

Typical markings on early 1950s production M1 rifle barrel made by Marlin.

The barrels, as made by Springfield after mid-1940, were marked on the right side with the month and year that the barrel was manufactured. These marking can be observed by retracting the operating rod. During the war, the time lag between the date the barrel was made and the rifle assembled was normally only one or two months. Any period longer than three months is cause to consider the originality of the receiver/barrel combination. There were certainly exceptions, but they were very much in the minority. The drawing number along with the heat lot number and various proof/inspection markings were also stamped on the barrels. Winchester barrels made during WWII were marked with the initials of the firm and the drawing number on top and cannot be seen without removing the rear handguard. Winchester barrels were marked on the right side with a punch mark and the Winchester "WP" logo. WWII Winchester barrels were not marked with the date of production.

A number of replacement barrels were made by Springfield Armory in the late 1940s and early 1950s for use with the extensive postwar rebuilding programs. When Springfield resumed production of new M1 rifles in the early 1950s, the barrels continued to be marked in

the same manner. Harrington & Richardson manufactured most of their own barrels, which were marked on the right side with the initials of the firm and the month and year of production. The barrels were also stamped with drawing numbers and various proof and inspection markings. International Harvester utilized barrels made by Line Material Corporation of Birmingham, Alabama. These barrels were marked "LMR" on the right side along with the month and year of production. The drawing and proof/inspection markings used on the LMR barrels were similar to those found on H&R and Springfield M1 barrels of the same period. Marlin also made some barrels in the late 1950s. Unlike the barrels, the company made in WWII, the postwar Marlin M1 barrels were of good quality. Most were used for overhaul purposes, but some are believed to have been utilized by Springfield in new production rifles.

Even after production of the M1 ceased in 1957, replacement barrels continued to be made for overhaul purposes. Winchester received a contract for replacement barrels around 1967. These are marked with the company's name on the right side and the year of production. They are, of course, not correct for use on a WWII vintage rifle. In the 1960s, some barrels chambered for the 7.62mm NATO cartridge were made by Springfield Armory for use in converting existing service rifles to the new cartridge by the Navy. Some of the original .30-06 barrels had chamber inserts installed to accept the NATO round, but this proved unsatisfactory and new barrels were eventually produced. All were marked with the caliber designation and the month and year of manufacture.

In the late 1940s, the gas port area of the barrel was chromed in order to reduce the likelihood of corrosion. Many of the earlier WWII vintage barrels were chromed in this area as part of the overhaul process. All new production barrels were chromed. Therefore, any WWII or earlier vintage M1 barrel with a chromed gas port has been modified from its original condition.

Lower Band

From the time of adoption until circa late 1940, early production M1 rifles were fitted with milled lower bands having a groove machined into them. Very early versions were stamped with the part's drawing number. A stamped and brazed band was developed to speed production time and reduce cost. As originally adopted, the profile of a stamped band had a slight arch until mid-1943 when it was changed to a flatter profile. This type of band remained in use through the end of the war and was used on post-WWII production rifles as well.

Early Winchester rifles also had the grooved milled band, which was eventually replaced by the later variant with an arched profile. Winchester retained the arched type of band until it was changed to the flat profile during the production run of the late WIN-13 rifles. As is the case with many parts made by Winchester, they can often be identified by the presence of machining marks.

Lower Band Pin

The lower band pin used by both manufacturers during WWII can be identified by its solid construction. Both blued and unfinished solid lower band pins will be found. Post-WWII lower band pins were of a spring type. A WWII Winchester or Springfield M1 rifle with the later type of lower band pin should be looked at more closely since this part is not original to the rifle. The possibility always exists that this could be the only part changed and everything else remains as it left the factory. However, as stated previously, the presence of even a small incorrect part means that the rifle has had at least one of its parts changed and increases the odds that other parts may have been changed as well.

Gas Cylinder

As originally adopted, the M1 utilized the so-called "gas trap" gas system with a screw-on type gas cylinder. A separate muzzle plug was attached to the gas cylinder. The "gas trap" rifle will be examined in detail later.

When the gas system was changed to the improved "gas port" type, a spline-type gas cylinder was adopted. Early production gas port cylinders (Springfield and Winchester) were stamped with a drawing number and had a narrow platform to which the front sight base was attached. The drawing number was soon deleted. By mid-1943, the sight platform was widened to allow for lateral movement of the front sight. This pattern gas cylinder was used for the balance of WWII and for all postwar production rifles. There was a difference in the configuration of the barrel ring between the Springfield and Winchester gas cylinders which will be discussed later.

Some gas cylinders may be found with a saw cut through the sight platform. Two types of cuts have been observed: a straight cut and an angled cut. This modification was done to salvage gas cylinders that were too loose for proper functioning. Some of these "saw cut" gas cylinders were used on a relatively small number of new production rifles beginning around mid-1943. Many more were subsequently used on Garands overhauled after WWII. There are no substantive differences found

Comparison of Gas Trap gas cylinder and front sight (top) and Gas Port gas cylinder and front sight (bottom).

in the post-1943 Springfield gas cylinders and those made by IHC and H&R in the 1950s.

There were problems encountered regarding the durability of the gas cylinder's finish. Since the part was fabricated of stainless steel, it couldn't be blued or parkerized and a paint-like coating ("Molyblack") was initially used. This finish was not very durable and many early vintage M1 gas cylinders can be observed today with little or no finish remaining. Eventually, the formulation of the coating and method of application were changed. This helped but never totally eliminated the problem.

Gas Cylinder Lock

Three distinct types of gas cylinder locks were used with the spline type gas cylinders. The first type, which was used throughout WWII, had a rounded top with a chamfered area at the front edge. In the latter part of WWII, the metallurgy was changed to harden the lock for use in launching rifle grenades. The chamfer on the front edge was eliminated on these locks, and a letter "M" was stamped on the right side of the lock. Apparently few of these "M"-marked locks were utilized in production rifles during WWII, but many show up on rebuilds from the postwar period.

In the early 1950s, the final variant gas cylinder lock was adopted. This style had a prominent "hump" at the top which was incorporated to improved the rifle's performance when launching rifle grenades. This final variant will only be found on rifles made after circa 1952 and those rebuilt after this period.

U.S. Army troops advancing during WWII. This photograph vividly illustrates the problems encountered with the finish wearing off the M1's gas cylinder thus exposing a shiny surface. The solider at front has apparently wrapped a piece of cloth around his rifle's gas cylinder to camouflage the surface. The shiny finish on the rest of the rifles is clearly visible.

(Credit: U.S. Army)

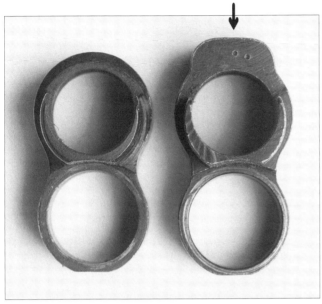

(Above, left) WWII (and earlier) gas cylinder lock.
(Above, right) Later pattern used from circa 1952 until the end of production. Note the high "hump" on top of the later lock.

Gas Cylinder Lock Screw

The first type of gas cylinder lock screw used with the gas port rifles is characterized by a single slot in the face to facilitate removal by the rifle's combination tool or a screw driver. This single slot screw remained in use until the adoption of the M7 grenade launcher. It was necessary to "bleed off" excess gas when using the M7 launcher. A gas cylinder lock screw with an internal spring valve was developed which opened when the launcher was fired to vent excess gas. Some of these were marked "S" on the face of the lock screw. Although some functioning problems were encountered, the design worked reasonably well. However, when the launcher was attached, the M1 rifle could not be fired semiautomatically since the gas system was essentially bypassed. In order to rectify the situation, a gas cylinder lock screw incorporating a "poppet" valve was devel-

(Above, left) Late production "poppet" gas cylinder lock screw.
(Above, right) Pre-1945 "single slot" gas cylinder lock screw.

oped in early 1944. This design allowed for the valve to open when launching rifle grenades and to close when the rifle was fired in the normal manner. Further refinements of the improved screw were forthcoming, and the component did not come into use until the latter part of WWII. After the war, the "poppet" valve gas cylinder lock screw was used on all production M1 rifles.

The poppet screws were normally marked on the face with the initials of the maker. Except for late production "WIN-13" rifles, all Winchester M1s were equipped with the single slot gas cylinder lock.

Front Sight

The front sight used with the original gas trap M1 rifles was markedly different in configuration and attachment to the gas cylinder as compared to the later gas port rifles. The first pattern front sight fitted into a dovetail slot on top of the gas cylinder and was secured by a screw on the right side. Two distinct variants of the gas trap front sight exist and will be discussed subsequently.

With the adoption of the improved spline type gas cylinder, a different front sight assembly was produced. The sight attached to a dovetail platform on the gas cylinder and was held in place by means of a socket head cap screw on the rear of the sight. When the improved front sight was adopted, a sheet metal cup type seal was placed over the head of the socket screw to prevent unauthorized removal of the screw to adjust the front sight. In early 1943, the seal was eliminated and a slightly different shaped socket screw was used. The adoption of a wider sight platform to allow the front sight to be laterally adjusted was the primary reason for elimination of the sight screw seal. The seal was removed when the rifles were overhauled and intact seals on rifles today are a strong indication that the front sight assembly is original. However, some reproduction front sight screw seals have been noted, so this feature is not necessarily irrefutable proof that the rifle is all original.

Some variance in the width of the front sight "ears" will be noted between the sights used by several manufacturers. For example, Winchester front sight ears are significantly wider than those produced by Springfield ($^{13}/_{16}$" vs. approx. $^{5}/_{8}$"). The sight ears as produced by International Harvester during the 1950s, measuring $^{7}/_{8}$", were even wider than those made by Winchester. The post-WWII front sight ears made by Springfield and Harrington & Richardson were the same width as those produced by Springfield during the Second World War.

(Above, left) Later production front sight screw without seal.
(Above, right) Early production with sight screw seal intact.

(Below, left) Winchester M1 front sight.
(Below, right) Springfield Armory M1 front sight. Note the much more prominently flared "ears" on the Winchester sight.

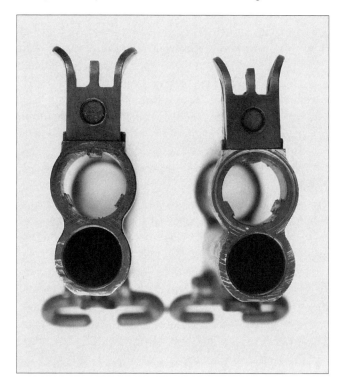

Stacking Swivel

The Garand was fitted with a somewhat anachronistic stacking swivel attached to the gas cylinder. Except for very early swivels marked with drawing numbers, there were no real differences in this part from the beginning of production until the end.

Follower

There were two basic types of followers used with the M1 rifle. The first variety has been dubbed the "long tail" type due to the configuration of the rear portion. This follower dropped from use fairly early, circa late 1941, when the "short tail" variety was adopted. Winchester continued use of the early variety follower longer than Springfield but changed to the "short tail"

version in late 1943. There were various revision numbers stamped on the followers. The highest follower revision number for WWII production is "13".

The followers used in post-World War Two production were of the later "short tail" type. These were generally unmarked except for some produced by International Harvester which were stamped with single digits or letters.

Follower Slide

There were two distinct types of follower slides. The first variety was utilized from the inception of production until circa mid-1940, and it is characterized by an approximately 20 degree angle of the rear section. Both blued and unfinished early slides have been observed. The second variety had a the rear section with an approximately 45 degree angle. This type of follower slide was used on all subsequent M1 rifles. Parkerized and unfinished examples may be encountered. The majority of the early slides were modified to the later pattern during overhaul and unaltered examples are very hard to find today.

Follower Arm

Follower arms are classified as "double bevel," "single bevel" or "no bevel" types. The double bevel follower arm was used from the beginning of production until

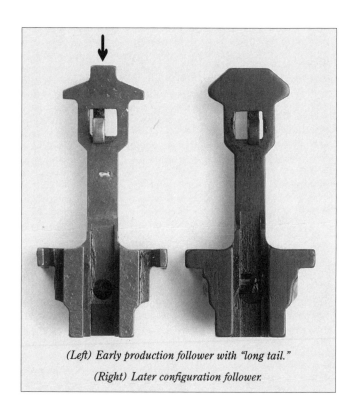

(Left) Early production follower with "long tail."
(Right) Later configuration follower.

Early production follower arm (marked with drawing number).

Later production follower arm. Note the difference in the bevels machined on both types.

the latter part of 1939 and was stamped with a drawing number. It was replaced by the single bevel follower arm which remained in use until early 1941. Only a relative handful of the single bevel follower arms were numbered. The final variant was used exclusively afterward. Some may be found with letter or digit markings, which were forge codes, not drawing numbers, used by the manufacturer. Interestingly, Winchester apparently only produced the single bevel type and never adopted the no bevel variety. All post-WWII follower arms were of the "no bevel" type.

Follower Arm Pin

Even a seemingly insignificant part such as a pin can hold important clues to the originality of a rifle. The follower arm pin used for WWII production can be identified from the type used in postwar M1s by the presence of a "step" below the head of the pin. Springfield and Winchester used this type of pin for all their Second World War production Garands. After International Harvester and Harrington & Richardson went into production in the early 1950s, the step was deleted from the follower arm pin. Springfield appears to have utilized the stepped variety of pin throughout production.

Follower Rods

There were five distinct variations of follower rods used with M1 rifles. The first, and certainly the rarest,

was the type used with early production rifles. It was of one-piece construction and characterized by a rounded body with a thin profile for use with the short-lived compensating spring. Extremely early versions were stamped with the drawing number. Springfield eliminated the separate compensating spring in the fall of 1940, but Winchester continued its use until mid-1941.

The second type had a rounded body with a profile much thicker than the first type of follower rod. Since the compensating spring did not have to be accommodated, the part could be made thicker (and stronger). This follower rod was only used by Springfield for a few months in late 1940 and, perhaps, very early 1941. Winchester did not produce any follower rods of this type.

The thick, rounded follower rod was replaced by a one-piece rod with a flat profile. This follower rod was manufactured and used exclusively by Winchester. Unmarked as well as coded variants ("CM" or "A") may be observed. Winchester used this type of follower rod from the time it dropped the compensating spring until the introduction of the WIN-13 rifle in early 1945.

Springfield produced a follower rod constructed of several pieces of stamped metal riveted together. This rod replaced the rounded profile type in late 1940 and was continued in use at least through the latter part of 1943. The "fork" in the rod was not as deep as later production rods, and some problems were encountered with the fork disconnecting from the follower arm. In order to eliminate this tendency, a very similar follower rod with a deeper profile "fork" was adopted in early 1944. It was used through the end of production and was the type adopted for postwar production as well. Winchester also utilized this type of follower rod in its late production WIN-13 rifles.

Some totally original pre-1944 production M1 rifles have been noted with all correct parts except for the later pattern follower rod. Undoubtedly, the problems encountered with disengagement and the ease with which the newer rod could be installed resulted in some rifles having the newer part substituted in the field. As the rifles were sent for arsenal overhaul, the newer follower rod was installed. Some collectors have grappled with the decision whether or not to replace a switched follower rod with the earlier type in rifles that are otherwise all original. While some may disagree, it is a simple matter to replace the exchanged rod with the type that it had when the rifle left the factory. It was "altered" at the time the newer rod was installed so this simple exchange does not destroy the originality of the piece as other more extensive (and questionable) forms of restoration.

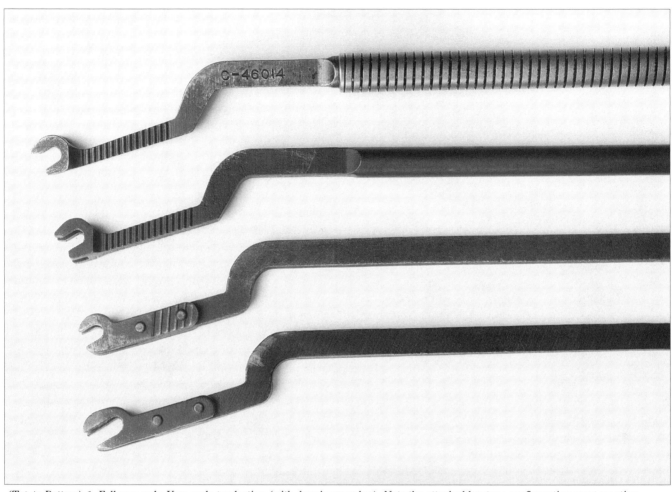

(Top to Bottom) 1. Follower rods. Very early production (with drawing number). Note the attached keystone configuration compensating spring; 2. Round body follower rod as found on 1940 vintage M1 rifles; 3. Typical early to mid-WWII follower rod with "short fork." Note the riveted construction as compared to earlier two rods; 4. Late WWII (and postwar) follower rod with deeper "fork."

Operating Rod Catch Assembly

The operating rod catch assembly was made up of three separate parts: the operating rod catch, accelerator and accelerator pin. There were two basic types termed the "early" and "late" varieties. The early type is characterized by the thinner and longer profile of the "forks." The later type had thicker forks and was the type installed in new production rifles from early 1941 onward. Winchester also used the early and late types but, as usual, did not change until two or so years after Springfield. There was a revision number ("0") stamped on the operating rod catch and accelerator. The number was soon deleted on the catch (but remained on the accelerator) and was eliminated altogether in early to mid-1941.

The postwar operating rod catch assemblies were all of the type used by Springfield and Winchester during the latter part of WWII. Except for some single letter codes found on some International Harvester assemblies, these were unmarked.

Bullet Guide

Though technically a misnomer, bullet guide was the official nomenclature of this part. There are several varieties of the component. Originally, the part was manufactured by Springfield by forging and had a narrow slot in which the follower arm was inserted. This type was marked with a "B-8875" drawing number. The next variant was also forged but the slot was enlarged and the drawing number changed to "B8875" (the dash was deleted). Later forged bullet guides will be found marked with drawing numbers that include the initials of the manufacturer ("SA" or "WRA") and/or raised forge codes. All markings were eventually eliminated.

Some of the unmarked bullet guides may be found with milled cuts in the middle of the guide. This variety was only used for a relatively short period of time.

In order to save machining time, a bullet guide constructed of stamped metal was substituted for the forged variety in late 1943 although the item didn't get into production until rather late in WWII. The stamped bullet guide was used in all post-WWII manufactured M1 rifles. The late WWII bullet guides can be identified from the 1950s vintage guides by the lack of a notch cut into the left side, which is found on the 1950s vintage bullet guides.

Clip Latch

There were two variations of clip latches. The first variety, as produced by Springfield Armory from the beginning of production until circa early 1944, had a rounded front end. Very early versions were stamped on the inside with a revision number ("0") with or without a preceding dash. The configuration of the clip latch was changed to a square front end. This was the pattern used for subsequent production, including all post-WWII Garands. Winchester continued with the rounded front clip latch throughout its production run of the M1 rifle. Some Winchester clip latches were marked "CM" or "A". In addition, a number of clip latches used on International Harvester M1s made in the 1950s were marked with a single code letter.

Operating Rod

A very important part to consider is the operating rod. There were two major variations of this part and numerous minor variations exist. Full drawing and revision numbers are stamped on the operating rod and are very important when attempting to determine if a particular rifle is all original or has been modified or restored.

The first pattern operating rod is characterized by the angled shape of the part which engages the bolt. The first thousand or less M1 operating rods were constructed with a welded seam along the bottom of the tube. However, this was soon changed to eliminate the welded seam. Early versions of the standard M1 operating rod were stamped with the drawing number on top next the handle, but this location was soon moved to the underside near the junction of the handle and tube. The "slant cut" operating rod was used by Springfield Armory from the beginning of production until around the low 30,000 serial number range when the configuration was changed to a "straight cut." Winchester utilized

the slant cut rod until circa mid-1943 when the company produced the straight cut rod. However, Winchester used both types concurrently for a period of time. There are two sub-variations of this operating rod identified by the cross section profile of the area. The first sub-variation has a curved profile on the side, while the second type has a flat profile in this area. Some overlap has been observed in the curved-sided and flat-sided types. Winchester used the straight cut "flat side" operating rod in very late production WIN-13 rifles. Again, however, there was some overlap in the use of the two types during this period.

Another key feature to observe on an operating rod is the presence of a milled-out area at the junction of the handle and tube. It was discovered that cracks could develop in this area. After WWII, the tooling was changed to mill away this area to prevent such cracks from forming. Many operating rods incorporating this improvement were produced in the late 1940s for use in rebuilding programs. However, no original production WWII M1 rifles were fitted with anything but the "uncut" operating rods. Large numbers of the original

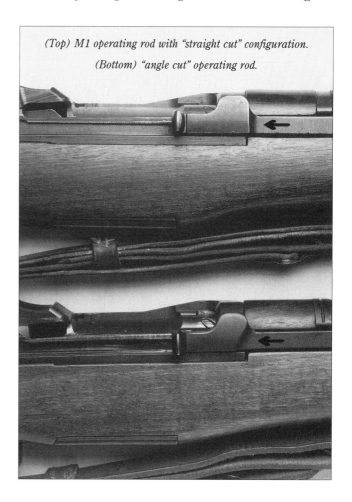

(Top) M1 operating rod with "straight cut" configuration. (Bottom) "angle cut" operating rod.

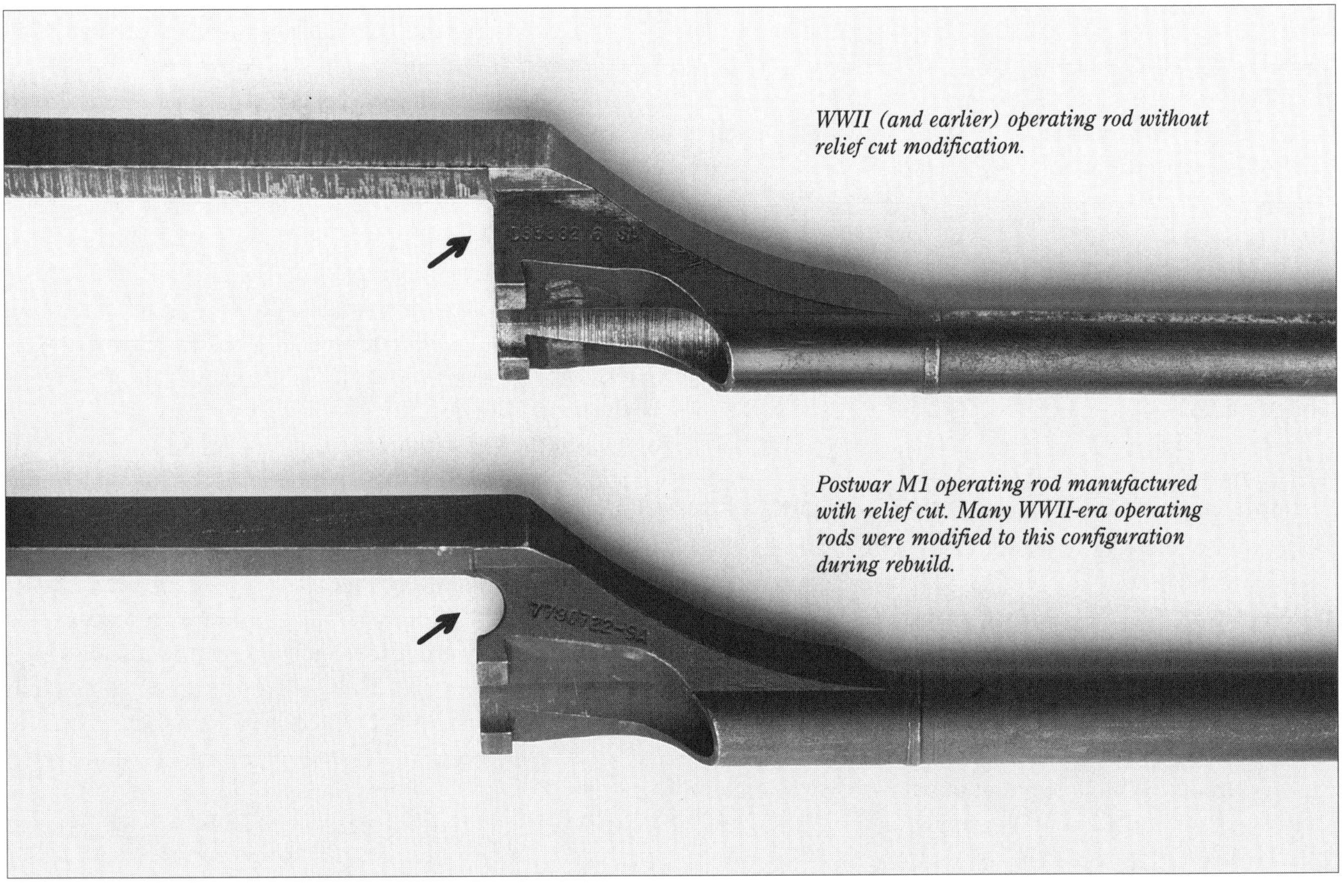

WWII (and earlier) operating rod without relief cut modification.

Postwar M1 operating rod manufactured with relief cut. Many WWII-era operating rods were modified to this configuration during rebuild.

rods were subsequently milled away in this area to salvage them for use with rebuilt rifles. Therefore, even if a WWII vintage M1 rifle is equipped with an operating rod having a proper revision code for the period, the rifle is not all original if the relief cut is present. Finding the correct "uncut" operating rod with which to restore a particular rifle can, at times, be difficult. Uncut Winchester operating rods are even tougher to find. One of the first things to look for on a supposedly original WWII M1 rifle is an uncut operating rod. This is a very key feature along with the proper barrel/receiver combination and the stock cartouche.

The post-WWII operating rods manufactured by Springfield, International Harvester and Harrington & Richardson will all have the relief cut modification and are marked with the initials of the manufacturer as well as the drawing number.

Operating Rod Spring

The original design for the M1 utilized an operating rod spring and a separate compensating spring. Both springs were of a "keystone" (a.k.a. "square wire") type. As mentioned under the discussion on follower rods, the compensating spring was dropped from use by Springfield Armory in late 1940. The use of the keystone operating rod spring continued for a short period of time (until perhaps very early 1941) after the compensating spring was eliminated. A more conventional round wire operating rod spring was adopted to replace the keystone configuration spring. This type was used for the balance of production, including all postwar variants. Blued and unfinished operating rod springs have been observed.

Trigger Housing Group

Trigger Housing

There are several distinct variations of trigger housings, and they are characterized primarily by two features. The first feature to observe is the small "pad" located on the upper left inside of the trigger housing. This feature was not found on the original model shop rifles but was added to production gas trap rifles. John Garand desired some means to retard excessive hammer force to the rear and incorporated the pad into production trigger housings. The pad was essentially a reinforced hammer "stop." When the later rounded top safety was adopted (to be discussed shortly), the front edge of the pad could interfere with the operation of the safety. Circa late 1940, the pad was reduced in size in order to eliminate this problem. The so-called "wide pad" and "narrow pad" trigger housings are key features in earlier and later rifles. There were several revision numbers found on the trigger housing made during WWII as this and other changes were incorporated. Many of the earlier housings had a portion of the wide pad milled away when rebuilt. Therefore, even if the drawing/revision number is correct for a particular vintage trigger housing, the size of the pad must be determined to be certain that the part wasn't subsequently modified. Except for the late production, WIN-13 rifles, Winchester utilized the wide pad trigger housing since the firm did not change to the round top safety. All post-WWII trigger housings were of the narrow pad variety.

The other key feature to observe on trigger housing is the configuration of the hole on the outside wall of the housing. Early production Springfield and Winchester trigger housings have a single small hole. Later in production, this was changed to a so-called "cloverleaf" shaped hole. This feature was changed at roughly the time that the narrow pad replaced the wide pad. All trigger housings were marked with the drawing number and appropriate revision number. After 1940, the trigger housings were also stamped with the initials of the manufacturer. Some Winchester trigger housings will be found with "CM" markings.

Trigger

From the beginning of production until the latter part of 1940, Springfield Armory M1 triggers were manufactured with a second hole. This second hole was presumably used to position the part in the manufacturing tooling as part of the production process. The hole was deleted after circa late 1940 on all Springfield M1 rifles as well as on those made after the war by Harrington & Richardson and International Harvester. Winchester

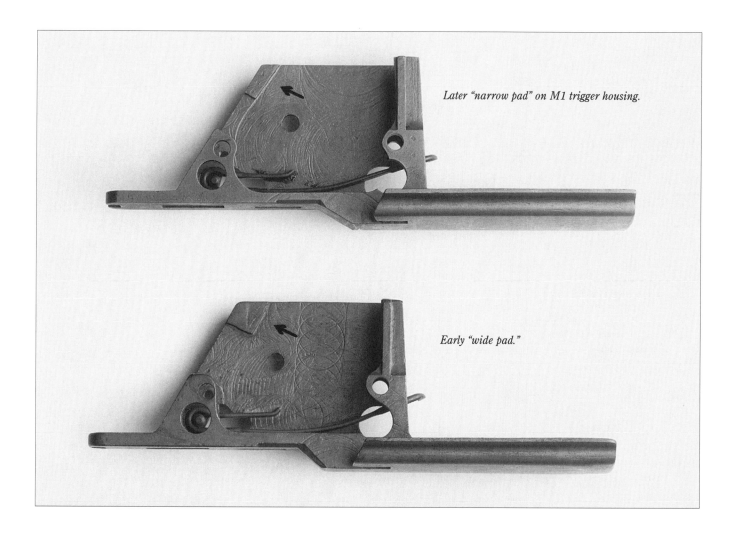

Later "narrow pad" on M1 trigger housing.

Early "wide pad."

continued using triggers with the second hole as late as the middle part of 1942 when this hole was deleted.

Very early Springfield triggers were marked with drawing numbers, but this was deleted early in production. Some Winchester triggers were stamped "A", but many were unmarked. As is frequently the case with parts made by Winchester, they can often be identified by the rough machined surface and the presence of a punch mark.

Triggerguard

Although there are only two basic types of M1 triggerguards, several sub-variations exist. The two basic types are the "milled" triggerguard and the later stamped variety.

The milled triggerguard was used by Springfield from the inception of Garand production. Early versions of this part had concentric rings on either side of the hole located at the rear of the triggerguard. The part was also stamped with the full drawing number. The concentric rings were eliminated fairly early in production. The drawing number (including subsequent revision numbers) continued to be stamped on the milled triggerguard until very late in 1941 or very early 1942 when the use of drawing numbers on this part was stopped.

The milled triggerguard was a rather time consuming item to produce and a guard made from stamped metal was developed in 1943. By early 1944, the milled triggerguard began to be used by Springfield Armory. As is normally the case when new parts were adopted, there was some overlap in the use of the milled and stamped triggerguards. Winchester did not use the stamped triggerguard and continued to utilize the milled

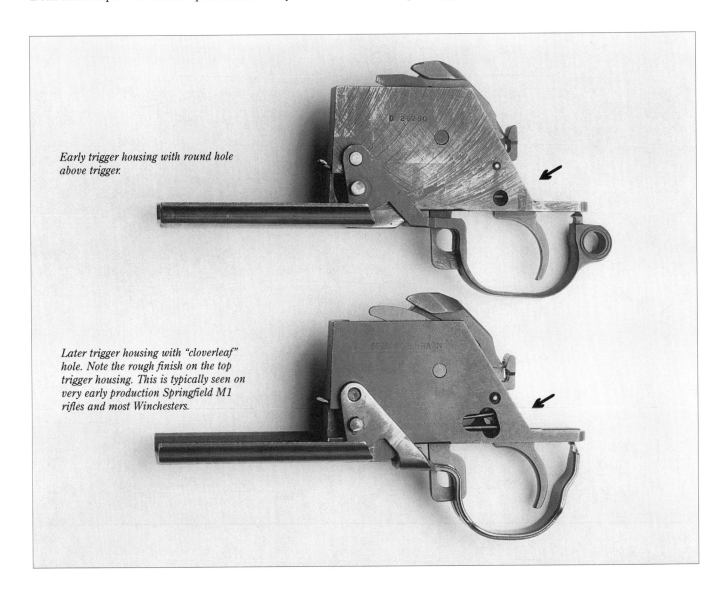

Early trigger housing with round hole above trigger.

Later trigger housing with "cloverleaf" hole. Note the rough finish on the top trigger housing. This is typically seen on very early production Springfield M1 rifles and most Winchesters.

type for all of the company's M1 production run.

There were some changes made in the design of the "hook" at the rear of the triggerguard that engaged the trigger housing to lock the part in place. A milled hook was used with the early production versions of the stamped triggerguard. In order to speed production even further, the milled hook was replaced by a tab of stamped metal bent into the proper contour. This is commonly called the "stamped hook" variety by collectors today. A third sub-variant had the milled hook but also had a small tab of metal welded onto the front of the triggerguard. There is no evidence that this third sub-variant was used on any production rifles and was likely developed as a replacement part for overhaul purposes.

The stamped hook triggerguard was used during the post-WWII era by Springfield Armory, Harrington & Richardson and International Harvester. Many of the pre-1945 milled triggerguards were utilized on rebuilds since they were as serviceable as the later stamped guards. None of the stamped triggerguards were marked with any sort of codes or manufacturers' initials so identification by maker is not possible.

Hammer

Early production hammers are characterized by an extra hole and a slightly different configuration of the "hooks" at the rear. By late 1940, the design of the hammer was revised by Springfield Armory to eliminate the extra hole and to improve the function of the hammer by redesigning the hooks. Winchester continued use of the early style hammer (extra hole and "early" hooks) throughout production. All post-1940 Springfield M1s and those made in the 1950s by International Harvester and Harrington & Richardson utilized the later type hammer.

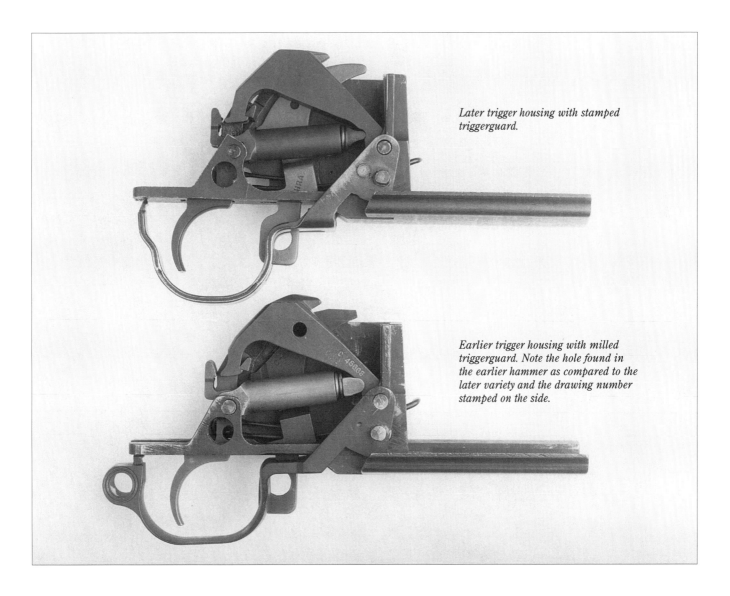

Later trigger housing with stamped triggerguard.

Earlier trigger housing with milled triggerguard. Note the hole found in the earlier hammer as compared to the later variety and the drawing number stamped on the side.

There are numerous marking variations to be found among M1 hammers. Early production Springfield Armory hammers (made by late 1940) had the drawing number stamped on the right side of the hammer. Afterward, the drawing number was stamped on the face of the hammer. Winchester continued stamping drawing numbers on the right side throughout production. Some Winchester hammers marked "CM" or "A" have been observed.

Post-WWII hammers were also marked on the face with the drawing number (but no revision numbers) as well as the initials of the manufacturer "SA", "IHC" or "HRA").

Hammer Spring Plunger

The hammer spring plunger is one of the sometimes overlooked parts. Prior to circa early 1944, the hammer spring plungers made by Springfield had "ears" on either side of the front. This was changed to the type without these ears. Winchester changed to the "no ears" hammer spring plunger in mid- to late 1944. All subse-

quent hammer springs plungers did not have the ears. There were also differences in the configuration of Springfield and Winchester hammer spring plungers.

Safety

There were two basic variants of M1 safeties along with a third sub-variant. There were a number of differences found in the marking format of the safety. The earliest pattern safety can be easily identified by its flat top profile. This safety was used by Springfield from the inception of production until circa late 1940 when it was replaced by the more familiar pattern with a rounded top profile. A sub-variation of this part was in use for about a year from circa mid-1941 to mid-1942 and was of the rounded top type but had a small hole into the top area of the safety. After mid-1942, the hole was deleted, and the rounded top safety (with no hole) was used by Springfield for the balance of its WWII production. This pattern safety continued in use when production again resumed in the early 1950s. Winchester, on the other hand, utilized the flat top safety for all of its production

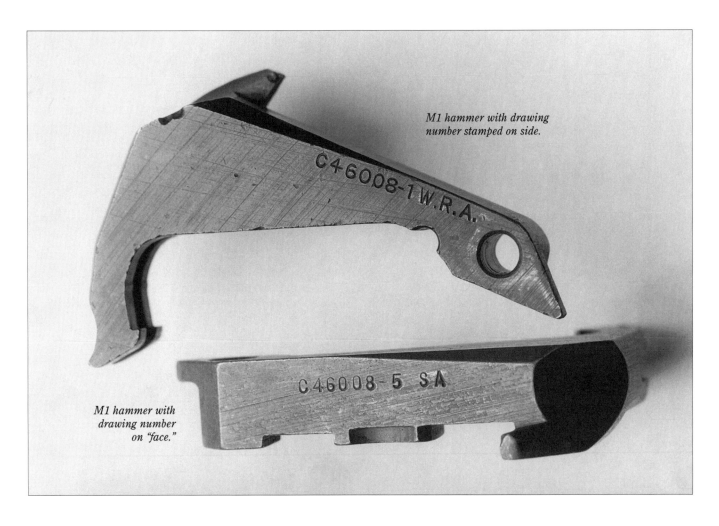

M1 hammer with drawing number stamped on side.

M1 hammer with drawing number on "face."

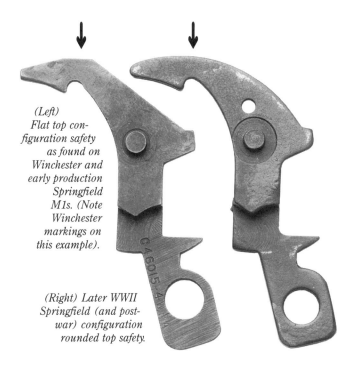

(Left) Flat top configuration safety as found on Winchester and early production Springfield M1s. (Note Winchester markings on this example).

(Right) Later WWII Springfield (and postwar) configuration rounded top safety.

Another overlooked feature of early production stock is the configuration of the so-called "barrel channel". This is the area at the front of the stock into which the operating rod fits. Prior to early 1942, stocks were of the "long channel" type. The "channel" area was approximately 2⅜" long. After early, 1942, the channel was shortened to approximately 1⅝" in length. A number of the early "long channel" stocks were subsequently modified as part of the overhaul process to the "short channel" variety. This was presumably done to prevent binding of the operating rod against the stock in this area. Winchester retained use of the "long channel" stocks until the latter part of 1943. The barrel channel area is very important to observe due to the extreme number

run of the Garand. Very early Winchester safeties had the full drawing and revision number stamped on the right side in a very high location. This was changed to the more commonly encountered location much lower on the safety. Winchester eventually deleted the full drawing and revision number and simply marked the part "WRA-1".

Stock Group (including Handguards)

Stocks are of particular interest to collectors today. Since wood is obviously more delicate than metal, stocks were much more likely to be worn or broken than other parts, hence the higher likelihood of replacement. An otherwise original M1 with an incorrect stock is seriously devalued as a collector item. The proper stock cartouche is also an extremely important feature. The correct cartouches will be explored later in this book when specific variants of the M1 are examined.

Stock

When originally adopted, the M1 rifle was not designed with a butt trap recess for the storage of cleaning implements, etc. Two holes were drilled into the butt to, presumably, reduce the weight. There were some variations noted in the diameter of the holes which will be discussed later in the section on the "gas trap" rifles. By late 1940, a butt trap recess was incorporated, and the rear of the stock was routed out to provide the necessary clearance. All subsequent M1 stocks utilized the butt trap recess. Winchester did not change to the butt trap recess stock until around mid-1942.

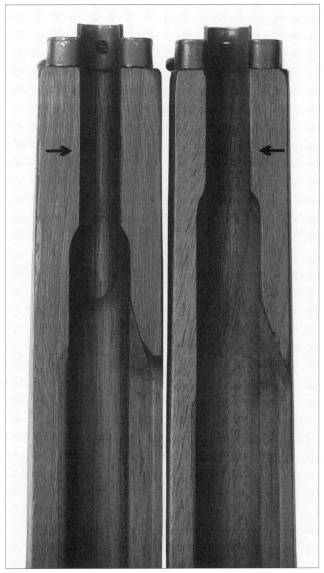

(Left) Early stock with long "barrel channel."
(Right) Later stock with short "barrel channel."

of fake cartouches stamped on stocks. For example, if a stock is stamped with a 1940 vintage cartouche but it has a short channel, the marking is fake. This feature is sometimes forgotten by the con artists. Some realistic looking fake cartouches have been identified as non-original by this method.

There are other rather more subtle features found in the stocks made by (or for) the various manufacturers. Winchester stocks will exhibit a more arched profile from the pistol grip to the floor plate area than will the stocks made by Springfield. There were also rather subtle differences found in some IHC and HRA stocks.

The cartouches and proof marks stamped on the stocks as part of the final inspection process are vitally important for collectors today. These will be discussed in depth in the sections that follow on each variation of the M1 rifle.

Front Handguard

There was very little difference found in the front handguard throughout the M1's production run. A sharp profile on either bottom edge is typically found on most WWII production front handguards and a rounded edge on later handguards. However, some M1s made later in WWII vintage rifles that appear to be all original may be found with rounded bottom edges. The time period that this changed is not known but earlier production rifles (circa pre-1944) will usually be found with sharp bottom edges although some exceptions may be encountered.

The early gas trap rifles had a unique front handguard ferrule with a "lip" spacer. This item will be discussed shortly. Very early front handguards were also stamped with the drawing number on the right side.

Rear Handguard

The most significant feature of the rear handguard to observe is the clearance cut at the bottom right edge. It is not widely known that very early rear handguards were made of rather thin wood which was prone to cracking. The tooling was changed to have the rear handguard made from thicker wood to reduce this tendency. However, when the slightly thicker rear handguards began to be used, the operating rod would often bind on the right rear of the handguard. This problem was eliminated by milling away small portion of the handguard in this area. The rear handguard clearance cut began to be used circa early 1941 by Springfield. Some of the earlier rear handguards still in use were modified by adding the relief cut. Winchester did not

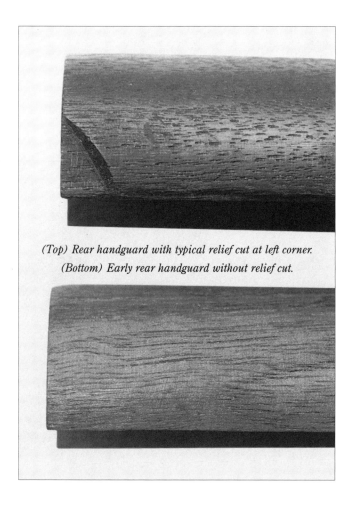

(Top) Rear handguard with typical relief cut at left corner.
(Bottom) Early rear handguard without relief cut.

incorporate the relief cut until sometime in the middle of 1944. A supposedly original pre-1944 Winchester should have a rear handguard without the relief cut modification. This is a key feature that is often forgotten. Very early "gas trap"-era Springfield rear handguards were also stamped with the drawing number. Numbered handguards are rare.

Rear Handguard Band

As was the case with the lower band, early rear handguard bands were of milled construction and had a groove machined into the surface. Very early bands were also stamped inside with the drawing number. The milled band continued in use by Springfield Armory until the introduction of a band made from stamped sheet metal in late 1942. The stamped band was used for all subsequent production bands including the post-WWII variants. Winchester used the grooved, milled band until circa early 1943 when the company changed to a milled band without the groove. After just a few months, Winchester changed to a stamped band for the remainder of its production run. The milled, ungrooved

Winchester band can be identified by a arched profile as compared to the Springfield bands. No milled, ungrooved Springfield rear handguard bands have been observed.

Buttplate Assembly

As mentioned, the M1's stock did not have a butt trap recess. Since there was no need to gain access, the original pattern buttplate was solid and did not have a hinged door as found on later rifles. Both Springfield and Winchester utilized the solid buttplate. Early versions of the Springfield solid buttplate were stamped with the drawing number on the inside and had a border around the edge. The drawing number was soon dropped, and the border was eventually deleted prior to adoption of the later type buttplate in the latter part of 1940.

Winchester solid buttplates had a slightly larger border area than did the early Springfield buttplates. No numbered Winchester buttplates have been observed. Winchester continued use of the solid buttplate until at least the middle of 1942.

Many of the earlier "no trap" buttstocks were later

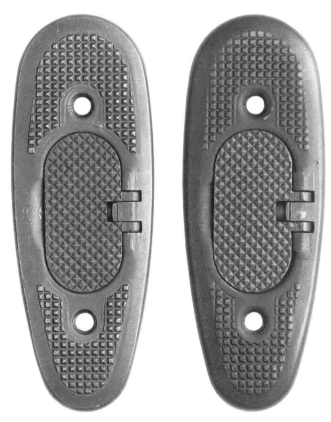

(Left) Winchester M1 buttplate.
(Right) Springfield Armory M1 buttplate. Note the more defined border around the checkering on the Winchester buttplate.

routed out and fitted with the later buttplates having the hinged door. The design of the later type buttplate remained essentially unchanged from the time of its adoption until the end of Garand production. Winchester buttplates can be distinguished from those made by Springfield and the other manufacturers by the presence of a more defined border around the checkering.

The buttplates made by Springfield Armory after 1940 and the postwar buttplates used by Harrington & Richardson and International Harvester were essentially identical, and it is not generally possible to distinguish between them. While the admonition that all parts should exhibit equal wear is true, buttplates can be an exception. This part often received an inordinate amount of use and some rather beat up buttplates can be found on rifles in otherwise excellent condition. Of course, if the reverse if observed, something is probably amiss since a pristine buttplate should not be found on a well used rifle.

Buttplate Screws

The M1's buttplate utilized two different type of screws. The long screw was only threaded near the end and engaged the rear sling swivel to secure it to the rifle. Very early gas trap-era long buttplate screws were stamped with drawing numbers/revision numbers. This practice was dropped early in the production run as it was difficult to stamp this part with a number, and it served no real purpose anyway. Virtually all original WWII production buttplate screws were blued although use of some parkerized ones cannot be categorically ruled out. The postwar screws were parkerized.

The short buttplate screw was a typical wood screw. Again, even this seemingly unimportant part can hold clues as to the originality of a rifle. All, or at least the overwhelming majority, of these screws were blued during WWII and earlier. While a supposedly original WWII vintage rifle with a parkerized short buttplate screw should not be dismissed out of hand as a non-original rifle, it should be looked at even closer. Likewise, a blued screw does not, by any means, indicate that the rifle in question is totally original. However, several incorrect features should raise real doubts as to a rifle's authenticity.

Many of the above-referenced components will be discussed in the sections that follow pertaining to their use on specific variants of the M1. Properly coded parts of the correct vintage and with original finish are highly desired for restoration purposes today. It is wise idea to obtain any parts that fall into this category even if you do not need them at the present time. You may run across a rifle that needs to have the correct parts added or the parts can make good trading material for what you may be looking for. The early numbered parts are especially in demand and staggering prices have been paid for some of them. If you need only one part to make an otherwise original M1 100% complete, then paying a seemingly exorbitant price may make sense.

➤ ➤ ➤ ➤ ➤ ➤ Variations of the M1 Rifle ◄ ◄ ◄ ◄ ◄ ◄ ◄

"Model Shop" Rifles

As stated, the first eighty rifles are known today by the descriptive, but unofficial, term "Model Shop" rifles. The model shop rifles were serially numbered consecutively beginning with "1". Rifle #1 resides in the Springfield Armory collection today and a handful of others are in private collections.

Identification of the model shop rifles is quite straightforward. The receiver was marked:

U.S.
SEMIAUTO. RIFLE
CAL. .30 M1
SPRINGFIELD
ARMORY
SERIAL #

Receiver markings on "Model Shop" M1. Note use of the word "Semiauto." (Credit: Garand Stand Collection)

Other unique features of the model shop rifles include the configuration of the lower portion of the receiver, the gas cylinder and front sight assembly. Table #3 will list the features found on the model shop rifles.

The Model Shop rifles were originally tested with the T1/T1E1 8-round clip. This prototype clip differed from the type eventually standardized in that a portion of the middle of the clip was cut away.

Upon completion of the testing and evaluation process, the model shop rifles were withdrawn from service. Except for a few in museums and reference collections, the remaining rifles were destroyed. Only a handful of model shop rifles, in varying degrees of completeness, are in private hands today, so the odds of encountering an example for sale are quite remote. Any model shop M1 would be a very valuable and desirable collector's prize.

"Gas Trap" M1s
1936–Early 1940 Production

When the M1 rifle was approved for production, a few changes from the original model shop rifles were instituted. One of the most obvious was the change in the receiver marking format that dropped the word "Semiauto." The receiver markings were changed to:

U.S RIFLE
CAL. .30 M1
SPRINGFIELD
ARMORY
SERIAL #

The configuration of the lower portion of the receiver was changed from the "V" shape of the model shop rifles to the now familiar square configuration. Other changes included a front sight with protecting "ears" on either side, changes in the configuration of the trigger housing and triggerguard and a slightly different type of gas cylinder. Otherwise, the early production M1 rifles were similar to the model shop guns. All M1 rifles were

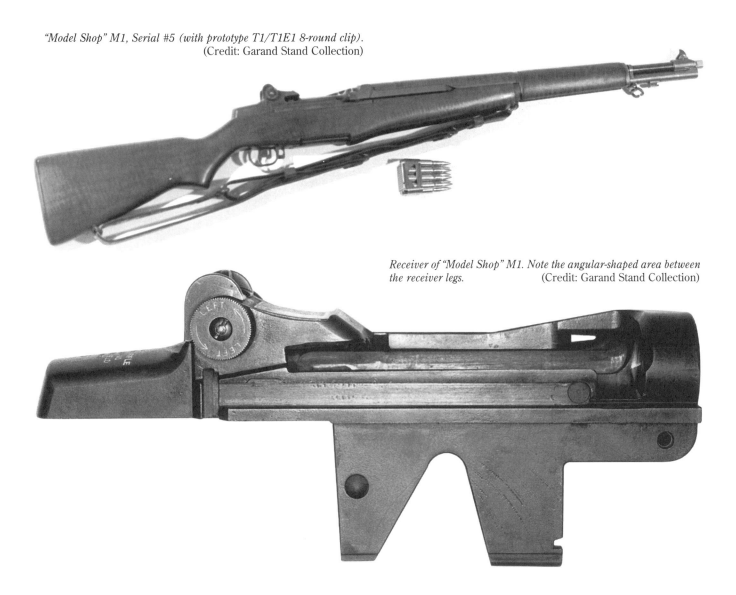

"Model Shop" M1, Serial #5 (with prototype T1/T1E1 8-round clip).
(Credit: Garand Stand Collection)

Receiver of "Model Shop" M1. Note the angular-shaped area between the receiver legs. (Credit: Garand Stand Collection)

finished in parkerizing. The tint and texture of this finish varied through the years but no production Garand rifles were finished in anything other than parkerizing.

As stated, the first production M1s also utilized a gas system which trapped the escaping gas at the muzzle that was used to operate the action. As we will subsequently discuss, this type of gas system was changed several years later. In order to differentiate the early production M1s with the original type of gas system from the later rifles, collectors have coined the term "Gas Trap" rifles. Those later rifles, equipped with the improved gas system, are generally referred to as "Gas Port" rifles. Like "Model Shop," these are unofficial but descriptive terms and are widely accepted by collectors today.

Production of the gas trap M1s began with serial #81 (although rifle #87 was actually the first to pass inspection) and continued until the change to the later type of

Close-up view of Gas Trap M1 receiver markings.

Original Gas Trap M1 serial #2126 as manufactured in April 1938 (Right and left views).

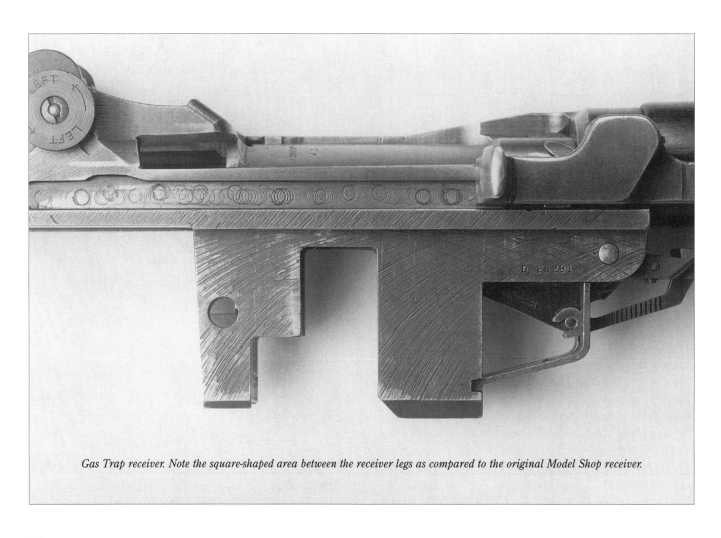

Gas Trap receiver. Note the square-shaped area between the receiver legs as compared to the original Model Shop receiver.

gas system in March of 1940 by which time serial numbers were into the low 50,000 range. Initial manufacture of the Garand rifle was very slow and laborious due to the difficulty in converting Springfield Armory's line over from M1903 to M1 production.

When these early gas trap M1 rifles began to be issued, several problems were noted. One of the most serious, and perplexing, was the so-called "Seventh Round Stoppage." This situation resulted in a jam when the seventh round was in the process of chambering. This vexing problem did much to contribute to the Garand's early "bad press" and had not occurred with the model shop rifles, which were extensively tested prior to the M1 going into production. Extensive trouble shooting eventually determined that a minor change in the production tooling for the receiver had resulted in the front guide rib, which supported the clip, being beveled at the top. This had not been done on the model shop rifles. If John Garand's original specifications had been followed, this problem would not have occurred. Once the cause was discovered, the tooling was changed, and the situation was rectified in short order. As mentioned previously, when the early rifles were overhauled, a bit of welding was added to build up the guide ribs to the proper contour.

There are a number of characteristics that identify original, unaltered gas trap M1 rifles. Table #4 details these features. The most apparent difference between these rifles and all subsequent variations is the early type of gas system which incorporated a special 22" barrel rather than the 24" barrel found on later M1s. There were several variants of the early gas cylinders. Early gas cylinders had machined "flutes" on either side, but they were eliminated later in production (estimated around serial #20,000). Also, the front sights of the gas trap rifles differed substantially from the sights found on the later gas port rifles. Very early gas trap rifle front sights had straight protective "ears." However, novice M1 shooters often mistook, with detrimental effects on accuracy, these ears for the sight blade. As this problem became apparent, the ears were flared to make them more easily distinguishable from the sight blade.

As we have discussed, the M1's rear sight was an excellent design and remains one of the best ever used on a military service rifle. The sight utilized a peep-type aperture and was fully adjustable for elevation by means of a knob on the left side and the windage by means of a knob on the right. A grooved pinion connected the elevation and windage knobs together and allowed the aperture to slide up and down. The windage knob was

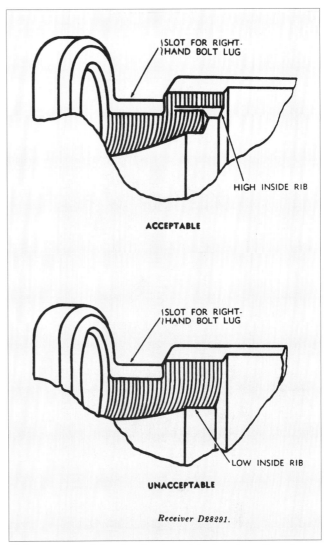

Ordnance manual drawing showing original configuration of gas trap receiver without built-up guide rib (bottom) termed "unacceptable" and the later receiver configuration with built-up rib (top) termed "acceptable."

secured to the pinion by means of a spanner nut. The only significant problem noted with the early M1 rear sights was the fact that the spanner nut did not always hold the adjustments securely. Most gas trap rifles had an indentation in the gas cylinder plug (often referred to as the muzzle plug). This was eliminated in later production gas trap M1s.

A metal ferrule having a prominent "lip" was used to separate the rear ring of the gas cylinder from the front handguard. The rear handguard did not have the small clearance cut as found on later rifles.

The gas trap rifle stocks lacked the buttstock recess found on the later rifles, which was used for storage of the thong and oiler case. These early stocks can be

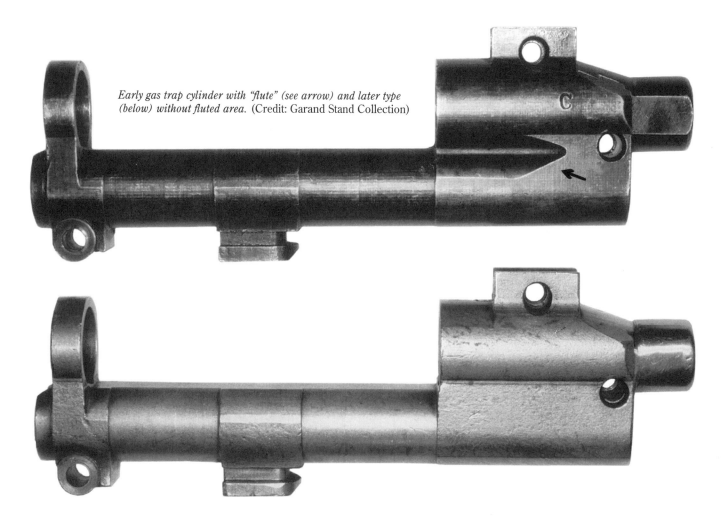

Early gas trap cylinder with "flute" (see arrow) and later type (below) without fluted area. (Credit: Garand Stand Collection)

identified by a 1" hole over a smaller (⁹⁄₁₆") hole drilled into the butt. These holes were presumably intended to reduce the weight of the stock, albeit to a very small degree. Later in the production run of the gas trap rifles, the large over small hole configuration was changed to two equal size ¹³⁄₁₆" holes. The reason for this change has not been discovered, but it was likely done to eliminate the necessity of using two different size drill bits.

Another key identification feature of these early rifles is the buttplates, which were solid and lacked the hinged door. Unlike the Model shop rifle stocks, which were not stamped with inspector cartouches, the production gas trap M1 rifles were stamped on the left side "SA/SPG". This represented Springfield Armory (SA) and inspector Stanley P. Gibbs (SPG). Gibbs was a civilian inspector who had been employed at Springfield since 1916. By the early 1930s, Gibbs had worked his way up to the position of an arms inspector. His cartouche can be found on a number of Springfield Armory weapons of the 1930s period including M1903A1 service and National Match

rifles as well as some .22 caliber M2 rifles and special presentation pieces. Unlike later Springfield Armory stock cartouches, the "SA/SPG" cartouches were not accompanied by the now familiar "cross cannons" Ordnance Department escutcheon. Gibbs' cartouche was used until October of 1940.

The cartouches on subsequent M1 rifles were stamped "SA" above the initials of Springfield Armory's commanding officer. After WWII, Stanley Gibbs inspected a number of M1 rifles, which were overhauled at Springfield, and resumed use of his "SA/SPG" stamp. Stanley Gibbs retired from Springfield Armory on December 31, 1951.

In addition to marking the stocks with inspector cartouches, a single letter "P" enclosed in a circle was stamped on the pistol grip. This mark signified that the rifle had been successfully proofed fired as part of the final inspection process. The proof mark used on gas trap rifles was a plain block letter "P" without the serifs used on later proof marks.

One of the most unique, and interesting, features

(Above, left) Windage knob as found on gas trap M1 rifles. Note the "flared" arrows. The square configuration bolt recess is also visible in this photo. The tool marks are commonly found in early gas trap rifles. (Above, right) Gas trap rifle elevation knob.

 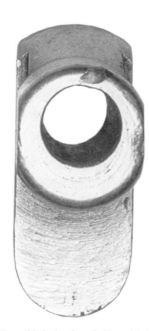 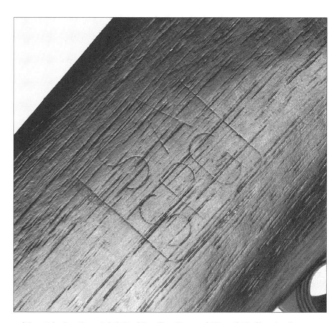

(Above, left) Early gas trap muzzle plug with indention (left) and later type without indention (right). (Credit: Garand Stand Collection)
(Above, right) Stock cartouche found on gas trap M1 rifles. "SA" indicates production by Springfield Armory and "SPG" represents the initials of inspector Stanley P. Gibbs.

found on the gas trap M1s is the presence of "drawing numbers" on most of the component parts. Each part of the M1 rifle was assigned a drawing number by the Ordnance Department. Each drawing number had a letter prefix "A" through "F", which identified the size of the part, followed by the specific number of each part. For example, the M1's bolt was assigned the drawing number " D 28291". If a part was revised for improved performance or easier production, a "revision" number was often stamped after the part's drawing number.

Rear of early gas trap cylinder marked with drawing number. Note the lip-type spacer between ring and the front handguard ferrule.

Thus, the first change in the M1's bolt was represented by the drawing/revision number of "D28291-1". The marking format for drawing numbers underwent some rather subtle changes during the first few years of Garand production. The progression of the drawing number format (using the sight cover as an example) was as follows:

B-8872

B 8872

B8872

No Number

There may occasionally be some exceptions to this format, but it can generally be stated that the earliest parts will have a dash between the letter and number. The next variation will have a space (no dash) between the letter and number. This format is followed by one with no space or dash between the letter and number. Parts revised subsequently were often identified by a "revision number" that was preceded by a dash between it and the drawing number.

Example of early component part (rear handguard band) stamped with drawing number.

In addition to the drawing number, the receiver, bolt and barrel were normally marked with a "heat lot" code. This code generally consisted of a letter and one or two digits identifying the firm that supplied the steel and the specific "lot" of steel used to produce the part. For example, the heat lot marking on the bolt of rifle serial number 2126 is "J 1", and the lot number is "1". The receiver of the same rifle has a heat lot marking of "J 11". It has been theorized (but not confirmed) that "J" represents the firm of Jones & Laughlin Steel Company. If a particular batch of steel from a certain supplier proved to be unsatisfactory, this code would identify the parts produced from the batch of steel in question. Parts bearing this heat lot number could be withdrawn from service. The reason for only marking the heat lot codes on the receiver, barrel and bolt is because these are the most critical from a strength/safety standpoint. The use of heat lot codes on these three components continued throughout the M1's production.

While such information regarding the marking format of drawing numbers may seem quite esoteric, it is actually very important to collectors for determining if a specific part is correct for a particular rifle.

Initially, virtually every part large enough to be stamped was marked with the drawing number. Serial numbers aside, the vintage of a particular gas trap rifle can be determined by the number of numbered parts. That is, the earlier the rifle, the greater the number of numbered parts. On the early gas trap rifles even the wood components (stock and both handguards) were stamped with drawing numbers until around the 20,000 serial number range.

As production continued, fewer and fewer parts were stamped with complete drawing numbers. Sometimes only the revision ("dash") number was stamped, and eventually most drawing numbers were eliminated altogether. Even when drawing numbers were retained on some parts, the location to which they were applied was sometimes changed. For example, very early production M1 operating rods (approximately under serial number #5000) had the drawing number applied to the top of the handle. Slightly later, the same drawing number ("D 35382-0") was stamped on the bottom of the operating rod near the junction of the tube. Operating rods from the beginning of production until somewhere in the low 30,000 serial number range were machined with a slanted area just ahead of the handle. All Springfield M1 operating rods from this point until the end of production in 1957 are of the "straight cut" variety. These rods are generally known by today's collectors as "angle cut" and "straight cut" operating rods. As discussed, following WWII, some operating rods were prone to small stress cracks near the junction of the tube and handle. After the war, the tooling was changed to mill a "relief cut" in this area to eliminate the problem. Large numbers of WWII and earlier vintage operating rods were subsequently modified during overhaul to incorporate this feature. Operating rods without the relief cut are indicative of unmodified WWII (and earlier) production rifles and are a key feature to examine when evaluating a 1945 or earlier vintage Garand.

It was determined by the Ordnance Department that the time and trouble required to stamp so many parts with drawing numbers was not worth the effort involved. Eventually, only the major component parts such as the receiver, operating rod, trigger housing and bolt were marked with drawing numbers. However, the appearance of other numbered parts continued into the production run of the early gas port rifles as well. Following World War II, the drawing number code was revised. The specifics of this drawing number format change will be discussed later.

Another key characteristic of these early rifles is the configuration of the operating rod spring and the presence of a "compensating" spring. These springs were of a "keystone" or square configuration rather than the familiar round springs found on the later M1s. It has been reported that John Garand derisively referred to these springs as "screen door springs." The compensat-

Very early production operating rod drawing number. This number was soon moved to the bottom of the operating rod at the junction of the handle and tube.

ing spring was dropped soon after the adoption of the later gas system, although the use of keystone operating rod springs continued on early gas port rifles.

Gas trap M1s utilized early "long tail" followers and first type of follower slides (20 degree angle at rear). Followers were marked on the bottom with a revision number. Post-World War II followers were generally unmarked.

Beginning as early as the latter part of 1937, the new M1 rifles began to be issued to selected units of the U.S. Army, even though few were on hand. Although the semiautomatic action was obviously a desirable feature, the initial reception of the M1 by some in the U.S. Army, particularly those "in the ranks," was far from universally positive. The venerable '03 Springfield had been a known quantity for the past 30 plus years, and the soldiers were intimately familiar with the weapon. The army, like virtually any institution, does not tolerate change well, and the new Garand rifle certainly represented change. Officially, the introduction of the Garand rifle into U.S. Army service was embraced as a quantum leap forward in military weaponry. From the units initially equipped with M1s, each commanding officer presented reports at the conclusion of the field testing period regarding the rifle's efficacy to General George C. Marshall. For example, the commander of the 3rd Division, Maj. Gen. W.C. Sweeney, stated:

"It is the consensus of opinion of myself, the chief of the Infantry Section, and the commanders of the 4th, 7th and 15th Infantry Regiments, that the rifle, caliber .30 M1, is greatly superior in combat efficiency to the rifle, caliber .30, Model 1903 and is a highly satisfactory infantry weapon…

The mechanical functioning of the Garand rifle is considered satisfactory. There were a few breakages of firing pins due to a considerable amount of dry firing while training for marksmanship. Modification of training procedure reduced these breakages to a very low figure.

From my personal observation I find that the enlisted personnel of the division armed with the new rifle find it entirely satisfactory and are greatly pleased with the results they are obtaining with it. This applies to both enlisted men of long service and to young soldiers who have only fired the Springfield one or two years. As mentioned above, this new weapon has been in the hands of the division for only a short period, but I think that we are all satisfied that with further opportunity to use it, the Garand will prove to be a much superior combat weapon to the old Springfield."

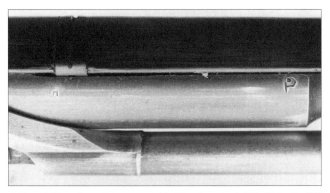

(Above) Barrel markings on right side of gas trap M1. Note the "P" proof with punch mark and the lack of manufacturing dates. The drawing number was stamped on top of the barrel and can only be seen with the rear handguard removed.

(Below) Early production gas trap barrel marked "SA" and dated February 1941. Note the inverted position of the markings.

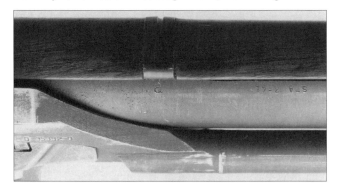

The same sort of sentiments were echoed in the report authored by Brig. Gen. L.R. Frendenhall, Chief of Infantry Section for the 5th Division:

"After observation of the firing of the Garand rifle, both on the known-distance range and on the combat-firing range, it is my opinion that this rifle is definitely superior to the Model 1903 Springfield for combat use for the following reasons: 1. The Garand rifle has reduced the time necessary to train a satisfactory military shot approximately fifty percent. 2. Within the ranges of ordinary military combat firing, the Garand rifle is as accurate as the M1903 Springfield. 3. During critical phases of combat, the Garand rifle is capable of delivering three times the volume of effective fire of the bolt-operated weapon. 4. Men are much less fatigued after firing the semiautomatic rifle over long periods of time than they are after firing the Springfield.

The number of malfunctions have been negligible. All the Infantry company officers consulted are enthusiastic about the performance of the new type rifle."

All of the reports from circa late 1938 to early 1940

period were similarly positive. However, there were definitely opinions to the contrary regarding the new rifle, particularly on an unofficial basis. Some of these were perceived and others were real. The early problems encountered such as the "Seventh Round Stoppage" and the deficiencies with the gas trap system contributed to the M1's image problem. An illustrative passage in the book *There's A War to be Won…The United States Army in World War II* by Geoffrey Perret aptly describes another side to the reaction of the M1's introduction:

"The remaining bugs were worked out one by one. All the while, however, rumors were spreading among the infantry, encouraged by NCOs, that the new rifle wasn't worth a damn. The reason why NCOs disparaged the new rifle was that it had brought with it a more difficult marksmanship course that made it harder to qualify as an expert rifleman. An expert rating was worth five dollars a month. To a sergeant making thirty dollars a month, that was worth getting upset about. A lot of NCOs, fearing for their five dollars a month, bad-mouthed the new rifle rather than try to get used to it."

Perret goes on to report that some marines purposely sabotaged the M1:

"…The Marine Corps held a shooting competition of its own in San Diego. Marine NCOs were determined to hang onto their Springfield — and their five dollars. By dropping the eight round clips into the sand, they got the result the wanted, the weapon jammed…"

As was the case with the Army a couple of years earlier, the Marine Corps' eventual adoption of the M1 was not without controversy. An extensive "selling job" had to be done before the Garand was, at first, reluctantly accepted

In addition to the general fear of anything new, there were a number of flaws inherent with the M1's original gas system design. Common complaints were that gas system was rather hard to clean and a patch could become lodged inside of the gas cylinder. In addition, the relatively loose fit of the gas cylinder on the barrel often resulted in the front sight shifting, which obviously had an adverse effect on accuracy. Also, it was widely felt that, as an attachment for the bayonet, the gas cylinder might not be strong enough. However, the primary problem was that the attachment of the muzzle plug to the gas cylinder was found to be weak. This resulted in some instances of the gas cylinder being blown com-

*Soldier with a "gas trap" M1. The pattern of
the soldier's helmet dates the photograph at
likely no earlier than 1942. A number of
unaltered gas trap Garands saw active use
during the Second World War.*

(Credit: U.S. Army)

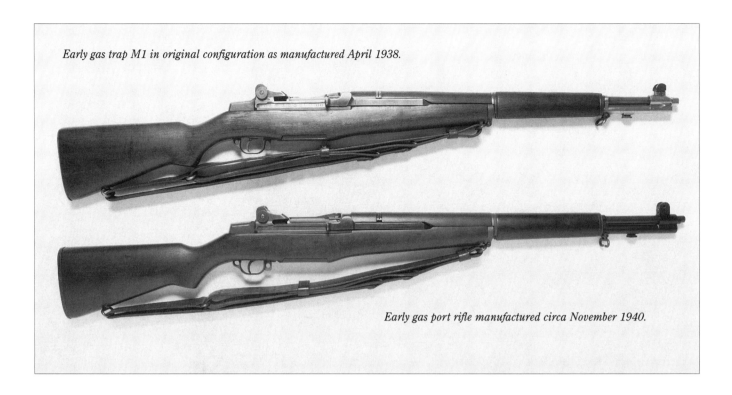

Early gas trap M1 in original configuration as manufactured April 1938.

Early gas port rifle manufactured circa November 1940.

pletely off the rifle when the muzzle plug became loose. These occurrences were rather uncommon but the potential was quite serious. Despite the excellence of John Garand's rifle, some changes in the type of gas system were clearly needed in order to make a good rifle even better.

Garand/Johnson Rifle Controversy

The U.S. Army was less than candid when questioned about these early problems as they began to surface. Their position of "stonewalling" inquiries on the perceived deficiencies of the Garand rifle resulted in further questions regarding the wisdom of adopting what appeared to be, in the eyes of some, a trouble-prone rifle. Proponents of a competing semiautomatic rifle, the Johnson, seized upon this opportunity to push their weapon in favor of the M1. Developed by a Marine captain, Melvin M. Johnson, the Johnson rifle did have several favorable design features. In February of 1940, the *Washington Evening Star* newspaper ran a three-part series of articles titled "Battle Efficiency of the Garand Rifle Provokes Controversy." Other media sources, including newspapers and national magazines, picked up the topic as well. Some civilian shooters at the National Matches held at Camp Perry, Ohio, had previously brought up some concerns about the M1.

In order to inform its membership and in an attempt

to put the matter to rest, the National Rifle Association met with Army representatives and requested permission to borrow an M1 rifle for extensive testing and critique. The Army responded in an almost insulting manner and not so subtly suggested that the shooters didn't know how to use the rifle. The *American Rifleman* published an editorial on the subject and also ran an article favorable to the Johnson rifle. Eventually, the mini-furor had reached the point that a Congressional committee held hearings on the subject. An informal "shoot off" between the Garand and Johnson rifles attended by some members of Congress was held and both weapons acquitted themselves well. Since the M1 was already adopted and in production, it was decided to retain it and concentrate on fixing the problems. The Johnson rifle later saw a small amount of use by the Marine Corps in the early Pacific fighting of WWII. The M1, of course, was eventually thoroughly vindicated. However, due primarily to the Army's high handed approach, the Johnson rifle came surprisingly close to becoming a serious rival to the Garand. *Life* Magazine called the Garand/Johnson controversy "...one of the greatest military squabbles in U.S. history..."

These early problems with the M1 pointed out the need for refinement. Eventually, the annoying bugs were worked out one by one to the point that the Garand became arguably the most reliable semiautomatic service rifle of all time.

On October 26, 1939, the Ordnance Department adopted an entirely new type of gas system to replace the original gas trap system. Rather than trapping the escaping gas at the muzzle, it was decided to utilize a port drilled into the bottom of the barrel, almost 1½" from the muzzle, to divert the gas required to operate the action. This necessitated a different type of gas cylinder and a longer 24" barrel. The new pattern gas cylinder was a spline type rather than the screw-on gas cylinder utilized with the gas trap rifles. A different pattern front sight assembly was also adopted for use with the new gas system.

"Direct Conversion" of Gas Trap Rifles ca. late 1940 to mid-1941

After adoption of the new type of gas system, the Ordnance Department ordered the conversion of the gas trap M1s to the gas port system. Unlike the situation with the original "rod bayonet" M1903 rifles over three decades earlier, there was not a general recall of the gas trap M1s for conversion to the new specifications. Rather, the early rifles were to be modified as they were cycled into depots for maintenance and/or other reasons. The conversion of the 50,000+ gas trap rifles began soon after adoption of the new type of gas system and continued on during, and even after, World War II. Generally, the early rifles were torn down, and the gas trap related parts scrapped. Often, only the receiver was used to rebuild another rifle and even that part was modified by adding a spot of welding to the guide ribs. It is believed that some early gas trap rifles were rebuilt at Springfield Armory in early 1940 primarily to modify the receiver guide ribs. These rifles remained in their gas trap configuration after this rebuild procedure.

However, beginning in very late 1940 or early 1941, Springfield Armory converted a limited number of gas trap M1s directly to gas port configuration and utilized as many of the original parts as possible. Generally, the only new parts found on these rifles are the barrel, gas cylinder and related parts (such as front sights). Therefore, one of the hallmarks of the "direct conversion" rifles is the presence of many parts marked with drawing numbers which would not normally be found on gas port type M1s. The one main exception to the use of the original parts on such rifles is the stock. Springfield fitted these "direct conversion" gas trap rifles with new production stocks having the butt trap recess and hinged buttplate rather than the original "no trap" stocks. By this time, the armory had begun the practice of using cartouches with the initials of the commanding officer. In early 1941, such stocks would have a cartouche marked "SA/GHS" (for Col. Gilbert H. Stewart) stamped next to the ordnance "crossed cannons" escutcheon. It was undoubtedly easier to put new production stocks on these rifles than delay the process by modifying the original stocks. Most of these early "no trap" stocks were eventually modified and used on later rebuilds. The receiver guide ribs were built up by welding as part of the conversion process. In addition, even though the original operating rods were retained, the early keystone configuration operating rod springs were replaced by the later round wire variety.

After modification, these rifles were issued concurrently with new production M1s. Other than the low serial number and the presence of many parts marked with drawing numbers, these rifles were indistinguishable from early 1941 production M1 rifles. See Table #5 for a list of the typical characteristics found on the scarce "Direct Conversion" M1s.

These "direct conversion" gas trap rifles are a little-known and extremely interesting variant M1 for today's collectors. Few of these rifles have survived in their original early 1941 conversion configuration due to the widespread rebuilding programs carried on during, and after, World War II. Original production 1941 vintage M1s, as

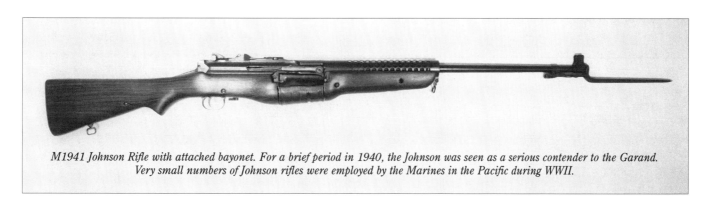

M1941 Johnson Rifle with attached bayonet. For a brief period in 1940, the Johnson was seen as a serious contender to the Garand. Very small numbers of Johnson rifles were employed by the Marines in the Pacific during WWII.

well as the "direct conversion" variants are quite scarce today. Fewer of the converted rifles will be found since only a relatively few were converted during this period. Whether a surviving early 1941 gas trap conversion or an original production M1 of the same vintage is more or less desirable as a collector's item is an individual decision. However, it is probably fair to state that both are in approximately the same value/desirability category given comparable condition.

The goal of acquiring an original gas trap M1 remains an elusive one for most collectors. Even though slightly over 50,000 M1 rifles were made in the gas trap configuration, they are extremely rare due to the fact that practically all the rifles were overhauled before, during and after World War II. The overhaul procedure consisted of removing and scrapping the gas trap related parts and replacing them with updated components. The exact number of rifles that somehow escaped modification is not known, but some students of the subject estimate the number of such rifles in private hands as no more than a couple of dozen. Others exist in various museums and reference collections but, of course, these are not available to collectors. Only those rifles that were removed from the system by theft or other unofficial means prior to rebuild were spared. Previously unknown gas trap M1s rarely show up today, but several have surfaced within the past few years.

Unfortunately, the very high prices that original gas trap M1s normally fetch on the market recently have attracted the attention of con artists. A number of altered early M1s have been "restored" in an attempt to pass them off as original gas trap M1s. Receivers numbered in the gas trap range are not particularly hard to find, but virtually every one has been modified by the guide ribs being built up by welding. It is possible to remove the added welding but generally this can be spotted by careful examination. The hardest parts to find are the original 22" barrels, the gas cylinder and muzzle plugs and the unmodified "SA/SPG" stocks. Not surprisingly, some individuals have produced "reproductions" of these parts. The following fake gas trap rifle parts are known to have been manufactured within the past few years:

- Barrels
- Gas cylinders
- Muzzle plugs
- Front Sights
- Front sight screws
- Front handguard ferrules
- Rear handguards (no clearance cut)
- "No Trap" stocks (generally with *perfect* "SA/SPG" cartouches)
- Bogus drawing numbers stamped on previously unmarked early parts
- Keystone configuration operating rod and compensating springs
- Original operating rods with the later relief cut modification welded up
- Rear sight spanner nuts

Some makers or sellers have openly admitted that the parts are not original and have attempted to mark them in some manner to indicate that they are newly produced items. Other more unscrupulous individuals have not been as forthcoming and have assembled rifles with bogus parts in an attempt to defraud collectors. It should go without saying that someone knowledgeable in the subject should be consulted before a substantial sum is paid for a supposedly original gas trap M1 since some of the crooks can do a remarkably good job of putting together a fake. Original gas trap rifles are exceedingly rare and quite desirable today. Some extremely high prices have been paid for the very small number that have changed hands in the past few years. As is always the case with high-dollar collectibles, *caveat emptor*!

While it can be extremely difficult, if not impossible, to locate an original gas trap M1, other very collectible and interesting variants exist. While far from common, the "direct conversion" M1s (circa early 1941) can serve as an excellent example of the transition from the gas trap to the gas port M1s since these rifles contain features of both variants. While not easy to find, they are certainly more available and less expensive than original gas trap M1s.

The "Gas Port" M1 Rifle Springfield Pre-WWII Production

Although adopted in October of 1939, it was not until March 15, 1940, that the new type of gas system began to be used on new production M1s. Except for the longer barrel with the gas port and the different type of gas cylinder, front sight and handguard ferrule, the modified rifle was identical to the earlier gas trap variety. The production tooling had been corrected to cure the aforementioned "Seventh Round Stoppage" problem prior to incorporation of the new gas system.

Due to the change in gas systems, a new type of front

Prewar production (early 1941) M1 Gas Port rifle.

sight was required. The new pattern sight was secured to a platform on top of the gas cylinder by means of a cap screw. In order to prevent the front sight from being moved, a thin metal cup or seal was placed over the screw. The front sight screw used with these early rifles was beveled in order for the seal to fit tightly over it. The sight screw seal was utilized until mid-WWII. When the early M1s were modified, the sight screw seals were removed and discarded. Generally, later pattern front sight screws were substituted for the early variety. Therefore, the presence of a front sight seal is one of the indications that an early rifle has not been modified.

However, it should be noted that reproduction front sight seals have appeared on the market in the past few years.

The gas cylinders used on the early gas port rifles had a narrower front sight base than found on the rifles made from mid-WWII and later. The early narrow base did not allow the front sight to be shifted to any perceptible degree. Initially, this was not considered to be a problem since the front sight was not supposed to be moved, hence the utilization of the sight screw seal. Later pattern gas cylinders utilized a wider front sight base that allowed for minor adjustment of the front sight's position.

Comparison of front areas of gas port (left) and gas trap (right) gas rifles including front sight.

By this time, it was apparent to all but the most myopic that the United States would eventually be drawn into the war raging in Europe. Almost reluctantly, the United States increased production of all manner of armaments, including M1 rifles, which flowed from Springfield Armory in ever-increasing numbers.

Concurrent with adoption of the new type of gas system, production of the M1 steadily increased at Springfield Armory. Initially, the only substantive changes to the M1 rifles were those directly related to the incorporation of the new gas system. As mentioned previously, these items included the new pattern barrel, gas cylinder, front sight and front handguard ferrule. The same type of stock found on the gas trap rifles was used on the early production gas port rifles. These had the solid buttplate and were stamped with the same "SA/SPG" cartouche. The presence of numbered parts also continued to some extent, although to a much smaller degree than found on the early and mid-production gas trap rifles.

In June 1940, Col. Gilbert H. Stewart was posted to Springfield Armory as the new commanding officer. As stated above, shortly after his arrival, the practice of stamping M1 stocks with a cartouche containing the initials of the commanding officer along with the Ordnance Department's "crossed cannons" escutcheon was instituted. This cartouche consisted of "SA/GHS" enclosed in a box with the ordnance escutcheon stamped to the right. Two variants of this escutcheon may be encountered. The original type was $^{23}/_{32}$" in diameter and was used until sometime in early 1942 (roughly in the high 400,000 serial number range) when a smaller $^{7}/_{16}$" escutcheon came into use. Collectors today generally refer to these as large and small "cannons" (or "wheels"). One must be cautioned, however, that there can be a great deal of overlap in this range as a few examples of totally original rifles as high as the mid-700,000 range have been noted with the "large wheel" escutcheons. A rifle that appears to be totally correct except for the size of the escutcheon should not, by any means, be arbitrarily ruled out as an original piece.

At about the same time that the "small wheel" cartouche came into use, the length of the so-called "barrel channel" was also changed. The "SPG" and earlier "GHS" cartouched stocks had channels approximately 2.275" in length while the later ("small cannon") "GHS" had the channel shortened by about ½". The reason for this change was to provide more clearance in this area. All subsequent M1 stocks were of the "short channel" variety. Some of the early M1 stocks had the long barrel

Cartouche used during the tenure of Col. Gilbert H. Stewart as Commanding Officer of Springfield Armory. Note the large "crossed cannons" escutcheon.

Solid buttplate (left) as used on gas trap and very early gas port rifles and later buttplate (right) with hinged door for access to stock recess.

channel altered to the short variety during postwar overhaul. Such stocks are correct only for rebuilt rifles and will not be found on original rifles. All early stocks had the long barrel channel and, under no circumstances can a short channel stock be found on an original early rifle, regardless of what type of cartouche it may have. This is one of the positive methods of identifying a supposedly original early ("SPG" or "large wheel" "GHS" cartouche) stock. Side-by-side comparison of early and later stocks will readily reveal the difference in barrel channel lengths.

During this period, the now familiar hinged butt trap recess, used to hold cleaning equipment, was adopted. A metal buttplate having a hinged door was standardized. This change occurred at approximately the high 70,000 serial number range. Many of the older "no trap" buttstocks were modified to incorporate the new type of butt trap recess. This was done by routing out the appropriate areas in the butt and modifying the lightening holes accordingly.

One section of the butt trap recess was designed to hold a cylindrical metal oiler and thong case as used with the M1903 rifle. The case was constructed of nickel-plated brass. One compartment of the case held a bore brush attached to a thong, and the other end was an oil reservoir with a dropper built into the cap. Both compartments of the case were secured by screw caps. The other section of the M1's butt trap recess could hold a combination tool, a small container of rifle grease and cleaning patches.

Another feature of the early "SA/GHS" rifles was the continued use of the "keystone" configuration operating rod and compensating springs as were utilized on the gas trap M1s. Eventually, the compensating spring was dropped but the keystone operating rod spring continued in use for a period of time. A follower rod with a thick, rounded profile was adopted for use with the keystone operating rod spring after the elimination of the compensating spring. This pattern follower rod was only used during the mid- to latter part of 1940. After the adoption of the now familiar round wire operating rod spring, a riveted follower rod with a flat profile was used. There were several variants of this later follower rod.

Very early gas port rifles utilized the "long tail" follower (unmarked) and first type (20 degree angle rear) slide. By early 1941, the later "short tail" follower and second type of slide came into use.

At first, the gas port barrels (like the gas trap barrels) were not marked with the date of production. Beginning in mid-1940, the gas port barrels were

stamped with the month and year of production and with the initials "SA" (Springfield Armory). Other parts also began to be stamped "SA" since the Winchester Repeating Arms Company began mass production of the M1 rifle during this period.

Winchester Repeating Arms Company Pre-WWII Production

By early 1939, Springfield Armory began to slowly but steadily increase its output of M1 rifles. However, due to the war heating up in Europe, it was feared that the eventual demand for rifles by our allies and our own armed forces would overwhelm Springfield's production capacity. In order to have another source of M1 rifles available, the Ordnance Department solicited bids from several civilian arms manufacturers to produce the weapon under government contract. Winchester Repeating Arms Company of New Haven, Connecticut, was awarded the contract for M1 production. Winchester was a long time supplier of small arms to the United States military, and the company had a good working relationship with the Ordnance Department. Winchester was given an "Educational Contract" on April 4, 1939, (Contract #W-ORD-343) for 500 M1 rifles and one tool, fixture or gauge for each part. The contract gave specific cost allocations for all labor and materials. This initial small contract was to determine the suitability of the firm for production of the Garand rifle prior to any large scale contracts being granted.

During the period Winchester was tooling up for M1 production, several changes in the production specifications were mandated by the Ordnance Department. Two of these changes involved different steel specifications. The most significant was the change in gas systems. The original contract specifications called for the early gas trap system. The change to the improved gas port system occurred on July 13, 1940, when an additional $9,050 was appropriated to Winchester for the necessary manufacturing changes in gas systems. These changes were accomplished prior to the start of production, and all of the rifles made by the firm were of the gas port variety. Since Winchester was a civilian entity, any changes from the original contract specifications had to be negotiated by the government, and the firm compensated for any additional labor or materials cost.

Although there were the normal "bugs" and "glitches," Winchester delivered the first 100 of its M1 rifles to the government on December 27, 1940, and the balance of the first contract rifles were completed on March 10, 1941.

Winchester rifles were marked on the receiver:

U.S. RIFLE
CAL. .30 M1
Winchester
TRADEMARK
"Serial Number"

The block of serial numbers assigned to Winchester for M1 production began with serial number 100,001, and the first five hundred rifles were numbered consecutively (100,001–100,500).

The first 500 "Educational Contract" Winchester M1 rifles were very similar to the rifles made by Springfield Armory during the same period. However, there were a number of differences between Winchester and Springfield M1 rifles that are of interest to collectors today. They will be discussed later.

Surviving examples of unmodified "Educational Order" Winchester M1 rifles are quite rare and are seldom encountered. It has been reported (apparently erroneously) that the rifles from first block of Winchester M1s had blued finishes. However, the very first production Winchester M1 rifle, serial number 100001, which shows every indication of remaining in its

Receiver markings of early "Second Contract" Winchester Garand manufactured circa October 1941.

original condition, exhibits a black-tinted, parkerized finish on the receiver.

The early Winchester M1 stocks were of the "no-trap" variety with two equal size holes drilled in the butt and fitted with the solid buttplate. These stocks were stamped with a "WRA/RS" cartouche enclosed in a 1" x .875" box on the left side next to the "crossed cannons" ordnance escutcheon. This cartouche was used on the Winchester Garand rifles produced prior to June 1941. "RS" represents Col. Robert Sears, the head of Winchester's Ordnance District (Hartford) at the time. A "circle P" proof mark was stamped on the pistol grip. It should be noted that the use of the previous inspection cartouche stamp did not cease abruptly on the day that a new ordnance district chief was assigned. Use of the previous cartouche could, and did, continue for weeks or even months after a new ordnance head was posted.

Unlike the practice at Springfield Armory since mid-1940, Winchester did not stamp their barrels with the month and year of production. A number of component parts such as the receiver, barrel, trigger housing, operating rod, bolt, triggerguard, safety, bullet guide and hammer were marked "WRA" as a prefix to the drawing number. The early Winchester rifles had numbered gas cylinders and incorporated the front sight screw seal. The front sights of all Winchester M1s had noticeably wider ears than found on Springfield Garands. The early Winchester M1 rifles utilized keystone-shaped operating rod and compensating springs as found on the gas trap and very early gas port Springfield M1s.

Even before the first 500 "Educational Contract" rifles were manufactured, Winchester was awarded a second contract for Garand production. On September 20, 1939, the firm was given an order for 65,000 M1s. Springfield Armory assisted Winchester in setting up its assembly line for mass production of the Garand rifle. Sometimes dubbed the "Second Contract" Winchester M1 rifles by collectors today, they were assigned serial numbers in sequence with the "Educational Contract" rifles. This block of serial numbers was 100,501– 165,500. Although production began in February 1941, the first "Second Contract" Winchester M1s were not shipped from the factory until April 15 of the same year. The last rifles under this contract were completed in May of 1942. Initially, the "Second Contract" Winchester M1 rifles were very similar to the first 500 "Educational Contract" Garands. The keystone compensating spring was soon discontinued and other relatively minor changes followed. The stocks were still of the no-trap variety and stamped with "WRA/RS" cartouches.

Early production Winchester stock cartouche. This is the first pattern "WB" cartouche. "WRA" is for Winchester Repeating Arms and "WB" represents the initials of Col. Waldemar Broberg, head of Winchester's Ordnance District. This is a rarely encountered cartouche. The second pattern cartouche does not have the "WB" enclosed in a separate box.

When Col. Waldemar Broberg assumed Col. Sears' duty in July 1941, the cartouche was changed to "WRA/WB". The first "WB" cartouches had a unique marking format with the initials being enclosed in a small rectangle inside of a larger box containing the "WRA" marking. Broberg's cartouche was later changed to the familiar variety with "WB" and "WRA" enclosed in a single large box. The use of the no-trap buttstock continued early in Broberg's tenure but the incorporation of the butt trap recess was approved just prior to Broberg's departure in July of 1942. The rifles with "WRA/WB" stock cartouches (of both variants) will have serial numbers in the (approx.) 111,500 to 1,219,000 serial number range.

The buttplates used by Winchester throughout production can be identified from those made by Springfield Armory by the much more defined border between the edge of the buttplate and the checkering.

The final contract given to Winchester prior to our entry in WWII was for 60,000 M1 rifles on November 18, 1941. The company was still in the midst of the building the "Second Contract" rifles when the Japanese attacked Pearl Harbor, and the United States was actively at war. Winchester was awarded additional contracts for M1 production during WWII, and the firm eventually deliv-

Early production "Second Contract" Winchester M1 rifle.

ered some 513,880 Garand rifles to the government before production was terminated in 1945.

Surviving examples of pre-World War II production Winchesters are seldom encountered today and are highly desirable collector items. The most difficult to find are examples of the Educational Contract rifles in unaltered condition. Surviving unaltered examples of the 65,000 "Second Contract" Winchester M1 rifles are almost as scarce.

As is the case with pre-WWII Springfield M1s, many collectors desire examples of early production Winchester Garands. The very limited supply and high demand have resulted in very high prices for the relatively few original examples and an increase in the practice of "restoring" overhauled rifles. Restoring any early Garand, particularly a Winchester, can be a frustrating and difficult task as many of the necessary parts are in extremely short supply today.

The most difficult items to find are the genuine, unaltered early "no trap" Winchester stocks and the keystone configuration springs. As stated, there are a number of fake keystone springs on the market today. There are also some stocks with bogus (sometimes imaginatively referred to as "enhanced" or "refreshed") "WRA/RS" cartouches on the collector market today. Winchester receivers in the Second Contract block of numbers are not especially common but can be found from time to time. Almost invariably, these are on rebuilt rifles that have few, if any, of the original Winchester parts left. Original, unaltered "Second Contract" Winchester rifles are rare and highly desirable collector pieces. The fact that some of the receivers may be found means that they can serve as a starting point for a legitimate restoration or as a "rip-off" project by a crook. Likewise, many of the early Winchester M1 parts are far from common but do turn up from time to time. Any pre-WWII Winchester Garand purported to be original and with a price tag to match should be examined very closely by a knowledgeable collector or student of the subject.

There are several things to look for when evaluating such a rifle. One of the first is to determine if the stock is actually of Winchester origin. There are some slight dimensional differences between Winchester and Springfield M1 stocks that are apparent to a trained eye. The stock should then be examined to be certain that it is an early stock. This will be evidenced by the long barrel channel and a butt that has not been routed out for the butt trap recess. Almost all of the early Winchester (and SA gas trap) stocks were later modified by routing out the butt for the recess and its hinged buttplate. Any

attempt to fill in this area is usually pretty obvious. The buttplate should always be removed, and the butt area examined very closely. Likewise, the "WRA/RS" or "WRA/WB" cartouche should be closely scrutinized. Many of the bogus cartouches are absolutely perfectly aligned and very deeply struck as compared to the originals which were often slightly askew with varying degrees of indention in the wood. An original cartouche could be perfectly aligned as well but this would be the exception and certainly not the rule. A good rule of thumb is, "If it looks too good to be true, it probably is."

Any example of an original "pre-Pearl Harbor" M1 rifle, either Springfield or Winchester, is an excellent addition to a collection. The low survival rate of M1s made during this period is attributable to relatively low production quantities and the fact that such weapons saw widespread use beginning in the early days of America's entry into WWII. Therefore, the pre-WWII production M1 rifles were much more likely to have been overhauled by the government one or more times than rifles produced near the end of the war. Since the original pattern gas trap and early gas port rifles (pre-1942) were the only ones in inventory at the time of Pearl Harbor, they were immediately in the thick of fighting. The first combat use of the M1 occurred in the Philippines. Contrary to some published reports, a number of unmodified gas trap M1s were used during this period. An interesting cablegram dated February 20, 1942, from General Douglas MacArthur to Chief of Staff General George Marshall stated:

"Garand rifles giving superior service to Springfield, no mechanical defects reported or stoppages due to dust and dirt from foxhole use. Good gun oil required as lubricant to prevent gumming, but have been used in foxhole fighting day and night for a week without cleaning and lubricating. All these weapons are excellent ones even without any modifications such as suggested."

Undoubtedly, the "modifications" referred to by Gen. MacArthur included the change in gas systems.

Since it is all but impossible to obtain an original gas trap M1, many collectors take the reasonable approach of acquiring a pre-1942 Garand as the earliest example in their collection. The limited number of original surviving examples of these rifles, both Springfield and Winchester, and the steady demand have resulted in ever-escalating prices for such weapons. The demand for pre-WWII Garands will surely continue to increase as will the unfortunate problem of fakes.

Pre-World War II
Accessories and Accouterments

In order to make use of existing equipment, the M1 was designed to utilize several of the accouterments and accessories of the M1903 rifle. The ability to utilize existing stocks of equipment was an important consideration in the budgetary climate of the 1930s. Among the most important of these are the M1907 sling and the M1905 bayonet and M1910 bayonet scabbard.

Slings

The leather M1907 sling was adopted just a few years after the introduction of the M1903 rifle. Large numbers were left over from the First World War and remained on hand in the government's inventory. Many of these slings were dated so it was normal to find "1917"- or "1918"-dated slings on original pre-WWII M1 rifles. The pre-WWII M1907 slings can be identified as they had brass hardware rather than the steel hardware found on most of the slings made during the Second World War.

Bayonets and Scabbards

The M1905 bayonet had originally been adopted concurrently with the modifications of 1905 that eliminated the M1903's original "rod bayonet" mechanism. The M1905 had proven to be a very serviceable bayonet, and it saw wide use during the First World War. At the time of the M1's adoption, sufficient numbers of these bayonets were on hand to equip the new rifles. The majority of the WWI and earlier vintage M1905 bayonets had their original bright blades refinished by parkerizing during the 1920s and 1930s. This partially accounts for the relative scarcity of 1917 and earlier vintage M1905 bayonets retaining the original bright finish on their blades.

The M1910 scabbard had been standardized for use with the M1905 bayonet prior to World War I in order to replace the original leather M1905 scabbard. The M1910 was the current issue bayonet scabbard at the time of the M1 rifle's adoption. The M1910 scabbard had a hard rawhide body under a canvas cover with a leather tip. The scabbard was equipped with cartridge belt hooks. Some of the old M1905 scabbards had previously been modified by the addition of these hooks. These modified scabbards were classified as "Substitute Standard." Such modified M1905 scabbards can technically be considered as correct for use with early M1 Garand rifles.

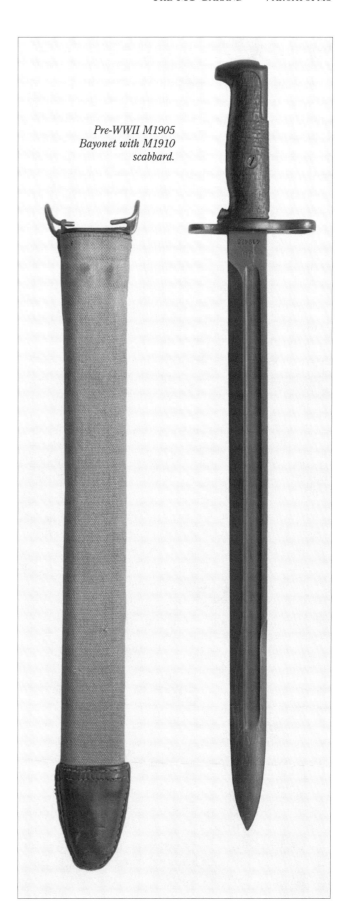

Pre-WWII M1905 Bayonet with M1910 scabbard.

Cartridge Belts

There were sufficient stocks of cartridge belts left over from the First World War to meet the needs of the pared-down U.S. Army prior to 1940. The standard issue cartridge belts at the time of the M1's adoption were either M1918 belt, as adopted during WWI, or the M1923 belt. Few of the latter belts were produced prior to 1942. Both models were similar and could be utilized to carry two '03 five-round chargers or one eight-round Garand clip in each pocket. Grommets on the bottom of the belt allowed for bayonet scabbards, canteens, first aid pouches and the like to be attached to the belt. Suspenders could also be fastened to the top row of grommets to help support the weight of the belt. If a collector wishes to display an early M1 rifle as issued prior to WWII, the use of First World War vintage accessories such a slings, bayonets and cartridge belts would be proper. It may be surprising to some just how much of the older 1917–1918 vintage equipment was still on hand and widely issued during the early days of the Second World War.

➤ ➤ ➤ ➤ ➤ ➤ ➤ World War II Production ◄ ◄ ◄ ◄ ◄ ◄ ◄

At the time of the attack on Pearl Harbor, production of the M1 rifle was well underway at Springfield Armory. The U.S. military was still woefully short of Garand rifles during this period due to the tremendous increase in demand. To further compound the problem, a number of new production M1 rifles had been diverted to fill Lend-Lease requirements to our British allies.

M1 rifle production at both Springfield Armory and Winchester took on even greater urgency with the active involvement of the United States in the war. For a number of collectors today, the "Pre-Pearl Harbor" and "Post-Pearl Harbor" Garands are sometimes thought of as distinct and separate variants. This is pushing things a bit as the rifles made on December 8th did not differ one bit from the rifles produced on December 7th. On the other hand, there is some validity to the differentiation between rifles made prior to the United States' declaration of war and those made during the course of the war. As production increased at Springfield and Winchester, growing numbers of Garand rifles began to appear in combat around the globe. Table #6 gives the general characteristics of Springfield M1 rifles produced during WWII and Table #7 covers the Garands produced by Winchester.

Although the U.S. Marine Corps adopted the M1 in early 1941, the early Pacific campaigns were fought primarily with the venerable '03 rather than the M1 due to initially slow procurement of the Garand by the Marine Corps. The following is the text of a letter from Maj. General Thomas Holcomb, Commandant of the Marine Corps to Maj. General Charles Wesson, U.S. Army, Chief of Ordnance, regarding the Corps' adoption of the Garand rifle. Due to its historical significance, the letter is reproduced here in its entirety.

HEADQUARTERS U.S. MARINE CORPS
WASHINGTON, March 5, 1941

Dear General Wesson:

Three additional copies of the report of the board which conducted tests of rifles at San Diego during the period November 12 to December 21, 1940 were sent to you this day by messenger. As a result of these tests, the Marine Corps has decided to adopt the M-1 [sic] rifle. There is available under 1941 appropriations $2,213,960 for the purchase of these rifles. Included in the 1942 appropriations bill now before Congress is an item of $1,080,000 for the purchase of additional rifles.

At the present time the Marine Corps has approximately 52,000 serviceable M-1903 [sic] rifles; 4,000 awaiting reconditioning for which the Marine Corps has been unable to get spare parts from the Army; and an additional 3,000, each component of which is unserviceable.

The present enlisted strength of the Marine Corps on active duty is 46,048, which will be increased to 50,566 not later than April 5th

The Marine Corps has a directive to submit at the earliest practicable date estimates for an additional 25,000 men.

Will you please inform me at what rate the M-1 [sic] rifles can be furnished the Marine Corps in order that the Quartermaster may place formal order for same. It is urgently recommended that not less than 3,000 a month be delivered, commencing in April, 1941.

Very sincerely,
(signed) Thomas Holcomb
The Major General Commandant

Major General Charles M. Wesson, U.S.A.

Chief of Ordnance Return to:
Munitions Building   Small Arms Division
Washington, D.C.   Industrial Service

A Navy Bureau of Ordnance Report dated November 5, 1941, stated:

Attention is invited to the substitution of the U.S. Rifle, Cal. .30, M1 for the M1903 rifle, as the M1 Rifle is now the standard rifle.

A Marine Corps memorandum from the Commandant to the Director of Plans and Policies dated January 26, 1943 stated:

M1 rifles are now being received at a rate that will not only permit the equipping of all new Fleet Marine Force organizations but the gradual replacement of M1903 rifles now in the hands of other units. M1903 rifles, as received will be turned over to the Navy.

There was quite a bit of dissatisfaction during this period regarding American troops being the in the same armament class as the Japanese. As was often the case, the needs of the Marine Corps took a back seat to the army when it came to scarce and desirable equipment such as the M1 rifle. The Marines Corps' desire for the M1 rifle increased steadily as the weapon's combat superiority over the '03 became apparent. Some marines were initially a bit anxious about giving up their beloved '03 Springfields but soon became die-hard proponents of the Garand. An official Marine Corps volume on the operations in WWII discusses this subject:

The M1 rifle was issued to the 1st Division in April, 1943, after it had left Guadalcanal, and was in Australia training for the impending New Britain operation. Nostalgia for the reliable '03 was widespread, but the increased firepower of the M1 would not be denied. This is not to say that no Marines had M1s on the 'canal, for some acquired them through a "moonlight requisition" after Army units arrived on the island. Others obtained the new rifle by picking up the dropped weapons of soldiers who had been wounded and evacuated.

Col. John George relates several anecdotes regarding the Garand's superiority over the M1903 rifle on the battlefield in his interesting book, *Shots Fired in Anger.* Col. George landed on the Guadalcanal with the army troops who were sent to relieve the beleaguered

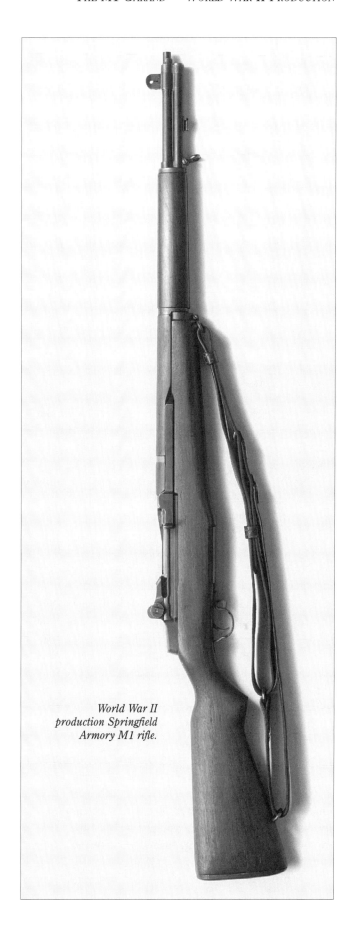

World War II production Springfield Armory M1 rifle.

marines. There were numerous occasions for the Marines who had been armed with the bolt action '03 to observe the effectiveness of the Garands in the hands of the U.S. Army troops who came later. Col. George confirms the "unofficial" use of the M1 by Marines on Guadalcanal:

By the time we landed, we had to keep ours (M1s) tied down with wire. Leathernecks were appropriating all they could lay their hands on by "moonlight requisition". In daylight, they would come over to our area to barter souvenirs with the freshly landed doughboy units; any crooked supply sergeant who had an extra M1 could get all the loot he wanted.

The actions of one marine participating in a joint operation with the army aptly summed up the desire to replace the slow and laborious '03 with the fast-firing M1:

I saw this Marine, a member of the 2nd Raider Battalion, place and keep himself squarely behind one of the army sergeants in the advance platoon. When the march was well underway the sergeant inquired as to why the leatherneck kept treading on his heels.

The answer came quickly; "You'll probably get yours on the first burst, Mac. Before you hit the ground I'll throw this damn Springfield away and grab your rifle."

A 1943 U.S. Marine Corps report on various infantry weapons used by a raider outfit on New Georgia Island contained the following passage regarding the M1, "U.S. Rifle, cal. .30 M1: Turned in an excellent performance, and held up very well under all conditions. It is recommended that the modified rear sights be procured for all rifles." The "modified rear sights" referred to in the report were undoubtedly the improved "locking bar" sights.

The first combat use of the Garand by the U.S. Army in Europe took place during the "Operation Torch" campaign in North Africa against Vichy French troops in November of 1942. The first combat action against the Germans in which the M1 rifle played a part was in Tunisia in early 1943. The M1 eventually served with distinction in every theater of the war and gained an overwhelmingly positive reputation with its users. From the onset, the M1 rifle provided a very real "edge" against enemy troops armed primarily with bolt action rifles. The early "bugs" were soon forgotten, and the various minor improvements made during the war only increased the Garand's already excellent efficiency.

Despite the Garand's unquestioned success of the battlefield, some problems became apparent as the rifle was used with increasing frequency. It was often noted that the rear sight would not hold its setting as securely as it should. In mid-1942, the spanner nut used on the original design was replaced by a bar that could be hand-tightened to prevent the elevation and windage knobs from moving. The same short pinion was used on the first "lock bar" rear sights. A longer pinion utilizing the same type of bar was introduced a short time later. The "short pinion" locking bar rear sights were only in use for a relatively brief period of time and are much less commonly seen than the later long pinion variety. In late 1944, the "T105E1" rear sight (to be discussed later) was adopted although not put into production before the end of the war. Even with the problems encountered, the Garand's sights were superb. As stated by Roy Dunlap in his book, *Ordnance Went Up Front*, "The Garand's sights…are in my opinion better than those on any other standard military rifle in existence."

Another potentially less serious but still troublesome problem was that the finish applied to the M1's gas cylinder wore off very quickly with even a modest amount of use. The gas cylinder was constructed of stainless steel, therefore it could not be blued or parkerized in the conventional manner. Originally, a paint-like coating ("Molyblack") was applied to the shiny gas cylinder but this coating was not very durable. Various formulations and methods of application were tried that helped a great deal, but the problem was never totally solved. This issue was more than cosmetic in nature. Obviously, a shiny gas cylinder on the end of a rifle's barrel was not conducive to camouflage and could conceivably reveal a soldier's position with disastrous results.

Generally speaking, the earlier the rifle, the less durable the finish of the gas cylinder. It is quite common to see pre-1943 vintage M1 rifles in extremely nice condition but having gas cylinders with little or no finish remaining. On later rifles, the degree of finish found on the gas cylinder is normally directly proportional to the wear and tear found on the rest of the rifle.

Another vexing problem with the M1 was noted when the weapon was subjected to prolonged periods of rainfall. Such conditions could cause the action to "freeze," and the rifle become unserviceable. Eventually, it was determined that a special grease applied to the camming surfaces of the bolt would reduce the problem a great deal. Small containers of this grease (called "Lubriplate") were carried in the buttstock recess of the

Marines on Peleliu. Note the M1 held by the Marine in the foreground and the carbine carried by the Marine behind the wounded Marine.
(Credit: USMC)

U.S. Marines on the range with their M1 rifles. Although many "old salts" initially believed that the Garand was far inferior to the Corps' beloved '03 in accuracy, experience soon revealed that the M1 was actually easier to shoot than the '03, and its accuracy was entirely adequate for a combat rifle. (Credit: USMC)

M1. The use of Lubriplate prevented this tendency of the M1 from becoming a significant problem.

Other complaints against the M1 were due to the basic design itself and little could be done to correct these. The Garand's weight of some ten pounds was widely criticized, particularly compared to the eight plus pounds of the '03 rifle. Soldiers carrying the M1 on extended marches and similar duties frequently groused about the weight of the rifle. On the other hand, such complaints tended to become less frequent when the Garand saw front line combat service. The rifle's weight actually wasn't excessive for a semiautomatic rifle of the period, but this was probably the most common gripe against the weapon. As stated by Roy Dunlap, "The weight of the blasted rifle got me down — 10 pounds is about two and a half too much for an army rifle."

The M1's method of loading also came in for a great deal of criticism in some quarters. John Garand designed his rifle with an "en bloc" loading system by which eight cartridges contained in a sheet metal clip were loaded into the open bolt at the top of the receiver. Such a method allowed for manual seating of the cartridges and the design did not have a magazine protruding under the stock. It did, however, require that the section of the stock containing the magazine be noticeably thicker than the rest of the stock. There were many contemporary complaints lodged against the "en bloc" system.

The opinions of Marine Colonel W.J. Whaling on the subject are reported in Hatcher's *Book of the Garand*:

The clip, as it is now designed, is a waster of ammunition. When one, two or three rounds have been fired, the user naturally wants to replenish his magazine so that he will have the full eight rounds ready for the next target, or perhaps for a Banzai charge. But after one or more shots have been fired, it is so difficult to reload that the remaining four, five or six rounds are invariably fired at once, and a fresh clip is inserted. Such excessive firing wastes ammunition, and discloses positions, especially at night. The Garand clip loading system should be replaced by a magazine similar to the BAR or the carbine.

This same sentiment is echoed by Roy Dunlap in *Ordnance Went Up Front*:

A eight round clip is fine — it's nice to be able to fire that many times without reloading. But it is not so good to

U.S. soldier posing with his newly issued M1 Garand rifle with fixed M1905 bayonet. (Credit: USMC)

have *to fire that many — to be obliged to completely empty the gun before it can be reloaded, which is almost a necessity with the M1.*

The Garand's method of loading was probably the weapon's weakest design point. One contemporary rival of the M1, the Johnson rifle, was designed with an integral 10-round rotary magazine that could be easily "topped off." This was touted, with some justification, as a great improvement over the M1's loading system. Undoubtedly, John Garand felt that the lack of a protruding magazine under the M1's stock was a reasonable trade off for the inability to easily reload a partially empty clip. Obviously, this is debatable. It should be noted that the M1's successor, the M14, utilized a detachable 20-round box magazine.

Another problem sometimes cited concerning the Garand was of a rather questionable nature. This oft-repeated "deficiency" was the distinctive pinging noise made by the M1's ejected clip when the last round was fired. Supposedly, this caused the unnecessary deaths of many American servicemen as it signaled the enemy that the rifle was unloaded, and the soldier vulnerable until his M1 could be reloaded. The Japanese or, in some tales, the Germans could instantly charge across open ground and kill the hapless American while he wrestled with his unloaded Garand. The problem with this scenario is that such a turn of events is rather unlikely as solider with even a modicum of training (not to mention lots of incentive) could easily reload his M1 much quicker than a enemy could leave his position and charge across even a few dozen yards of ground.

Despite this alleged serious problem being bandied around from the early days of WWII until now, there have been few, if any, *documented* cases where the noise of an ejected M1 clip resulted in the death of an American serviceman. This story was the likely result of barracks bull sessions or from some other similar

Pfc. Frank Vukasin, Company C, 331st Infantry Regiment, 83rd Division, reloading his M1 rifle near Houffalize, Belgium, during the "Battle of the Bulge." Note the dead Germans in front of his postion. (Credit: U.S. Army)

Photograph dated July 20, 1944, showing an American infantryman firing his M1 rifle at a German sniper in France.
(Credit: National Archives)

Marines "coming ashore" in the Pacific during WWII. The Marine on the far right is carrying an M1 with an M1905 bayonet attached. (Credit: USMC)

source. Nevertheless, some soldiers took the issue quite seriously and were concerned about the noise caused by the M1's ejected clip. It has been reported that the Ordnance Department looked at several methods of correcting the situation including a suggestion that plastic clips be used to silence the noise caused by the standard sheet metal clips. In spite of such concern in some quarters, this alleged deficiency of the M1 rifle did not reduce its effectiveness one iota.

Despite the above enumerated problems, the M1 rifle performed superbly on the battlefield. The weapon definitely gave the American GI an edge as compared with our allies and adversaries. Only two nations fielded semiautomatic service rifles in any appreciable quantities; the German G41/G43 and the Soviet M1938/40 Tokarev. These weapons were not in the same class as the Garand regarding reliability and utility and were only issued in limited numbers. On the other hand, by mid-1943, the majority of American infantrymen, army and marine, were well equipped with M1s.

From the onset of America's entry into WWII, the demand for M1 rifles was high and remained constant for the first few years of the war. The rifles being produced by Springfield Armory at the time of Pearl Harbor

were in the low 400,000 range with "SA/GHS" stock cartouches. Winchester Garands of the same period were in the low 130,000 serial number range and were marked with "WRA/WB" stock cartouches

Barrel dates are not a definitive indicator of the exact date of production as might be imagined by some people. For example, barrels used on the Springfield assembly line on December 7th were taken from storage bins of barrels produced weeks or months earlier. It should be remembered that the date stamped on the barrel was the date that the *barrel* was manufactured, not the date that the rifle was assembled. A general rule of thumb for WWII production M1 rifles is that the barrel date could precede the date of assembly by two to three months. Therefore, a rifle assembled in early December of 1941 could have a barrel dated October or November of the same year. Many collectors who have November '41 (or earlier) dated barrels could well have a rifle that was made after Pearl Harbor. The best indication of the date of assembly is the vintage of the receiver. Table #1 gives the estimated month and year of receiver production by serial number.

Actually, there is very little, if any, difference in value between M1 rifles made in late 1941 and early 1942 assuming comparable condition and degree of originali ty. However, by mid-1942 several noteworthy changes, from the collector's point of view, were incorporated into new production M1 rifles.

Collectors often seek distinct "variants" in order to differentiate the rifles in their collections. Some collectors consider any M1 rifle made from 1941 to 1945 as a "World War Two Garand," while others are of the opinion that there are a number of separate and distinct WWII variants The problem with this latter approach is the identification of variants was never officially recognized as such. While there were some true variants such as the M1C and M1D sniper rifles (to be discussed later), the M1 service rifles were all officially considered the same.

Many collectors consider the rifles produced during the tenure of each commanding officer of Springfield or, in the case of Winchester, Hartford's Ordnance District as distinct variants of the Garand. The different stock

cartouches are the principal identifying characteristics for such "variants." While this approach can be criticized as overly simplistic and lacking any official recognition, it is nevertheless a popular approach. Table #2 gives the approximate serial number ranges and dates of tenure for the cartouches of Springfield's commanding officers or the heads of Winchester's Ordnance District during World War II.

In June of 1942, Col. Earl McFarland replaced Col. Stewart as commanding officer of Springfield Armory. Soon after McFarland's posting to Springfield, the final inspection cartouche was changed from "SA/GHS" to "SA/EMcF". There were two minor variations in McFarland cartouched stocks. The earlier stocks had a rounded recess for the clip latch, while later stocks had a square recess. Otherwise, the stocks were essentially identical. Stocks with the "EMcF" cartouche will be found on rifles in the (approx.) serial number range of 639,000 to 1,790,000

Marines battling the Japanese on "Suicide Ridge", Peleliu. Note the M7 rifle grenade launcher on the M1 Garand at the right.

(Credit: USMC)

 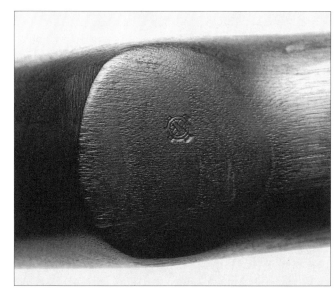

(Above, left) Cartouche of Col. Earl McFarland, Commanding Officer of Springfield Armory circa June 1942 to July 1943. (Above, right) Small "crossed cannons" Ordnance Department escutcheon on the bottom of the pistol grip as found on many Springfield Armory M1 stocks made during the mid-WWII period.

Another interesting, but often overlooked, feature began to appear during Col. McFarland's tenure. A small (approx. ¼") "crossed cannon" insignia was stamped on the bottom of the pistol grip on many Springfield M1s. The meaning of this marking has not been documented and several theories have been advanced. One theory is that stocks bearing this marking were procured by Springfield from outside sources. Another theory is that Springfield Armory started the practice of stamping stocks with stock inspector markings during this period. Other theories have been advanced as well. No definitive information has yet been discovered to explain the purpose this marking or why it was started and later stopped. However, the "crossed cannons" escutcheon typically indicates that a part so marked has been approved by an ordnance inspector. Therefore, the most reasonable explanation is that the marking represents that of a stock inspector.

During this same general period, the front sight seal was eliminated. It was eventually realized that the seal served no real purpose, and its elimination was one less part of the M1 that had to be manufactured. A front sight screw without a bevel to accommodate the seal was incorporated to replace the earlier variety. As the pre-1943 rifles underwent rebuild, the seals were removed and discarded. It is relatively uncommon to find a WWII rifle from this vintage that has not been overhauled, and the presence of the seal is one key point to observe. It should be mentioned that some very good reproduction front sight seals have been on the market for several

years. Therefore, the condition of the seal should be looked at very closely to determine whether it matches the general condition of the rest of the rifle, particularly the gas cylinder and front sight. A seal that appears brand new would not be expected to be encountered on a well used rifle with a very worn finish on the gas cylinder and front sight areas.

As production continued, there were numerous engineering changes made to most of the M1 components. Many of the changes are not readily apparent but can be identified by the change in the drawing/revision number. Virtually every major part including receiver, barrel, operating rod, trigger housing, bolt and many others will show revision number changes during the course of the war. The time frame for such changes should track the general vintage of the rifle. There was some overlap in the general time period that the various revision number changes were instituted since the earlier parts were used until the supply became depleted and new revision parts came into use. Collectors sometimes get a little too focused on exact cut-off points for the revision changes on certain parts. It should be remembered that the only concern for workmen at Springfield or Winchester during the war was to turn out as many acceptable rifles as possible in the shortest period of time. If a part with an earlier revision number was available, it was used. On the other hand, a part with a revision number differing from the vintage of the receiver by more than a few months is suspect. For example, an operating rod with a revision "-3" would not be correct for a 1945 vintage rifle.

"British-Proofed" M1 Rifles

As previously stated, a surprising number of M1 rifles were supplied to Great Britain under Lend-Lease and related programs during the late 1941 and early 1942 periods. This practice was not widely known at the time due to national security considerations. Also, some of these rifles were sent to England prior to Pearl Harbor at a time when isolationist feelings in the United States still ran high. If it was revealed that thousands of our newest service rifles were being sent to Great Britain at a time when our own rapidly expanding armed forces were faced with severe shortages of weapons, a great hue and cry would have been forthcoming.

The M1 rifles supplied to Great Britain during this period were standard production Garands as made circa mid to late 1941 and early 1942. When the rifles arrived in England, the common practice was to paint a large red band around the front handguard to identify the fact that the rifle was chambered for a non-standard cartridge (i.e., something other than the British .303 round). A painted ".30" (representing .30 caliber) was also generally applied as well. These "Lend-Lease" M1s saw very little, if any, active use by the British and were mainly relegated to duty with the Home Guard. Other than possibly shooting at passing German aircraft, it is doubtful if any of these rifles were fired in anger by the British. Nevertheless, they probably served as a bit of a morale booster to the beleaguered English during a most difficult time in their history.

The "Lend-Lease" M1s remained in storage until most were purchased by American arms dealers in the early 1960s and sent back to the United States for sale on the commercial market. These weapons will invariably be found stamped with various markings on the receivers and barrels indicating inspection and/or ownership by the British government. Many people erroneously assume that these markings were applied by the British when the rifles arrived in Great Britain during WWII. Actually, the markings were applied to the rifles just prior to their departure from Great Britain fifteen to twenty years after the war. Garand rifles marked in this manner are generally referred to today by collectors as "Brit-proofed" M1s.

It is interesting to note that the vast majority of such rifles found today remain in their original 1941–1942 factory configuration. Since these rifles stayed in Great Britain during much of the postwar period, they were not subjected to the extensive overhaul and rebuild programs as were the M1s remaining in Uncle Sam's arsenal. It is relatively uncommon today to find a late 1941 or very early 1942 vintage M1 remaining in its original configuration without British proofs.

Despite little opportunity to use M1 rifles during the war, the weapon was favorably looked upon by our British allies. As former English army officer John Weeks related in his book *Infantry Weapons*, "The Garand, or M1 to give it its proper title, was a simple and robust self loading rifle. The outline appearance is highly attractive and it is slim and well balanced. In fact, it looks right, just as in the same way a properly designed railway locomotive looks right, and is obviously functional."

Just a few years ago, the presence of British markings on an M1 was considered a rather serious flaw from a collector's perspective. However, the fact that such rifles generally remain in their unaltered condition has elevated them in the eyes of many collectors today. In fact, a legitimate "Brit-proofed" Garand is widely considered as a distinct collector variant of the M1. On the other hand, most serious collectors will agree that all things being equal, an original M1 without British markings is more desirable and more valuable than one with the markings.

The reverse is also true. A late production "-9" operating rod would unquestionably be incorrect for a 1942 vintage Garand.

Many mid-1943 and earlier Garands, both Winchester and Springfield, will exhibit a two-tone appearance to the finish of the receiver characterized by a darker color on the "heel" as compared to the rest of the receiver. This was due to the results of annealing the receiver in order to prevent cracking from the added stress of firing rifle grenades. The M7 grenade launcher was standardized on February 11, 1943, and some problems were soon reported. These related primarily to the rear portion of the receiver cracking due to the bolt recoiling harder than normal when firing rifle grenades. In mid-1943, Springfield began annealing the rear area of the M1 receiver to make the steel less brittle and reduce the chances of stress fractures. The heel of the receiver was dipped in molten lead in order to anneal it in this area and make it less susceptible to cracking. The heat treatment process was eventually modified to make the separate annealing step unnecessary. Therefore factory annealed receivers will only be found during a relatively short mid-1943 production period. It is not known if Winchester incorporated similar procedures during this period. As the pre-1943 rifles were overhauled or rebuilt at ordnance depots during and after WWII, many of the receivers were annealed to reduce the possibility of fracture. "Unannealed" receivers are more desirable for collecting purposes since they have not been altered from their original condition. Reparkerizing will not hide the darker color of the annealed area.

On August 1, 1943, Col. George A. Woody replaced Col. McFarland as commanding officer of Springfield Armory. Shortly after Woody's arrival, the final inspector's cartouche was changed to "SA/GAW". Otherwise, the stocks produced under Col. Woody's tenure were the same as the later production "SA/EMcF" cartouched stocks. The presence of the small "crossed cannons" marking on the bottom of the pistol grip continued during this period. In fact, few (if any) "SA/GAW" stocks will be found without this marking. M1 stocks with the "SA/GAW" cartouche will span the serial number range of (approx.) 1,790,000 to 3,250,000. The "crossed cannons" Ordnance Department escutcheon continued to be stamped next to the cartouche on the left side of the stock.

The peak production of M1 rifles during WWII occurred during Col. Woody's tenure at Springfield and the "SA/GAW" cartouched stocks are seen more often than any other WWII cartouche. The tremendous

increase in Garand production under Col. Woody's tenure was acknowledged in a October 5, 1943, letter from the Undersecretary of War to the Chief of Ordnance:

I was pleased to hear that over 100,000 Garand rifles were produced in the Springfield Armory during September. This is a fine record and I congratulate the Ordnance Department on its accomplishment. Will you please convey to Colonel George A. Woody, Acting Commanding Officer, and those at the Arsenal, the congratulations of the War Department on this work, and tell them that we look forward to a continued record at the Armory. We are proud of the Springfield Armory.

Despite the amazing achievement of 100,000 rifles produced in a single month, the actual peak of production occurred in January of 1944 when 122,001 rifles were delivered to the government.

The tremendous rate of production during this period dictated that every avenue possible be explored to reduce manufacturing time and cost. Although John Garand had originally designed his rifle with an eye toward ease of mass production, there were a number of components that could be redesigned to assist in speeding up production. From the time of the rifle's adoption, the M1's triggerguard was of the "milled" variety. This meant that it was forged from a single piece of steel which was obviously a time consuming process. By late 1942, a triggerguard produced from stamped sheet metal was considered to replace the milled guard. Approval for this component was granted

Cartouche of Col. George A. Woody, Commanding Officer of Springfield Armory circa July 1943 to October 1944. M1 rifle production reached a peak during Col. Woody's tenure. This the most commonly encountered WWII cartouche.

Ninth Army infantrymen searching for German snipers near Reckingham, Germany, April 7, 1945. Two of the soldiers are armed with M1 rifles while the one in the center has an M3 submachine gun.
(Credit: U.S. Army)

on October 7, 1943, but it was not until the middle of 1944 that the stamped triggerguard began to appear on production rifles. There was some overlap in the use of the milled and stamped triggerguards, and for a while, both types appear to have been used concurrently by Springfield. The first type of stamped triggerguard had a milled "locking hook." A stamped triggerguard with a welded metal tab added to the front was also fabricated. By early 1945, an all stamped variety came into use. This pattern was used by Springfield Armory on subsequent production rifles for the remainder of WWII and afterward.

The stamped triggerguard was a good example of a redesign which was quicker and cheaper to produce but didn't negatively affect the utility of the rifle. It is interesting to note that Winchester continued to use the earlier milled triggerguard throughout its production run.

Prior to the incorporation of the stamped triggerguard, the M1 "SA/GAW" cartouched rifles differed little from the weapons produced during Col. McFarland's tour of duty. The "long pinion" locking bar rear sight remained in use.

As was the case since the beginning of production, all M1 rifles produced during WWII were finished in parkerizing. A hallmark of the rifles made during this period was the grayish/green-tinted parkerizing. We will discuss this aspect of the Garand in greater detail later.

Col. Woody remained at Springfield until his death in October of 1944 when he was replaced by Brig. Gen. Norman F. Ramsey. General Ramsey was the highest ranking commanding officer of Springfield Armory during the time that the Garand was in production at that facility. As would be expected, the rifles produced under Ramsey's command were stamped with a "SA/NFR"

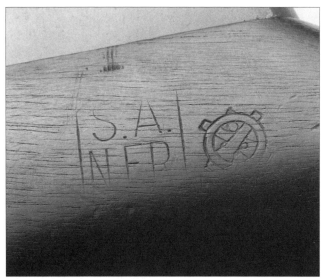

Cartouche of Brig. Gen. Norman F. Ramsey. Gen. Ramsey assumed command of Springfield Armory after Col. Woody's death, and his cartouche will be found on Garands made through the end of WWII.

cartouche. Interestingly, the small ¼" ordnance escutcheon on the bottom of the pistol grip began to disappear during this period. Otherwise, the rifles produced during Gen. Ramsey's tenure at Springfield were essentially the same as those made while Col. Woody was in command. Stocks with the "NFR" cartouche will be found on rifles in the (approx.) serial number range of 3,250,000 until the end of WWII production (around #3,880,000). It should be noted that some "GAW" cartouched stocks may be found on original rifles after the time that Gen. Ramsey was at Springfield. This is likely a case of using the prior cartouche stamp until the new one could be fabricated. If a very late 1944 or very early 1945 vintage M1 remaining is its original configuration is encountered with what appears to be its original stock but with a "GAW" cartouche, it's probably best to leave it alone.

In late 1944, an improved rear sight, designated as

Soldiers of the 75th Infantry Division firing on Germans January 7, 1945, during the Battle of the Bulge.
(Credit: U.S. Army)

the "T105E1", was adopted to replace the earlier "locking bar" sight. This design did not require a bar that had to be tightened to hold the sight's adjustments. It appears that few, if any, M1 rifles were fitted with T105E1 rear sights during WWII. Some students of the subject are of the opinion that late production M1C rifles were equipped with T105E1 sights. However, there is little evidence to support this assertion beyond the appearance of the sight in some very late WWII ordnance photographs. Any assembly line use of the T105E1 rear sight during WWII is doubtful.

The T105E1 rear sight was utilized on all post-WWII Garands. In addition, beginning after WWII, the earlier sights were retrofitted with the new T105E1 sight during the extensive rebuild programs carried on during this period.

Winchester WWII Production

Production of the M1 rifle at Winchester paralleled that at Springfield in many ways. The tremendous increase in demand after Pearl Harbor resulted in additional Garand production contracts being awarded to the firm. Contracts were granted in February of 1942, July of 1943, March and August of 1944 and a final contract in February of 1945. A total of 513,880 M1 rifles was produced by Winchester during WWII. Even with Winchester at peak capacity, the production rate was only a fraction of Springfield's output during the war. As an example, the peak production rate at Springfield and Winchester occurred in January of 1944. Springfield turned out some 122,000 rifles during this period, while Winchester produced about 15,000. This ratio was relatively consistent throughout the M1's WWII production run.

Col. Waldemar Broberg was replaced as head of the Hartford Ordnance District by Lt. Col. Guy H. Drewry in July of 1942. Winchester's change from the solid buttplate to the type with a hinged trap door occurred in May of 1942, just prior to Col. Broberg's departure. The rifles produced during Col. Drewry's term of office were stamped with a "WRA/GHD" cartouche in the same manner as the previous rifles. Two variations of Col. Drewry's cartouche may be observed. The first was enclosed in a 1" square while the later and, by far, most common cartouche was enclosed in a slightly smaller ¹³⁄₁₆" square. The "crossed cannons" ordnance escutcheon continued to be used by Winchester through the end of production.

As stated, Winchester buttplates had a more defined border than the ones produced by Springfield. This was true even after the change from the solid buttplate to the later variety with the hinged door. Many later Winchester buttplates were stamped "2S" inside.

The M1s produced by Winchester were essentially equal in quality to the rifles turned out by Springfield during the war. Winchester reportedly experienced some problems with the quality of their operating rods, but this did not cause any appreciable problems. There were, however, a number of differences beyond the obvious markings between the rifles made by the two manufacturers. One difference that is often observed is the rough finish found on many M1 parts produced by Winchester due to the lack of careful polishing prior to finishing. Springfield M1 parts, particularly early production rifles, sometimes exhibit similar rough machining marks, but it is much more commonly seen in Winchester Garands. It is rather surprising that a firm noted for its meticulously crafted sporting weapons would have such a feature as a hallmark for their M1 rifles. On the other hand, it is logical that such cosmetic touches as careful polishing would be dispensed with during the rush of wartime production. However, as we have discussed, Springfield Armory produced many more rifles under equally pressing conditions, and the SA rifles typically exhibit much better finished parts than Winchester.

In addition to the rough finish found on many Winchester parts, the presence of a punch mark in many parts made by the company will be observed. It is assumed that these punch marks were done to measure the hardness of the component as defined by the "Rockwell test". The depth of indentation by a punch was measured to ascertain if a particular part was within hardness specifications. While Springfield used the Rockwell tests on some parts, these punch marks are typically seen much more often on Winchester parts. While the presence or absence of these punch marks, like comparatively rough finishes, do not, in and of themselves, constitute definitive identification, they do tend to point to Winchester rather than Springfield origin. Of course, many of the larger components parts were marked with the prefix of the manufacturer ("SA" or "WRA") which positively identify the maker. A number of Winchester M1 parts may also be seen marked "A" or "CM". Collectors and students of the subject are still trying to sort out the meaning of these markings. There are a number of theories possible but the most logical explanation is that they are subcontractors' code.

There were three distinct variations of Winchester

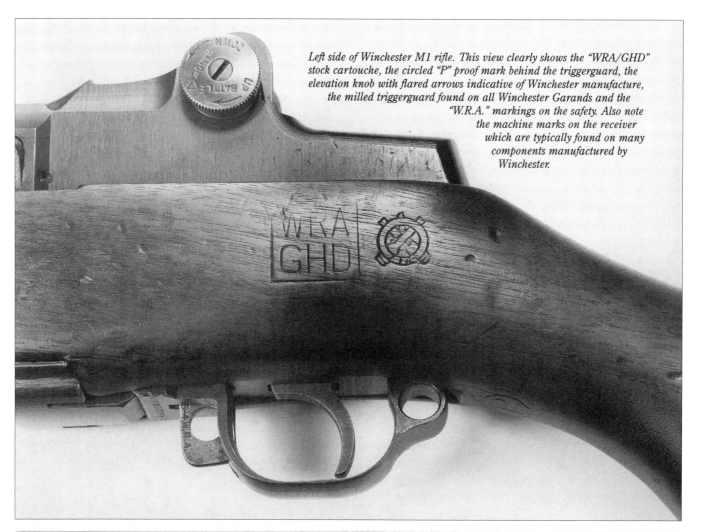

Left side of Winchester M1 rifle. This view clearly shows the "WRA/GHD" stock cartouche, the circled "P" proof mark behind the triggerguard, the elevation knob with flared arrows indicative of Winchester manufacture, the milled triggerguard found on all Winchester Garands and the "W.R.A." markings on the safety. Also note the machine marks on the receiver which are typically found on many components manufactured by Winchester.

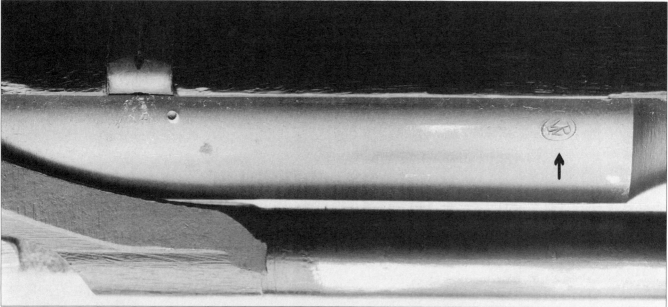

World War II production Winchester M1 barrel. Note the entwined Winchester "WP" proof marking and the deep punch mark. WWII Winchester Garand barrels were not dated. The drawing number and manufacturer's markings were stamped on top of the barrel and can only be seen with the rear handguard removed.

Cartouche as found on mid-1942 to 1945 Winchester stocks. "GHD" stands for Col. Guy H. Drewry, head of Winchester's Ordnance District during this period. Note how the top edge of the box is not indented into the wood. This is typical of original cartouches as few were perfectly aligned or evenly struck on all sides.

receivers produced. The first type used on approximately the first 65,000 production rifles is characterized by a square-shaped bolt lug recess and flat area below the rear sight. The second variation had the same square-shaped bolt lug recess, but the area below the rear sight had a larger profile in order to strengthen the receiver in this area. Winchester M1s in approximately the 1,200,000 to 2,400,000 serial number ranges will be found with this type of receiver. The final variant had a round profile bolt lug recess. This pattern was used after approximately 2,400,000 through the end of production. All "WIN-13" rifles will be found with this type of receiver.

There were also three variations found in the area of the receiver just behind the rear sight on Winchester Garands. The first type had a slight "V"-shaped area; the second had a rounded profile; and the third was rounded with a very slight "V" in the middle. These changes seem to track the changes in the bolt lug recess fairly closely.

M1 stocks produced by Winchester display several rather subtle differences from Springfield stocks. These include a "V-shaped" notch area behind the trigger-guard notch on the stock and a more arched or curved area between the pistol grip and recess for the trigger housing. These features can identify a Winchester M1 stock even if the cartouche has been totally removed.

Another feature that is sometimes overlooked by beginning collectors is the lack of a clearance cut on the rear handguard on Winchester Garands. This modification was instituted by Springfield to prevent the operating rod from binding on the right rear portion of the handguard. This change was implemented prior to our entry into WWII. However, Winchester continued use of

the rear handguard without the clearance cut until introduction of the "WIN-13" variant. Therefore, a Winchester rifle made prior to 1945 should have this feature. Even some of the very late production "WIN-13" rifles (to be discussed shortly) utilized rear handguards without clearance cuts.

The rear sight knobs on Winchester rifles also differed slightly from those found on Springfield Garands. The most obvious feature is the more prominently "flared" arrows on the windage knobs. Except for very early rifles, the arrows found on the Springfield Garand windage knobs had smaller triangular heads.

In addition to the configuration of the arrows on the sight adjustment knobs, the "locking bars" on the later Winchester rear sights can be distinguished from their Springfield counterparts by the shape of the ends. Winchester locking bars are rounded on the ends while Springfield-made bars are square.

Winchester rear sight apertures differed from those made by Springfield primarily in a noticeably more curved profile and the absence of two sets of grooves on the bottom. Many Winchester apertures are stamped "CM" and have the typically seen punch mark on the bottom.

The front sights of Winchester M1 rifles were noticeably different from their Springfield counterparts due to the more prominently flared protective "ears." Winchester front sights' ears are $^{13}/_{16}$" apart while Springfield's range from about $^{5}/_{8}$" to $^{11}/_{16}$".

Another difference between Winchester and Springfield Garands is the configuration of the barrel ring on the gas cylin-

Mid-WWII production Winchester M1 rifle.

der. Springfield gas cylinders were milled flat on top of the ring while Winchester gas cylinders are rounded. Also, Winchester gas cylinders will exhibit a somewhat subtle bluish tint to the finish as compared to Springfield gas cylinders. This is due to abandonment of the "Molyblack" coating used by Springfield, and the utilization of an iron plate and "Dulite" finish on Winchester gas cylinders. The iron plating on the stainless steel gas cylinder allowed for the application of the bluish Dulite finish.

The hammer spring plunger used on Winchester M1 rifles was flat on the side of the component as compared to the more rounded side of the Springfield Armory plungers. As is the case with many other parts discussed, such minor changes can help identify original rifles from ones that have been altered or subsequently restored.

Winchester Garands were finished in parkerizing that normally has a greenish tint to the finish. This greenish tint is not readily apparent if the rifle is devoid of oil or grease but is generally quite obvious otherwise. This finish can be hard to duplicate today and is a hallmark of World War II production Garands.

As can be seen, there were actually fewer component changes found in Winchester M1 rifles than those produced by Springfield Armory. This was primarily due to

the fact that Winchester was a civilian contractor and each change in the production specifications required contract changes and, in most cases, additional compensation for the firm. Production changes at Springfield Armory could be accomplished with little more than issuing the appropriate orders through ordnance "channels."

Winchester M1 receiver manufactured circa July 1942.

Right side of Winchester M1 showing the rounded ends of the "locking bar" rear sight. Note also the square bolt recess.

Comparison of Springfield Armory M1 gas cylinder (right) and Winchester M1 gas cylinder (left). Note the flat section on the rear ring of the Sprinfield gas cylinder that is not found on those made by Winchester. Also note the wider "ears" on the Winchester front sight as compared to the Springfield front sight.

Winchester Garand rifles being inspected at the factory. (Credit: Winchester Repeating Arms Co.)

"WIN-13 Rifles"

One of the more interesting and significant variants of the Winchester M1 (from a collecting viewpoint) are the so-called "WIN-13" rifles. These were the last production M1 rifles made by Winchester and differ from earlier production WRA Garands in a number of ways. The most significant feature of the WIN-13 rifles is the serial number range of approximately 1,600,000 through 1,640,000. This range is much lower than the previous block of serial numbers used by Winchester in December of 1944 and January of 1945 (2,534,000 range). This is an obvious departure from the normal practice of ascending serial numbers as production continues. In other words, WIN-13 rifles have significantly lower serial numbers than Winchester M1 rifles made much earlier.

Another readily apparent difference is the drawing number stamped on the right side of the receiver which, which was changed from "D28291-2" to "D28291WIN-13". As can be seen, the marking format was modified by the addition of "WIN" and the revision number changed from "-2" to "-13". The reason(s) for such a numerically large change in the revision number in a very short period of time is not known. The rear portion of the receiver bolt recess was also changed from the square configuration to a round profile. Other slightly less noticeable changes were the use of later pattern parts not found on Winchester Garands produced previously. Examples of such items include handguards with the clearance cut on the right rear area and "straight cut" operating rods. Interestingly, these later parts are commonly found on WIN-13 rifles assembled early in the variant's production run, but earlier vintage parts show up near the termination of Winchester's M1 program in June 1945. For this reason, later examples of original WIN-13 rifles often reveal an interesting combination of early and late parts. This includes earlier "long barrel channel" stocks, rear handguards with-

Original late WWII Winchester "WIN-13" M1 rifle.

out the clearance cut and earlier pattern operating rods mixed with some of the later parts typically found on in the WIN-13 rifles. This can be attributed to the fact that Winchester was using up all parts on hand so they would not be stuck with unusable (and unsaleable) components when the contract was terminated. Therefore, particularly on later production rifles, it is not possible to state that a particular part is "correct"

for a WIN-13 rifle. As long as it is of Winchester manufacture and the general condition matches the rest of the rifle, it may very well be original. It is interesting to note that few original WIN-13 rifles contain "A" or "CM" marked parts. All WIN-13 rifles acquired by the government will have "WRA/GHD" stock cartouches. Occasionally, a WIN-13 rifle that appears to be in virtually new condition but without an inspector's cartouche

Receiver leg markings on "WIN-13 rifle."

will show up. It is speculated that such rifles were left over after Winchester's contract was canceled, and the company eventually disposed of the weapons. The lack of the final inspector's cartouche indicates that such weapons were never accepted into government service.

As stated, collectors are prone to categorizing some M1 rifles as distinct "variants" when such distinctions may be questionable. The WIN-13 rifle, on the other hand, is unquestionably a separate and distinct collector variant of the M1. Original examples are highly sought after and many dubious restorations may be encountered. One problem with evaluating a WIN-13 is the fact that, particularly on later production rifles, there are many seemingly inconsistent features even on totally original pieces.

As is the case with the prewar Winchester Garands, there are numerous fake rifles and bogus parts floating around on the market today. The fact that, all things being equal, a Winchester M1 will normally bring more money than a Springfield M1 of comparable vintage and condition makes faking WRA rifles an attractive option for some of the crooks. All sorts of counterfeit Winchester Garand parts may be found, including stocks with fake or "enhanced" cartouches and parts made by other manufacturers with WRA markings overstamped. Fake Winchester M1 barrels are a particular problem and any barrel purported to be original should

Receiver markings of late production "WIN-13" rifle manufactured circa June 1945.

be examined very closely. Comparison, if at all possible, with a known original WRA barrel is wise. Such things as the markings on top, the gas cylinder threads and index lines are among the features that should be compared. Often, the original markings on a non-Winchester barrel are ground off and the fake WRA markings applied. The metal under the markings should be felt to ascertain if it is a smoother surface than the surrounding metal. If so, the odds are extremely high that the markings have been faked. All WWII M1 barrels, including Winchester, did not have the chromed area around the gas port. This is a feature of post-WWII M1 barrels or barrels of 1940–1945 vintage that were rebuilt following the war. In any event, a chromed gas port area would never be proper for a supposedly original World War II vintage Garand.

In June 1945, the government canceled Winchester's M1 rifle contract, and the firm permanently ceased Garand production. As was the case with Springfield Garands, the vast majority of Winchester M1 rifles were subsequently overhauled after World War II. Such overhauled rifles lost virtually all of their originality as most of the parts were refinished and/or replaced during the rebuild process. Today, the only Winchester part found on the average government rebuilt Garand is the receiver. Occasionally, a few other WRA components may be found, but this is coincidence as no effort was made to re-install Winchester parts on Winchester receivers as the rifles were overhauled. A relatively small number of Garands, Springfield and Winchester, have survived through the years in their original factory configuration. When rifles were cycled through the ordnance depots for inspection and overhaul, a rifle in otherwise excellent condition might receive no more than a visual inspection and a cleaning. Such rifles would not have any parts replaced and would generally be prepared for long term storage. Even with the subsequent increased demand during the Korean War, some of these WWII vintage rifles remained in various ordnance storage facilities and were not issued. On occasion, such rifles surface today through the CMP sales program. Some fortunate individuals have obtained totally original rifles in excellent to near new condition. Such rifles are in direct contrast to the typical DCM/CMP Garand which is almost invariably a hodgepodge of refinished parts of varying vintages and manufacturers. Interestingly, a fair number of original Winchester M1s, including some WIN-13 rifles, have surfaced via the DCM/CMP in the past few years. While still very desirable and valuable weapons, original Winchester Garands are now seen a

An American soldier occupying a well-prepared defensive position in a German forest late in WWII. Note his M1 rifle placed between two sets of forked sticks and the other M1 rifle to his right.   (Credit: U.S. Army)

bit more often than just a few years ago.

Winchester's record in manufacturing Garands under the trying conditions of wartime is a testament to the professionalism and resourcefulness of the company. As stated, the quality and utility of Winchester's Garands were equal to those made by the government's Springfield Armory. Given comparable condition and degrees of originality, Winchester M1s are generally more valuable than Springfield M1s of like vintages on the collector's market due chiefly to the smaller numbers made and the indisputable attraction of the Winchester name. The early production Winchester Garands (with "WRA/RS" and "WRA/WB" cartouches) are quite uncommon and highly desirable weapons. Due to the desirability of Winchester Garands, potential purchasers should be wary as many "restored" rifles of this

type are on the market today. A number of fake WRA parts have been noted including stocks with bogus cartouches. Some WRA operating rods with the postwar relief cut modifications have been observed with the cut area welded and the rod refinished in an attempt to pass it off as a more valuable "un-cut" rod. Likewise, some of the much more common Springfield gas cylinders have had welding added to the flat portion of the ring in an attempt to pass them off as Winchester gas cylinders. Some trigger housings that were modified during rebuild by having the original wide "pads" cut down have been altered by welding. Generally the discoloration caused by the welding process will reveal such altered items. Winchester M1s are certain to continue their steady increase in value in the future, and the problem of fakes will surely continue as well.

World War II M1 Sniper Rifles

Among the most interesting and highly sought after variants of the M1 are the sniper rifles. As we have discussed, the time from the adoption of the M1 in 1936 until the beginning of America's active involvement in WWII was a period of refining and "debugging" the Garand. Due to the necessity of putting the rifle into mass production, little thought was initially given to a sniping version of the Garand. When U.S. troops were deployed to overseas combat zones, the need for sniping rifles became evident rather quickly. The Ordnance Department began research and development of a sniping version of the Garand. However, this project was given a rather low priority. As an interim measure, in 1942 the Ordnance Department contracted with Remington Arms Company for a slightly modified version of the simplified M1903A3 bolt action service rifle that was currently being produced by the firm under government contract. The modified rifle was adopted as the "U.S. Rifle, Caliber .30, M1903A4, Snipers." In order to speed the production rate, readily available commercial components were used with the '03A4 rifle. These included Weaver 330C telescopes (designated "M73B1" by the government) and Redfield "Junior" scope mounts.

While the Army fielded the M1903A4, the U.S. Marine Corps pressed into service a few First World War (and earlier) M1903 rifles fitted with Winchester A5 or Lyman 5A telescopes. Many of these were rifle team weapons that saw double duty as sniper rifles. In order to meet the increasing demand, the marines briefly considered standardizing the Winchester Model 70 as a sniper rifle but eventually settled on a slightly modified M1903A1 fitted with a target-type telescope made by the Unertl Company. Many of the M1903A1 Springfields converted to sniping weapons by the Marines during this period were National Match rifles.

The various '03 rifles served the needs of the Marine Corps and Army reasonably well but the desirability of a semiautomatic Garand sniper rifle seemed apparent. The Ordnance Department's Experimental Division continued work on the development of a sniping version of the M1. The most immediate problem to be overcome was the Garand's en bloc loading method. This effectively ruled out the standard practice of mounting the telescope directly over the center of the receiver. In order to circumvent the problem, a prismatic type telescope with the body of the scope mounted on the left side of the receiver but with the eyepiece in line with the rear of the receiver was considered. This design was designated as the "M1E2." Subsequent testing revealed that this was a somewhat flawed concept, and the design was abandoned. After considering other options, it became apparent that the best course of action would be to mount a conventional telescope directly to the left side of the receiver. This would permit the M1 to be loaded and fired in the normal manner and also permitted the alternate use of the iron sights. The primary drawback was the necessity of the shooter to assume a rather awkward position, but this was considered to be an adequate trade-off for the advantages that accrued. A design with a telescope mounted on the left side of the receiver and with an experimental rear sight similar to

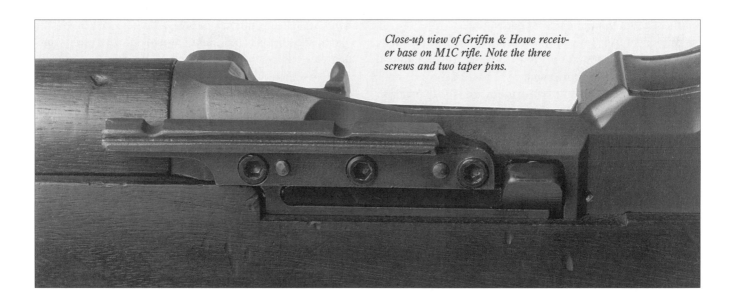

Close-up view of Griffin & Howe receiver base on M1C rifle. Note the three screws and two taper pins.

THE M1 GARAND — WORLD WAR II PRODUCTION

the peep sight used on the M1903A3 rifle was given the designation "M1E6" and thoroughly tested. The test results validated the concept of an offset scope, but the non-standard rear sight was not found to be necessary.

The next experimental variant, the "M1E7," was essentially an issue M1 rifle (including the standard rear sight) fitted with a conventional telescope mounted on the left side of the receiver. A commercially developed scope mounting system patented and produced by the firm of Griffin & Howe was chosen for use with the M1E7 design. The G&H system had been in use for a number of years and was a strong and well designed scope platform. It also had the big advantage of being readily available. The Griffin & Howe design allowed the scope to be removed and reattached to the rifle with no loss of "zero" (at least theoretically). The only modifications required to the M1 rifle was the drilling of five holes in the left side of the receiver. Three of these holes were threaded for attachment of screws to hold the base to the receiver. The other two holes were for taper pins that held the base in alignment while the screws were tightened. The three screws were staked after installation to hold them securely in place.

The Ordnance Department selected the 2.2X power Lyman Alaskan telescope for use with the M1E7 rifle. As was the case with the Griffin & Howe mount, the Alaskan scope was a successful commercial design that had been in use for a number of years prior to the Second World War. The Lyman Alaskan telescope was given the military designation of "M73."

The M1E7 rifle met the requirements and passed all preliminary tests necessary for official adoption.

However, the Infantry Board expressed a desire for an M1 sniping rifle that did not require any modifications to the rifle's receiver. A mounting system, designated as the "M1E8," designed by John Garand was tested in conjunction with the M1E7. Rather than mounting the telescope base to the rifle's receiver, the M1E8 utilized a mounting block attached to the rear portion of the barrel. A bracket held the telescope and was secured to the mount by a large knurled knob. Like the M1E7, the M1E8 system allowed the telescope to be easily removed from the rifle. The M73 scope was also approved for use with the M1E8. The M1E8 design allowed for the necessary offset mounting of the scope but did not require the receiver to be modified. However, the fact that the barrel had to be modified by

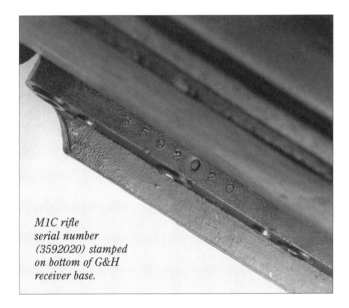

M1C rifle serial number (3592020) stamped on bottom of G&H receiver base.

View inside M1C receiver showing staking punch marks on the three screws.

having the block attached to it did not offer any substantive advantages over the receiver-mounted M1E7 design. However, it was believed that it would be easier to convert existing M1 service rifles into the M1E8 configuration than the M1E7 configuration. As we will later discuss, this feature played an important role in subsequent utilization of the M1E8 design after World War II.

The Infantry Board subjected the M1E7 and M1E8 rifles to extensive testing and both were deemed satis-

factory for service use although the M1E7 was felt to be a somewhat sturdier design. On July 27, 1944, the M1E7 was standardized as the "U.S. Rifle, Caliber .30, M1C (Snipers). Concurrent with adoption of the M1C, slightly modified versions of the Lyman M73 telescope were adopted as the "M81" and "M82." These scopes differed from the commercial Lyman chiefly in the incorporation of a sliding sun shade on the front of the tube and the addition of a rubber eyepiece. The M81 featured a cross-

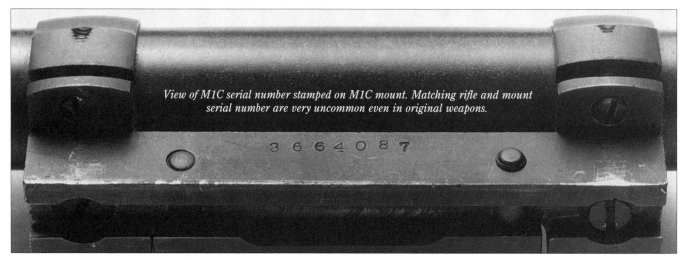

View of M1C serial number stamped on M1C mount. Matching rifle and mount serial number are very uncommon even in original weapons.

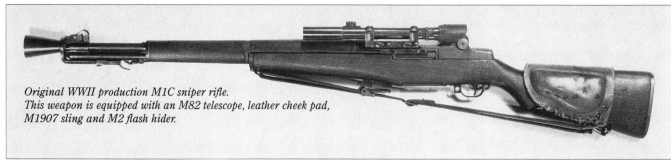

Original WWII production M1C sniper rifle.
This weapon is equipped with an M82 telescope, leather cheek pad, M1907 sling and M2 flash hider.

Close-up view of M1C mount and M82 telescope.

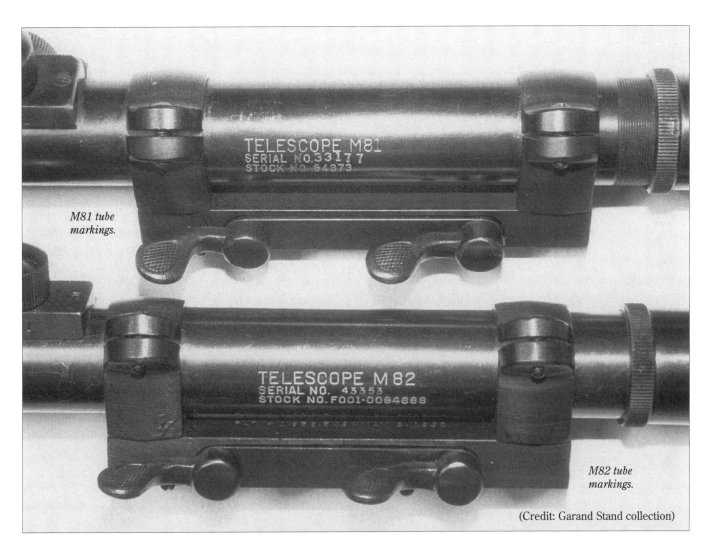

M81 tube markings.

M82 tube markings.

(Credit: Garand Stand collection)

hair reticle, and the M82 utilized a tapered post. The nomenclature, serial number and Federal stock numbers were marked on the left side of the scope tube. The M81 scopes and the vast majority of M82 scopes were blued. Occasionally, an M82 scope with a phosphate finish may be observed. These are believed to be late war production scopes.

Due to the offset position of the telescope on the M1C and M1D rifles, a pad to properly position the shooter's head was deemed to be desirable. A leather cheek pad, designated as the "T4," was adopted in October 1944. The cheek pad had several felt inserts that could removed as necessary to suit the preferences of the user. The T4 pad fastened to the stock by means of a leather thong. The pad could be further secured by two wood screws. The Kay Leather Products Company was given a contract for production of the T4 pad during the war. These pads can be identified by the "K Line" logo stamped on top. It is believed that the "K Line" marked

"K Line" (Kay Leather Products) marking on WWII production leather cheek pad.

variety are the sole type of T4 pads used on the WWII M1C rifles. After adoption, the "T4" test designation was dropped. The item was not assigned a model ("M") designation and was referred to as simply "Pad, Cheek."

Another accessory standardized for use with the Garand sniper rifles was a flash hider. Several designs were tested for use in engaging targets in low light environments. A funnel-shaped design, tested as the "T18," was officially adopted on January 25, 1945, as the "Hider, Flash, M2." The M2 flash hider attached to the rifle in the same manner as the M7 grenade launcher. The M2 flash hider was produced during WWII by Springfield Armory and the commercial firm of Hart Manufacturing Company. The Springfield made M2s were marked "SA" on the bottom of the mounting bracket, and those made by Hart were marked with the name of the firm. It was eventually determined that the M2 flash hider could actually be detrimental to the rifle's accuracy and many were removed in the field and not used.

Even though the War Department had settled on the M1C as the preferred variant, the M1D was adopted in September of 1944 and given the designation "Substitute Standard." This was done in order to have the M1D approved for immediate procurement if production delays or if other problems were encountered with delivery of the M1C. However, other than a few prototype rifles that were fabricated, the M1D was not manufactured during WWII and cannot be properly considered as a Second World War weapon.

Springfield Armory began preparation for production of the M1C soon after its official adoption in July 1944, and by late 1944 the first Garand sniper rifles began to come off the assembly line. A contract was given to Griffin & Howe for modification of the receiver and attachment of the M1C base. Springfield shipped receivers that had not yet been heat treated to the Griffin & Howe facility in New York City where the five holes were drilled and the bases attached. The "green" receivers were then returned to Springfield for heat treatment and final finishing including parkerizing. Initially, the receiver and bases were heat treated and parkerized together as a unit. However, it was found that corrosion could form between the receiver and base so the procedure was changed and the two components were heat treated and finished separately then joined together as a unit. Some collectors and students of the subject have questioned why, in the middle of wartime, it was necessary to pull unfinished receivers from Springfield's assembly line and ship them several hundred miles to simply have five holes drilled in the receiver then returned to the Armory for finishing. The craftsmen at Springfield were certainly capable of drilling five holes in an M1 receiver. The reason(s) for this seemingly incongruent practice is not known but several theories have been advanced including patent considerations and political patronage.

After assembly, the M1C rifles were fitted with telescopes and other accessories. It is interesting to note that although specifications called for slightly greater accuracy requirements for the Garand sniper rifles, there was apparently little real difference in manufacturing techniques or tolerances of these weapons as compared to standard M1 service rifles. While the standard M1 was certainly capable of decent accuracy, it did not possess the type of accuracy that one would normally expect from a sniping arm.

M2 flash hider.

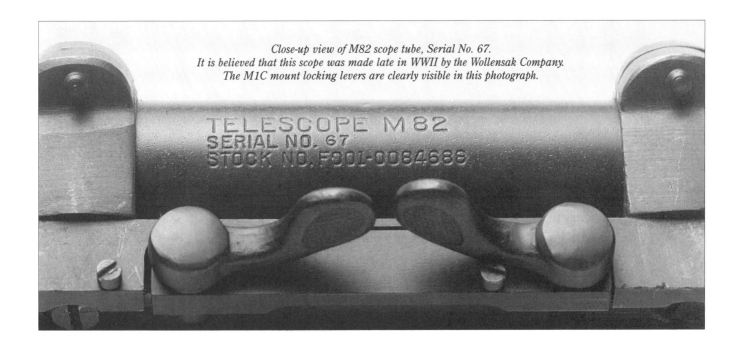

Close-up view of M82 scope tube, Serial No. 67.
It is believed that this scope was made late in WWII by the Wollensak Company.
The M1C mount locking levers are clearly visible in this photograph.

By the end of calendar year 1944, the first M1C rifles were scheduled for shipment from Springfield Armory. Unfortunately, the actual production rate lagged far behind the initial estimates. As an example the combined total of M1Cs delivered in November and December of 1944 was just eleven. Delivery schedules continued to be seriously delayed for the first few months of 1945 as well. As stated, the M1D had been standardized in case there were delays in the M1C production program. However, putting the M1D into production instead of, or in addition to, the M1C would not have helped matters because much of the delay with delivering M1Cs was caused by difficulty in obtaining sufficient numbers of M81 and M82 telescopes from Lyman. In order to supplement Lyman's production efforts, the Wollensak Optical Company was given a contract for production of M82 scopes. Details concerning these late war Wollensak M82 scopes are sketchy. None of the M81 and M82 scopes were marked with the name of the maker. However, the Wollensak scopes have a slightly different marking format and much lower serial numbers than the Lyman scopes. In addition, at least some of the Wollensak M82s had a phosphate-like finish rather than the blued finish as typically found on the Lyman scopes. Eventually, increased scope production at Lyman augmented by the Wollensak scopes helped alleviate the troubling shortages.

Some 4,960 M1C rifles were delivered by the first half of 1945 rather than the target goal of 11,000. By June 1945, production had increased sufficiently, allow-

ing delivery of 1,251 M1C rifles in a single month.

The production delays meant that very few M1C rifles were actually fielded during the Second World War. None of the weapons are believed to have arrived in Europe before Germany's surrender. A few of the weapons were employed in the Pacific by the U.S. Army before V-J day, but their use was quite limited. There has been very little recorded concerning the M1C's use in WWII. The book *Ordnance Went Up Front* by Roy Dunlap contains the following passage regarding the M1C:

They (M1Cs) were beautiful outfits and I would have given anything to have one during the war, but they arrived in the Philippines just before the Japanese surrendered. The rifles were selected, the best-finished and tightest M1s I ever saw.

By the end of the war when all outstanding M1C contracts were canceled, a total of 7,971 M1C rifles had been manufactured by Springfield. Although, as stated, few M1Cs were fielded during WWII, these rifles saw use a few years later in Korea. We will discuss post-WWII use of the Garand sniper rifles later.

Basically, an M1C rifle will contain all the features found on late 1944 to mid-1945 vintage M1 service rifles. The Griffin & Howe base attached to the receiver was generally serially numbered to the rifle (except perhaps in very late vintage rifles) as was the G&H mount. The other accessories included the leather cheek pad, M2 flash hider and M1907 leather or M1 web slings.

M82 scope and M1C mount.

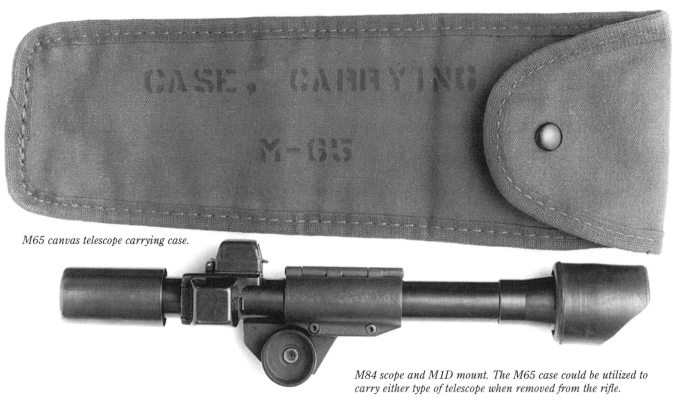

M65 canvas telescope carrying case.

M84 scope and M1D mount. The M65 case could be utilized to carry either type of telescope when removed from the rifle.

Original M1C rifles have always been extremely scarce items since very few were released by the government. Unfortunately, collector interest has been dampened a bit due to the extreme number of fake M1C rifles around today. It is a relatively simple matter for a reasonably competent gunsmith to attach a surplus G&H receiver base to an M1 receiver. Fortunately, there are several key features that will help identify the genuine articles from the fakes. Without question, the most useful is a data base, which several dedicated researchers have assembled, of authentic M1C serial numbers which, by applying statistical analysis, a particular serial number can be ruled out or ruled in as an authentic M1C with an estimated 95% confidence level. This verification should be obtained before paying the typically substantial sum that a supposedly original M1C will bring. Table #13 details the specific features of original M1C rifles and will give information on how this verification service might be obtained.

World War II Accessories and Accouterments

In addition to the rifles, there are many interesting and varied Second World War vintage accessories associated with the Garand rifle. The inclusion of such items can add much interest and color to the rifles in a collection. Only the major accessories will be discussed in this section. All of these items can be found today with varying degrees of difficulty and expense but are well worth adding to one's collection.

Slings

The M1 rifle is technically incomplete without its proper sling. There were two basic types of slings standardized for use with the M1 during WWII. The leather M1907 sling had been the standard sling utilized with the M1903 rifle since before WWI and was retained for use with the Garand rifle as well. There were sufficient supplies of the First World War and earlier vintage M1907 slings on hand to equip the M1 rifles made prior to America's involvement in WII. These slings can be

However, one of the earlier slings with brass hardware would not be incorrect on any vintage WWII M1 since many of these slings remained in the supply system and used on an "as needed" basis.

ATTACHING U.S. SLINGS

Q *After purchasing a surplus M1 Garand, I picked up a bayonet and sling to complete the rig. The sling is a two-piece leather job with brass fittings, that, for the life of me, I can't figure out how to attach properly. Can you help?*

A The sling to which you refer is the U.S. Model 1907. It has two leather straps, one long and one short, two brass hooks and two leather keepers. The short strap has a D-ring with a sewn fold on one end and a brass hook on the other. The long strap has another brass hook on one end, with the other being a tab or "feed end."

To attach the sling, in the "prescribed military manner," begin by turning the rifle upside down on a flat surface with the muzzle pointing to the right. Lay both straps flat with the smooth sides down: the short with the brass hook on the left and the D-ring on the right and; the long with feed end on the right and the hook on the left.

Pick up the sewn fold in your left fist and the hook of the long strap in the right hand, and work the D-ring down over the hook. Push one of the keepers, sewn side up, over the long strap's hook. Pick up the feed end of the long strap with the right hand and push the entire length through the keeper. After laying the long strap down, take up the second keeper, again sewn side down, with the right hand and insert the feed end.

Then, run the feed end through the rifle's front sling swivel and pull the strap toward the muzzle. With the feed end in the right hand, run the end through the second

keeper and pull the strap toward the butt. With the hook of the long strap in your left hand, count off nine sets of holes, beginning with those nearest the feed end, and insert the two prongs into the ninth pair. Take the hook end of the short strap and insert the prongs into the nearest set of holes rearward of the long strap's hook.

Once attached, the sling may be tightened by grabbing the feed end (now between the doubled over long strap) and pulling it firmly toward the butt while at the

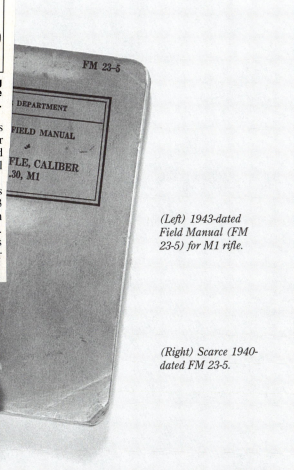

Components of the U.S. Model 1907 leather sling (above) and M1 improved web sling are shown here in their proper arrangements as they would be used.

same time pulling the outside strap towards the muzzle. To keep it taut, force the upper keeper against the front sling swivel and slide the lower one toward the muzzle until the feed end passes through it.

Though the Model 1907 sling was intended for the U.S. Model 1903 Springfield rifle, it was commonly used on M1917s, M1s and other U.S. military rifles. Today, original and modern-made versions of this sling are often used in highpower rifle competition.—MARK A. KEEFE, IV

The "M1" sling was also standardized early in WWII use with the M1 as well as the M1903 and M1917. It should be noted that the designation "M1" was intended to convey that it was made specifically for Garand rifle. Rather this indicates that it was the first sling (**M**=Model and **1**=1st) adopted after the nment changed the nomenclature of such items the year of adoption to the "Model" designation. M1 sling was constructed of canvas web material simple stamped sheet metal adjustment buckles. sling was lighter in weight and could be made faster and cheaper than the M1907. The web ial was better suited than the leather M1907 sling

(Left) 1943-dated Field Manual (FM 23-5) for M1 rifle.

(Right) Scarce 1940-dated FM 23-5.

22

Marine firing his M1 rifle. Note the M1907 leather sling and the M1923 cartridge belt.

(Credit: USMC)

supplies of the First World War and earlier vintage M1907 slings on hand to equip the M1 rifles made prior to America's involvement in WII. These slings can be identified by their brass hardware, and many, but not all, were dated. The most commonly observed dates on such slings are "1917" and "1918". Therefore, an M1907 sling bearing a First World War date is the correct item for pre-1941 vintage Garands. With the rapid increase in demand following Pearl Harbor, the M1907 sling was put back into production. Since brass was in critically short supply at the time, the WWII vintage M1907 slings were made with steel hardware. Thus, such slings can be readily identified from their prewar counterparts. Again, many, but not all, of the WWII M1907 slings were marked with the date of production and the name of the maker. The M1907 slings with steel hardware would be properly found on 1942 and later vintage M1 rifles.

However, one of the earlier slings with brass hardware would not be incorrect on any vintage WWII M1 since many of these slings remained in the supply system and were used on an "as needed" basis.

The "M1" sling was also standardized early in WWII for use with the M1 as well as the M1903 and M1917 rifles. It should be noted that the designation "M1" was not intended to convey that it was made specifically for the Garand rifle. Rather this indicates that it was the first model sling (**M**=Model and **1**=1st) adopted after the government changed the nomenclature of such items from the year of adoption to the "Model" designation. The M1 sling was constructed of canvas web material with simple stamped sheet metal adjustment buckles. This sling was lighter in weight and could be made much faster and cheaper than the M1907. The web material was better suited than the leather M1907 sling

(Left) 1943-dated Field Manual (FM 23-5) for M1 rifle.

(Right) Scarce 1940-dated FM 23-5.

Marine firing his M1 rifle. Note the M1907 leather sling and the M1923 cartridge belt. (Credit: USMC)

for use in the harsh Pacific climate as well. Although the M1907 was a superb sling for use on the target range, the light and simple M1 sling was a better choice for use on a battle rifle. The WWII vintage M1 slings were made of a khaki colored canvas material, and the sheet metal adjustment buckles had a flat profile. The date of production and name (or initials) of the maker were stenciled in black ink inside many of these slings.

The M1 sling remained the standard rifle sling following WWII, while the M1907 slings were dropped from use when the existing supply was exhausted in the late 1940s. The post-1945 M1 slings differed from the WWII variety in several respects. The later slings were constructed of much darker colored and slightly heavier canvas material. In addition, the metal adjustment buckles were made of heavy metal and had a raised ridge rather than being flat on top. Some of the postwar M1 slings were marked "MRT" for "Mildew Resistant Treatment" and some were stamped with the year of production and/or the year that the MRT was applied. Obviously, one of the later M1 slings would not be correct for a World War II vintage Garand displayed in its original configuration.

Two other slings (in addition to the M1907 and M1 slings) were approved for use with the M1 rifle during WWII but were seldom employed on the weapon. The M1917 Kerr sling was put into mass production during the First World War for use on the M1903 and M1917 rifles. Fairly large numbers were made and used during WWI, and the sling remained a substitute item for use with the M1 rifle during the Second World War. The canvas M1923 sling was adopted before WWII as an improvement over the leather M1907, but it proved to be an overly complicated and cumbersome sling and saw little field use. Although both the M1917 and the M1923 slings would be technically correct on a WWII vintage Garand, from a practical standpoint, the M1907 and M1 slings are more historically accurate choices.

The WWII M1907 and M1 slings are in increasingly short supply today since they are actively sought after by collectors wishing to have the proper accessories for their rifles. Unfortunately, this desirability has resulted in a number of fake slings on the market, particularly the more expensive M1907 sling. Most of these are complete with the date (1943 seems to be the most commonly seen) and manufacturers' names or initials. While a few "like new" original M1907 slings may still occasionally surface, most will show some evidence of a half century of wear, tear and/or storage. A sling that appears as if it was made yesterday very likely was! In

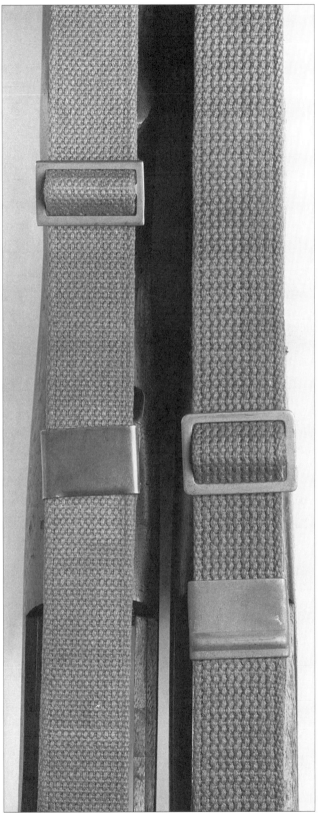

(Left) WWII production M1 sling.
(Right) Postwar production M1 sling. Note the thicker weave pattern in the later sling and the differences in the sling hardware. The WWII slings were khaki colored and the later slings darker olive green.

addition, close comparison of the metal hardware between the fake slings and the genuine article will normally reveal differences in construction and, most importantly, the method of riveting the hardware to the leather. While the dated slings are the most desirable for collecting purposes, a correct vintage unmarked original sling of either type (M1907 or M1) adds a lot to an original WWII M1 rifle.

Bayonets and Scabbards

As was previously mentioned, the M1905 bayonet was standardized for use with the M1 upon the rifle's adoption in 1936. A modified version of the prewar M1905 bayonet was placed into production by several commercial firms. These differed from the earlier bayonets made by Springfield Armory and Rock Island Arsenal in several respects. Among the most obvious differences was the fact that the WWII vintage bayonets were not nearly as well crafted as their prewar, arsenal-made counterparts. In addition, the wooden grips found on the SA and RIA bayonets were replaced by plastic grips. The WWII M1905 bayonets were marked with the initials of the maker (i.e. "UC" for Utica Cutlery), a "flaming bomb," a "US" and "1942" (the year of production) on the reverse ricasso. The obverse was unmarked. Some problems were encountered on certain batches of these bayonets due to blades that were too brittle and prone to breakage because of improper heat treatment. Otherwise, even with the cosmetic items left off, these bayonets were as useable as the ear-

lier arsenal-made M1905 bayonets. Some writers today refer to these WWII variant bayonets as the "Model of 1942," but this designation is not correct. Such bayonets retained the "M1905" designation. A total of 1,540,578 M1905 bayonets were made during WWII.

The increase in bayonet production naturally required a corresponding increase in the need for scabbards. At the beginning of the war, the standard scabbard issued with the M1905 bayonet was the M1910. This scabbard replaced the earlier leather-covered M1905 scabbard and featured a canvas cover with a leather tip. The scabbard attached to the cartridge belt by metal hooks. A few modified M1905 scabbards were also in inventory at the time. There had been sufficient numbers of M1905 bayonets and M1910 scabbards on hand to meet the limited demand prior to World War II, but subsequent events quickly revealed the need for tremendous numbers of new bayonets and scabbards. In order to help alleviate the shortage of M1910 scabbards, the M1917 Enfield bayonet scabbard was approved for use as an interim measure since it would fit both the M1917 and M1905 bayonets. Also, some 48,000 of the modified M1905 scabbards were found and issued, although they had not been classified as "Standard" since the early 1920s. Therefore, the modified M1905 scabbard and the M1917 scabbard can be considered as technically correct for use with early M1 Garands rifles, although the M1910 scabbard saw much wider use.

Contracts were given for production of new M1910 scabbards, while the search began for a suitable replace-

Second World War production M1905 bayonet and plastic M3 scabbard.

ment scabbard that could be produced faster and cheaper than the older variety. The WWII M1910 scabbards differed from the earlier versions primarily in the dark green color of the canvas rather than the khaki color of the pre-WWII scabbards.

In addition to being time consuming and expensive to manufacture, the M1905 and M1910 scabbards were found to be prone to deterioration. Clearly, an improved type of bayonet scabbard was needed. The Beckwith Manufacturing Company developed a bayonet scabbard fabricated from a composite plastic material for consideration by the Ordnance Department. The scabbard was far superior to the early leather and canvas-covered scabbards from a durability and ease of production standpoint, and the scabbard was formally standardized as the "M3" bayonet scabbard. On November 17, 1941, Beckwith and the Detroit Gasket & Manufacturing

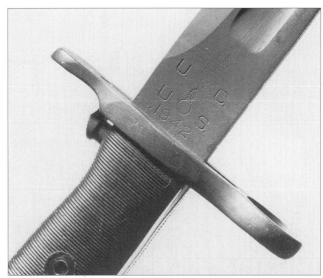

Typical blade markings on WWII production M1905 bayonet. This example was manufactured by Utica Cutlery Co. in 1942.

Troops "training" with M1905 bayonets. (U.S. Army)

Company were given contracts for production of the new M3 bayonet scabbard. Adoption of the M3 resulted in the earlier modified M1905, M1910 and M1917 scabbards being reclassified as "Substitute Standard."

It is interesting to note that production of the bayonets and scabbards actually lagged behind manufacture of M1 rifles. The situation had reached a point in April of 1942 that the Ordnance Department ordered that the rifles be shipped as soon as possible even though they weren't accompanied by sufficient numbers of bayonets. The bayonets and scabbards were to be subsequently shipped when they became available.

Although the M1905 bayonet had proven its worth, its long blade was the cause for criticism in some quarters during WWII. The most common complaint was that the 16" blade was cumbersome for troops riding in vehicles — a common mode of transportation by this time. In addition, less emphasis on bayonet fighting during WWII further reduced the perceived need for the long-bladed M1905. To this end, in late 1942, a bayonet similar to the M1905 but with a shorter 10" blade was under active consideration. It was felt that such a bayonet would be entirely adequate for fighting and would be more practical and less cumbersome than the M1905. It was also pointed out that the reduction in blade length would save a lot of badly needed steel. A number of M1905 bayonets had their blades shortened to 10" and were field tested. The modified bayonet, designated as the "M1905E1," met with very favorable results, and on February 11, 1943, the design was standardized as the "Bayonet, M1" and approved for use with the M1 and M1903 rifles. As was the case with the M1 sling, the M1 bayonet's nomenclature did not mean that it was adopted for use specifically with the M1 rifle, rather, it was the first bayonet standardized since the Model ("M") designation was adopted. The newly adopted M1 bayonet was essentially identical to the WWII production M1905 except for the shorter blade length. Most M1 bayonets

Army troops in the Pacific. Note the soldier firing his M1 rifle with fixed M1905 bayonet.

(Credit: U.S. Army)

Interesting photo of a U.S. Army solider undergoing winter training in Alaska in 1942. Note the M1905 bayonet carried in an M1917 scabbard attached to his pack. It is not widely known that the M1917 scabbard was authorized for use with the M1905 bayonet during WWII due to a shortage of standard M1910 scabbards. Note also that the M1's bolt is open. (Credit: U.S. Army)

were made with black plastic grips, but brown grips may be seen on occasion.

Manufacture of the M1 bayonet began in April 1943 and continued at varying production levels through August 1945. A total of some 2,948,649 M1 bayonets was made during the war. Large numbers of the M1905 bayonets were modified to M1 specifications by doing nothing more than shortening the blade and adding plastic grips. Two different methods of shortening the blades have been noted. The most common method utilized the normal spear point as found on the M1 bayonet, while some will evidence a so-called "Bowie" configuration blade tip. The initials of the firm contracted to modify the bayonets were generally stamped on top of the tang between the grips. Such modified M1905 bayonets can be identified by the Springfield Armory, Rock Island

Arsenal or 1942 vintage commercial contractor markings and by the fullers, which run the entire length of the blade. On original M1 bayonets, the fuller stops about 3 inches before the tip of the blade. Just over one million M1905 bayonets were modified to M1 specifications.

A scabbard virtually identical to the plastic M3, but with a correspondingly shorter length, was adopted on February 10, 1943, as the "M3A1." The nomenclature was changed to the "M7" on April 6 of the same year. Some of the M3 scabbards were shortened to M7 length, but most were newly made.

The M1 bayonet and M7 scabbard were widely used in World War II and remained standard issue into the 1950s and early 1960s. The canvas-covered M1910 scabbards and, to a lesser extent, unaltered M1905 bayonets are getting to be quite hard to find today. Both the

Text continued on page 102

Marine Corps private (San Diego, 1943) preparing his pack. The 1905 bayonet (with plastic grips) is carried in a WWII vintage M3 composition (plastic) scabbard attached to the pack. (Credit: National Archives)

THE M1 GARAND — WORLD WAR II PRODUCTION

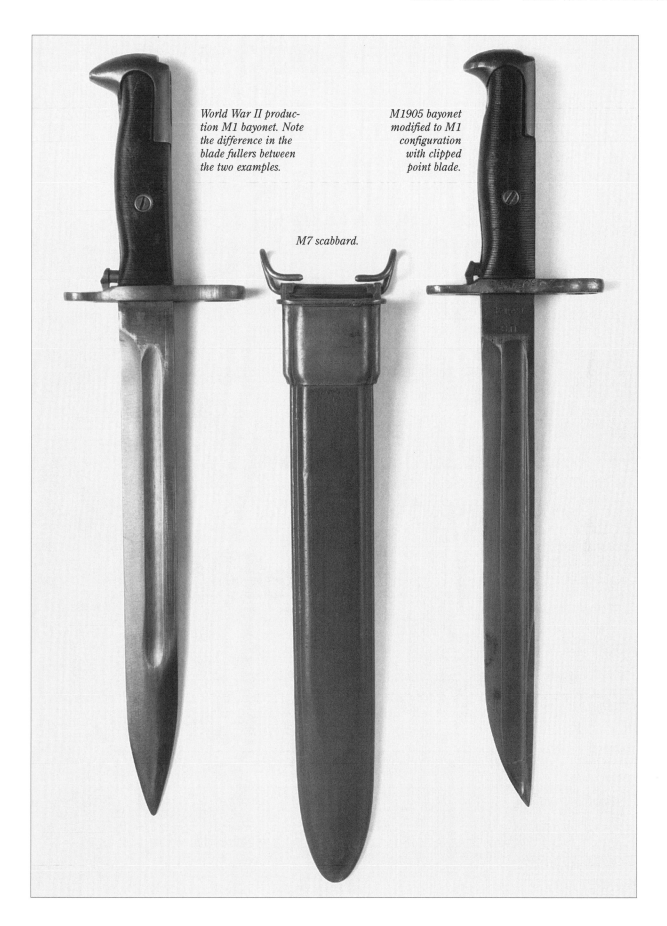

World War II production M1 bayonet. Note the difference in the blade fullers between the two examples.

M1905 bayonet modified to M1 configuration with clipped point blade.

M7 scabbard.

101

Text continued from page 99

M1905 and M1 bayonets would be correct for any WWII vintage Garand rifle. If one wished to display an M1 rifle made prior to the middle of 1943 in its "as issued" configuration, the M1905 would be the only type technically correct since the M1 bayonet did not come into use until sometime after April of that year. Of course, any 1945 or earlier vintage Garand rifle could have been used with either type of bayonet during the course of its tenure of service. On the other hand, from late 1943 until the end of the war, the M1 bayonet saw much wider use as compared to the M1905. Fortunately for today's collector, original M1 bayonets and M7 scabbards are still relatively common and affordable. There is little difference in price between original M1 bayonets and the shortened M1905 bayonets. The correct bayonet is a fine addition to an M1 rifle in a collection or display.

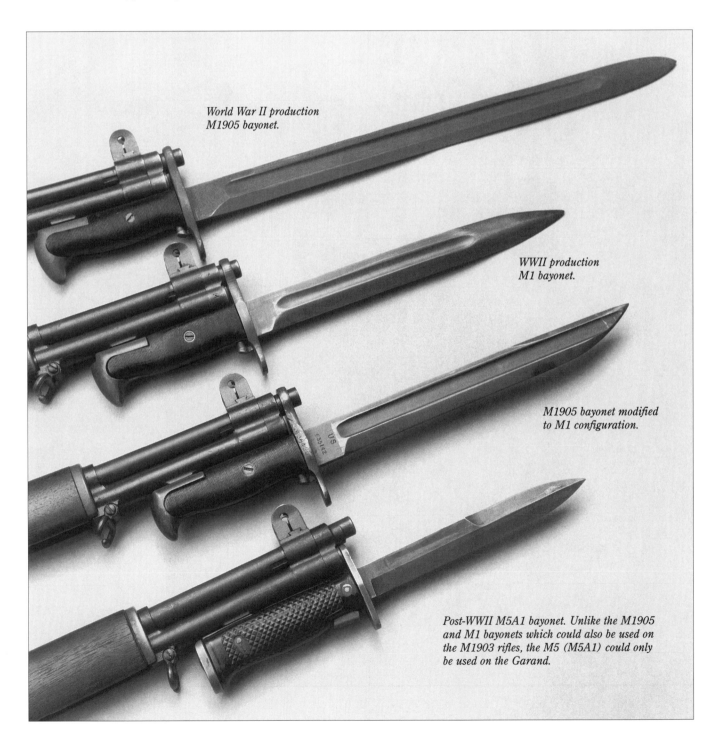

World War II production M1905 bayonet.

WWII production M1 bayonet.

M1905 bayonet modified to M1 configuration.

Post-WWII M5A1 bayonet. Unlike the M1905 and M1 bayonets which could also be used on the M1903 rifles, the M5 (M5A1) could only be used on the Garand.

Infantryman of the U.S. Army's 1st Division crossing the Rhine in 1945. Note the M1 bayonet in an M7 scabbard attached to his belt. (Credit: U.S. Army)

Bruce Canfield's Complete Guide to The M1 Garand and The M1 Carbine

(Above) Marine firing his M1 rifle with fixed M1 bayonet. Note the M7 scabbard on the left side of his pack.

(Below) Marines in the Pacific. Note the M1 bayonet on the M1 rifle in the foreground.

(Credit: USMC)

(Credit: USMC)

WWII production M7 grenade launcher.

M7 Grenade Launcher

Another interesting accessory used with the M1 rifles during much of WWII was the M7 rifle grenade launcher. Soon after our troops were employed in combat in the early days of WWII, requests for a grenade launcher capable of being used with the M1 rifle began to come in. The Garand's gas system, however, posed vexing problems for designers working on the project, because it was necessary to "bleed off" excess gas in order to reduce operating pressures to a safe level when firing rifle grenades. While these problems were being tackled, grenade launchers for the M1903 and, to a much lesser extent, the M1917 rifles were put into production. These bolt action rifles could be adapted to a grenade launching system much easier than could the gas operated M1. Therefore due to their utility as grenade launching platforms, many M1903 rifles stayed in service longer than would otherwise be expected.

Several experimental models of grenade launchers, designated by a "T" prefix, were tested for use with the M1 rifle. The "T14" design was found to be the most

acceptable, and the launcher was officially standardized on February 11, 1943, as the "M7." The M7 attached to the M1's bayonet lug by means of a hinged clamp. Excess gas was vented from the rifle by utilizing a stud, which fitted into a special gas cylinder lock screw that held it open at all times. A special gas cylinder lock screw was issued along with an instruction sheet with each M7 launcher. One big drawback of the M7 was that the rifle would not function as a self-loader when the launcher was attached. The early lock screws remained open after the launcher was removed from the rifle and closed only when the first round was fired afterward. An improved lock screw, which closed as soon as the launcher was removed, was adopted in January 1944.

The M7 launcher utilized a blank-type cartridge without a bullet. This grenade launching round was standardized as the "Cartridge, Rifle Grenade, Cal. .30, M3." The M3 round was used with the M1903 and M1917 rifles as well as the M1. It was designed to propel the standard M9A1 anti-tank rifle grenade approximately 180 feet per second. An auxiliary cartridge, the "M7," was standardized to boost the range of the M3 round. Quickly dubbed the "vitamin pill," the M7 auxiliary cartridge increased the effective range of the M7 launcher although it had the negative element of causing more recoil.

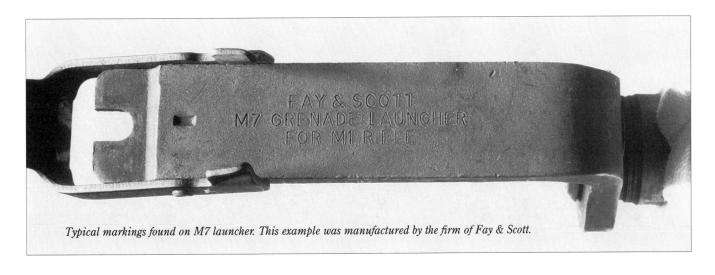

Typical markings found on M7 launcher. This example was manufactured by the firm of Fay & Scott.

The commercial firm of Knapp-Monarch Company was awarded a contract for 250,000 M7 launchers. The contract called for production to begin in May 1943 and set a target goal of 50,000 launchers per month. The company experienced some problems in getting underway due in large measure to the fact that the company was still producing grenade launchers for the M1903 rifles. As a result, only ten M7 launchers were produced in July 1943, none in August, and just 1,500 in September. Obviously, additional sources of M7 launchers were needed, and other firms were given contracts to supplement the production at Knapp-Monarch. These firms were International Business Machines (IBM), Fay and Scott, Arrow-Hart & Hegman, Hawley Smith Machine Company and Mitchell & Smith. Government records also reflect that Alfred Hoffman & Company was given a contract to produce M7 launchers, but no examples made by this firm have been observed. M7 launchers began to be delivered in quantity by February

of 1944 and by August of that year some 795,699 had been manufactured. The nomenclature of the item and the name of the maker were stamped on the bottom of the mounting bracket.

There was one major design changed in the M7 launcher. The early examples made by Knapp-Monarch prior to December 1943 were made with a removable nut on the front that held the flat retaining spring in place. All following M7 launchers had a solid tube and a coil spring instead. There were only 35,678 of the first variant M7 launcher made.

Due primarily to practices employed in the field, the actual number of M7 launchers needed exceeded the original estimates. Since the M1 rifle would not fire semiautomatically with the launcher attached, the typical practice was for a soldier to attach the launcher to fire the grenade and then remove it as soon as possible in order to have his rifle ready for normal fire. Naturally, this resulted in many lost launchers since they were

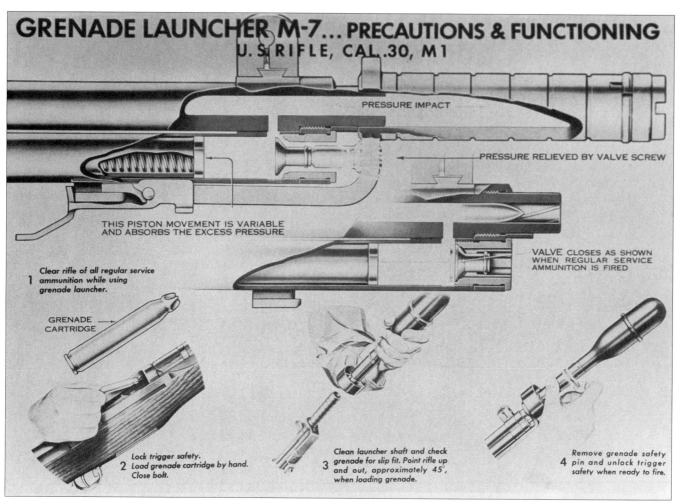

U.S. Army Ordnance poster depicting the operation of the M7 grenade launcher.

(Credit: U.S. Army)

often dropped in the heat of combat and never retrieved.

The Ordnance Department continued work on an improved design that would enable the Garand to fire with the launcher still attached. A revised model, tested as the "T95," was adopted in July 1945 as the "M7A1." Two firms were given contracts to produce the M7A1, but since neither was able to get into production before the end of the war, the outstanding contracts were canceled. The M7A1 was placed into production at Rock Island Arsenal after the war. With the pending adoption of the new grenade launcher, the M7 was declared as "Limited Standard" on June 14, 1945. The only type of grenade launcher used with the M1 rifle during World War II was the M7.

Even with its drawbacks, the M7 was a valuable addition to the M1 rifle during the latter years of WWII since it enabled the Garand to fire all sorts of fragmentation and anti-tank grenades, in addition to many types of to pyrotechnic devices.

A grenade launching sight, tested as the "T59E3," was adopted as the "M15" in March 1944 for use with the M7 launcher as well as with the M1 launcher used with the M1903 rifle and the M8 carbine launcher. The M15 sight attached to the left side of the rifle's stock by means of a round metal mounting plate and featured a leveling bubble, front post bar and rear peep sight. Large numbers of these sights were made and issued late in the war. A black rubber recoil boot was made primarily for the M1903 rifle but could also be used with the M1 as well. It was seen more frequently on the former.

The improved M7A2 and M7A3 grenade launchers were made in fairly large numbers in the 1950s. For today's collectors, the M7 launchers still remain relatively available and inexpensive. The M7A1 is, by far, the hardest of the M1 grenade launchers to locate, but, as stated, it was not manufactured or issued during WWII. Some interesting collections of the M7 launch-

Text continued on page 110

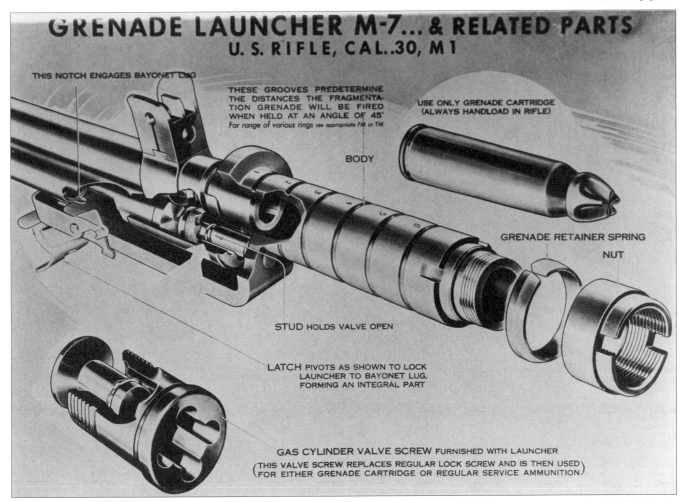

U.S. Army Ordnance poster depicting the operation of the M7 grenade launcher. (Credit: U.S. Army)

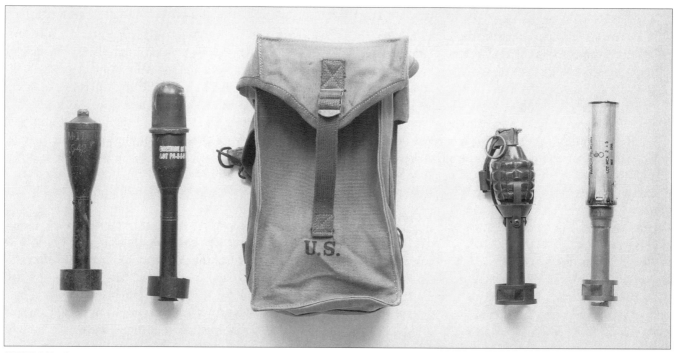

WWII Rifle Grenades — (Left to right) M11 practice grenade, M11 A1 practice grenade, Rifle grenade carrying bag, MkII fragmentation hand grenade on M1 adapter; ground signal parachute flare.

Marines help a wounded comrade. Note the MkII fragmentation grenade and adapter on the M7 launcher in the foreground. (Credit: USMC)

Two American soldiers with M1 Garand rifles and M7 grenade launchers with M9A1 rifle grenades.   (Credit: U.S. Army)

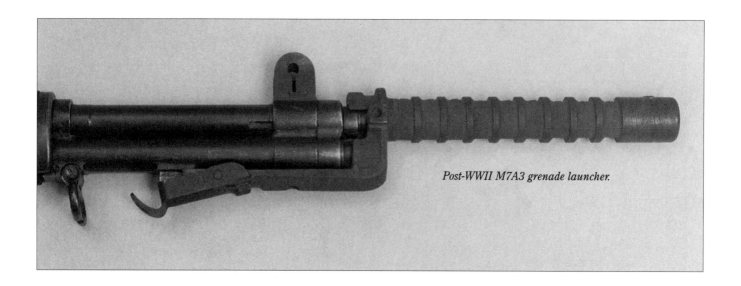

Post-WWII M7A3 grenade launcher.

M7A1 grenade launcher for M1 rifle. This variant allowed for the rifle to be fired semiautomatically with the launcher attached. The M7A1 was developed from the T95 design and was standardized in July of 1945, too late for service in WWII.
(Credit: Garand Stand Collection)

Text continued from page 107

ers have been assembled. Some examples of a launcher made by one firm with the original markings crossed-out and the markings of another firm added have been observed. This would be a good field for a collector on a modest budget who is looking for something a little different. The M15 sights are still around in unissued condition in very large numbers at extremely low prices. The rubber recoil boots are not as common but can still be found. These items as well as the various grenades and pyrotechnic items used with the rifle grenade launchers during the war are thoroughly covered in my book, *U.S. Infantry Weapons of World War II*. An M1 rifle fitted with an M7 launcher and an inert anti-tank or fragmentation rifle grenade is an impressive addition to a martial arms collection and vividly illustrates the versatility of John Garand's original design.

Leather Scabbard

Another interesting accessory for the WWII Garand rifle is the leather carrying scabbard. These items were originally intended to carry the M1 attached to a saddle. However, by the time the weapon was in widespread use, the horse cavalry was virtually a thing of the past. The scabbards were utilized for carrying M1 rifles on all manner of mechanized vehicles including motorcycles,

jeeps, trucks, weapon carriers and half tracks. Very early versions of the scabbard had a leather guide to accommodate the operating rod handle, while later versions had a steel guide. Two leather straps with metal snap hooks served to secure the scabbard. The name of the maker and year of production was stamped on the scabbard near the operating rod guide. Many of these scabbards are missing one or both straps, which obviously devalues the item for collecting purposes to some extent. Such scabbards, particularly in excellent condition, make very good additions to a collection and can still be found though prices are rising.

Cartridge Belts

The standard cartridge belt issued with the M1 rifle during WWII was the M1923 Dismounted belt. This belt was made of canvas web material and had ten pockets, which could each hold two 5-round '03 chargers or one 8-round M1 clip. Earlier versions of this belt had a dividing strap that fastened by a snap in each pocket and featured brass hardware. Colors of the material ranged from

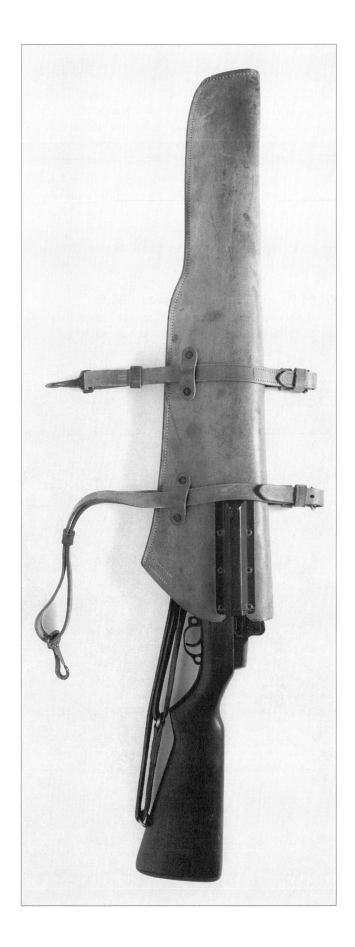

(Left) M1 rifle in WWII leather scabbard. Note the metal operating rod guide next to the lower strap.

(Below) Photograph taken in early WWII of the author's father, Charles K. Canfield, Sr., holding an M1 rifle in a leahter scabbard. Although originally developed for the "horse cavalry," the leather Garand scabbard was used on jeeps and other vehicles during WWII.
(Credit: Charles K. Canfield, Sr.)

khaki to olive green. Later versions omitted the dividing strap and utilized steel rather than brass hardware. Most of the WWII M1923 belts were marked "US" and stamped with the name of the maker and year of production inside. Some of the First World War vintage cartridge belts such as the M1918 remained in inventory during WWII and could have been used with M1 rifles, especially the earlier variants. A little known and very interesting variant WWII cartridge belt is the type produced for the U.S. Navy. This belt is essentially identical to standard Second World War M1923 belts, but it is made from dark blue canvas material rather than the khaki or olive drab material seen on the infantry belts. Most collectors like to have WWII production belts accompany their Second World War vintage rifles. Fortunately, decent condition M1923 belts of 1942–1945 vintage are still around today in fair numbers and can usually be found at reasonable prices.

Ammunition

One often overlooked item that was intimately associated with the M1 rifle are the myriad types of ammunition. The Garand rifle used many different kinds of ammunition during the war including standard ball, armor piercing, tracer, incendiary, incendiary/tracer, M3 grenade launching, M7 auxiliary and blank cartridges. These rounds can be identified by the headstamp, which identifies the maker and the year of production. Such ammunition still in its original factory boxing is much more desirable for collecting purposes. Original boxed WWII ammunition of all types is becoming harder to find with each passing year.

Other Accessories and Accouterments

The list of items used in one capacity or another with the M1 rifle during WWII is too lengthy to cover in this book. Such items as cleaning equipment and

Selection of ammunition issued with M1 rifle. Grouping includes M2 ball, armor piercing, tracer, grenade launching, auxiliary grenade launching cartridges, match and a sealed metal can containing 24 eight-round clips of armor piercing ammunition in bandoleers.

"Lubriplate" containers carried in the stock recess, the various types of ammunition and bandoleers are all interesting and appropriate additions to a collection. Anyone interested in pursuing this subject in depth should consult the book *Ordnance Tools, Accessories & Appendages of the M1 Rifle* by Billy Pyle. This book illustrates and briefly describes virtually all of the items associated with the M1 rifle before, during and after World War II. A collection consisting of nothing more than the rifles themselves can sometimes be a bit dull, and the many and varied items associated with the Garand can add much interest and value.

WWII Experimental M1 Rifles

There were a number of experimental M1 rifles, which were fabricated in varying quantities to test and evaluate various changes to the standard Garand design. As we have discussed, several of these were prototype or experimental versions with telescopic sights intended for sniping use. Others were designed to test various improvements or changes to the gas system, to improve general functioning of the weapon, to test selective fire capabilities and to evaluate the feasibility of a "carbine" version of the Garand. These weapons are informally referred to as "E models" or "T series." The "T" and "E" experimental rifles will be briefly profiled in Tables #17 and #18. Since few of these weapons were produced and none officially released by the government, the odds are extremely high against encountering any of these weapons on the collector's market today. Even if one did show up, most of the "T series" were selective fire weapons, which makes their possession subject to very strict federal rules. None of these weapons were fielded during WWII except for the M1E7, which was standardized as the M1C sniper rifle. These experimental variants notwithstanding, the M1 rifle as manufactured and issued throughout the war was little different than the pattern that had been in production since late 1940.

Although over four million were made, World War II M1 rifles remaining in their original "as issued" configuration are surprisingly scarce today since the majority were rebuilt after the war. The desirability of unaltered WWII Garands has resulted in a large number of the previously rebuilt rifles being "restored" to approximate their 1941–1945 factory configuration. The term "restoration" as used today can be a very misunderstood and abused word. In some instances, when only a few minor parts have been replaced, the term "restoration" may be proper. In many other cases, however, the

term "restored" is used to describe a rifle that has been totally assembled from parts. Such a non-original assembly of parts is more properly described as a "put-together" rifle. While some purists may scoff at anything other than a totally original and untouched rifle, there is really nothing wrong with adding a few parts to bring a rifle back to its factory configuration.

As an example, some of the WWII M1 rifles that were cycled through ordnance depots may have had nothing more done to them than the replacement of the "locking bar" rear sights and a new replacement stock installed. It would seem totally appropriate to replace the later T105E1 rear sights with the correct WWII type and install a stock of the properly cartouched variety *if* the presence of such replaced parts is disclosed to a subsequent buyer. There is a problem, of course, in the fact that later buyers may not have this information disclosed to them, and the rifle could be passed off as totally original. On the other hand, a rifle that has been subjected to only minimal restoration (if properly done) is surprisingly close to the same value of a totally original piece. However, a "put-together" rifle has no real value beyond the sum of its parts. Without question, the more restoration work done to a rifle, the more its value and desirability are reduced. It should not be inferred, however, that there is anything inherently wrong with the practice of restoring rifles if the fact that the weapon is not totally original is duly disclosed. Restoration can be an enjoyable and rewarding enterprise and will continue to be popular as the already small supply of original rifles continues to decrease.

All weapons of World War II are enjoying an increase in interest and popularity, and the M1 rifle is certainly at the head of the group. Its role in the war is well known and the Garand's place in the history of our armed forces is secure.

The United States concluded the Second World War as, unquestionably, the best equipped military fighting force in the history of mankind. The M1 rifle performed superbly in the war and vindicated the Ordnance Department's decision to stick with the weapon in spite of the early problems that were encountered. John Garand's legacy to his adopted nation should not be forgotten. His magnificent weapon was a key component of the American GI's triumph over the forces of oppression. Although repeated in virtually every book and article written about the M1 rifle, it is difficult to praise the M1 rifle with any higher accolade than bestowed by Gen. George S. Patton, Jr. when he proclaimed the Garand as…

"The greatest battle implement ever devised."

A member of an ordnance unit on New Guinea cleaning stacks of salvaged rifles. This photo clearly illustrates one of the reasons why relatively few WWII rifles have survived in their original "factory" configuration. (Credit: U.S. Army)

➤ ➤ ➤ ➤ ➤ ➤ ➤ ➤ Post-World War II ◄ ◄ ◄ ◄ ◄ ◄ ◄ ◄ ◄ ◄

Following the cessation of hostilities after V-J day, all outstanding contracts for M1 production were canceled. Winchester soon reverted to producing sporting weapons for the civilian market. Springfield Armory's mission shifted from mass production to overhaul and rebuild of the massive number of M1 rifles and other weapons that were in inventory following the conclusion of the war. The majority of M1 rifles that had seen use during the war required some sort of refurbishment in order to be put back into serviceable condition. Beginning soon after V-J Day, Springfield Armory embarked on a large scale program of overhaul and rebuild of M1 rifles and other infantry weapons.

Post-WWII Rebuilds

As the rifles were shipped to Springfield from myriad sources around the globe, the normal procedure was to tear the weapons down and sort the serviceable parts

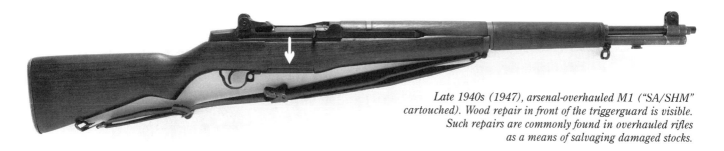

Late 1940s (1947), arsenal-overhauled M1 ("SA/SHM" cartouched). Wood repair in front of the triggerguard is visible. Such repairs are commonly found in overhauled rifles as a means of salvaging damaged stocks.

from the unusable components. The salvageable parts were inspected and subsequently assembled into complete rifles. Any parts that were defective, superseded or otherwise not usable were discarded. The receivers were often reparkerized and other metal parts refinished as necessary. Due to improper cleaning and, in many cases, maintenance procedures, the corrosive-primed ammunition of the period corroded large numbers of barrels necessitating their replacement. In order to meet this demand, Springfield began production of new M1 barrels for replacement and overhaul purposes soon after the war. Government records indicate that the Armory produced a combined total of 331,854 new M1 barrels in Fiscal Years 1946 and 1947. This large number illustrates the need for such items during this period. It should also be noted that some of the serviceable barrels salvaged from otherwise defective rifles were recycled and used on other rebuilt rifles as well.

In addition to the need to replace many barrels, a large number of M1 stocks required repair or replacement during overhaul. There were large numbers of stocks on hand that, with some repair, could be salvaged for use on rebuilt rifles. It is common to find stocks of this type with such features as inletted wood to replace serious chips or gouges, "plastic wood" to fill small spots, brass pins to strengthen damaged areas and similar evidences of repair. Springfield Armory's commanding officer from late 1945 to August 1947 was Col. Stephen H. McGregor. A cartouche with his initials ("SA/SHM") was stamped on the left side of the stock of each rifle overhauled at Springfield during McGregor's tenure of service. During overhaul, the stocks were frequently sanded or otherwise refinished, which often obscured the original cartouche. However, there were some stocks that retained the original cartouche and subsequently had the "SA/SHM" cartouche applied.

It is very likely that a number of the early gas trap M1s were overhauled during the 1946–1950 period as well. Unlike the "Direct Conversion" rifles discussed previously, there was no effort made to use as many of the original parts as possible. The only remaining component of the gas trap M1s rebuilt after WWII in most cases was the receiver. Even this part was modified by welding to build up the guide ribs.

Other than the presence of the "SA/SHM" cartouche, there is normally little conformity found in the M1s rebuilt by Springfield during this period. As stated, though the 1946–1947 replacement barrels are quite commonly found, some overhauled M1s were fitted with WWII vintage barrels that were salvaged from other rifles. The balance of the components could be of any vintage and could be of Springfield or Winchester origin. Operating rods were modified by milling out a section at the junction of the tube and handle to eliminate stress cracks as called for by regulations. In addition to the modified salvageable rods, some 817,947 newly made operating rods, which incorporated this modification, were made by Springfield Armory from 1948–1951. The configuration of the milled out area differed between the

Cartouche of Col. Stephen H. MacGregor. Col. MacGregor commanded Springfield Armory circa November 1945 through the summer of 1947. Although no new M1 rifles were manufactured during this period, many thousands were overhauled at Springfield and stamped with Col. MacGregor's cartouche.

modified rods and the newly made variety. In addition, the post-WWII replacement operating rods can be identified by their drawing number (D 35382SA). Another common modification during overhaul was to convert the early "wide pad" trigger housings to the "narrow pad" configuration. Rebuild regulations also called for newer components such as the latest pattern "T105E1" rear sights to be installed in place of the earlier types.

Springfield Armory records reveal that 98,487 M1 rifles were overhauled at the facility during Fiscal Years 1946–1947 (July 1, 1945 to June 30, 1947). This is the approximate time period in which the "SA/SHM" cartouched stocks were used.

Following Col. McGregor's departure from Springfield, the practice of stamping stocks with the initials of the commanding officer of the Armory was apparently discontinued for several years. However, Springfield continued to rebuild large numbers of M1 rifles. Records indicate that 92,477 M1 rifles were overhauled there in Fiscal Years 1948–1949 (July 1, 1947 to June 30, 1949). A number of M1s rebuilt during this time frame may be encountered with "SA/SPG" stock cartouches. As we discussed in the section dealing with the early gas trap Garands, this was the cartouche of civilian inspector Stanley P. Gibbs. Mr. Gibbs inspected some M1s that were rebuilt at Springfield during the late 1940s. This is an interesting variation that is much less commonly seen than the "SA/SHM" cartouche. However, other than the slightly later 1948–1949 barrels (if used), the rifles inspected by Gibbs varied little from those rebuilt under McGregor's tenure. Such rifles were generally a mixture of new replacement and serviceable salvaged parts.

Springfield Armory continued to overhaul M1 rifles into the early 1950s. In July 1950, Col. James L. Guion was posted to Springfield as commanding officer. Soon after Col. Guion assumed his new duties, the practice of stamping stocks with the commanding officer's initials resumed. The new "SA/JLG" cartouche began to be used on M1 rifles overhauled at Springfield beginning after Col. Guion's arrival. There are at least two variants of the "JLG" cartouche. The first appears to be a modified stamping die in which the "SA" portion appears well aligned and essentially identical to the previous Springfield cartouches. The "JLG" portion of the die is somewhat mis-aligned and struck much deeper than the "SA" marking. One would speculate that this was a interim stamping die that was used until a permanent die could be fabricated. The result is an unusual cartouche that could easily be mistaken for a bogus stamp. The

Cartouche of Col. James L. Guion, Commanding Officer of Springfield Armory circa July 1950 to May 1953. Many M1s were overhauled during Col. Guion's tenure. New production M1s were also stamped with his cartouche during the early 1950s. This was the last cartouche used by Springfield containing the initials of the Commanding Officer.

Typical early 1950s stock cartouche stamped on overhauled M1 rifles. Most M1D stocks were marked with the pattern cartouche.

period of time that this cartouche was used is not known but was likely the latter part of 1950 into early 1951. The later, and much more common, "SA/JLG" cartouches conform to the same general format as the previous Springfield cartouches. The first variant "JLG" cartouche would be properly found on the M1 rifles rebuilt by Springfield Armory during Col. Guion's tenure of duty.

In addition to the stock cartouche, the rifles overhauled at Springfield during this period can be identified by the 1950–1951 dated SA barrels. Although, as was the case previously, serviceable WWII barrels salvaged from other rifles were also occasionally used.

While on the subject of the post-WWII rebuilt Garands, mention should be made of one other variant. A number of M1 rifles rebuilt at Springfield in 1952 were marked on top of the receiver, just behind the rear sight, with the initials of the Armory and the year of rebuild ("SA-52"). The use of markings stamped into the receiver differed from the previous practices of stamping the stocks to indicate that a rifle had been cycled through the Armory for overhaul. Some WWII vintage M1C sniper rifles were altered to service rifle configuration

"SA-52" marking stamped on receiver as found on M1s overhauled at Springfield Armory in 1952.

during this period. These converted rifles are easy to identify as the five holes drilled into the left side of the receiver were plugged as part of the overhaul process. The plugged receivers were then assembled into service grade M1s. Occasionally, one of these altered M1C receivers may still be encountered today on rebuilt M1 rifles coming out of the DCM (CMP) program. Since such receivers are invariably genuine M1C receivers, they can be "restored" to their original configuration with little difficulty and are desirable items for this reason. However, many of the plugged M1C receivers have the "SA-52" marking stamped behind the rear sight which would prevent them to being restored back to their original WWII configuration. In any event, M1 rifles with the "SA-52" marking on the receiver are found only in the rifles overhauled at Springfield Armory during 1952.

After 1952, Springfield began stamping the stocks with a rebuild mark generally consisting of a "SA over a single letter" enclosed in a three corner box or square. M1s overhauled at Springfield in the post-1952 period had this mark stamped on the left side of the stock approximately midway between the pistol grip and the end of the butt. M1 rifles overhauled at facilities other than Springfield Armory often had various types of rebuild marks stamped on the stocks or, later, engraved by "electric pencil" on the receiver legs. Table #19 lists the various markings used to identify ordnance facilities that overhauled M1 rifles during and after World War II.

All of these 1946 to 1952 rebuilds outlined above are interesting and often unappreciated collector variants. While none of them approach the gas trap "direct conversion" rifles in scarcity or value, they are nevertheless distinct and historically significant collector variants of the M1 rifle. Of course, given a properly cartouched stock, it is all too easy to assemble a mixture of various pre-1950 parts and come up with what appears to be an original Springfield rebuild. However, this hasn't really been a problem for collectors as even the original post-WWII rebuilds have rather limited value as compared to rifles remaining in their 1940–1945 factory configuration. However, as the supply of the WWII rifles continues to decrease and the significance of the original rebuilds is recognized, this may become more of a problem. As is the case with undocumented sniper rifles, a good rule of thumb is not to pay any more for a rebuild than the sum of the value of the parts. The inclusion of the "SHM", "SPG", "JLG" and "SA-52" marked rebuilds can add some interesting variants to a collection at generally modest cost. Table #8 lists the attributes of M1 rifles rebuilt in the post-WWII period.

Japanese "Type 5" Copy of the U.S. M1 Rifle

During the latter stages of World War II, the Japanese produced a rough copy of the M1 rifle. It is estimated that 100 to 125 of the rifles were fabricated at the Yokosuka Naval Arsenal sometime in 1944. The war ended before any were put into production, if that was, in fact, Japan's intent. A few made it back to the United States in the hands of the conquering GIs.

Known as the "Type 5 Rifle", the "Japanese Garand" was chambered for the 7.7mm service cartridge. Rather than the M1's 8-round en bloc clip, the Type 5 rifle loaded by means of a 10-round charger ("stripper clip"). The basic action and gas system were clearly based on the M1, but the differences were at least as great as the similarities. These weapons are rarely encountered today. While not technically an M1 variant, the Japanese Type 5 rifle would be an interesting conversation piece in a Garand collection. Due to the very small numbers made, this rifle is rarely encountered on the market today.

Post-World War II Production M1 Rifles

The M1 rifles produced after the Second World War are interesting weapons but do not have the same degree of collector interest as the 1945 and earlier rifles. In addition, scholars of the subject find the post-WWII Garands to be confusing and, occasionally, even enigmatic rifles. Curiously, there is much less documentary data available on the rifles made from 1952 to the end of production in 1957 than on the WWII production rifles. There is also much less uniformity in these weapons than those produced previously. For example, Table #1, which enables the determination of the date of production by serial number for the WWII and earlier Garands, is quite accurate. However, efforts to produce a similar table for the post-WWII M1 rifles are still continuing with rather frustrating results. Much of the information known about the post-1945 production M1 rifles has been gathered from the observation of existing specimens believed to be original. However, this is less reliable than much of the information that has been garnered on the WWII and earlier rifles. This field is the subject of continuing research by several M1 scholars, and it is hopeful that additional reliable information with be uncovered. Nevertheless, the post-WWII Garands are quite interesting weapons and are certain to gain greater interest with collectors as the supply of original WWII rifles continues to decrease.

Korean War Springfield Armory Production

The continuation of the rebuild program at Springfield into 1952 was due in large measure to the outbreak of hostilities in Korea in the summer of 1950. There were ample supplies of M1 rifles and other weapons left over from the Second World War to meet the immediate demand. As the war in Korea dragged on longer than expected, the resulting depletion of our small arms inventory required a new supply of weapons.

In 1951, Springfield Armory commenced plans to resume mass production of the M1 rifle. The serial number range assigned to the Armory began with 4,200,000. Even though Springfield Armory had manufactured well over three million M1 rifles during WWII, the process of getting back into production was more difficult than might be imagined. One of the most serious problems encountered during this time was the difficulty in procuring suitable steel for barrels. Armory records indicate that over 120,000 barrel blanks were rejected during the first half of 1952 because the metal developed serious cracks during the metallurgy process. Partly as a result of this problem, the Marlin Firearms received a contract in 1952 for production of M1 barrels. It is a little known fact that Marlin

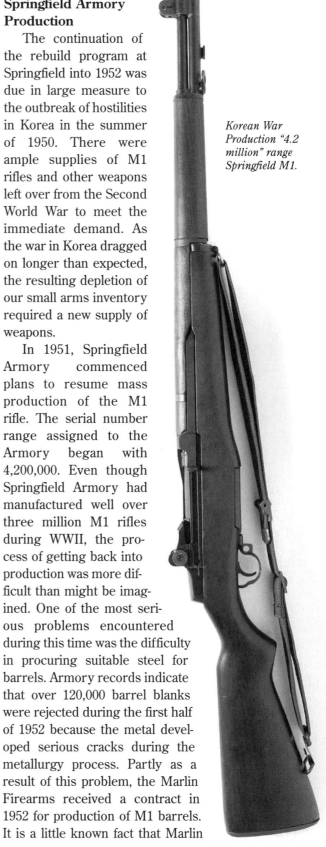

Korean War Production "4.2 million" range Springfield M1.

produced over 40,000 M1 barrels during World War II. These WWII Marlin barrels were finished in blue rather than parkerizing and were dubbed "Blue Marlins." However, the quality control was terrible. Many, if not most, were rejected by the government, and none are believed to have been used during WWII on production rifles, although some were used after the war for overhaul purposes. The barrels made by Marlin in the 1952 to 1953 period were of much better quality and some were utilized by Springfield on new production M1s. This is the only confirmed use of barrels made by an entity other than Springfield Armory on newly manufactured SA Garands. The Marlin barrels made at the start of production in 1952 were marked with the drawing number and "Marlin" on top and were not dated. In late 1952, the markings were relocated to the right side of the barrel and can be seen when the operating rod is retracted. The later Marlin barrels were also marked with the month and year of production. Springfield eventually corrected the problem with the steel blanks and the use of Marlin barrels ceased. It should not be inferred that the use of Marlin barrels was extremely widespread during this period as the vast majority of M1 rifles made during the 1952–1953 had SA barrels.

Although the basic design of the M1 rifle did not change after WWII, there were a number of differences in the "Korean War" Garands and the WWII variants. Among the most obvious is the 4,200,000 range serial numbers. The highest serial number utilized in WWII was in the very high 3,800,000 range or, perhaps, into the very low 3,900,000 range.

The M1s produced at the start of renewed production in 1952 were fitted with the latest pattern parts including the T105E1 rear sight assembly, the "poppet"-style gas cylinder lock screw, "high hump" gas cylinder lock, operating rod with the integral relief cut and other features not found on WWII production Garands. Also, the format of the drawing numbers was changed in this period with the addition of a "55" or "65" prefix to the part number. For example, the drawing number for the trigger housing as used during WWII and earlier was "D28290" with various revision ("dash") numbers following. When the format was changed in the early 1950s, the trigger housing drawing number became "6528290" with a "SA" suffix. There will be variances found in the drawing numbers during this period such as a "SA" prefix rather than suffix and changes to the marking format.

Examples of M1 rifles still in their original factory condition as made during the early 1952 through the mid-1953 period are surprisingly uncommon today. The best

Receiver markings of Korean War production M1 ("4.2 million" range).

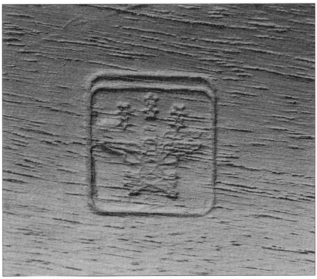

Defense Acceptance Stamp stock cartouche as used after 1952 until the end of production.

U.S. Army solider in Korea, circa 1950, with an M1C sniper rifle equipped with M81/M82 telescope, M2 flash hider and M1 sling.
(Credit: U.S. Army)

estimates are that between 123,000 to 124,000 rifles were made by Springfield Armory during this period. Serial numbers for these rifles ranged from the very low 4.2 million range into the low 4.3 million block. These "Korean War" Garands were subjected to the extensive rebuilding programs in the mid-1950s and into the early 1970s. Table #9 lists the general characteristics found on original rifles of this vintage.

The success of the M1 rifle in the Korean War mirrored that of World War II. The weapon proved to be the best battlefield rifle in the world and served our fighting men well during the often brutal conditions in Korea. The noted military historian, S.L.A. Marshall wrote the following evaluation of the M1's service in Korea in his book, *Battlefield Analysis of Infantry Weapons*:

The issue rifle (M1) has performed adequately in

Korea and is regarded by troops with a liking amounting to affection. This is true of all forces, Army and Marines alike. They have found it stands up ruggedly against the most extreme tests by terrain, weather, and rough handling. They want the weapon left as it is now, and they have no suggestions to make as to how it might be changed for the better.

The rifle is sufficiently accurate for the purpose intended. Its record of high serviceability remained unimpaired during the worst storms of the winter.

Of all the weapons carried by the infantry, the M1 appeared to be the least sensitive to heavy frost, extreme cold, and icing.

Its "durability" is the greatest reason why it stands in such high favor with the men. They no longer mind the weight of the piece because of its consistent performance.

Photo dated September 22, 1950, depicting an infantryman of the U.S. Army's 5th Regimental Combat Team firing his M1 rifle at North Korean troops from behind the cover of a tank. The M1 saw wide use in the Korean War. (Credit: U.S. Army)

The harsh winter climate of Korea often played havoc with many infantry weapons. The M1 rifle was notable in its ability to function in such extreme conditions. A Korean War-era Army report regarding the M1 rifle stated that:

In infantry company data from Korean operations there are numerous examples wherein the retention of the position depended finally on fire from the M1.... The M1 works equally well in bitter or moderate cold. In fact, it is the "old reliable" of infantry fighting during winter operations, and is not less dependable in other seasons. There are occasional mechanical failures for one reason or another. But outside of an occasional broken firing pin, the rifle structurally stands the gaff phenomenally well."

Many M1s were also supplied to our United Nations allies during the Korean War. One of the major recipients of Garands during this period was the Republic of Korea which received large numbers of Garands from the early 1950s into the 1960s. These former ROK M1s constitute the bulk of the so-called "imports" mentioned previously. These weapons provided to our allies under various military aid programs was one of the reasons that it was necessary to put the M1 back into production during the early and mid-1950s. As was the case in United States service, the Garand proved to be a reliable and popular weapon for many of our allies. Some problems were reported when the typically smaller Asians such as Koreans, Filipinos and Vietnamese found the size and recoil of the M1 to be objectionable. However, the power and durability of the M1 offset these perceived deficiencies somewhat, and the rifle was in active use by many of our allies long after it was replaced in United States service.

Accessories and Accouterments for Post-WWII Rifles

In most cases, the ancillary items issued with the M1 were the same as used in World War II. Although the leather M1907 sling was superseded by the web M1 sling, large numbers of the earlier sling were on hand and saw use well into the 1950s. Likewise, large numbers of the M1923 cartridge belt were left over from WWII, but the item was put back into production in the early 1950s to meet the increased demand caused by the war in Korea. Some changes were made in the combination tool and other cleaning implements carried in the butt trap. The previously referred to book, *Ordnance Tools, Appendages and Accessories of the M1 Rifle*, details the various changes.

One of the most interesting items adopted for use with the post-WWII M1 was the M5 bayonet-knife. Although large numbers of the M1 bayonet were issued after WWII, a smaller edged weapon that could function as a bayonet and combat knife was developed for the M1. The resulting weapon was very similar to the M4 Bayonet-Knife developed for the M1 carbine. The new bayonet was designated as the "M5." The "M5A1" was the same design but with an improved locking lever. The M5A1 was produced in much larger numbers than the M5 variant. Its chief distinguishing feature was its lack of the typical barrel ring, and it had a rearward facing stud that fitted securely into the Garand's gas cylinder screw. This meant that it could only be used with the Garand rifle. The now familiar Defense Acceptance Stamp was generally marked on the guard of the M5/M5A1 bayonets. The patent for the M5 bayonet was granted on December 27, 1955, and the weapon began to be issued the following year. Although large numbers of the older M1 bayonets were still on hand, a fairly large number of the M5(A1) bayonets were issued. The bayonet was accompanied by the M8A1 scabbard, but the older M8 scabbard could also be used. The M5A1 bayonet remains quite available to collectors today.

The M7A2 and M7A3 rifle grenade launchers are around in fairly large numbers today, so finding a decent example at a good price is not normally difficult. The launchers are not in high demand by collectors since they were not actively employed in warfare like the M7, and they are not as rare as the M7A1 launcher.

Post-World War II Garand Sniper Rifles

Although the M1C sniper rifle saw extremely limited use at the very end of WWII, the weapon was rather widely used in Korea during the 1950–1953 time period. Both the U.S. Army and U.S. Marine Corps fielded the M1C in Korea where it was used alongside the M1903A4 and M1903A1/Unertl bolt action sniper rifles. The wide open terrain found in much of Korea was an ideal environment in which to employ sniper rifles. While the scope-mounted Garand was not an optimum sniping rifle, it was definitely superior to iron-sighted service rifles for sniping use.

Most of the Garand sniper rifles used in Korea are believed to have been standard M1Cs, as produced late in WWII, which still remained in inventory. The Marine Corps had officially adopted the M1C at the end of WWII and acquired a number between 1945 and 1950. The M1C sniper rifles fielded in Korea were fitted with the standard WWII vintage accessories including M81/M82 telescopes.

M1D

Although not manufactured during WWII except in small prototype quantities, large numbers of M1D rifles were converted at Springfield Armory from standard M1 service rifles during the 1952–1953 period. It is interesting to note that the government's official position regarding the preference of the M1C over the M1D did an "about face" from 1945 to 1951. During World War II, the M1C was clearly the preferred variant, but just a few years later the M1D was favored instead and

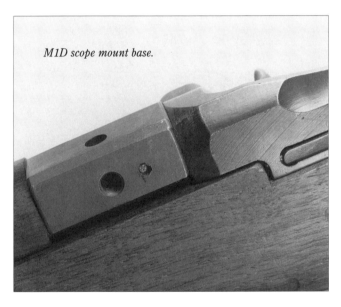

M1D scope mount base.

was approved for future procurement in much larger numbers. The primary reason for the M1D's renewed favor was that standard Garand rifles could be converted to this configuration much easier and faster than new M1Cs could be manufactured. An M1D sniper rifle could be produced by doing little more than removing a standard M1 barrel and installing the special "D" barrel, while the M1C was a specially manufactured weapon.

Government records reveal that the first large scale order to convert M1s to M1Ds occurred on December 10, 1951, with Springfield Armory Expenditure Order No. 1868. This document requisitioned the first M1Ds and ordered that 14,325 M1 rifles be converted into M1Ds. Springfield produced large enough numbers of the special M1D barrels during this period to meet the immediate demand and also provided enough barrels for subsequent M1D conversion programs at other ordnance facilities. The precise number of M1D rifles eventually made is not known, but several ordnance depots converted M1 rifles into M1Ds as late as the 1960s.

As initially produced, most of the Korean War vintage M1D rifles were equipped with leather cheek pads, M2 flash hiders and M84 telescopes. The M84 was adopted late in WWII as a replacement for the M81/M82 scopes but did not see production until the early 1950s. Some commercial production Lyman Alaskan scopes were acquired in the very early 1950s for use on early M1Ds until the sufficient numbers of M84 scopes became available to meet the demand. A few of these commercial scopes were also believed to have been used on M1Cs during this period as replacements for unserviceable M81/M82 scopes. The Libby-Owens-Ford Company was the primary manufacturer of M84 scopes. The Hart Metal Products Company pro-

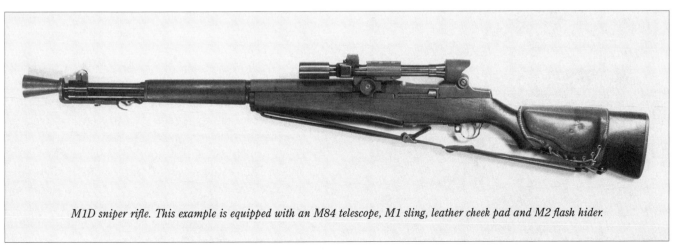

M1D sniper rifle. This example is equipped with an M84 telescope, M1 sling, leather cheek pad and M2 flash hider.

Close-up view of M1D mount and M84 scope.

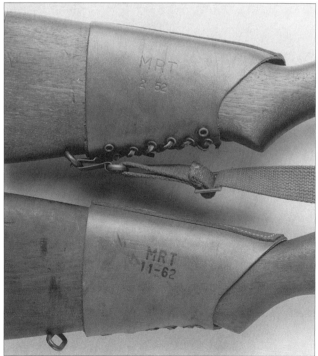

(Top) "MRT" (Mildew Resistant Treatment) markings and February 1952 date on leather cheek pad. This marking is impressed into the leather. (Bottom) "MRT" marking and November 1962 date. These markings are stamped in black ink on the leather.

duced large numbers of M2 flash hiders in the early 1950s. Most of these flash hiders had stamped metal mounting brackets rather than the forged brackets found on the WWII vintage M2s. The leather cheek pads produced during the 1950s (and later) were generally stamped in black ink "MRT" and dated. This indicated that the item had been treated for mildew resistance (**M**ildew **R**esistance **T**reatment). The date indicated the month and year that the pad was treated, not necessarily when it was manufactured.

As was the case with standard M1 service rifles, the M1 web sling was the standard issue rifle sling issued with the Garand snipers during the Korean War. However, large number of the earlier leather M1907 slings were on hand and saw wide use, although none are believed to have been produced after the late 1940s.

Table #14 lists the general characteristics of original M1D rifles. As will be noted, the parameters of M1D rifles are much wider than for the M1C and MC 1952 weapons. The key item to look for on an M1D rifle is the barrel marked with the proper "D7312575" drawing number. Early M1D barrels were marked with the drawing number on top, and later barrels had the number stamped on the right side.

Adjustment knob cover open on M84 scope. Note the nameplate and serial number below the adjustment knob.

Photo dated October 5, 1951, showing the U.S. High Commissioner for Germany, John J. McCloy, examining an M1C sniper rifle. The rifle is equipped with an M81/M82 telescope, M2 flash hider, leather cheek pad and M1 sling.
(Credit: U.S. Army)

1951 Conversion M1C

One little known variant M1 sniping rifle was also produced during the time that the M1D was first put into mass production (or, more correctly, mass conversion). The same Springfield Armory Expenditure Order No. 1868 that requisitioned the first M1Ds also called for the conversion of 3,087 M1 rifles into M1C configuration. This official order is not widely known today, even by some advanced M1 collectors and scholars. This was obviously a radical change from the WWII practice of building the M1C "from the ground up" as a sniper rifle. It is rather surprising that the government would order over three thousand M1 rifles to be converted to M1C configuration given the fact that it would have been easier just to convert more of the standard service rifles into M1Ds.

The M1D remained unproven as a combat weapon. Perhaps this fact dictated that some additional M1Cs should be on hand in case the M1D turned out to be unsatisfactory in service. In any event, few details regarding these 1951 vintage conversion M1C rifles are known. They were almost certainly converted from WWII-era rifles on hand at the time since the Armory had not pro-

duced any new M1s by then. It may seem foolish to someone not accustomed to bureaucratic reasoning that the government would order Springfield Armory to convert service rifles into M1Cs one year and then turn around and order many M1Cs to be modified into standard service rifles the next year by plugging the receivers (as discussed previously). However, according to official government documents, this is exactly what occurred.

Marine Corps "MC 1952" Sniper Rifle

During the time that the M1D conversion program was going on at Springfield Armory, an interesting sub-variant of the M1C rifle was also being produced. As stated, the USMC standardized the M1C sniper rifle at the end of WWII but did not use the weapon in combat until the Korean War. The issue M81 and M82 scopes lacked sufficient power and light gathering capabilities to meet the Marines' needs, and the search for an improved telescope resulted in the consideration of several commercial rifle telescopes. The Stith Bear Cub scope met the specifications, and a slightly modified version of the scope was put into production by the Kollmorgen Optical Company under Marine Corps con-

Text continued on page 129

Close-up view of Kollmorgen 4X MC-1 telescope and special MC-1 mount. The receiver base is the standard Griffin & Howe type used on WWII M1C rifles.

USMC 1952 sniper rifle. This rifle is fitted with a USMC issue Kollmorgen 4X "MC-1" scope and special mount, M2 flash hider and M1 sling. Note the lack of a leather cheek pad as this item was not issued with the rifle according to Marine Corps equipment lists. All USMC 1952 rifles were modified from WWII Production M1C sniper rifles.

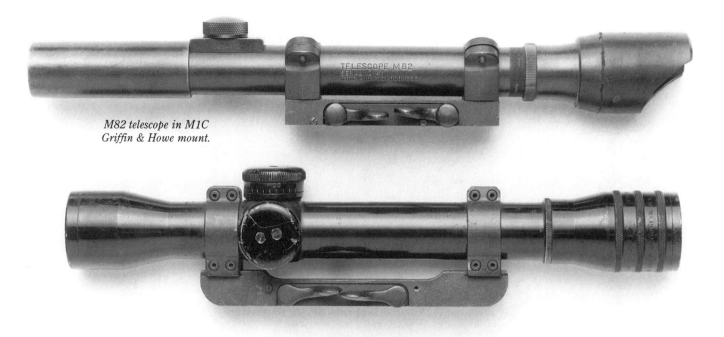

*M82 telescope in M1C
Griffin & Howe mount.*

*USMC Kollmorgen MC-1 scope in special MC-1 mount. Note the difference in size between
the M1C and MC-1 mounts, although both will fit on the G&H receiver base.*

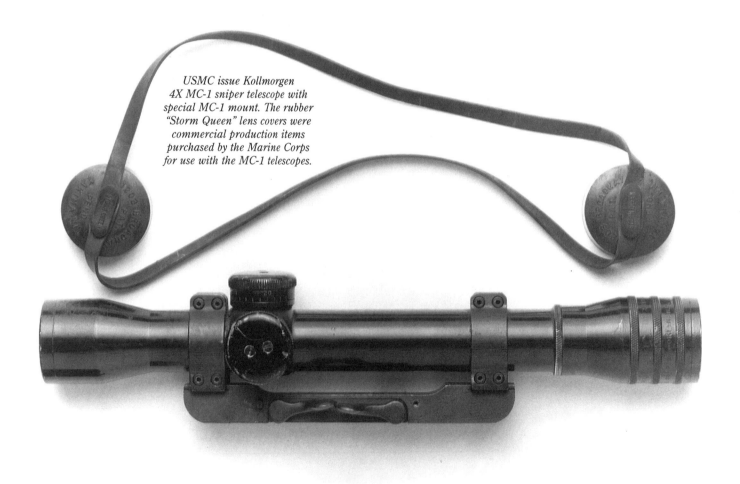

*USMC issue Kollmorgen
4X MC-1 sniper telescope with
special MC-1 mount. The rubber
"Storm Queen" lens covers were
commercial production items
purchased by the Marine Corps
for use with the MC-1 telescopes.*

(Left) Marine Corps markings on top of Kollmorgen MC-1 telescope tube.

(Below) Typical markings found on eyepiece of USMC Kollmorgen MC-1 scope.

Text continued from page 126

tract. The USMC Kollmorgen scope was 4X power and featured excellent light gathering characteristics. It was officially adopted as the "MC-1" telescope. The scope had an aluminum alloy tube, which could not be blued or parkerized in the normal manner and was painted black. Early variants of the scope had Marine Corps markings stamped on top of the tube, and later models had U.S. government markings on the eyepiece. Commercial "Storm Queen" rubber lens covers were procured for use with the new Marine scopes.

A modified Griffin & Howe mount was also adopted by the Marine Corps as the "MC-1" for use with the Kollmorgen scope. It could be used with the standard M1C receiver base with no modification.

The M1C rifles equipped with MC-1 scopes and mounts were designated as the "MC 1952" or "USMC 1952" sniper rifle. Most of these weapons were overhauled at Springfield Armory in 1952 and fitted with new production replacement barrels dated in the early 1950s. If the original WWII barrel was still serviceable, it would possibly be retained. Most of the USMC 1952 rifles were also fitted with replacement stocks that were typically marked with a boxed "SA" on the left side sev-

eral inches behind the grip. Some of the rifles are believed to have been stamped "SA-52" on the receiver behind the rear sight as was done on other Garands overhauled at Springfield in 1952. The M2 flash hider was approved for use with the USMC 1952 rifle. Curiously, the leather cheek pad is not shown as an accessory or component for the weapon in any of the Marine Corps manuals or stock lists for the USMC 1952 rifle. Table #15 details the characteristics of original USMC 1952 rifles.

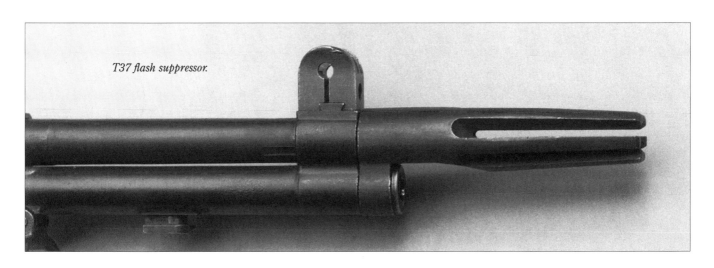

T37 flash suppressor.

As was the case with the M1D, no MC 1952 rifles are believed to have seen active service in the Korean War prior to the cessation of hostilities in 1953. However, the weapon did remain in Marine Corps service into the 1960s when it was replaced by sniper versions of the M14 and bolt action sniper rifles such as the "M40." It should be noted that the Marine Corps utilized some M1D rifles as well.

After the mid-1950s, the M1D was the primary sniper rifle in the U.S. Army's inventory, and there were much larger numbers on hand as compared to the M1C.

Upon America's active involvement in Vietnam, some M1Ds were sent to Southeast Asia where they saw a fair amount of use early in the war by our troops and our South Vietnamese allies. Virtually all of these were fitted with the 1950s vintage M84 scopes and many had the later T37 flash suppressor. The demand for sniper rifles resulted in a depletion of the inventory and several ordnance depots turned out M1D rifles in the early to mid-1960s. The Tooele (Utah) Depot converted a number of M1 rifles into M1Ds during this period. These later depot converted M1Ds typically show inferior

M1D sniper rifle equipped with Weaver K-4 telescope in 1" mount. Rifle is also fitted with an M1 sling, leather cheek pad and T37 flash suppressor.

(Top) M84 telescope in standard ⅞" M1D mount.

(Bottom) Weaver K-4 telescope in special 1" M1D mount.

U.S. Marine sighting an M1D rifle in Vietnam. This rifle is equipped with an M84 telescope and leather cheek pad but does not have a flash hider or flash suppressor attached. (Credit: USMC)

U.S. Army Special Forces advisors in South Vietnam in the early 1960s. These "Green Berets" are armed with M1 Garand rifles. The M1 saw a surprising amount use early in the war in Vietnam in the hands of U.S. personnel and our South Vietnamese allies. (Credit: U.S. Army)

craftsmanship when compared to the rifles assembled at Springfield in the early 1950s. Even though the M1Ds produced in the 1960s generally utilized existing 1951–1953 dated barrels, they can usually be identified by the initials of the ordnance depot and the date of conversion engraved by "electric pen" on the right front receiver leg. These rifles also will typically be found with dull gray parkerizing rather than the greenish tinted, WWII-style parkerizing usually found on the early 1950s M1Ds.

As stated, the M84 telescope was standardized for use with the M1D rifles as well as the M1Cs still in inventory. The M84 does not fit the M1C mount very well but can be used nevertheless. In the early 1960s, the government procured a quantity of commercial Weaver K-4 telescopes for use with some of the M1D rifles being assembled at the time. It is not known if this was done because of an inability to acquire sufficient numbers of M84s or if the Weaver was intended to be an improvement over the issue scope. The Weaver scope required a larger 1-inch mount rather than the standard ⅞" mount utilized with the M81/M82 and M84 scopes. Some have speculated that the M1D rifles with K-4

scopes were intended for issue in Vietnam. There is no evidence to support this theory, and it is believed that these scopes stayed stateside throughout the war. It has been theorized that the M1D rifles with these scopes were acquired for potential use during the widespread civil unrest rampant in the United States during this period. This is certainly possible, but specific details regarding the M1D/Weaver K-4 rifles are sketchy. Relatively few of these scopes and special 1" mounts were acquired by the government. Some of the mounts, many complete with Weaver K-4 scopes, were sold in the mid-1990s through the auspices of the Director of Civilian Marksmanship (DCM). Prior to the release of these scopes, the 1" M1D mounts were very scarce. They are still far from common but can found a bit more easily now. Such scopes and mounts would probably be found most often on one of the depot-converted, 1960s vintage M1Ds, but conceivably they could have been utilized on any M1D.

After the conclusion of the war in Vietnam, the M1D rifles along with the few M1Cs still in the government's inventory saw little use. It has been reported that a small number of M1Ds saw service in the Gulf War, but any

U.S. Army soldier identified as Sfc. R. Remp of Akron, Ohio, firing on retreating Communist North Korean forces with an M1C sniper rifle from a hill top near the Naktong River on August 18, 1950. The M1C does not have an M2 flash hider attached. (Credit: U.S. Army)

THE M1 GARAND — POST-WORLD WAR II

Barrel markings on original M1D sniper rifle barrel. Note the drawing number with the special "D731" prefix identifying it as an original M1D barrel. The example pictured was manufactured in November 1952.

U.S. soldier firing an M1D sniper rifle from a rooftop during the Dominican Republic intervention in 1965. The M1D is equipped with an M84 telescope and an M2 flash hider.   (Credit: National Archives)

U.S. Marine reloading his M1C sniper rifle while keeping watchful eye on the enemy during the Korean War. The rifle is fitted with an M81/M82 scope and does not have an M2 flash hider.   (Credit: USMC)

such use was quite limited. In late 1993, the government authorized the release of a number of M1D rifles, which had been in storage for some time at the Anniston (Alabama) arsenal. These rifles were sold through a lottery system to qualified individuals under the auspices of the DCM (later renamed CMP). In 1995, one hundred M1C rifles were also sold through the DCM by means of a sealed bid auction. Although none of these M1C rifles remained in their original WWII configuration and most had been extensively overhauled, many sold for surprisingly high prices. A few other M1C or M1D rifles have trickled out of the government's inventory primarily through the "Title 10" program.

While collector interest in all variants of the Garand sniper rifle has been very high for the past decade or so, the M1C is certainly the most desirable. However, the unfortunate problem of fakes has plagued the collector fraternity with respect to the M1 snipers. Unquestionably, the bulk of purported original M1C rifles seen for sale today are bogus. As mentioned previously, several dedicated and talented researchers have painstak-

ingly assembled a data base of authentic M1C serial numbers. It enables a particular serial number to be verified as original or fake with an approximate 95% confidence level. USMC 1952 rifles may also be verified through this procedure since they were made from the original batch of Springfield Armory M1C rifles produced in late WWII. Table #13 gives information on how this verification may be obtained.

Some of the fake M1Cs look very good indeed, but if a rifle does not have *original* government documentation or cannot be otherwise verified as original, its value is no more than the sum of its parts. There have been some attempts to fake photocopies of original government sale documents by altering the serial numbers on the paper. It is unfortunate that some desirable WWII vintage M1 service rifles have been ruined by someone attempting to fake an M1C. The five holes drilled into the receiver of such a rifle forever destroys its collector value.

Occasionally one of the legitimate M1C receivers that had the holes plugged circa 1952 will be found on a

Text continued on page 137

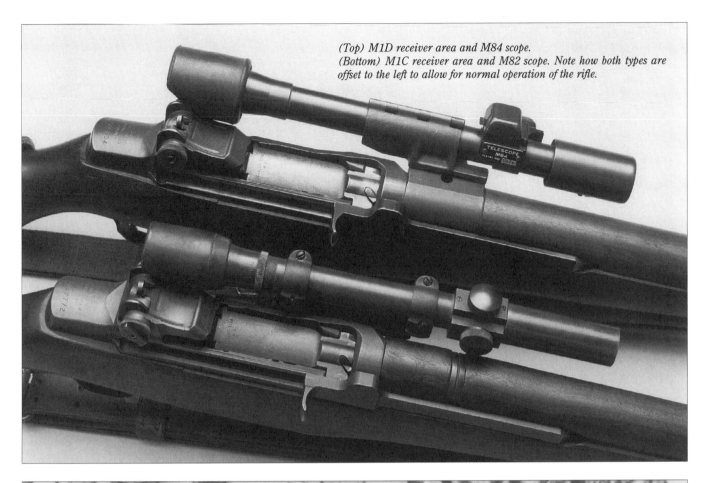

(Top) M1D receiver area and M84 scope.
(Bottom) M1C receiver area and M82 scope. Note how both types are offset to the left to allow for normal operation of the rifle.

Korean War-era photo depicting an M1C rifle. Note the firing position required due to the offset location of the telescope.

(Credit: National Archives)

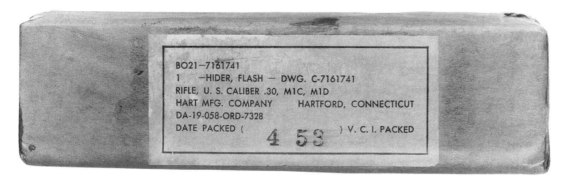

M2 flash hider produced by the Hart Manufacturing Company accompanied by its original factory shipping box dated April 1953.

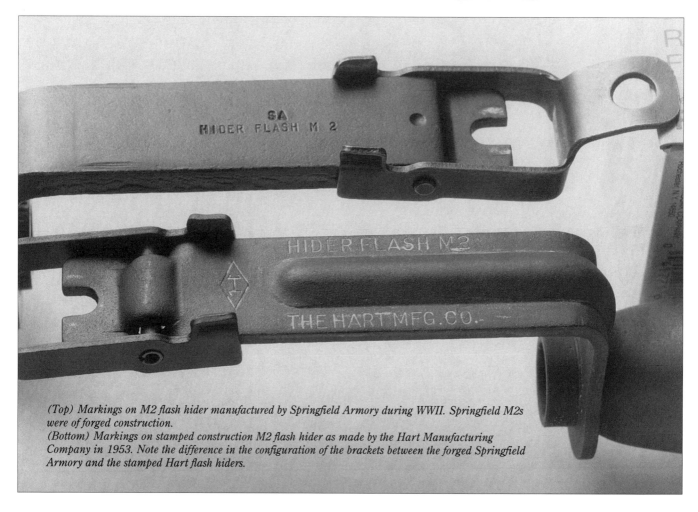

(Top) Markings on M2 flash hider manufactured by Springfield Armory during WWII. Springfield M2s were of forged construction.
(Bottom) Markings on stamped construction M2 flash hider as made by the Hart Manufacturing Company in 1953. Note the difference in the configuration of the brackets between the forged Springfield Armory and the stamped Hart flash hiders.

Text continued from page 134

rebuilt service rifle. Such receivers are desirable for restoration purposes since they can often be verified as original. Of course, a restored M1C is not as desirable or valuable as a totally original piece, but it is infinitely preferable to a bogus "reproduction" (i.e., outright fake). MC 1952 rifles are also faked today, and the same caveats as mentioned pertaining to the M1C apply equally.

The problem with fakes is also rampant with M1D rifles. It can be difficult, if not impossible, to spot a fake M1D since even the originals were converted from existing service rifles. Surplus M1D barrels are still around, and it is a simple matter to fit such a barrel into a receiver. Virtually any vintage and make of receiver could be used since there were no distinctive serial number ranges for M1D rifles. Therefore, a rifle assembled last week in a basement workshop often cannot be distinguished from a rifle converted forty-five years ago by an ordnance facility. The M1Ds sold through the DCM (CMP) should bring a premium if accompanied by their original bills of sale since their provenance can be determined. Again, any M1D that cannot be positively verified as original is worth no more than the value of the sum of the parts. If original documentation is not available, the most important feature to look for is an *original* M1D barrel. Some fake M1D barrels have been noted where a standard M1 barrel, possibly properly dated (early 1950s), was turned down on the rear portion and an M1D barrel mount installed. Cosmetically, this barrel might appear to be a legitimate M1D barrel. However, the originals were stamped with a special drawing number "D7312575" (marked on the top or side). If this drawing number is not present, the barrel is not an original M1D.

Many of the accessories related to the Garand snipers are in demand today. M81 and M82 telescopes are particularly sought after as are original M2 flash hiders and WWII "K Line" cheek pads. The Springfield Armory M2 flash hiders are particularly hard to find and generally rather expensive. A fairly large number of early 1950s vintage Hart flash hiders surfaced several years ago and can generally be found. The Hart flash hiders typically sell for somewhat less than the SA flash hiders. Some reproduction flash hiders may be found from time to time and can usually be spotted by the crude workmanship and the lack of "SA" or Hart markings. Of course, such markings could be added, so the item should be examined closely prior to purchase. Likewise, some newly made leather cheek pads with bogus markings have been seen. The general condition

and age of a pad should be considered. Even if the pad was never issued, forty or fifty years of storage will generally impart some measure of patina to a leather item. An M1 sniper cheek pad that looks absolutely brand new should be suspect.

In spite of the problems encountered with fakes, collecting the various M1 sniper rifles can be an extremely interesting and rewarding hobby. With such exceptions as original gas trap rifles, genuine M1C and USMC 1952 sniper rifles are among the most sought after collectible examples of the Garand. An experienced collector or reputable dealer should be consulted prior to the consummation of a purchase since such rifles generally sell for fairly sizable sums. Nevertheless, few examples of the Garand are more interesting or desirable for martial arms collectors than the sniper rifles.

Post-WWII Commercial Contract Rifles (H&R/IHC)

In 1948, the government awarded a contract to the Winchester Repeating Arms Company for an assessment of the prospect of resuming manufacture of the M1 rifle at a rate greatly exceeding the firm's WWII production. A second contract was given to the firm's parent company (Olin Industries) in June 1949 for a feasibility study regarding the suitability of utilizing the closed St. Louis Ordnance Plant for new Garand production. On June 30, 1951, the Remington Arms Company was given a contract for a pilot production run of nineteen M1 parts. Winchester did not resume M1 production after World War II nor was the St. Louis plant reactivated for M1 production. The Remington contract was canceled before completion although some of the tooling and production equipment made by the firm was delivered to the government and used for later production.

With the outbreak of the Korean War and the increased demand for M1 rifles, it was determined that additional sources of the weapons were needed to supplement production at Springfield. Government records of the period reveal that much thought was given to the perceived vulnerability of the American arms makers' geographic concentration in the New England area. This concentration of manufacturers in the newly dawned nuclear age was a major consideration for the dispersal of arms production to other areas. Many of these same concerns had been previously voiced during World War II regarding the possibility of Axis sabotage. Despite the fact that no major problems resulted from this concentration, geographic considerations did play some role in the awarding of new M1 production contracts.

On April 30, 1951, the first step was taken to resume new production of the M1 rifle. It was recognized early on that one of the most critical items would be barrels. The Line Material Company of Birmingham, Alabama, was granted a contract on this date for the production of M1 barrels. It was anticipated that Line Material could supply barrels to other firms engaged in Garand production and thus speed manufacturing time. On June 15, 1951, a contract for new production of M1 rifles was awarded to a civilian firm, the International Harvester Corporation of Evansville, Indiana, for the first time since the Second World War. Known primarily as a major manufacturer of farm equipment and trucks, International Harvester was a rather unusual choice since the company had never previously produced small arms. As we will subsequently discuss, International Harvester's M1 production program was plagued virtually from start to finish with many problems. Engineers at International Harvester began setting up their production facilities with a great deal of assistance from Springfield Armory and the Ordnance Department. It was soon determined that the bulk of the Line Material barrels would be utilized by International Harvester in a effort to ease the company's production problems.

On April 3, 1952, the Harrington & Richardson Arms Company of Worcester, Massachusetts, was also given a contract to produce 100,000 M1 rifles. This initial contract was followed by a second order for 31,000 rifles on June 25, 1952. Harrington & Richardson had been a long-time manufacturer of small arms for the commercial market. The company had also manufactured the ill-fated Reising .45 caliber submachine gun for the U.S. Marine Corps during World War II.

The first rifles made under International Harvester's contract were delivered in December 1952, and Harrington & Richardson began delivery in early 1953. It is interesting to note that H&R did not receive its contract until almost a year after International Harvester yet was able to begin delivery just a few months after IHC.

In order to help coordinate production of the M1 between Springfield Armory, the two civilian prime contractors and the various subcontractors, an Ordnance production "integration committee" was formed in late 1952. This was similar, albeit on a much smaller scale, to a committee formed during WWII to help coordinate production of the M1 carbine. A number of issues were addressed regarding production of the M1 during this period. Some non-critical tolerances were eased in order to boost production. Other thorny problems, including shortages of steel and other materials due to labor strikes, were addressed.

International Harvester

Even though IHC's first rifles were delivered in late 1952, it was not until sometime in the second quarter of calendar year 1953 that the firm was at a point which could reasonably be called "mass production." As stated, International Harvester experienced many serious production delays. The firm acquired thousands of receivers from Springfield in order to help alleviate its difficulties. This helped but did not solve the problem. The situation reached a climax in early 1955 when the company negotiated an end to its contractual commitments for M1 production and closed its manufacturing line. As we will discuss, the myriad of problems encountered by International Harvester has resulted in some interesting variants of the M1 made by the company for today's collectors. There are three distinct receiver marking variants of International Harvester Garands and a number of minor variants as well. IHC was assigned two blocks of serial numbers:

4400000–4660000
5000501–5278245

The most common marking variant is found on the receivers actually manufactured by International Harvester. All four lines of text above the serial number are of equal length. A typical drawing number of this variant receiver is "IHC D6528291-A". Several letter suffixes may be noted. Unlike M1 receivers made by Springfield Armory, the IHC-made receivers are not marked with heat lot codes.

A second variant are the first batch of receivers produced by Springfield Armory under contract for International Harvester. These can be easily identified by the lines of varying lengths of text above the serial number in much the same manner as Springfield Armory marked Garand receivers. Some collectors refer to this variant as an "arrowhead" shaped marking format. Receivers of this type have "D6528291" drawing numbers with a two digit suffix (i.e., "42" or "43"). As is the case with Springfield Armory made receivers, these are marked with heat lot codes.

Another variant are the so-called "Gap Letter" receivers. These were also made by Springfield Armory for IHC but have a distinctive space between the two top

Markings on receiver manufactured by International Harvester. This type of receiver has a "IHC" prefix to the drawing number.
(Credit: Bob Seijas)

Markings on receiver manufactured by Springfield Armory for International Harvester. Note the uneven length of the lines as compared to the IHC-made receivers.
(Credit: Bob Seijas)

Second variant receiver manufactured by International Harvester. This type does not have an "IHC" prefix to the drawing number.
(Credit: Bob Seijas)

"Gap letter" receiver. These receivers were also made by Springfield Armory for International Harvester.
(Credit: Bob Seijas)

139

lines in order to have all four lines of equal length. Collectors have speculated as to the reason for this change in marking format. The most commonly accepted assumption is that this was done in order to have all lines of the same length as found in the "standard" receivers made by International Harvester. If this was in fact the case, it can certainly be argued that this cosmetic touch was not worth the effort. In any event, the "gap letter" Springfield/IHC Garands are an interesting and somewhat sought after variant. The drawing number for these receivers is "IHC F6528291." The receivers are marked with heat lot codes.

Unlike the WWII Springfield and Winchester M1s, it is difficult, if not impossible, to formulate a serial number/production date table for the International Harvester Garands. Several serious researchers are working on such a project and, in time, a somewhat clearer picture may emerge. The serial number blocks assigned to IHC are well established, but actual production was apparently very inconsistent regarding the utilization of assigned serial numbers.

Until the late 1970s, International Harvester M1 rifles were very scarce on the collector's market since few had been released by the government. However, by this time a fairly large number of M1 rifles were imported back into the United States primarily from Central America for sale to qualified law enforcement officers. Curiously, the majority of these rifles were International Harvesters. While condition of these rifles varied greatly (many were in excellent shape), most remained in their original factory configuration and had not been arsenal overhauled. Many police officers availed themselves of the opportunity to buy original M1 rifles at very attractive prices. Since the law did not forbid subsequent resale of these weapons, most changed hands rather quickly as collectors were only too glad to pay several times the original price for what had previously been a hard-to-find variant of the M1 rifle. Eventually the regulations were changed and the flow of rifles was cut off for several years. However, enough IHC Garands had made it back into the country to go a long way toward satisfying the demand.

As stated, there are several distinct variants of International Harvester M1s. While not as popular as the WWII rifles or even the Korean War Springfield rifles, IHCs are interesting collector items. Other than the receiver markings, there are several features which identify IHC Garands. International Harvester is believed to have used the "LMR" barrels exclusively. There is ongoing research to correlate barrel dates with

Typical markings found in barrel channel of International Harvester M1 stocks. Many were also stamped with a two letter prefix such as "OR" or "HR."

International Harvester M1 receiver markings.

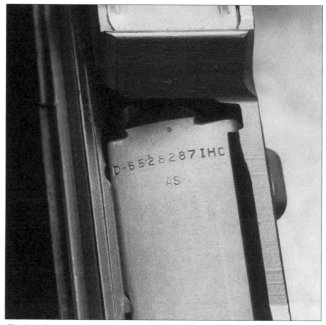

Typical International Harvester M1 bolt markings.

receiver vintages. Typically, on original production rifles, the barrel dates range from very late 1952 to mid-1955.

The stocks of International Harvester M1s are also distinctive. They have the Defense Acceptance Stamp (eagle & stars) cartouche stamped on the left side in the same manner as post-1952 Springfield Armory Garands. However, the "barrel channel" of IHC stocks are stamped with a four digit number, which is often preceded by the letters "OR" or "HR". Researchers have postulated several theories regarding the meaning of these markings. The most generally accepted ideas are that the numbers represent a Julian calendar date and the stocks marked "OR" were made by the Overton-Richardson Company. In any event, such barrel channel markings are unique to International Harvester rifles and are a sure means of identification.

Most of the other component parts are marked "IHC" next to the drawing number to signify the prime contractor. Of course, when rifles were overhauled, many of the original parts were removed. Restoration of rebuilt IHC rifles is generally not too difficult if the receiver/barrel combination is original. International Harvester M1 stocks are not extremely common but do turn up from time to time. Most of the other parts are generally not too difficult to find. Table #11 details the typical features found on original IHC Garands.

Despite the tremendous difficulties faced by IHC during its M1 production run, the completed rifles were satisfactory in quality and performance. By the time the IHC rifles began to come into inventory, the fighting in Korea was over. However, many International Harvester M1s were in service from the mid-1950s onward. An International Harvester M1 in excellent condition with all original features is a worthwhile addition to any martial collection. The several interesting variants also adds to the IHC's collector appeal.

Harrington & Richardson

Besides International Harvester, the other post-WWII commercial M1 prime contractor was the Harrington & Richardson Arms Company of Worcester, Massachusetts. H&R had a great deal less trouble than International Harvester during the course of their M1

(Above) Typical Harrington & Richardson M1 barrel markings. This example is also dated March 1953.

(Below) Line Material barrel (LMR) dated March 1953 as found on original International Harvester M1. LMR barrel markings were often lightly stamped.

production contract. This was due primarily to the fact that Harrington & Richardson was an established firearms manufacturer where IHC had no prior experience in the field.

Although H&R had not made large numbers of guns for the government (with the aforementioned exception of the Reising SMG), the firm's management and work force were well versed in the intricacies of small arms production. As stated, although H&R received its M1 contract well after IHC, the firm was able to begin delivery of finished rifles in early 1953, only a short time after International Harvester was able to complete its first production rifles.

There were less inconsistencies and variants among the H&R Garands than the IHC Garands. The firm made most of its own barrels (marked "HRA"). Harrington & Richardson actually produced barrels prior to the production of complete rifles which helped the company efficiently get into mass production. It is believed that H&R procured some LMR contract barrels in the mid-5 million serial number range to help alleviate production bottlenecks. However, the vast majority of original Harrington & Richardson rifles will have HRA barrels.

Harrington & Richardson was assigned two blocks of serial numbers:

4,660,001–4,800,000
5,488,247–5,793,847

Interestingly, the firm used a few serial numbers into the low 6 million range, and at least several hundred rifles have been confirmed with numbers this high. However, the vast majority will have serial numbers within the two assigned blocks. Unlike the receiver markings variants found in the International Harvester M1s, the Harrington & Richardson receivers were generally consistent in their markings.

As was the case with the other contractors, Harrington & Richardson marked their initials on many of the components. The "HRA" marking was used as either a prefix or suffix to the part's drawing number. For example, the hammer was typically marked "HRA 5546008" while the operating rod was marked "654582 HRA". The company also procured some parts from subcontractors which were often marked with single letter codes in addition to the drawing number and/or HRA markings.

The Harrington & Richardson M1 stocks have several differences which distinguish them from stocks

Harrington & Richardson M1 receiver markings.

Typical Harrington & Richardson M1 bolt markings. Note the steel and heat lot codes.

made by other entities. There are actually three rather subtle variants of H&R stocks. The first is characterized by a noticeably thick profile in the wrist and pistol grip areas and a noticeably rounded pistol grip. The stock also had a distinctive "horseshoe" shape on the part of the stock behind the rear of the receiver. This stock was stamped with a ½" Defense Acceptance Stamp cartouche and a "circle P" proof mark without serifs. A second variant had a thinner profile in the wrist and pistol grip areas, although the pistol grip itself was still noticeably rounded but with a somewhat flatter base. The distinctive horseshoe area behind the receiver remained the same. The Defense Acceptance Stamp cartouche was a larger ⅜" and the proof mark still lacked serifs. A third variant H&R stock was similar to the second, but the pistol grip was less rounded, and the proof mark had serifs added. The cartouche remained the same ⅜" size. Both the second and third variant stocks are found primarily on later production rifles (in the 5 million) range, and it is probable that these stocks were procured by H&R from subcontractors.

Like their IHC counterparts, the Harrington & Richardson M1 rifles were fairly uncommon on the collectors market until fifteen or twenty years ago. Quite a few were imported from overseas, and a number have also been released through the DCM program over the past few years. Many of these rifles retain all, or most, of their original parts. Restoring a H&R Garand is normally not too difficult since the parts are still available, and the weapons are not as much in demand as are the earlier rifles. Table #12 lists the general characteristics found in H&R M1 rifles. As is the case with all post-WWII rifles, there are many frustrating inconsistencies which makes the development of a reliable receiver/barrel date table difficult.

Despite few distinctive variants, Harrington & Richardson M1 rifles are still interesting weapons and at least one example should reside in every Garand collection.

National Match M1 Rifles

Another interesting and desirable variant of the Garand rifle is the National Match. The genesis of the National Match M1 began in March 1953 when the Ordnance Department ordered Springfield Armory to produce 800 M1 rifles for use at the National Matches held at Camp Perry, Ohio. This was the first new order for National Match rifles since the late 1930s when the M1903A1 was the mandated rifle for National Match use. The demands of WWII had put the development of

"NM" barrel marking as found on original, unmodified "Type 1" National Match M1. This was the only special marking found on these early National Match Garands. Note the star marking next to the "NM".

a NM version of the M1 rifle on hold. Furthermore, some competitive shooters questioned the Garand rifle's ability to perform up to acceptable match standards. However, by early 1953, the time was right to produce a match version of the M1. Since Springfield Armory was producing new M1 rifles at this time, the production of a few hundred National Match rifles was not a particularly onerous task. The quality of the standard service rifles in production at the time was such that it was believed only modest "tuning" would be required to give satisfactory match accuracy.

The sequence of production for National Match M1s varied through the years that the weapon was in production (1953–1963). The first variant, termed the "Type 1" by collectors started out as essentially nothing more than a finely tuned service rifle. The only readily apparent National Match feature was the "NM" stamped on top of the barrel. Otherwise, despite the superior gunsmithing, it was difficult to distinguish the early "Type 1" National Match Garands from standard service rifles in comparable condition. Such rifles had the same Defense Acceptance Stamp cartouche found on service rifles of the period. Serial numbers began in the 5,800,000s with barrel dates from 1953 to 1957. "Type 1" National Match rifles were assembled using new production receivers,

Although capable of better accuracy than the standard service rifle, the first National Match Garands were something of a disappointment to the experienced competitive shooters. One problem was that the rules specified that National Match rifles must be "...the service rifle as issued." There was a great deal of contention regarding how much the Garand could be modified as a match rifle without jeopardizing its status as an "as issued" service rifle. Nevertheless, the vocal critics of the M1 as a match rifle couldn't be ignored and fur-

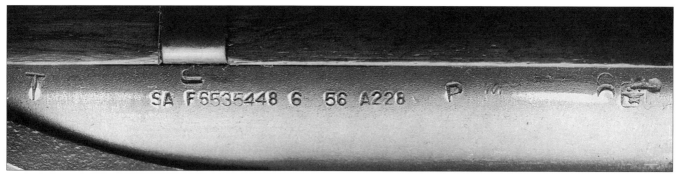

Late production Springfield M1 barrel dated June 1956. This barrel was used on an original "Type 1" National Match rifle. Note the full drawing number, "P" proof mark and Defense Acceptance Stamp (arrow).

ther modifications were forthcoming to help solve the accuracy deficiencies of the Garand.

By 1958, National Match rifles began to lose their service rifle appearance due to the addition of non-standard parts. At first, these changes were rather subtle but became more and more extensive each year. Among the first changes was the introduction of a specially made National Match gas cylinder with a larger diameter rear ring to eliminate contact with the barrel. Special sight blades and other refinements became common. These refinements helped marginally but were not enough to satisfy the demands of the users. By 1960, the M1 National Match had changed sufficiently from the original "Type 1" configuration to become a distinctive and easily recognizable variant. The subsequent rifles have been dubbed "Type 2" by today's collectors and

will evidence many special National Match features such as hooded rear sights, glass bedded stocks and "NM" markings on many parts. The special parts and extensive modifications resulted in greater accuracy over the earlier models, and eventually the M1 National Match rifle was recognized as a satisfactory competitive shooting instrument.

The number of new and rebuilt National Match rifles from 1953 to 1963 is listed below:

Year	New	Rebuilt	Total
1953	800		800
1954	4,184	499	4,683
1955	3,003	314	3,317
1956	5,050	550	5,600
1957	4,184	499	4,683
1958	1,295	731	2,026
1959	2,877	2,652	5,529
1960		8,663	8,663
1961		1,410	1,410
1962		4,500	4,500
1963		3,639	3,639

Receiver markings of late production M1 rifle manufactured in 1956. This rifle is an original National Match M1 still in "Type 1" configuration.

As can readily be seen, many of the earlier rifles were rebuilt beginning in 1954. After 1959, no new National Match M1s were manufactured, and the rifles made after were all rebuilt from existing weapons. Thus, many of the earlier "Type 1" rifles were modified to "Type 2" configuration and forever lost their service rifle appearance. Unlike the original "Type 1" NM rifles, which were all made from new production receivers, many of the later National Match M1s utilized earlier vintage receivers taken from salvaged Garands. Table #16 lists the specifications for M1 National Match rifles.

Unfortunately, many fake National Match Garands are on the market today. Some look very good and many are capable of extremely good accuracy. As is the case with the sniper rifles, the only definitive way to prove the authenticity of a National Match M1 is if the weapon is accompanied by its *original* government documentation. Since many of these rifles were legally sold to competitors at the National Matches, this important paperwork was often retained. It is certainly more common to find a National Match Garand accompanied by its original documents than a sniper rifle. If someone is offered a NM Garand, and the seller says he will send the paperwork later, it might be wise to pass on the purchase. Rock Island Arsenal retained the serial numbers of all National Match rifles, and at one time a person could contact the Arsenal to determine if a particular serial number was that of an original NM rifle. However, this program is reportedly no longer in operation. A good rule of thumb is that a purported National Match M1 without the original papers is worth no more than a standard service rifle in comparable condition. The "Type 1" rifles in unmodified condition are much harder to find and in more demand by collectors than the later, more extensively modified rifles. In any event, an original National Match rifle is a good addition to a collection.

7.62mm NATO Conversions

When the M14 rifle was adopted in 1957, plans were formulated to phase the venerable Garand out of service and replace it with the new rifle. Manufacturing difficulties with the M14 resulted in a delay of several years before getting the new weapon into mass production. It is noteworthy that the M14 was actually a "product improved" M1. The new rifle was chambered for the 7.62mm NATO cartridge, which was also adopted for use with the M60 machine gun.

By the early 1960s, the U.S. Army had almost totally rearmed with the M14, and the M1s in inventory were relegated to the reserve stockpile. The U.S. Marine Corps adopted the M14 soon after the army. The U.S. Navy was well equipped with M1 rifles at the time and didn't feel the need to expend vitally needed funds on new rifles. Small arms were an ancillary part of the Navy's arsenal, and the demand for the latest type of rifle was not overwhelming. However, logistical considerations dictated that the Navy rifles should be chambered for the new standard 7.62mm NATO cartridge. As early as 1959, the Navy looked for ways to convert its M1 rifles to the newly standardized cartridge without the necessity of acquiring new weapons.

The most logical course of action seemed to be conversion of the original .30-06 M1 barrels to 7.62mm NATO. A bushing that would fit into the chamber of the original .30 caliber barrel was developed by the H.P. White Laboratory. After firing several rounds, the bushing would theoretically become permanently wedged into the chamber, and the barrel would be thus chambered for the 7.62mm NATO cartridge. The gas port was also enlarged to the proper diameter. A plastic spacer was attached to the M1's bullet guide to prevent the loading of a .30-06 round. The Navy rifles converted in this manner were designated as the "Mark 2 Model 0."

The first hundred or so newly modified Mark 2 Model 0 rifles were boldly stamped "7.62 NATO" on the left side of the receiver below the rear sight. This marking was soon deleted, and the new caliber designation was moved to the right side of the barrel. The American Machine and Foundry Company (AMF) was given a contract to convert approximately 17,000 M1 rifles to Mark 2 Model 0 specifications by the Navy.

While good in theory, the Mark 2 Model 0's bushing technique did not work out very well. Subsequent testing revealed that the bushing could become dislodged and ejected with a fired cartridge case. This would obviously result in a serious, or even potentially deadly, malfunction. A "fix" was tried that called for the chamber of the rifle to be grooved prior to installation of the bushing in an attempt to anchor it more securely. Another batch of

Text continued on page 148

Original National Match M1 manufactured in 1956.

Markings on M1 barrel manufactured in 7.62mm NATO by Springfield Armory in March of 1966. Most of these barrels were used by the U.S. Navy. Note the Defense Acceptance Stamp at the right.

White plastic spacer used on M1 rifles converted to 7.62mm NATO in order to prevent a longer .30-06 cartridge from being inserted into the rifle.

Barrel markings on U.S. Navy "Mark 2, Mod. 0" rifle converted by Harrington and Richardson Arms Co. to the 7.62mm NATO cartridge by means of a chamber sleeve. Note the original barrel date of October 1942 ("SA"). AMF also received a navy contract to convert M1 rifles to Mark 2, Mod. 0 configuration.

(Credit: Garand Stand Collection)

U.S. Navy landing party members practice with their M1 rifles from the deck of the USS Kearsarge (CVS-33). Photo dated July 2, 1969. The Navy used M1s both in the standard .30 caliber (.30-06) and rebarrelled to the 7.62 NATO round. (Credit: U.S. Navy)

Text continued from page 145

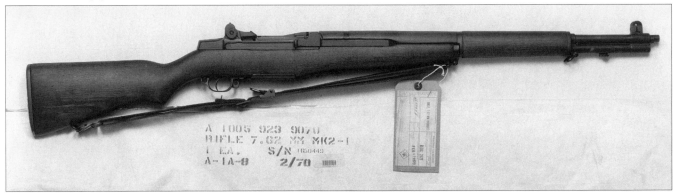

7.62mm "Mark 2, Mod. 1" rifle (serial #1650449) converted by the U.S. Navy Depot in Crane, Indiana. This rifle was awarded as a Match trophy by the Navy. The rifle is accompanied by its original shipping wrapper and depot rebuild tag dated February 12, 1970.

some 17,000 rifles was modified by AMF using this new technique. These rifles retained the Mark 2 Model 0 nomenclature. Unfortunately, the new procedure only helped marginally, and the problems continued.

Clearly another method of converting the Navy M1 rifles was called for. The only reasonable alternative seemed to be rebarrelling the weapons with newly made barrels chambered for the 7.62mm NATO round. Although this method would be considerably more expensive than the bushing technique, it would solve the previously encountered problems and would be much cheaper than acquiring all new weapons.

In 1964, the Navy contracted with Springfield Armory for the production of 30,000 newly made M1 barrels chambered for the 7.62mm NATO cartridge. These barrels were delivered in 1965 and 1966. The barrels were marked "7.62mm NATO" along with Springfield Armory markings and the month and year of production. 1965-dated barrels had a drawing number of "11010457," and the 1966 barrels' drawing number was "11686514". Other than the dates, the primary difference between the two barrels was the diameter of the gas port. The Navy rifles with the newly made 7.62mm NATO barrels were designated as the "Mark 2 Model 1." In addition to the new barrels, these rifles utilized a plastic spacer attached to the bullet guide to prevent the use of the longer .30-06 ammunition.

AMF and Harrington & Richardson received contracts from the Navy for the conversion of existing M1 rifles into the Mark 2 Model 1 configuration. The new barrels were procured from Springfield, and the initials of the firm doing the conversion work were stamped on the right side. In addition to the rifles modified by these two civilian firms, the Naval Weapons Command at Crane, Indiana, converted a number of M1 rifles to Mark 2 Model 1 configuration. The Mark 2 Model 1 rifles were

Left-side receiver markings of a U.S. Navy "7.62mm Conversion." Only the first 100 rifles would be marked this way after which the marking swould be moved to the right side of the barrel. (See GSR #12, p. 2). (Credit: Garand Stand collection)

entirely satisfactory and met the Navy's needs for many years. The converted 7.62mm NATO rifles were used as auxiliary weapons and training arms. Some were modified to match condition and used in competitive shooting. Fairly large numbers have been awarded as match trophies during the past decade or so. Most, but not all, of the Navy's M1 rifles were converted to 7.62mm NATO. Most are overhauled weapons with a mixture of WWII and later parts with the only special features being the new barrels and the plastic cartridge spacer.

The U.S. Air Force also acquired several hundred 7.62mm NATO barrels for use in match rifles. The barrels made for the Air Force were produced at Rock Island Arsenal to match grade specifications. They were marked with a different drawing number ("11686320") than found on the Springfield Armory-made 7.62mm Navy barrels. Air Force armorers extensively modified their rifles for match shooting and many were marked "AFPG" for "Air Force Premium Grade." Authentic

"AFPG" rifles are seen much less often than the Mark 2 Model 0 or the Mark 2 Model 1 Navy rifles. None of these Navy or Air Force match rifles should be confused with the National Match M1s previously made by Springfield Armory.

Although not extremely common, the converted 7.62mm NATO Garand rifles are not especially popular with collectors. The rifles awarded to Navy match winners complete with their original paperwork are probably the most desirable. Surplus 7.62mm NATO barrels can still be found so a rifle without accompanying documents should be valued only as a "shooter."

The converted 7.62mm M1 rifles saw little active use by the Navy but were entirely serviceable weapons. A number of these rifles saw secondary service in Vietnam, and some were on hand as late as the Gulf War of the early 1990s. It is a tribute to the genius of John Garand that the rifle he developed in the early 1930s was still in use some six decades later.

With the exception of the sniper rifles and a few other variants, the post-World War II Garands are, as a rule, not as highly sought after by collectors as the earlier rifles are. The WWII rifles are the most popular to the majority of today's collectors and prices for Garands of this vintage are typically quite a bit higher than the later variants. Nevertheless, any M1 rifle in original configuration and decent condition is a candidate for collecting. Except for the National Match rifles, the problem of fakes and bogus "restorations" does not seem quite as widespread among the later M1s as it is with the earlier vintages. This is due to typically lower prices plus the fact that more of the post-1945 rifles remained in their original factory configuration as they were less apt to have been overhauled. This does not, by any means, indicate that all such rifles are unquestionably authentic. The desirable "4.2 million" serial number Korean War vintage Springfield Garands are especially susceptible to faking or questionable restoration work. In addition, some of the IHC and HRA rifles have been subjected to some form of restoration. The most commonly changed part is the stock. Some of these rifles sold through the DCM are essentially original except the stock was replaced. If a proper stock of matching condition is substituted for a non-original stock, the restoration cannot generally be spotted. Even if it were, the price difference between such a weapon and a totally original piece probably wouldn't be significant. On the other hand, if wholesale changes such as a replaced barrel and/or refinished metal were evident, such a weapon would be much less desirable and much less valuable than an original piece.

Italian M1 Rifles

After the conclusion of the Second World War, the Italian government adopted the M1 as the standard service rifle. The Italians were originally supplied with surplus U.S. Garands, and the available supply was soon exhausted. Two Italian firms, Beretta and Breda were given contracts for production of the M1 rifle. Beretta began to manufacture the M1 rifle in 1952, reportedly using some surplus tooling acquired from Winchester. Some Beretta M1s were sent to Korea for use by United Nations troops. The firm later sold a number of these rifles to several foreign governments. It is estimated that Beretta manufactured a total of some 100,000 M1 rifles.

Breda began production of the M1 rifle for the Italian government in the 1950s. Like the Beretta rifles, the Breda rifles were close copies of the United States M1 and were also chambered for the .30-06 cartridge. The name of the manufacturer and serial number were stamped on the receivers of the Italian M1 rifles.

After adoption of the 7.62mm NATO round, Italy adopted a modified version of the M1 rifle chambered for the NATO round. The new Italian rifle was adopted as the "BM59" and was produced by Beretta. It superficially resembled the U.S. M14 and shared a 20-round detachable box magazine as well as selective fire capability. It certainly was not, by any means, a copy of the M14 as there were many physical and operational differences. Beretta initially converted existing M1 rifles into the BM59 configuration starting around 1962. Italy also converted some standard configuration M1 rifles to take the new 7.62mm NATO round in much the same manner as did the U.S. Navy in the 1960s.

The Italian rifles are not extremely common but are certainly not rare. The name of the manufacturer on the receiver makes identification of these rifle quite straightforward. Many of the parts are marked "PB" (Pietro Beretta) or "BMR" (Breda Meccanica Romana). The Italian M1 rifles have never been extremely popular with U.S. collectors. This is due, no doubt, to the fact that the majority of American collectors desire to collect rifles made and used by Americans. The BM59 variants are also uncommon and must be registered with the ATF due to their selective-fire capability. Nevertheless, some collectors wishing to acquire new and underappreciated variants of the Garand rifle are taking a second look at the Italian rifles, and they seem to be gaining in popularity.

Commercial Production M1 Rifles

Beginning in the late 1950s, several commercial firms produced M1 receivers in order to make use of the vast amount of surplus Garand parts available at the time. The original receiver was the only component of the rifle that was controlled regarding surplus sales, but all the other parts were available in vast numbers at extremely low prices. Various names were used on the receivers including Santa Fe and National Ordnance (among many others). Fairly recently, private individuals have acquired the terms "Springfield Armory" and "Rock Island" and have manufactured newly made Garand and carbine receivers using these names. It is a simple matter to ascertain that the serial numbers of the commercial "Springfield Armory" Garand receivers are not in the government's assigned ranges. Of course, Rock Island never made any Garands (or carbines) for the government so identification of such receivers as non-military production is easy. The fact that many of the parts used to assemble such commercial rifles are "GI" production can be confusing to a novice collector. One should remember that unless a receiver was made by Springfield Armory (the National Armory), Winchester, Harrington & Richardson or International Harvester, it is *not* government issue. Likewise, a Springfield Armory receiver with a serial number outside of the government's assigned range is a commercial item.

Many of these commercial Garands are of decent quality and can serve as good "shooters." However, none are suitable for martial arms collecting and should be avoided if one is seeking a collectible piece.

"Tanker" Model

While on the subject of commercial M1 rifles, mention should be made of the so-called "Tanker" Model. This is the most common name used to identify M1 rifles with shortened stocks and barrels. These arms are seen quite frequently on the market today and are the subject of confusion and misunderstanding by some people. These weapons are not, and never have been, items of issue by the U.S. military. There were an extremely small number (possibly only two or three) of shortened M1 rifles fabricated by Springfield Armory and tested late in WWII for potential use by airborne forces. These weapons were designated as the "T26" (See page 158). Also, the Pacific Warfare board requested permission to convert a small quantity of standard M1 rifles to T26 configuration. One was sent to Springfield Armory for testing but the design was not approved for production or

issue. At least one other is reported to have been fabricated for informal field testing. The handful of rifles shortened under the auspices of the Pacific Warfare Board were all supposedly converted back to standard M1 configuration after the unsuitability of the weapon became apparent. someone may claim that they have an original PWB rifle that escaped reconversion. Without some definitive documentation, such claims are impossible to prove and any rifles of this type claim to be legitimate should be viewed with the utmost suspicion. No *documented* originals have ever been verified outside of government museums.

The shortened M1s exhibited excessive muzzle blast and flash. The concept was soon dropped and further developmental work was not forthcoming. As stated, no original T26 rifles or Pacific Warfare Board rifles are known to be in private hands. However, thousands of standard M1 rifles, some with welded "demilled" receivers, have been altered during the past twenty or thirty years to approximate the T26 configuration and sold on the commercial market. someone gave such rifles the imaginative nickname of the "Tanker" Garand as some sort of sales pitch. As stated, none of these rifles are genuine U.S. military issue and have no place in a martial collection. A valuable guideline to remember is, "If it's not in the Springfield Armory Museum, it's not an original T26". The same thing can safely be said for the Pacific Warfare Board rifles. At least one fake with bogus PWB markings has been reported. However, a rifle of this type with special markings can be easily identified as bogus since standard M1 receivers without special markings were undoubtedly used to fabricate the handful of shortened rifles (both T26 and Pacific Warfare Board). Unless you want one of the so-called "Tanker" Garands as a curiosity, save your money for a legitimate GI M1 rifle.

The fact that Garand production spanned the period of time from 1936 to 1957 and that the rifle was made by Springfield Armory and three commercial contractors means that there are many interesting and desirable variants available to the collector today. In addition, the Garand's widespread use in WWII and its subsequent utilization by two generations of American servicemen insures the continued collector interest in the weapon. Few military arms combine the historic significance of the Garand with the wide array of variants that are still available today. While collector-grade specimens are getting harder to find and more expensive with each passing year, the rewards of collecting one of the premier American battle rifles of all time is well worth the effort involved.

TABLE #1
Serial Numbers and Dates of Production

This table will enable the month and year of production to be ascertained by the serial number. Serial numbers are as of production at month end. (Reproduced from *The M1 Garand: World War II* by Scott A. Duff. Used by Permission.)

Springfield Armory

Date	Serial Number	Date	Serial Number	Date	Serial Number	Date	Serial Number
1937		September	17010	October	377258	September	1978407
August	120	October	19410	November	401529	October	2092825
September	307	November	21293	December	429811	November	2204430
October	539	December	23567			December	2305849 &
November	696						2410000–2420191
December	1034	**1940**		**1942**			
		January	26729	January	462737	**1944**	
1938		February	30008	February	498216	January	2543412
January	1186	March	33790	March	542494	February	2634316
February	1338	April	38034	April	588879	March	2723004
March	1809	May	41679	May	638679	April	2810628
April	2213	June	46221	June	691401	May	2900312
May	2406	July	51970	July	749779	June	2981126
June	2911	August	59868	August	809016	July	3051952
July	2911	September	68054	September	872343	August	3114434
August	3537	October	78306	October	940250	September	3180532
September	4386	November	90177	November	1008899	October	3242497
October	5242	December	100000	December	1090310	November	3302641
November	6072		166501–169073			December	3359159
December	6972						
		1941		**1943**		**1945**	
1939		January	183519	January	1169091	January	3450503
January	7715	February	197811	February	1200000 &	February	3531489
February	8762	March	211228		1377474–1396255	March	3627442
March	9893	April	228527	March	1469177	April	3717867
April	10703	May	248757	April	1547452	May	3797768
May	11511	June	269686	May	1629565	June	3875601
June	12848	July	296252	June	1710012	July	Unknown
July	12911	August	324301	July	1786469	August	Unknown
August	14823	September	349442	August	1877654	September	Unknown
						October	3888081

Winchester Repeating Arms Company

Date	Serial Number	Date	Serial Number	Date	Serial Number	Date	Serial Number
1941		November	131130	July	1218972	April	1323872
January	100501	December	137960	August	1228982	May	1336882
February	100831			September	1241002	June	1349982
March	102701	**1942**		October	1254002	July	1364982
April	104901	January	144110	November	1266502	August	1380000 &
May	107801	February	149130	December	1276102		2305850–2305932
June	111501	March	155310			September	2318032
July	115501	April	162190	**1943**		October	2334032
August	120111	May	165500 &	January	1282762	November	2349632
September	122081		1200001–1203692	February	1294762	December	2364642
October	126130	June	1210472	March	1309772		

TABLE 1 continued on next page

Winchester Repeating Arms Company • *(Cont'd.)*							
Date	**Serial Number**	**Date**	**Serial Number**	**Date**	**Serial Number**	**Date**	**Serial Number**
1944		July	2469642	**1945**		February	1607100
January	2379642	August	2484642	January	2534232	March	1613000
February	2394642	September	2499642	and 1600000–1605600		April	1620000
March	2409642	October	2513822	(Beginning of		May	1627000
April	2424642	November	2523942	"WIN-13" Block)		June	1640000
May	2439642	December	2533142				
June	2454642						

TABLE #2
M1 Rifle Stock Cartouches

Springfield Armory

Cartouche	Name and Dates of Production	Approximate Serial # Range
SA SPG	Stanley P. Gibbs 1936 — Mid-1940	81–80,000
SA GHS	Col. Gilbert H. Stewart Mid-1940–June 1942	80,000 –700,000
SA EMcF	Col. Earl McFarland June 1942–July 1943	700,000 –1,800,000
SA GAW	Col. George A. Woody July 1943–Oct. 1944	1,800,000 –3,260,000
SA NFR	Gen. Norman F. Ramsey Oct. 1944–Nov. 1945	3,260,000 –3,900,000*

Some overlap with "GAW" cartouches very late 1944 or very early 1945.

Cartouche	Name and Dates of Production	Approximate Serial # Range
SA SHM	Col. Stephen H. MacGregor Nov. 1945–Aug. 1947	Any range from 1936–1945* *Rebuilds only
SA JLG	Col. James L. Guion July 1950–May 1953	4,200,000 –4,300,000**** New production

Some M1 rifles overhauled in the very late 1940s may be found with "SPG" or "JLG" rebuild cartouches.

Winchester Repeating Arms Company

Cartouche	Name and Dates of Production	Approximate Serial # Range
WRA RS	Col. Robert Sears July 1940–June 1941	100,001 –110,000
WRA WB	Col. Waldemar Broberg July 1941–June 1942	110,000 –1,200,000
WRA GHD	Col. Guy H. Drewry June 1942–July 1945	1,200,000 –Termination of production (including WIN-13).

Post-World War II

Attempts to compile a table similar to Table #1 above have proven to be unsuccessful due to the extreme inconsistencies in the serial number ranges and date correlation between receiver vintages and barrel dates for the post-WWII manufacturers.

Below are assigned serial numbers for 1950s production. Not every serial number from each block was used.

Manufacturer	Assigned Serial Number Block
Springfield Armory	4200001–4399999
International Harvester	4400000–4660000
Harrington & Richardson	4660001–4800000
Springfield Armory	5000001–5000500
International Harvester	5000501–5278245
Springfield Armory	5278246–5488246
Harrington & Richardson	5488247–5793847
Springfield Armory	5793848–6099905

Beginning in the later 4,200,000 serial number range, the use of a cartouche containing the initials of the Commanding Officer of Springfield Armory was discontinued and use of the Defense Acceptance Stamp was instituted. This stamp was used from c.1952 until 1957 by all manufacturers including Springfield Armory, International Harvester and Harrington & Richardson.

TABLE #3
Model Shop Rifles
Manufacturer: Springfield Armory

Serial Number Range: 1 to 80
Stock Cartouche: None
Distinguishing Characteristics:
    Receiver markings: "Semiauto. Rifle" rather than "Rifle"
    "V-shaped" configuration of receiver legs
    "Gas trap" system
    Weld seam operating rod
    No protective ears on front sight
Comments: Extremely rare and valuable variant

TABLE #4
Gas Trap Rifles
Manufacturer: Springfield Armory

Approximate Serial # Range: 81 to the very low 50,000 range.

Receiver: Guide ribs not built up except on very late examples.

Barrel: 22" gas trap type. Drawing number marked on top. "P" marking on right side. Not dated.

Finish: Parkerizing.

Stock: Not routed for butt trap recess. "Long barrel channel." Large over small size holes in butt.

Stock Cartouche: "SA/SPG" (Stanley P. Gibbs). No "crossed cannons" escutcheon. Circled "P" proof (without serifs) on grip.

Front Handguard: "Lip type" spacer. Handguard marked with drawing number to approx. serial #20,000.

Rear Handguard: No relief cut modification. Handguard marked with drawing numbers up to approximately serial #20,000.

Rear Sight: Original "spanner nut" rear sight. "Flared arrows" on adjustment knobs. Short sight pinion with drawing number.

Front Sight: Original pattern front sight. Straight protective "ears" on early production gas trap rifles. Later changed to flared ears.

Operating Rod: Slant type, changed to straight cut around serial #30,000, without relief milling at junction of tube and handle. Very early production examples had drawing number stamped on top of handle.

Gas Cylinder: Original screw-on gas trap cylinder. Early examples had flutes on both sides, which were late deleted. Drawing number on rear ring on early examples.

Triggerguard: Milled type with concentric rings. Marked with drawing number.

Comments: Virtually all parts stamped with drawing numbers on early production gas trap rifles. Some drawing numbers deleted as production continued, but all gas trap M1s will have more numbered parts than WWII production Garands. Original unaltered gas trap M1 rifles are rare. Caution should be exercised as there are a number of fake rifles on the market today.

TABLE #5
"Direct Conversion" from Gas Trap to Gas Port
Manufacturer: Springfield Armory

Approximate Serial # Range: Same as gas trap rifles.

Receiver: Guide ribs built up by welding (if required).

Barrels: Dated very late 1940 or early 1941. Marked "SA".

Finish: Same as gas trap rifles. Few, if any, were reparkerized.

Stock: New production with butt trap recess. Long barrel channel.

Stock Cartouche: Normally "SA/GHS" with large "crossed cannons" escutcheon.

Rear Sight: Same as gas trap.

Front Sight: New production for use with gas port system. Seal on front sight screw.

Operating Rod: Same as gas trap.

Gas Cylinder: New production spline-type gas port cylinders installed. Narrow sight platform and generally marked with drawing number.

Triggerguard: Same as gas trap.

Comments: Retains most gas trap parts marked with drawing numbers. This is a very scarce variant and one of the few examples in which a rebuilt rifle has a value and desirability rivaling an original piece of the same vintage.

TABLE #6
Springfield Armory M1 Rifles
WWII Production

Serial Numbers: Approximately 402,000 (early Dec. 1941) to 3,888,000 (Aug. 1945).

Barrel: Dated on right side from December of 1941 ("12/41") to August 1945 ("8/45"). Also marked "SA". Gas port area not chromed.

Finish: Parkerizing typically with a distinctive greenish tint.

Stock: Butt trap recess with hinged buttplate in all WWII production rifles.

Stock Cartouches: SA/GHS, SA/EMcF, SA/GAW or SA/NFR depending on vintage. "Crossed Cannons" Ordnance escutcheon next to cartouche. Circle "P" proof mark on grip.

Rear Sight: "Spanner nut" type prior to late 1942. "Locking bar" type used afterward.

Front Sight: Seal over the front sight screw until early 1943 when seal was eliminated. Front sight had narrow protective ears compared to Winchester M1 front sights.

Operating Rod: No relief cut modification. Rod marked with drawing number and "SA".

Gas Cylinder: Narrow front sight platform until mid-1943. Springfield gas cylinders had a flat area on top of the rear ring.

Triggerguard: Milled type until early 1944 when stamped variety came into use.

TABLE #7
Winchester Repeating Arms Co.
M1 Rifles
World War II Production

Serial numbers: Approximately 131,200 (early Dec. 1941) to 2,536,000 and 1,600,000–1,640,000 ("WIN-13" range).

Barrel: Marked "WRA" and drawing number on top. Cannot be seen with rear handguard in place. Right side marked with intertwined "WP" logo. Not dated. No chrome gas port.

Finish: Same as Springfield Armory production.

Stock: Solid buttplate with no butt trap recess until circa mid-1942 when the hinged buttplate and butt trap recess were incorporated.

TABLE #7 continued on next page

TABLE #7 continued from page 153

Stock cartouche: WRA/RS, WRA/WB or WRA/GHD depending on vintage. Ordnance "crossed cannons" escutcheon next to cartouche. Circle "P" on grip.

Rear Handguard: No relief cut at right rear until late in production.

Rear Sight: "Spanner nut" type until early 1943 when "locking bar" sight were used. Arrows on windage knob are flared.

Front Sight: Wide protective "ears" compared to Springfield M1 front sights.

Operating Rod: No relief cut modification. Marked with "W.R.A." and drawing number.

Gas Cylinder: Narrow front sight platform until circa mid-1943. Rounded rear ring. Winchester gas cylinders have a bluish tint to the finish.

Triggerguard: Milled type throughout production marked "W.R.A."

Components: Many parts will show rough machining and punch marks. "CM" or "A" marked parts will also be encountered.

TABLE #8
Post-WWII Rebuild M1 Rifles
Circa 1946–1951

Manufacturer: Springfield Armory or Winchester

Serial Number: Any 1945 or earlier vintage

Barrels: Either serviceable 1945 or earlier vintage Springfield or Winchester barrels or newly made replacement barrels (marked "SA" and dated prior to 1952). A few WWII made Marlin barrels were also used. Gas port area chromed on most overhauled barrels.

Finish: Parkerizing. Many receivers were reparkerized when overhauled but workmanship should be arsenal quality.

Stock: Normally refurbished issue stocks. A rebuild cartouche such as "SA/SHM" (the most commonly seen), "SA/SPG" or "SA/JLG" was stamped on the reconditioned stock. The original cartouche was often obscured by refinishing, but sometimes it remained visible, thus such stocks may reveal two different cartouches. Overhauled stocks often show evidence of repair such as spliced wood, areas filled in with plastic wood and/or brass repair pins.

Rear sight: Rifles rebuilt during this period were normally fitted with the new "T105E1" rear sight.

Front sight: WWII type (either Springfield Armory or Winchester).

Operating rod: If the original operating rod was retained, it was modified by having the cut milled into it. Many new production operating rods that incorporated this modification were installed during this period as well. These can be identified by the "D 35382SA" drawing number.

Gas cylinder: Standard WWII type. Many were modified by "saw cuts" to salvage loose gas cylinders.

Triggerguard: Either milled or stamped.

Comments: An M1 rifle overhauled in the late 1940s or early 1950s and remaining in this configuration is a very collectible rifle that is often overlooked by some collectors.

TABLE #9
Korean War Springfield M1 Rifles
New Production

Approximate Serial Number Range: 4,200,000 range.

Barrel: Dated 1952 or 1953. Marked "SA".

Finish: Parkerizing with black tint rather than WWII greenish tint.

Stock Cartouche: "SA/JLG".

Rear Sight: T105E1.

Front Sight: Standard late production Springfield type with narrow ears.

Operating Rod: Made with relief cut. "6535382SA" drawing number.

Gas Cylinder: Late production type with wide sight platform.

Triggerguard: Stamped.

Comments: Original unaltered Springfield M1 rifles in the 4.2 million serial number range are surprisingly scarce and quite desirable.

TABLE #10
Post-Korean War Springfield M1 Rifles
New Production

Serial Number Range: 4,300,000 and higher.

Barrel: Dated 1953 and later. Marked "SA". (A few new production Marlin barrels were also used.)

Finish: Parkerizing.

Stock Cartouche: Defense Acceptance Stamp ("Eagle & Stars").

Rear Sight: T105E1.

Front Sight: Standard Springfield late production with narrow ears.

Operating Rod: With relief cut. Marked "SA" by drawing number.

Gas Cylinder: Late production Springfield type with wide sight platform.

Triggerguard: Stamped.

Comments: Late production Springfield Garands are among the most finely crafted M1s.

TABLE #11
International Harvester M1 Rifles

Serial Number Range: Approximately 4,400,000 to 5,200,000.

Barrels: Marked "LMR" and dated circa 1953 to 1955.

Finish: Parkerizing.

Stock: Two letter "OR" or "HR" on many with four-digit code stamped in barrel channel.

Stock Cartouche: Defense Acceptance Stamp.

Rear Sight: T105E1 with "IHC" code markings on knobs.

Front Sight: Wide protective ears similar to WWII Winchester front sights.

Operating Rod: With relief cut. Marked "IHC" by drawing number.

Gas Cylinder: Standard late production Springfield type with wide front sight platform.

Triggerguard: Stamped.

Comments: Most components will be marked "IHC". All original International Harvester M1s can be tough to find.

TABLE #12
Harrington & Richardson M1 Rifles

Serial Number Range: Approximately 4,600,000 to 5,700,000.

Barrel: Marked "HRA" and dated 1953 to 1956.

Finish: Parkerizing.

Stock Cartouche: Defense Acceptance Stamp (⅜" size).

Rear Sight: T105E1 with "HRA" code markings on knobs.

Front Sight: Standard late production Springfield type.

Operating Rod: With relief cut. Marked "HRA" by drawing number.

Gas Cylinder: Standard Springfield type with wide sight platform.

Triggerguard: Stamped.

Comments: While not quite as hard to find as IHC rifles, all original unaltered H&R are sometimes a bit difficult to turn up.

TABLE #13
M1C Sniper Rifles

Manufacturer: Springfield Armory.

Serial Number Range: 3,000,000 to 3,800,000 range.

Receiver: Griffin & Howe base screwed and pinned to left side. Base normally marked with the rifle's serial number.

Barrel Date: Very late 1944 to mid-1945. "SA" marked.

Finish: WWII-type parkerizing.

Stock: Standard late M1 with short barrel channel.

Stock Cartouche: Normally "SA/NFR" with "crossed cannons" escutcheon. Early examples may have "SA/GAW" cartouches.

Rear Sight: Late WWII "locking bar" type. Few, if any, T105E1 sights used in WWII.

Front Sight: Standard Springfield type.

Operating Rod: No relief cut. "9" revision to drawing number. "SA" marked.

Gas Cylinder: Standard late Springfield type with wide sight platform.

Triggerguard: Stamped.

Accessories: Telescope dovetail mount stamped with rifle serial number (Few matching examples will be encountered); M81 or M82 telescope; T4 leather cheek pad marked "K-Line and M2 flash hider ("SA" or Hart).

Comments: Original M1C rifles remaining in WWII factory configuration are rare. Many fakes will be encountered.

Note: Members of the Garand Collectors Association may obtain verification of an M1C serial number. Anyone interested in this service and in Garand collecting in general should join the GCA. The current address is P.O. Box 181, Richmond, KY 40475.

TABLE #14
M1D Sniper Rifle

Manufacturer: Any maker (SA, WRA, IHC or HRA). SA most common.

Conversion Facility: All 1951–1953 M1D rifles were converted at Springfield Armory. Other Ordnance facilities converted M1 rifles into M1Ds in the 1960s including Toole (Utah).

Serial Number: Any range. (early 1950s conversions will have WWII serial numbers).

Barrel: Special M1D barrel (Drawing #D7312575) with integral base.

Finish: Parkerizing. Many were reparkerized when overhauled.

Stock: Usually new production.

Stock Cartouche: Rifles converted by Springfield Armory will normally have a boxed "SA" marking on the left side (hidden by the T4 cheek pad). Other facilities normally engraved the initials of the arsenal and date of conversion on right receiver leg.

Rear Sight: T105E1.

Front Sight: Any type. Normally late Springfield.

Operating Rod: Either new production (normally "SA") or overhauled operating rod with relief cut.

Gas Cylinder: Normally late production Springfield type.

Triggerguard: Normally stamped type.

Accessories: M84 telescope in 7/8" mount (some Weaver K-4 telescopes with 1" mounts used in 1960s); leather cheek pad (usually stamped in black ink "MRT" and dated); M2 flash hider or T37 flash suppressor.

Comments: All M1D rifles were converted from issue M1 rifles. Unless accompanied by an original government bill of sale, proving authenticity is often impossible.

TABLE #15
USMC 1952 Sniper Rifle

Manufacturer: Originally Springfield Armory (also converted to MC 52 specs by Springfield).

Serial Number Range: Same as M1C.

Barrel: "SA" marked. Same as M1C or new production dated 1951–1953.

Finish: Parkerizing. Some were reparkerized when refurbished.

Stock Cartouche: Normally box "SA" on right side. Some WWII cartouched stocks may be seen.

Rear Sight: T105E1.

Front Sight: Late production Springfield type.

Operating Rod: Typically early 1950s vintage new production with relief cut.

Gas Cylinder: Late production Springfield type with wide sight platform.

Triggerguard: Stamped (generally).

Accessories: USMC issue Kollmorgen 4X "MC 1" telescope, special G&H mount (not serially numbered); M2 flash hider (T37 used later). The T4 cheek pad was not an item of issue with MC52 rifle.

Comments: All USMC 1952 rifles were converted from WWII production M1C rifles. A very scarce variant. Some marked "SA-52" on receiver behind rear sight.

TABLE #16
Specifications for M1 National Match Rifles
(Circa Post-1956)

Stocks and Handguards

Stock shall be of solid heartwood with the direction of the grain parallel to the longitudinal axis of the stock.

Stocks shall be heavy in weight.

Stocks shall have no open grain which might swell excessively in high humidity.

Protective finish (chinawood) tung oil.

Stock shall be free from contact with barrel.

The stock shall have a .005" minimum clearance in the area between rear of receiver bedding surface and receiver rail surfaces.

All stocks shall be glass bedded and custom fitted to receiver and barrel assemblies and trigger housing assemblies. The stock assembly and the triggerguard assembly shall be identified with last four digits of receiver serial number. These assemblies shall not be interchanged after glass bedding has been completed.

Rear end of receiver shall bed squarely on the stock bedding surface.

The rear handguard may be free to move longitudinally.

The front handguard shall have no longitudinal movement.

Stock ferrule shall not contact lower portion of lower band. There shall be approximately 1/64" minimum clearance.

After proof firing, 5/16" high letter "P" shall be stamped on grip within a ½" diameter circle.

Defense Acceptance Stamp (1/2" high) stamped on left hand side of stock.

Sights

Elevating knob must be on 100 yard setting when aperture is elevated 8 clicks from lowest position.

Sight must be free from excess oil.

Screw, rear sight, shall be tightened within 20 to 25 inch lbs.

The aperture assembly produces 1/2 minute change of elevation by 180 degrees rotation of the eyepiece. Apertures within .0595 and .0520 diameter peep holes will be issued.

Front sight blade edges shall be sharp and well defined by selection only. The front sight shall be identified by the letters and numerals "NM/.062" which are 1/16" high inscribed on the right side. The front sight shall be assembled securely.

Top of front sight blade shall be square with side and all edges and corners sharp to .005" maximum. Front sight shall not overhang the sides of the gas cylinder.

Threads on the windage knob shall measure 5/16-64NS-3A.

Threads on the base, rear sight, shall measure 5/16-54NS-3B. Identification mark shall consist of letters "NM" inscribed on each part.

Barrel and Gas Cylinder, Assembly

The barrel shall be line straightened to meet the requirement of optical straightness gage.

The barrel must be crowned concentric with bore (60 degrees included angle) to remove burrs. Straightness of the barrel shall be such that the bore centerline established by a self-aligning expansion plug (2-1/2" long with pilot diameter of .2993-0001) that fits and aligns itself in the bore at the muzzle end. The maximum allowable deviation from that centerline shall not exceed 0 degrees 2' 23" throughout the length of the bore. Any resultant taper of the bore shall be within dimensional limits and be diminishing from breech to muzzle.

Identification mark shall consist of the letters "NM" approximately 1/8" inscribed on the barrel approximately midway between the front handguard and front sight.

In assembly, the gas cylinder lock shall be hand tightened against the shoulder of the barrel with a range of slightly beyond the 6 o'clock position.

Gas cylinder shall fit tightly on the barrel bearing diameter and splines. There shall be no rotational movement.

Gas cylinder shall be brought forward against the lock before tightening the gas cylinder lock screw.

Gas cylinder splined hole and rear rings shall meet requirements of alignment gage.

Triggerguard, Operating Rod, Proof Marks, Etc.

Clamping of the triggerguard shall have a definite resistance at a minimum distance of 3/8" of an inch from the full lock position.

The trigger pull required to release the hammer shall be smooth, free from "creep" and within the limits of four and one-half pounds.

Operating rod assembly shall function freely without binding during a simulated firing cycle with the operating rod spring removed.

Headspace shall be 1.940 to 1.943. Light finger pressure shall be used in checking headspace.

Prick punch receiver after proof firing.

Prick punch bolt after proof firing.

After proof firing, the headspace with component bolt shall be from 1.940 min. to 1.943 max.

After proof firing, prick punch barrel within loop of letter "P" exposed when operating rod is in rearmost position.

TABLE #17
"E Series" M1 Rifles

M1E1. The first officially designated experimental Garand. This weapon was tested to assist in finding a cure for the tendency of the rifle to "freeze" under certain conditions of extended rainfall or other forms of extreme moisture. A number of dimensional changes to the operating rod were tried. None of these modified operating rod designs significantly improved the problem and further development of the M1E1 was not forthcoming.

M1E2. The M1E2 was the first prototype sniping version of the Garand. This design utilized an unusual offset mounted prismatic telescope. The M1E2 was not looked upon favorably, and the concept was abandoned for a more conventional telescope mounting system.

M1E3. This weapon represented another attempt to rectify the propensity of the M1's action to "freeze" under certain conditions of extreme moisture. Rather than only changing the angle of the operating rod, like the M1E1, the bolt was also modified with the addition of a roller attached to the lug. Although this design did improve the problem, it was not felt that the benefits would justify interrupting M1 production at a critical time.

M1E4. The M1E4 was an attempt to reduce the speed at which the operating rod struck the bolt. It was felt that a less violent action would reduce recoil. However, the M1E4 design subjected the operating rod and spring to much higher temperatures and caused heating problems. The project was dropped rather quickly after this tendency became apparent.

M1E5. One of the most interesting of the "E series" rifles was the M1E5, which was intended to be a more compact "carbine" version of the Garand. As originally tested, the M1E5 featured an 18" barrel and a straight grip panatograph folding stock designated as the "T6." However, early testing revealed the need for a pistol grip, and it was recommended for use on any subsequent variants. The revised stock was designated as the "T6E3." Testing revealed that the accuracy of the shortened rifle was on a par with the standard M1 but that the flash and muzzle blast were unacceptably high.

In July 1945, the Pacific Warfare Board requested permission to send an M1 that had been field modified by reducing the barrel length comparable to the M1E5 but with a standard length stock. Springfield Armory evaluated the field modified M1 and deemed it superior to the folding stock M1E5. Testing resumed on an M1E5 action mounted in a standard length M1 stock. The resulting rifle was designated as the "T26" (See "T series").

M1E6. The M1E6 was essentially a standard M1 rifle with a telescope mounted on the left side of the receiver and with a specially designed rear sight similar to the M1903A3 sight. Testing validated the concept of the offset mounted conventional telescope but determined that there was no real need for the modified rear sight.

M1E7. The M1E7 was based on the M1E6 concept but retained the standard Garand rear sight. This design was selected for standardization as the "M1C." The M1E7 is noteworthy as it represents the first "E series" rifle to be officially adopted, put into production and issued.

M1E8. The M1E8 was tested as an alternative to the M1E7 rifle. Rather than mounting a conventional telescope to the left side of the receiver as was done with the M1E7, this design featured a mounting block attached to the rear of the barrel. Although subsequently adopted as the "M1D" and given the designation of "Substitute Standard," no M1D rifles were produced during WWII except for the handful of M1E8 prototypes, but many were produced in the early 1950s and later.

M1E9. The M1E9 was a refinement of the M1E4 that was intended to rectify the heating problems encountered with the original design. The results were not sufficient to warrant further development of the concept.

M1E10. The M1E10 was tested to determine if substantial improvements could be made to the standard M1 gas system by using a gas system based on the Swedish Ljungman rifle.

The modifications included a long tube that ran from the gas port into a short piston in order to work the operating rod. Therefore, the propellant gases impinged directly on the operating rod. Subsequent testing proved that this was not an improvement over John Garand's design. Furthermore, it had the drawback of generating excess heat, and the idea was soon forgotten.

M1E11. This was still another attempt to improve the M1's gas system. The Garand's gas cylinder was modified by incorporating an integral expansion system and cut-off and relocated the barrel's gas port some 3" to the rear. A special one-piece handguard made of aluminum was tested to help reduce the heat generated during firing. The results were not particularly impressive, and the concept was shelved.

M1E12. The M1E12 was the final "E series" variant and was designed to improve the performance of the Garand's gas system. It was a somewhat less radical approach than used in the M1E10 and M1E11 designs and consisted primarily of relocating the gas port about six inches to the rear. An aluminum one piece handguard similar to that used on the M1E11 was fitted. Again, the improvements (if any) were of such a marginal nature that disruption of Garand production was not warranted and refinement of the design was dropped.

TABLE #18
"T Series" Rifles

Combat action in World War II had clearly shown the desirability of selective fire weapons in many applications. In early 1944, the Ordnance Department issued directives for development of a selective fire version of the Garand rifle. Springfield Armory and Remington Arms were selected to design and fabricate various test versions of selective fire M1s. These weapons were assigned "T" prefix designations.

T20. This was the first prototype of a selective fire M1 and was developed and fabricated by Springfield Armory. The original test model was a standard M1 service rifle that was modified to allow fully automatic fire from an open bolt while retaining the normal mode of firing semiautomatically from a closed bolt. The rifle was further modified to allow it to function with a standard Browning Automatic Rifle (BAR) 20-round magazine and a rather rudimentary muzzle brake. The T20 was extensively tested at the Aberdeen Proving Ground and several weaknesses including attachment of the magazine were found. While theoretically desirable, the ability to fire from an open bolt during automatic operating and from a closed bolt during semiautomatic operation proved to be more trouble than it was worth. However, by early 1945, the general concept of the T20 was deemed worthy enough to warrant development of improved models.

T20E1. This was an improved version of the T20. The T20E1 was tested at Aberdeen Proving Ground in late January 1945. The design featured an improved magazine and modifications to assist in cooling the weapon. While some reliability problems were noted and a number of minor recommendations made, the tests were overall positive. Springfield Armory was ordered to manufacture one hundred refined versions of the T20E1 for additional testing.

T20E2. The refined version was designated as the T20E2. The chief differences from the previous T20 and T20E1 weapons were changes intended to improve feeding and reliability problems. The T20E2 performed very well in the tests, and in May 1945, the evaluation committee recommended that the weapon be approved for limited procurement and issue. To this end, Springfield Armory was directed to tool up to produce 100,000 T20E2 rifles and concurrently scale back production of the M1. Prior to mass production getting underway, ten new rifles were sent to Aberdeen for additional testing. Some minor refinements were indicated but the rifles performed satisfactorily. The end of the Second World War spelled an end to the T20E2, although developmental work continued into 1949, albeit at a greatly reduced level.

T20E3. This was essentially nothing more than a heavy barrel version of the T20E2 that was intended for use as a replacement or supplement to the BAR as a squad automatic weapon. Only a handful of T20E3 prototype rifles were fabricated.

T22. All of the "T series" discussed were products of the government owned and operated Springfield Armory. The T22, on the other hand, was developed by the commercial firm of Remington Arms Company. The T22 was somewhat similar to the T20 as it was a modification of the standard M1. Remington had hoped to be granted a contract for new production of the T22 rifle or, at least, a contract to modify existing M1 rifles into the new configuration.

T22E1. This was a refined version of the T22 which was developed to correct some of the problems noted with the original design. Rather than utilizing the standard M1 receiver, the T22E1 utilized the slightly longer T20 receivers which were supplied to Remington by Springfield Armory. Continued testing proved that the basic design premise was sound but revealed the need for further refinements.

T22E2. The T22E2 incorporated many of the improvements recommended when the T22E1 was tested. These included changes to the gas cylinder, trigger assembly, muzzle brake, magazine catch and bipod. One significant change was the utilization of the standard M1 receiver rather than the lengthened receiver used with the T20 and variants. This permitted existing M1 service rifles to be easily modified to T22E2 specifications if the need arose. However, the end of WWII resulted in an end to the involvement of commercial firms in further development of the "T models" by 1948.

T24 and T25. These were slightly modified T22E2 rifles. Further development of the designs was dropped by Remington in 1948 when the government canceled the R&D contracts for the firm.

T26. As discussed, this was the designation given to a short barreled M1E5 action put into a standard length M1 stock. This weapon was the inspiration for the so-called "Tanker Garand" which is a commercially produced item and is commonly encountered today. Only a couple were fabricated.

T27. The T27 was yet another modification of the standard M1 rifle. This weapon was chambered for what was eventually adopted as the 7.62mm NATO cartridge. The T27 was selective fire and was capable of 600 rounds per minute. However, one definite drawback to using the weapon in the fully automatic mode was that it retained the 8-round en bloc clip and the project was dropped in early 1948.

T28. The T28 was one of several "T models" that were not based on the M1 design. This design was a lightweight rifle chambered for the 7.62mm cartridge.

T31. The T31 was designed by Springfield Armory. It was an unusual weapon and not based on the Garand, although a few of the M1's design features were utilized.

T33. The T33 was another lightweight design not related to the M1 Garand.

T34. This was a Browning Automatic Rifle (BAR) chambered for the 7.62mm cartridge.

T35. The T35 was a standard M1 Garand fitted with a newly manufactured barrel chambered for the 7.62mm NATO cartridge. The weapon also featured an insert in the magazine to adapt it to the shorter cartridge. The T35 was the least altered of all the "T series" from the basic M1 rifle. Fifty of these weapons were manufactured and tested. Some functioning problems were noted during the tests.

T36. The T36 was the T20E2 rifle chambered for the 7.62mm NATO round.

T37. This was a T36 fitted with a lightweight stock and shortened, 22" barrel. The cyclical rate of fire in the fully automatic mode was approximately 750 rounds per minute.

T38. The T38 was a substantially modified T35. The weapon featured an integral magazine that loaded from the right side rather than a detachable box magazine.

T44. The T44 series was basically a T20E3 that utilized some of the features found in the T25, T31 and T37 rifles. Externally, it resembled the M14 rifle. Other rifles in the T44 included the T44E1, T44E2, T44E3, T44E4 (which became the prototype M14), T44E5 and T44E6.

The selective fire nature of the "T series" rifles, and the fact that none were ever released for sale makes in highly unlikely that any will ever be encountered by collectors today. As is the case with any weapon capable of fully automatic operation, it must be properly registered with the Treasury Department (BATF) before legal possession is possible. If a weapon is not now currently so registered, it cannot subsequently be registered. My book *U.S. Infantry Weapons of World War II* contains a section on the legal aspects of machine guns and other selective fire weapons.

TABLE #19
Arsenal Overhaul (Rebuild) Markings

As discussed numerous times, the majority of M1s existing today have been subjected to overhaul/rebuild one or more times by various ordnance facilities. These markings were normally stamped on the left side of the stock either beneath the rear portion of the receiver or below the comb (between the pistol grip and butt). A rebuild "P" proof mark will also be found on most rebuilt stocks to indicate that the weapon was successfully proofed fired as part of the overhaul process. These generally differed from the factory proof markings by lacking serifs and/or by not being enclosed in a circle. However, a few ordnance facilities utilized circled "P" proof markings very similar to those found on factory original rifles.

MARKING	FACILITY	LOCATION
AN	**Anniston (Alabama) Army Depot**	Left side of stock below comb
AA	**Augusta (Georgia) Arsenal**	Left side of stock under receiver
AAG	Same	Same
AA1111*	*Numbers may vary	On right side, vertically aligned
BA	**Benicia (California) Arsenal**	Left side of stock below receiver
BA/JPL*	*other initials such as CAB may be encountered	
HOD	**Hawaii Ordnance Depot**	Left side of stock below receiver
	Note: Normally accompanied by inspector's initials stamped adjacent to the "HOD" marking.	
MR	**Mt. Ranier (Wash.) Ordnance Depot**	Left side of stock below receiver
OG	**Ogden (Utah) Arsenal**	Left side of stock
O.G.		
O.G.E.K.	This is the cartouche of inspector Elmer Keith	

TABLE #19 continued on next page

TABLE #19 continued from page 159

OGEK	This is the cartouche of inspector Ed Klouser	
RA	**Raritan (New Jersey) Arsenal**	Left side of stock below comb
RA-P		Left side of stock below receiver
R.R.A.	**Red River (Texas) Arsenal**	Left side below comb
RRAD	**Red River (Texas) Army Depot**	Different letter sizes may be noted
RIA	**Rock Island (Illinois) Arsenal** Inspector's initials such as "EB" enclosed in a box with "RIA" marking	Left side below comb
SAA	**San Antonio (Texas) Arsenal**	Left or right side below receiver
C-SAA*		
C SAA*	*other letters such as "L" or "H" may be seen preceding the "SAA" marking.	
SA	**Springfield (Mass.) Armory**	Left side below comb
	A single letter may be found stamped below the "A" in "SA". This marking is normally enclosed in a square or a three sided box.	

Regulations generally called for the rebuild facility to stamp its initials and those of the inspector on the left side of the stock. However, as can be seen, there were some exceptions to this practice.

A fairly commonly seen rebuild mark is "SA-52" stamped into the metal behind the rear sight base of some M1 rifles, including a number of overhauled M1Cs. This was only done by Springfield Armory in 1952. Some similar "0-66" markings may be seen. Such rifles were overhauled by the Naval Weapons Command at Crane, Indiana in 1966.

In the 1960s, some ordnance facilities etched their initials and the month and year of overhaul by "electric pen" on the right front receiver leg. Some M1D rifles converted in this period will also be found with such markings. Examples of ordnance facilities, which marked rebuilt M1s with initials and dates on the right receiver leg, include:

"SA" — Springfield Armory
"LEAD" — Lake Erie Army Depot
"RA" — Raritan Arsenal
"RIA" — Rock Island Arsenal
"RRA" — Red River Arsenal
"RRAD" — Red River Army Depot
"TE" — Tooele (Utah) Depot

Note: Most of these same facilities also rebuilt M1, M1 and M2 carbines. Some also converted a number of M1 carbines into M2 configuration. This table should also be referred to when identifying carbine rebuild markings.

The M1 Carbine

American paratrooper training with an M1 carbine. Despite the fact that the M1A1 variant was developed for use by airborne troops, many paratroopers fought with the standard M1 carbine.

(Credit: U.S. Army)

Introduction

Only one United States small arm of the Second World War surpassed the M1 rifle in numbers produced and issued. This weapon was the M1 carbine. While the Garand represented a quantum step forward for military service rifles, the carbine was actually an entirely new class of weaponry. Before 1941, the U.S. M1 carbine did not even exist and by the end of WWII in 1945, the weapon had been produced in greater numbers than any other U.S. military small arm. From August 1941 through June 1945, the staggering total of 6,221,220 carbines had been produced by ten different commercial contractors. Carbines saw action on all fronts during WWII and remained in front line service well into the Vietnam era. In addition to use by American armed forces, huge quantities of carbines were supplied to current and erstwhile foreign allies under various military aid programs. Carbines are in active military use in many nations even today.

Collector interest in the carbine parallels that of the Garand in a number of ways, although it was actually recognized as a great collecting theme several years earlier. Until some fifteen or twenty years ago, collector interest in the carbine was rather minimal. There was generally a feeling among collectors that one carbine was pretty much like any other, and the weapon was of interest to only a relatively small group of collectors. The earlier martial arms such as "Trapdoor" Springfields, Krags and '03s were looked upon much more favorably as collecting themes than was the M1 carbine. Gradually, as these other guns became harder to find and more expensive, many collectors took a second look at the carbine and discovered many interesting and scarce variants. It is noteworthy that the "Baby Boom" generation has embraced the carbine as a collectible much more than has the prior generation. This is due, no doubt, in large measure to the fact that many veterans of WWII saw the carbine (and the Garand) as a wartime tool and had no particular interest in collecting the weapon. On the other hand, some veterans remembered the trim little carbine with some fondness and may have wished to own one after the war. For these individuals, the acquisition of any carbine usually fulfilled their desire.

From the end of WWII until the early 1960s, however, carbines were extremely scarce on the open market since they had not been released by the government for sale to the general public. Occasionally, one of the few M1 carbines that had been legitimately sold through proper channels surfaced and was eagerly snapped up. Carbines that left the government's inventory via "unofficial" means sometimes changed hands during this period as well, although in usually a less forthright manner. However, even the rather limited demand at the time was not met by the even more minuscule supply of genuine GI carbines. Some enterprising persons took advantage of the situation by acquiring large quantities of the tons of surplus carbine parts available in the late 1950s and early 1960s and assembled the parts to commercially made receivers. Many of these receivers were investment cast and were not made to the same high standards are were the government issue carbines. Several firms produced ersatz "GI" carbines that superficially resembled the real thing. While not of interest to martial arms collectors, such commercially made carbines helped satisfy the demand for "shooters."

The situation drastically changed in 1963 when the government released some 240,000 M1 carbines through the DCM to qualified members of the National Rifle Association for the very attractive sum of $20.00 each. Sales were limited to one carbine per person. Almost overnight, genuine GI carbines went from being quite scarce to very common. This large scale release of the weapons also sowed the seeds, which allowed for the carbine to become a highly desirable collector's item a number of years later. The supply of the DCM carbines was quickly exhausted, and it didn't take long for the original $20.00 carbines to triple or quadruple in price as the weapons changed hands. However, even into the early 1980s nice condition GI carbines could be purchased for a hundred dollars or less.

As more and more collectors entered the field, the market price for collectible GI carbines began an

(Above) Marine "War Dog" handler, Cpl. Robert W. Lowe, on Okinawa. Note te M8 launcher fitted to his M1 carbine.   (Credit: USMC)

(Below) U.S. Army soldier armed with an M1 carbine at the Battle of St. Lô in WWII.

upward spiral. A national carbine collectors' organization ("The Carbine Club") was started in the mid-1970s and helped spur interest in the weapon. Several other carbine collector organizations were formed during the past decade or so. As more information became available, collector interest in the carbine continued to grow, and as the almost infinite number of major and minor variations became known, the erroneous perception that all carbines were pretty much the same was eventually dispelled. Most of the carbines sold through the DCM in 1963 had been subjected to one or more ordnance rebuild programs. This meant that relatively few of the weapons remained in their original WWII factory configuration. As was the case with the Garand, the practice of "restoring" carbines became increasingly popular with collectors. Some carbines had been "demilled" by the government during the 1960s and 1970s by torch cutting the receiver in two. Some of these demilled receiver sections were welded together and refinished in much the same manner as was done with the torch cut Garand receivers of the same period. As is true with the Garand, the subject of restorations is fraught with controversy, and the potential for collectors being duped is always present. The topic of restorations will be discussed later.

Within the past decade another type of carbine has come onto the market. Like the Garand rifle, very large numbers of carbines were supplied by the United States to various and sundry nations around the world through military assistance programs. After the carbines became disposable, many were acquired by American firms and "imported" back into the United States. Like the "imported" Garands, the majority of these carbines are in less than pristine condition, have been overhauled one or more times, and will almost invariably evidence refinished metal. Generally the name of the importer was stamped on the metal (typically the barrel). The wood is frequently in poor condition. Nevertheless, the influx of additional carbines into the market at generally attractive prices has introduced many new collectors to the field and has also proven to be a source of replacement parts.

One feature of the carbine that makes it a fascinating collecting theme is that the weapon was made by ten prime contractors with a vast network of subcontractors. Most of the component parts were stamped with a code marking that identified the prime contractor as well as the subcontractor who actually made the part. Collectors are most interested in carbines that not only have the correct vintage parts but parts that are properly coded as

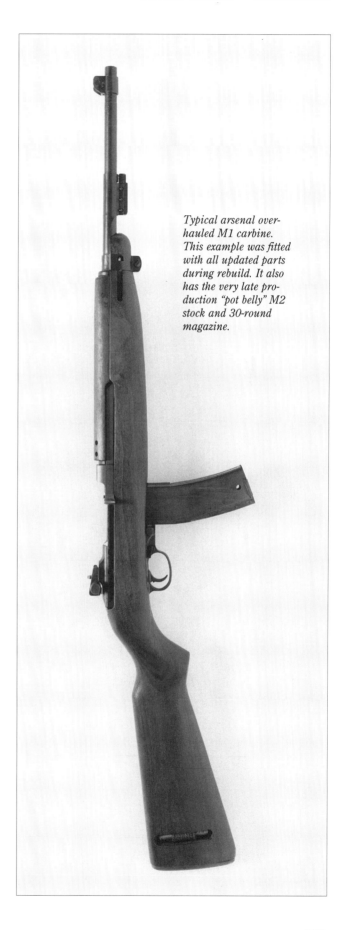

Typical arsenal overhauled M1 carbine. This example was fitted with all updated parts during rebuild. It also has the very late production "pot belly" M2 stock and 30-round magazine.

well. Collectors wishing to restore an overhauled carbine avidly seek parts of the correct type with the proper code markings. If someone is observed at a gun showing rummaging through a bin of carbine parts, the odds are very high that the person is a collector seeking a specific coded part to complete a restoration. Many of the early parts are now in short supply. The situation is compounded because, not only should the part have the proper code marking, it should be in comparable condition to the rest of the carbine as well. For example, a bolt in pristine condition would not be found on a well-worn original carbine even if it has the proper code markings.

There are probably as many approaches to collecting the carbine as there are collectors. One of the most common goals for beginning collectors is to acquire an example of a carbine made by each of the ten prime contractors. While several of the contractors may be hard to turn up, this remains a reachable goal for the majority of collectors today. As stated, there is a seemingly infinite

number of other variants to choose from. Among these include receivers made under subcontract by one firm and supplied to another. Some collectors concentrate only on the variants produced by a single prime contractor, while others pursue the objective of acquiring a specimen from every block of serial numbers assigned to each prime contractor. Still others seek only mint, unfired specimens. There is no right or wrong way to collect carbines. This is one of the many reasons why the carbine is an ideal collector's theme and why the weapon's popularity continues today.

Carbines are quite enjoyable weapons to shoot due to the low recoil and light weight. At one time surplus .30 caliber carbine ammunition was almost as cheap to shoot as .22 rimfire. However, this situation has changed. Today carbine ammunition is generally rather expensive, and carbines are less frequently used for plinking today as they were twenty or thirty years ago. Nevertheless, the carbine remains a popular recreation-

8th Armored division soldiers examining a target during training exercises at Ft. Polk, Louisiana, circa early 1944. The soldier at left has an M1 carbine and the one at right an M3 submachine gun. (Credit: Charles K. Canfield, Sr.)

al weapon and is used by some persons for hunting even though the cartridge is too under powered to give consistently good results on large game and such use is not recommended. The sporting demand for carbines has resulted in many thousands of the weapons being made over the past two or three decades by a number of commercial firms. Some of these are close copies of the original government issue weapons and others are markedly different in appearance. The carbine is certain to remain popular with collectors and gun enthusiasts well into the twenty-first century. The $20.00 DCM carbine of 1963 is now worth many times that amount. Unaltered specimens in collectible condition can be hard to find, and collector interest appears unabated. Like the Garand rifle, the carbine combines the historical significance of a major weapon of World War II (and later) with a seemingly endless number of variations. While some of the rarer and more desirable specimens are quite expensive, many very interesting and collectible carbines are still out there and accessible to even those on a modest budget. Few weapons offer as much to the collector and enthusiast as the M1 carbine.

➤ ➤ ➤ ➤ ➤ ➤ ➤ ➤ Historical Background ◄ ◄ ◄ ◄ ◄ ◄ ◄ ◄

The story of the carbine has it roots in the trenches of the Western Front of the First World War. Combat experience revealed that the typical service rifle cartridge was often overly powerful for some tasks. In addition, the rifle was too heavy and burdensome for use by such troops as crew-served weapons teams, Signal Corps personnel and myriad others. Typically such troops were armed primarily with handguns, but these were quite ineffective at any but point blank ranges. A few commercial Winchester Self Loading Rifles (SLRs) were acquired by the U.S. military during WWI to arm aviators, and some of these were informally tested by the infantry. The small and lightweight SLR which fired a rather modest cartridge appealed to many who otherwise would have been armed with a pistol. The war ended before any extensive evaluation of the "light rifle" concept was done, and the idea was soon shelved and all but forgotten.

Renewed development of the "light rifle" concept began as a response to Germany's Blitzkrieg tactics. The use of fast moving armored columns and vertical envelopment by airborne troops rendered the old strategy of heavily fortified fixed defensive positions obsolete. The rapid fall of France's vaunted Maginot Line is the most obvious example of this. This new type of warfare meant that troops previously considered as rear echelon non-combatants could all too quickly become engaged by enemy forces. A pistol would be of little use when support personnel became involved in active fighting. On the other hand, as determined during the First World War, a standard service rifle would be too great a hindrance to such troops in the performance of their normal duties. Clearly, a new type of weapon was needed, and the concept of the "light rifle" was revived. It was believed that such a weapon could not only replace the pistol but could also be used as a substitute for the sub-machine gun.

In June 1940, the Chief of Infantry proposed renewed development of a "light rifle." The Secretary of War approved this proposal and funds were allocated for the project. On October 1, 1940, the Ordnance Department took the first step in the acquisition of a "light rifle" for the United States military by issuing official requirements for such a weapon. Rather than develop the new weapon through government facilities like it had done at Springfield Armory with the Garand rifle, the Ordnance Department solicited proposals from both civilian and government designers. This approach allowed for innovative designs to be submitted. A five page circular was sent to potential arms manufacturers and private developers which gave the general characteristics required for the new weapon. These were:

(1) *Weight — not to exceed 5 pounds*
(2) *Range — effective up to 300 yards, semi-automatic fire essential, full-automatic desirable*
(3) *To be carried by sling or some comparable device*
(4) *Chambered for a cartridge of caliber .30 of the Winchester self-loading type with a case similar to that of the commercial Winchester self-loading cartridge, caliber .32.*

For the sake of consistency, the Ordnance Department decided early on that a standard "light rifle" cartridge should be adopted for which all test weapons must be chambered.

Since the Winchester .32 SLR cartridge was used as the "model" for the new round, it was no surprise that the Winchester Repeating Arms Company of New Haven, Connecticut, was selected to develop the new

A group of cold GIs in a chow line during the Ardennes campaign (late 1944–early 1945). The soldier in the front of the line has an M1 carbine slung on his back. The carbine became a widely used infantry weapon during WWII.   (Credit: U.S. Army)

Winchester Self-Loading Rifle (SLR). Small numbers of this commercial arm were acquired by the U.S. military in World War I for consideration as an infantry weapon. About a dozen had also previously been acquired by the fledging Army Air Service in 1916 for use in the Mexican Punitive Campaign. The First World War ended before any extensive evaluation could be done. However, the SLR served as the genesis for the M1 carbine of World War II.

light rifle cartridge. Winchester was a long-time supplier of firearms and ammunition to the U.S. military, and the firm enjoyed a good working relationship with the Ordnance Department.

The new cartridge proposed by Winchester would have a muzzle velocity of approximately 2,000 feet per second from an 18" barrel with a bullet weight of 100 to 120 grains. The Ordnance Department concurred with Winchester's recommendations and approved the further development of the light rifle cartridge with a 100 grain bullet. Winchester produced a small test quantity of the new round by altering some .32 SLR cartridge cases. It was decided to use non-corrosive primers in the new cartridge rather than the standard corrosive primers of the day. The smokeless powder that Winchester utilized was not capable of producing the necessary 2,000 fps, and the first test batch of ammunition only generated some 1,800 fps. Winchester representatives promised the Ordnance Department that the firm could procure suitable powder for subsequent cartridges. Initial testing began using the lower power cartridges. The tests revealed that the proposed cartridge was suitable in all respects except for the lower muzzle velocity. Winchester was able to acquire the necessary powder needed to meet the ballistic requirements. The first production drawings for the new "Light Rifle" .30 caliber cartridge were done in October of 1940. Some additional refinements were forthcoming, and the new cartridge was approved by the Ordnance Department on February 21, 1941. It appears as if the government had considered adoption of the proposed round a foregone conclusion since Winchester actually received a contract for the production of 50,000 of the new cartridge on January 9, 1941, over a month prior to formal approval. The company was given a second order in June 1941. These cartridges were intended to be used by designers of the various "light rifle" test weapons submitted for testing. With the selection of the cartridge finalized, the Ordnance Department began to look for the best weapon available to meet the mandated design parameters for the desired "Light Rifle."

A subcommittee of the Ordnance Technical Committee was appointed to test and evaluate the various designs submitted. The committee consisted of:

Maj. René R. Studler, OCO, Chairman
Maj. E.H. Harrison, Ordnance officer from
    Aberdeen Proving Ground
Lt. Col. W.F. Lee, Infantry
Lt. Col. John A. Steward, Field Artillery

Lt. Col. W.G. Layman, Infantry
Lt. Col. Frank R. Williams, Armored Force,
    Liaison Officer, A.P.G.
Maj. Charles F. Colson, Infantry, Liaison Officer, A.P.G.
Maj. J.H. Claybrook, Cavalry
Lt. James H. Dunbar, Jr., Ordnance (recorder)
Mr. Frank J. Jervey, Civilian employee of
    Ordnance Department
Mr. Charles E. Balleisen, Civilian employee of
    Ordnance Department

The original required date of submission for "light rifle" designs was February 1, 1941. However, because of the time lag required for development of a satisfactory cartridge, the date was extended to May 1, 1941. The committee convened in the old Social Security Building in Washington, DC. Nine designs had been formally submitted and were ready for testing by the committee. The test weapons and their representatives were:

(1) John C. Garand representing the government's Springfield Armory. Of course, Mr. Garand was a well-known individual because of his M1 rifle, which was the standard U.S. service rifle.

(2) Eugene C. Reising representing the Harrington & Richardson Arms Company. Reising had a good reputation as an arms designer and is best known for the .45 caliber submachine gun bearing his name that was adopted by the U.S. Marine Corps in World War II.

(3) V.A. Stevens with the Colt Patent Firearms Company. Colt's submission was a rifle designed by the legendary John M. Browning's son, Val.

(4) L.H. Hoover of the Auto Ordnance Company. Auto Ordnance held the manufacturing rights to the Thompson submachine gun.

(5) Fred Hickey representing the Savage Firearms Company. Savage's design was developed by a John Pearce.

(6) Clarence E. Simpson who was, like John Garand, affiliated with the government's Springfield Armory.

(7) F.H. Woodhull of the Woodhull Corporation. Woodhull's rifle was essentially a modified Winchester SLR.

(8) R.T. Hurley of the Bendix Aviation Corporation whose design was developed by George T. Hyde.

(9) Two individuals not associated with any established firm, a Mr. John J. Murphy and a Dr. Kohler.

Each inventor or representative appeared before the

committee individually to discuss their weapon. This allowed the committee to eliminate any obviously unacceptable designs prior to the actual tests. The gun submitted by Springfield Armory's Clarence Simpson was rejected as it greatly exceeded the permissible weight allowance. The weapon developed by Murphy and Kohler was eliminated from further consideration primarily because it was not of the required caliber. None of the weapons submitted were deemed acceptable by the committee, and a second round of tests was scheduled for September 15, 1941. This would permit sufficient time for refinement of the existing batch of weapons and the entry of additional submissions.

One glaring omission from the field of entries was a submission by the Winchester Repeating Arms Company. Although Winchester was very much involved in the light rifle project by virtue of developing the cartridge, the company was in the midst of gearing up for mass production of the Garand rifle. Winchester management determined that it should not devote the resources and capital required for the light rifle project in light of the daunting task of getting the M1 rifle into production.

Additionally, Winchester was involved in the research and development (albeit at a low level) of a .30 caliber service rifle of its own design which further taxed the firm's engineering capacity. This rifle contained some of the interesting and innovative design features of the firm's previous "G30" rifle and featured a novel short stroke gas piston developed by one of Winchester's designers, David M. Williams. Winchester dubbed the rifle the "M2" which was likely wishful thinking or tongue-in-cheek humor regarding the possibility that the weapon would eventually replace the M1 Garand. Only one full scale working prototype was fabricated. One of the weapon's main virtues was its light weight (for a full power service rifle) of just 7½ pounds. The rifle was never formally tested or evaluated by the government but was a good example of how Winchester continued to consider new and innovative gun designs.

During this same period, the .30 caliber test cartridge was slightly refined and in September 1941 was officially adopted as the "Cartridge, Caliber .30, Carbine." Initially the cartridge was slated to be given the nomenclature of "Cartridge, .30 Caliber, Short Rifle, M1." However, the Ordnance Department feared that such a designation could cause confusion between the new round and the ".30-06" M1 and M2 cartridges used with the M1 and M1903 rifles.

While arrangements were being made for the new round of tests, the Ordnance Department engaged in a bit of "behind the scenes" discussions with Winchester regarding the firm's decision not to enter the light rifle competition. The company had an excellent working relationship with the ordnance people and had proven to be a reliable supplier of small arms to the U.S. military for many years. Ordnance Colonel Rene R. Studler was aware of Winchester's work on its semiautomatic service rifle and the short stroke gas piston concept. On one of his visits to the New Haven plant, Col. Studler earnestly, but unofficially, requested Winchester's senior management to consider entering a weapon based on the "M2" rifle concept in the upcoming second round of tests. With such high level encouragement, the company changed its mind and decided that it could perhaps allocate sufficient resources to field an entry in the light rifle competition even with the constraints of limited working capital and the demands of Garand production.

Although Winchester had very limited time to design and fabricate a suitable prototype light rifle, the engineering team was able to assemble a rather crude working prototype light rifle utilizing the Williams' short stroke gas piston. This specimen was sent to Aberdeen Proving Ground for evaluation. The prototype was intended to demonstrate the basic design premise and was not suitable for extensive testing. Winchester's first prototype light rifle design was looked upon very favorably by the Ordnance Department representatives, and the firm was given a "green light" to proceed with building a test model for the upcoming second trial.

While this decision undoubtedly pleased the Winchester team working on the project, it created a problem for the company as there were only thirty days to refine the basic design and construct a weapon capable of sustained and grueling testing. In an amazing feat of engineering and managerial prowess, Winchester's engineers and designers literally rolled up their sleeves and worked around the clock on the light rifle project. Such a task was not totally unknown to Winchester. Back in 1917, the company was faced with a similar situation when it had to build a tool room model of John Browning's BAR for testing. However, at that time the firm was only copying Browning's design while, in the case of the light rifle, it was literally inventing and refining the weapon as it went along.

On September 12, just two days before expiration of the time limit, Winchester finally completed the working prototype. However, informal firing tests at the factory revealed some malfunctions and additional refinements proved necessary. By the night of September 13, the company felt that the problems had been corrected sufficiently to release the weapon for testing, and it was hurried to Aberdeen with little time to spare.

In addition to the Winchester entry, the second round of tests included four of the original entrants modified to some extent and four new designs. The new weapons consisted of a design by Howard Clarke of the Clarke Company, a gun designed by a private individual, R.J. Turner, a weapon produced by the High Standard Manufacturing Company and an unusual design by Colt based on a modified M1911 pistol. The Colt entry was quickly eliminated from consideration.

The subsequent testing which began on September 15, 1941, and continued through September 29, 1941, was thorough and exhaustive, and the field was eventually reduced to the Springfield Armory weapon designed by John Garand and the Winchester entry. Toward the end of testing, the Winchester weapon suffered a fractured bolt. However, due to its prior performance, the company was allowed to replace the broken component, and the testing continued. On September 30, 1941, the ordnance committee unanimously selected Winchester as the winner of the competition. The summary of the committee's report concluded:

That the Winchester rifle with the following minor modifications be adopted as the standard rifle for use in military service:

(a) Knurled buttplate.
(b) Stock to be of the same general type as the present service rifle except smaller in size.
(c) Strengthen forearm walls to increase rigidity.
(d) Improve direction of ejection.
(e) Install front sight similar to the present service rifle.
(f) The diameter of the aperture of the present sight is satisfactory. However, the rear sight should permit adjustment of 100, 200, 300 yards, inclusive. The sight should also be adjustable for deflection.

The success of Winchester's entry was a tribute to the technical expertise of the company. Few manufacturers could develop from scratch a rough working model and then refine it in a very short period of time to win a grueling competition. It is also worthy of note that it was exactly a year to the day that the Ordnance Department first announced requirements for the new weapon until such an arm was standardized.

An enduring myth exists regarding the development and subsequent adoption of the Winchester carbine. Popular legend, fostered by a early 1950s Hollywood movie, states that the carbine was invented by David Marshall Williams while he served time in prison. Most legends contain a grain of truth, and this one is no exception. Mr. Williams was an ex-convict who did work on some of his designs while serving a stint in prison. Williams was subsequently hired as a gun designer by Winchester and refined his short stroke gas piston concept while employed by the company. As stated, Williams' gas piston was utilized in the Winchester carbine. However, unlike the M1 rifle which was unquestionably conceived and developed by one man (John Garand), the Winchester carbine was very much a team effort by the entire Winchester organization. This is not to disparage either Mr. Williams or his talents but he did not "invent" the M1 carbine, contrary to popular legend.

The new weapon was formally standardized as the "U.S. Carbine, Caliber .30, M1." The "light rifle" designation was discarded as the War Department was concerned that some confusion between the new arm and the M1 Garand rifle could easily result. The term "carbine" was an interesting choice as the official designa-

Prototype Winchester trial "Light Rifle." A slightly modified version of this weapon was adopted as the M1 carbine.
(Credit: Winchester Repeating Arms Co.)

tion for the new weapon. Prior to adoption of the M1903 rifle, carbines were issued to the cavalry and were essentially shortened versions of the standard service rifle of the period. This was not the case with the Winchester .30 M1 carbine. The breech action of the carbine was similar to that of the M1 rifle and at the time of the weapon's adoption some persons dubbed the new arm a "Baby Garand." However, this was a very misleading and short-lived phrase since the carbine of 1941 was not a shortened Garand but represented an entirely new class of weaponry.

With the decision to standardize the Winchester design, plans were immediately formulated to begin mass production of the new weapon. It was apparent that Winchester's already burdened manufacturing facilities could not produce the required number of carbines. In order to facilitate production by other firms and to eliminate royalty payments, the government purchased manufacturing rights for the carbine from Winchester for $886,000. The Ordnance Department

negotiated with General Motors' Inland Manufacturing Division of Dayton, Ohio, regarding production of the new weapon concurrent with a contract to Winchester. Inland had previously planned to introduce an improved version of George Hyde's light rifle design for the second round of trials but was unable to finish the prototype in time for the competition. Representatives from Inland visited Winchester's New Haven plant for consultation and assistance in gearing up for quantity production of the newly adopted M1 carbine.

On October 5, 1941, the Ordnance Department requested that Winchester and Inland each fabricate five "toolroom" carbines for evaluation prior to going into mass production. The actual manufacture of Inland's five samples was subcontracted to the firm of R.F. Sedgley, Inc. of Philadelphia, Pennsylvania. The ten toolroom carbines were sent to Springfield Armory for evaluation and then to Aberdeen Proving Ground for function and firing tests. As might be expected, many nagging problems were encountered which had to be ironed out one by

WWII U.S. Army bazooka teams. Note the M1 carbine.

one. Each problem solved made the eventual mass production of the weapon more efficient. The results of the extensive evaluation of the Winchester and Inland toolroom carbines resulted in some changes in the production drawings for the weapons as well as recommendations for alteration of some components. By early April 1942, the modifications were deemed sufficient and the way was cleared to begin mass production of the new M1 carbine.

Not surprisingly, the first firms to receive contracts for production of the M1 carbine were Winchester and Inland. The Ordnance Department had originally entered into a letter agreement with Winchester on November 24, 1941, for the production of 350,000 carbines and related spare parts. The following day, Inland received a contract for the production of 336,698 carbines and related parts.

While the combined production of carbines by Winchester and Inland was deemed sufficient to meet the expected demand, the attack on Pearl Harbor some two weeks after the awarding of the contracts changed the situation dramatically. With America's active involvement in the war, the demand for all manner of war material, including carbines, increased virtually overnight. The rapid mobilization and expansion of our armed forces resulted in a corresponding increase in the need for small arms. Since the carbine was originally envisioned primarily to arm rear echelon and support troops and since such personnel outnumbered front line combat troops by a rather wide margin, it was apparent that larger numbers of carbines would be needed. The combined production of Winchester and Inland was inadequate to meet the suddenly increased demand and other sources of carbine production were clearly needed.

➤ ➤ ➤ ➤ ➤ ➤ ➤ Carbine Prime Contractors ◄ ◄ ◄ ◄ ◄ ◄ ◄

The near chaotic situation of early 1942 that resulted from the frenzied rush to equip our rapidly mobilizing armed forces made it extremely difficult to acquire the necessary raw material and trained work forces to produce new armaments. The Ordnance Department sought additional manufacturing sources for the carbine, and eventually, ten companies were awarded production contracts. The staggering total of 6,221,220 carbines was manufactured from late 1941 to mid-1945 when all outstanding contracts were canceled. The prime contractors represented a cross section of American industry in early 1942. The firms previously produced diverse items ranging from automotive equipment to office equipment to juke boxes. The fact that firms inexperienced in firearms production could produce so many modern weapons in such a short period of time while facing labor and materials shortages is nothing short of amazing. The fact that this was accomplished is a tribute to the managerial personnel and skilled workmen of the United States.

The firms that were awarded contracts to manufacture the M1 carbine during World War II were:

Winchester Repeating Arms Company, New Haven, Connecticut. As discussed, Winchester was the developer of the carbine and one of the first two firms to be awarded contracts to produce the weapon. Winchester was a well-known entity and long-time supplier of small arms and ammunition to the government. It is interesting to note that Winchester was the only firm among the ten prime contractors that had previously manufactured firearms. Winchester produced some 828,059 carbines which represented about 13½ percent of total production. Besides the standard M1 carbine, the company also made variants such as the T3 and M2. These will be discussed in a subsequent section of the book.

Inland Manufacturing Division of General Motors, Dayton, Ohio. Along with Winchester, Inland was the first recipient of a carbine production contract. The firm was an experienced manufacturer of automotive related products. Inland was, by far, the largest producer of the carbine. The firm made 2,632,097 carbines which represented approximately 43 percent of total production. Like Winchester, Inland made variants other than the standard M1 carbines. These included the M1A1, T3 and M2.

Underwood-Elliott-Fisher, Hartford, Connecticut. Underwood was a famous maker of typewriters and other office equipment. The company produced a total of 545,616 representing 8.9 percent of total production.

Rock-Ola Manufacturing Company, Chicago, Illinois. Rock-Ola produced juke boxes and other novelty related machines. Rock-Ola turned out some 228,500 M1 carbines — 3.7 percent of the total number produced.

Quality Hardware Machine Corporation, Chicago,

Factory workers preparing completed carbines for shipment during WWII.   (Credit: National Archives)

Illinois. This company specialized in the design of machine tools, dies, fixtures and related industrial machinery. QHMC made some 359,666 carbines (5.9 percent of the total). Quality Hardware was somewhat unusual among the prime contractors as the firm only produced a single part, the receiver. In some cases, production of that component was subcontracted to another firm.

National Postal Meter, Rochester, New York. As the firm's name implies, NPM was primarily a manufacturer of postal scales and metered mail machines. The company manufactured 413,017 carbines which was about 6.8 percent of the total.

Standard Products, Port Clinton, Ohio. This company manufactured automotive products such as weatherstripping, rubber bumpers and related trim items. Standard Products made a total of 247,100 carbines, about 4 percent of production. The company had initially accepted a contract to manufacture the M1903 rifle but changed to production of the carbine prior to producing any '03s as it was deemed a higher priority weapon.

International Business Machines, Poughkeepsie, New York. A well known maker of office equipment, IBM turned out a total of 346,500 M1 carbines during the war which was about 5.7 percent of the total. The company also made a number of M1918A2 Browning Automatic Rifles (BARs) for the government during WWII.

Irwin-Pedersen Arms Company, Grand Rapids, Michigan. A rather hastily organized subsidiary of an established furniture business (Irwin Brothers), the firm enlisted the services of the famous arms designer, John Pedersen. Mr. Pedersen's major contribution was apparently the lending of his name to the fledging arms producer. Irwin-Pedersen is the only one of the prime contractors who was unable to successfully produce the carbine. Irwin-Pedersen did manufacture some completed carbines and a fairly large amount of parts, including receivers, but none were delivered to the government by the company.

Saginaw Steering Gear Division of General Motors, Saginaw and Grand Rapids, Michigan. Saginaw was the only prime contractor to operate two separate carbine production plants when it took over the assets of the failed Irwin-Pedersen plant and re-opened operations at Grand Rapids. Saginaw's two plants had a combined total production of 517,212 M1 carbines, which was about 8.5 percent of the total. This includes the Irwin-Pedersen carbines that were on hand when Saginaw took over the I-P operation and carbines subsequently assembled using Irwin-Pedersen receivers.

Details regarding the carbines made by each of the ten prime contractors will be discussed in detail subsequently.

In order to help coordinate production between the various prime contractors, the "Carbine Industry Integration Committee" was formed. The entity enabled troublesome bottlenecks to be alleviated by allowing

prime contractors to provide parts to other contractors when required. Despite some inevitable friction, the cooperation between the manufacturers and the government was admirable.

Each carbine prime contractor was assigned one or more blocks of serial numbers for their exclusive use. This was done to prevent duplicate serial numbers on carbines made by different contractors. It should be noted that not all of the serial numbers in each block were necessarily used so it is not possible to ascertain a particular contractor's total production by simply adding up the serial numbers in each block. Some contractors used a large percentage of their assigned numbers and others only a relative few from certain blocks. The various assigned serial number blocks are listed in the section covering each prime contractor and in Tables #2 to #12.

U.S. Army litter party in the Pacific. The litter bearers are carrying M1 carbines which were less burdensome than the much heavier rifles and submachine guns.

(Credit: U.S. Army)

Typical WWII production M1 carbine with oval oiler slot in stock.

The various prime contractors utilized a vast network of subcontractors to produce the majority of the parts for the carbine. Some of the prime contractors made the majority of parts for their carbines while others made very few. As stated, Quality Hardware Machine Corporation manufactured only the receiver and, in some examples, even that part was manufactured by a subcontractor. Most component parts were stamped with a letter code to designate the prime contractor as well as a letter that identified the subcontractor who actually produced the part. In some cases, parts originally made for one contractor were diverted to another contractor to help alleviate production bottlenecks. For today's collector, the correct type and coded parts are very important to determine if a particular carbine remains in its original factory configuration or has been altered. Likewise, it is vital when restoring a carbine that the not only are the correct vintage parts used but that they are properly coded as well. Since the vast majority of carbines in existence today have been overhauled by the government at least once, this subject is extremely important for collectors today. As stated, it is common to see collectors rummaging through boxes of miscellaneous parts at gun shows looking for that one properly coded part still needed to restore a particular carbine. Finding such seemingly small treasures is one of the rewards of carbine collecting.

Locating parts with the proper prime contractor and subcontractor codes is only part of the problem. There were often numerous differences between the carbines made by the various prime contractors during the weapon's production run. Most of these changes were due to modifications of various parts for greater efficiency or to make production cheaper and/or faster. Therefore, not only does a part have to be marked with the proper codes, it must be of the correct vintage for

the carbine in question. The various parts changes and correct contractor and subcontractor codes will be discussed in the pages that follow. Each prime contractor will be discussed separately and a general summary of the proper parts for each manufacturer will be discussed. As stated, the fact that the vast majority of carbines on the market today have been overhauled one or more times makes the practice of restoration quite popular. The same caveats regarding ethics and proper disclosures as discussed about Garands also holds true for carbines. We will explore the subject of carbine restoration at length later.

As the M1 carbines began to come off the assembly lines and issued, the heretofore rumored, but somewhat mysterious, weapon soon became yet another familiar item in Uncle Sam's arsenal. Most servicemen were immediately taken with the lightweight and trim little carbine. One early WWII government report commented on the carbine's initial popularity with the troops: "Army Ordnance officers state that the carbine is one of the most popular weapons they have ever issued to the service."

The appeal of the carbine to soldiers previously armed with the rather heavy Garand or '03 rifles is easy to understand. The popularity of the carbine was not limited to support personnel but, at least initially, extended to many combat troops as well. Although not as powerful or accurate as the Garand, the carbine possessed a greater volume of fire. Soon after adoption by the U.S. Army, the Marine Corps and Navy standardized the M1 carbine as well. A January 19, 1942, Marine Corps document estimating specific weaponry requirements stated that 208,000 carbines would be needed while projecting a demand for just 10,000 Thompson submachine guns.

Another interesting early WWII Marine Corps document summed up the impression of one of its legendary officers, Lewis "Chesty" Puller after firing the carbine for the first time, "Lt. Col. Puller, after firing the carbine at Aberdeen, stated that he considered it an excellent combat weapon and could see no need for retaining submachine guns and pistols in combat units if they were armed with M1 rifles and carbines." The same report went on to state that the commanding officer of the 23d Marines preferred to have the carbine replace both pistols and submachine guns.

While the Army and Marine Corps were officially on the record as stating that the carbine should replace the submachine gun and pistol, it actually did neither during the war. All three weapons (carbines, submachine guns and pistols) were manufactured and issued in large numbers during the war and each filled a particular niche. It should be stated, however, that much larger numbers of submachine guns and pistols would have been required if carbines were not available.

As ever-increasing numbers of carbines were employed in front line combat roles, many soldiers changed their minds regarding the suitability of the weapon. Despite its light weight and rapid fire capability, many combat troops complained bitterly that the weapon lacked range, accuracy and stopping power. There were numerous instances recorded where enemy soldiers were not immediately stopped when hit one or more times by carbine bullets. One such example is related in the book *U.S. Infantry Weapons of World War II*:

A young U.S. Army sergeant went up a small ravine to relieve himself carrying his M1 carbine. He ran into a short, husky Jap infantryman coming down the same canyon. The Jap had a rifle with a bayonet. They were about 30 yards or so apart when the Jap charged. The sergeant unlimbered his carbine from its "quick draw" inverted carrying position and it took him nine shots to send the Jap on to his ancestors. The sergeant never carried a carbine in

U.S. Army troops on the beach in the Pacific Theater. All the soldiers in view are armed with M1 carbines.

(Left) M1A1 carbine.
(Center) Standard M1 carbine.
(Right) M2 carbine with all late features and fitted with a 30-round magazine and M4 Bayonet-Knife.

combat again because he had completely lost faith in its ability of stop a hostile.

This same sentiment was echoed in numerous WWII-era reports. One particular passage contained in *The History of U.S. Marine Corps Operations in World War II* reported, "On Saipan the M1 (rifle) continued as an excellent weapon, more durable than the carbine, and, although much heavier, it was preferred by most Marines. A carbine bullet would not always stop an enemy solider."

Subsequent use in the Korean War (1950–1953) resulted in many more unsatisfactory reports regarding the carbine. Most of the carbines used in Korea were the M2 selective fire type which seemed more prone to malfunction than the semiautomatic M1. Some interesting comments regarding this subject are contained in S.L.A. Marshall's book *Weapons Usage in Korea*. Below are several excepts from this work regarding the carbine:

In subfreezing weather, the carbine operates sluggishly and, depending upon the degree of cold, will require anywhere from 5 to 20 warm-up shots before it will fire full automatic

The weapon lacks power...is too delicate...its day-to-day operation is too variable according to changes in the weather. When fired full automatic it wastes ammunition...and when fired semi-automatic it isn't sufficiently accurate for aimed fire at moderate distance.

The 1st Marine Division takes (a) dim view of this weapon...they want it either eliminated or made over into a dependable weapon.

However, condemnation of the carbine as a combat weapon was, by no means, universal with the armed forces. Many combat veterans were proponents of the carbine and used it exclusively even when other weapons were available. A WWII report on various infantry weapons used by a Marine Raider battalion on New Georgia contained the following positive summation of the carbine as a combat weapon, "Carbine, Cal. .30, M1… This weapon held up very favorably, functioned well with but very few exceptions…" This report did not contain any negative statements regarding the carbine's lack of stopping power so it can be inferred that the Marine Raiders, at least in this unit, did not complain a great deal about this perceived problem. Likewise, another arms-wise combat veteran and author, Lt. Col. John George, wrote the following in his interesting book *Shots Fired in Anger*, "The carbine turned out to be an ace weapon of the war, as far as I am concerned. It was light and handy, powerful, and reasonably accurate…" Even the overall scathing report contained in Marshall's book contains a number of favorable comments regarding the carbine's use in Korea.

It should be noted that critics of the carbine are, for the most part, actually comparing it to the rifle. As com-

pared to a service rifle such as the Garand, the carbine certainly has less power, range and accuracy. On the other hand, the carbine was never intended to replace the rifle — only the pistol and submachine gun. Except in very close range fighting, few would argue that the pistol or submachine gun were superior to the carbine. Both the pistol and submachine gun are only effective at short ranges and require a great deal of practice for a person to become reasonably proficient. The carbine, on the other hand, can be effectively utilized at ranges exceeding a hundred yards with a modicum of training. The use of the carbine as a replacement for the rifle led to most of the above-mentioned instances where the weapon's relative lack of power (compared to a rifle) became apparent. It would be interesting to poll the combat veterans who denigrated the carbine to determine if they would have been willing to trade the weapon for a pistol instead. As one writer aptly noted, "Only those who mistake it [the carbine] for a rifle will find it wanting." Nevertheless, there seemed to be little middle ground regarding the combat soldier's opinion of the M1 carbine; it was either loathed or loved.

➤ ➤ ➤ ➤ ➤ ➤ ➤ ➤ ➤ ➤ **Variations** ◄ ◄ ◄ ◄ ◄ ◄ ◄ ◄ ◄ ◄ ◄

M1A1 Carbine

With the formation of airborne units early in the war, the need for a more compact version of the carbine was voiced. Inland developed a folding wire stock for the carbine. This allowed for a shorter and more compact weapon, which could be stowed away during a parachute jump and easily brought into action on the ground. A canvas carrying bag that strapped to the paratrooper's leg during his descent was produced for use with the new carbine.

In May 1942, this first major variant of the carbine was adopted as the "U.S. Carbine, Cal. .30, M1A1." A contract was awarded to Inland for production of the M1A1 carbine and deliveries began in October of 1942. The 82nd and 101st Airborne Divisions were among the first units equipped with the new M1A1 carbines. Eventually, all Army airborne units were equipped with M1A1 carbines, and some were also diverted to the Marine Corps. Inland was the sole manufacturer of this variant, and the firm eventually delivered a total of 140,591 M1A1 carbines to the government. The M1A1 variant will be discussed in detail in this book during the section covering Inland carbines.

Markings on bottom of early production M1A1 grip. Note the "OI" marking and the "crossed cannons" Ordnance Department escutcheon.

(Left) M1 carbine.

(Right) M1A1 carbine (with stock folded).

(Below) Marking found on later production M1A1 grip. As can be seen, this larger "crossed cannons" escutcheon was stamped on the side of the grip rather than the bottom.

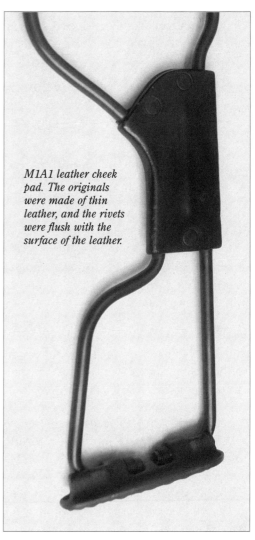

M1A1 leather cheek pad. The originals were made of thin leather, and the rivets were flush with the surface of the leather.

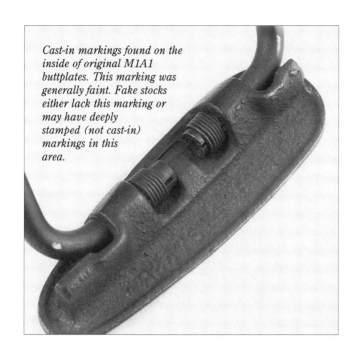

Cast-in markings found on the inside of original M1A1 buttplates. This marking was generally faint. Fake stocks either lack this marking or may have deeply stamped (not cast-in) markings in this area.

T3 Carbine

An interesting and rarely seen variant of the carbine is the "T3." The T3 carbine was the culmination of a June 1943 request by the Army for Inland to design a scope mount for the carbine. At least one prototype sniper carbine with a brazed-on, Redfield-type receiver mount was fabricated and thoroughly tested as the "M1E7." The M1E7 was teamed with the Weaver M73B1 telescope as issued with the standard M1903A4 sniper rifle. Extensive testing revealed that the concept of a lightweight sniping weapon based on the carbine was flawed due primarily to the carbine's lack of range and accuracy (for a sniping weapon), and the matter was eventually dropped. However, while the optical telescopic-sighted carbine didn't work out, another type of sighting device was utilized with the weapon.

The need for a night vision device, which would

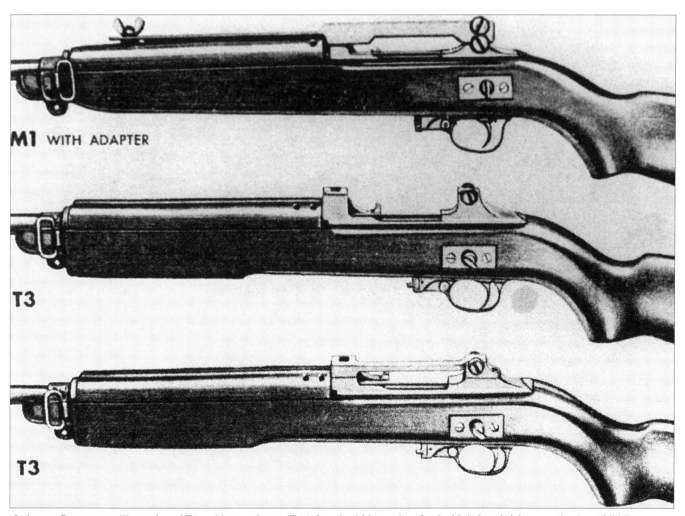

Ordnance Department illustration of T3 carbine receivers. (Top) Standard M1 receiver fitted with infrared sight mounting bar. (Middle) Winchester T3 receiver. (Bottom) Inland T3 receiver. Note the difference in configuration between the Winchester and Inland T3 receivers.

A member of the Army's 546th Engineer Detatchment (Ft. Lewis, Washington) sighting a T3 carbine with infrared scope. This weapon saw limited but effective use in the latter stages of the Pacific war. (Credit: U.S. Army)

allow an operator to acquire and engage targets without being observed by the enemy, spurred the development of infrared sighting equipment. The U.S. Army developed and refined a night vision sight that featured a lamp which emitted a beam filtered to remove all light waves from the spectrum except infrared. An electronic scope unit that was capable to converting infrared light to visible light was utilized. The arrangement resembled an oversized telescopic rifle sight teamed with an automobile headlight. As infrared light is invisible to the naked eye, an enemy would be unable to detect the use of an infrared scope unit. Since the infrared sighting equipment was quite heavy and bulky and since its range was rather short, it was believed that the carbine would be the ideal platform upon which to mount the new device. The light weight of the carbine helped mitigate the heavy infrared scope unit, and the limited range of the carbine's cartridge was not a factor due to the short range capability of the scope.

A carbine with a modified receiver was developed for use with the new infrared night vision sights and given the designation "T3." The T3 carbine featured an integral Redfield-type scope mount with one mounting point in place of the conventional rear sight and the other over the receiver ring. This was very similar to the configuration of the ill-fated M1E7 carbine. Inland and Winchester were the only manufacturers of the T3. The configuration of the receiver differed between the Inland and Winchester T3 carbines. The T3s made by each company will be discussed later.

The infrared night vision/T3 units were employed in the closing weeks of the war in the Pacific where they were put to limited, but quite effective, use. It has been reported that the Japanese were initially unable to ascertain why their previously successful night infiltration tactics were suddenly rendered ineffective. In addition to the infrared scopes mounted on T3 carbines, some hand-held infrared scopes were also fielded. The war ended before extensive issue of the T3 carbines could take place and many were subsequently destroyed by the government. Some of the torch cut "demilled" T3 receivers have since been welded back together and refinished. These welded T3 are seen from time to time and are not nearly as desirable for collecting purposes as unaltered T3 carbines. Any T3 offered for sale should be examined very closely for signs of welding on the receiver.

Any of the infrared carbine units make exceptionally interesting and colorful additions to a collection. While the electronic components are often deteriorated after a half century, they are still impressive items for a martial collector and should be obtained whenever possible if fairly priced.

M2 Carbine

Among the most significant changes to the M1 carbine was the addition of fully automatic capability. There are reports that some standard M1 carbines were field modified during WWII to be capable of fully automatic fire, but these modifications were usually rather crude. While the wisdom of a fully automatic carbine can be (and was) debated, the using services nevertheless expressed a desire for such a weapon. As mentioned, the original specifications for the "light rifle" included selective fire operation, but this feature was dropped before standardization of the carbine.

Several types of conversion kits were considered for retrofit to standard M1 carbines. One of the most promising of these was designated as the "Kit, Carbine, T17." When incorporated into a standard carbine, the weapon received the ordnance test designation of "Carbine, Caliber .30, T4." Several "T4" carbines fabricated by Inland were tested at Aberdeen Proving Ground in the summer of 1944. A 30-round magazine was also developed in order to increase the fully automatic carbine's effectiveness. Tests revealed that the weapon was only marginally heavier than the standard M1 carbine. The weapon

had a high rate of fire (750 to 775 rounds per minute) and was difficult to control. It was noted in the test report that accuracy improved as the shooters became accustomed to the weapon. Functioning and reliability were deemed satisfactory. On September 14, 1944, the "T4" was recommended for standardization. The request was approved, and the "U.S. Carbine, Caliber .30, M2" was formally adopted on October 26, 1944. The "T17" retrofit kit was also adopted concurrently with the M2 carbine. With formal standardization, classification of the M1 and M1A1 variants was changed to "Limited

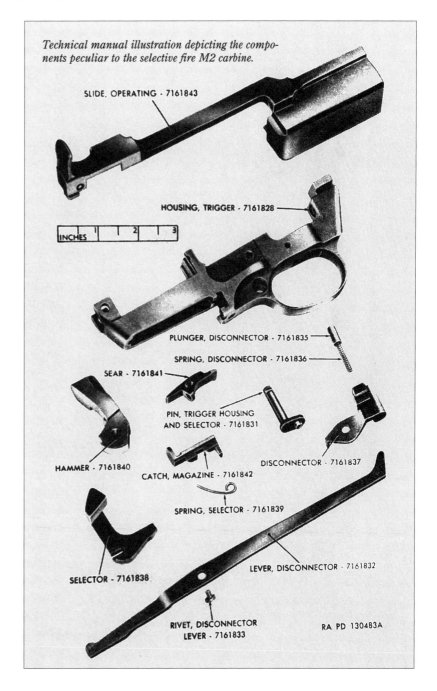

Technical manual illustration depicting the components peculiar to the selective fire M2 carbine.

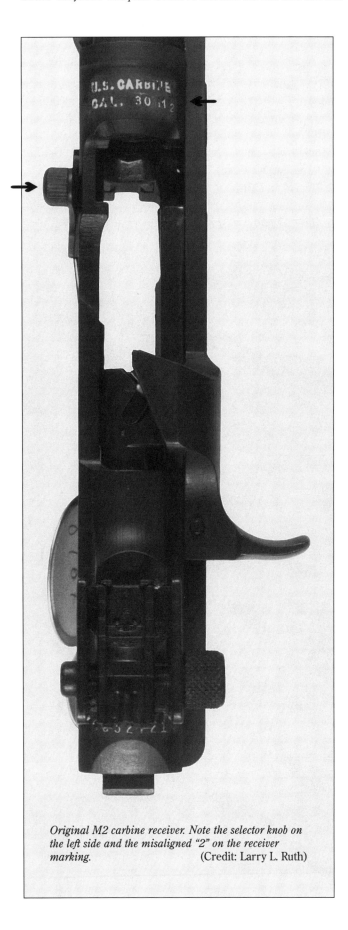

Original M2 carbine receiver. Note the selector knob on the left side and the misaligned "2" on the receiver marking. (Credit: Larry L. Ruth)

Standard." This meant that the weapons of this type on hand could continue in use but no more would be procured.

By the time manufacture of the M2 was scheduled to begin, only Inland and Winchester remained in production, and these two firms were the sole manufacturers of this variant. Many thousands of earlier M1 carbines were eventually converted to M2 specifications by use of conversion kits. Converted M2 carbines could be of any make and vintage. Most of the M1 carbines fitted with conversion kits had the "1" in the M1 marking on the receiver ring over-stamped with a "2".

There are several features which readily distinguish the M2 from the M1 carbine:

(1) "M2" marking on the receiver ring.
(2) Selector lever on the left side of the receiver.
(3) Stock with clearance cut to accommodate the selector lever.
(4) Special internal parts including trigger housing and sear.
(5) Late features including round bolt, adjustable sight, T4 band and rotary safety.

M3 Carbine

Following adoption of the M2, the next standardized variant was the "U.S. Carbine, Caliber .30, M3." The M3 carbine is the subject of some misunderstandings and confusion among a few collectors and students of the subject today. Simply put, the M3 carbine is a M2 carbine fitted with an infrared night vision scope. Undoubtedly part of the confusion surrounding this variant is the assumption that it was a variant of the specially manufactured T3 carbine. The T3 was manufactured strictly as a semiautomatic weapon and no selective fire variants were originally made by either Inland or Winchester. However, U.S. Army Technical Manual TM 9-1276 (February 1953) illustrates a M3 carbine that appears to have the same type integral receiver mounts as found on Winchester T3 carbines. The M3 illustrated in the manual has all late features including a "pot belly" stock. While this illustration may have been that of a single prototype, it is indeed possible that some T3 carbines were, in fact, converted to selective fire M3 configuration after World War II. In any event, most M3 carbines were produced by adding a mounting bar to either a M2 or converted M1 carbine (with T17 kit). Any selective fire carbine (M2, converted M1 or converted T3) fitted with any type of infrared scope can be technically

Group of U.S. Marines in Korea circa 1950. All are armed with M2 carbines equipped with 30-round magazines. (Credit: USMC)

Photo taken during the Tet Offensive, February 1968, in Vietnam. This shot is interesting in that it depicts U.S. Navy personnel armed with three different types of weapons: (From left) M16 rifle, M2 carbine (with 30-round magazine) and an M14 rifle. The carbine saw a surprising amount of service in Vietnam by American and South Vietnamese troops. (Credit: National Archives)

U.S. Army soldier in Korea firing his M2 carbine April 1951. Note the two 30-round magazines taped together in order to facilitate reloading. Note also the magazine pouch for two 15-round magazines. (Credit: U.S. Army)

designated as an M3 carbine.

The most commonly found type of scope fitted to M3 carbines was the M3 infrared (to be discussed later) which may also contribute to the confusion regarding this variant. While this improved night vision scope was designated as the "M3," the nomenclature had nothing to do with the M3 carbine. It was simply the third stan-

dardized type of infrared scope (**M**=Model; **3**=third type adopted). Again, this is coincidence, and the M3 carbine and M3 scope were not specifically made for each other. Some standard semiautomatic M1 carbines were also fitted with infrared night vision scopes after World War II. The various types of infrared scopes used with carbines will be discussed later.

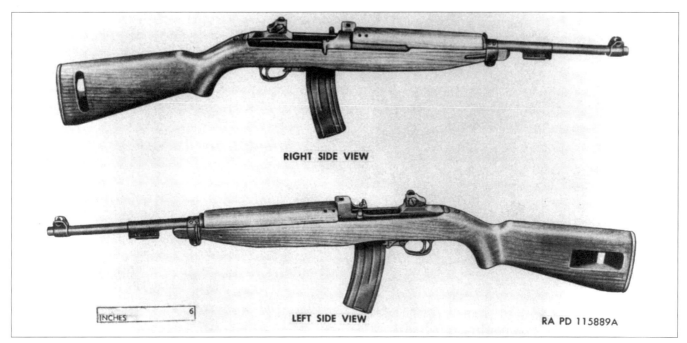

RIGHT SIDE VIEW

INCHES   6   LEFT SIDE VIEW   RA PD 115889A

Army Technical Manual showing a M3 selective fire carbine with Winchester-type T3 receiver. This was possibly a prototype weapon as there is no evidence of any official orders to convert semiautomatic T3 carbines to selective-fire M3 configuration.

➤ ➤ ➤ ➤ ➤ ➤ ➤ ➤ ➤ ➤ Components ◄ ◄ ◄ ◄ ◄ ◄ ◄ ◄ ◄ ◄ ◄

As the carbine saw greater and greater use, a number of deficiencies unrelated to the power of the cartridge became apparent, and a number of changes in various parts was forthcoming. Some of these changes were intended to speed production or reduce costs, and others were aimed at eliminating some problems that were being encountered as the carbine began to see service. Virtually every part of the carbine was revised to some extent.

Receiver

There were two basic types of carbine receivers characterized by the absence or presence of a detachable housing for the operating spring. Only a few manufacturers utilized the detachable housing and most of them changed to the type with an integral housing later in production. Receivers with the detachable spring tube housing fall into two general variants.

The first type had a projection or lug on the side of the tube that fitted into a corresponding hole milled into the right side of the receiver. It was discovered that the hole in the receiver could weaken and cause cracking in this area. This has been dubbed the "Type 1" detachable spring tube receiver by some collectors.

The variant is characterized by deletion of the lug on

the tube and elimination of the troublesome hole milled into the receiver. Some of the earlier tubes were modified by grinding off the projection. This variant is less commonly seen than the first type as it was a transition feature in use for a relatively short period of time. This is sometimes referred to as the "Type 2" detachable spring tube receiver.

The most commonly encountered type of carbine receiver is the later variant with an integral spring tube hole drilled into the right side of the receiver. Some collectors refer to this final major receiver variant as the "Type 3." Production delays were initially encountered due to problems inherent in setting up the machine tooling to drill such a deep hole. However, these difficulties were eventually overcome, and the integral tube housing proved to be an improvement in the strength and reliability of the carbine.

Other sometimes overlooked features found in some carbine receivers include the width of the rear tang that fitted into the recoil plate (wide or narrow) and the configuration of the handguard retaining "lip" (long or short). Wide tang receivers were made by Saginaw Steering Gear (including some made by this firm for Inland) and receivers made under subcontract by Auto-Ordnance Corporation. There were other seemingly

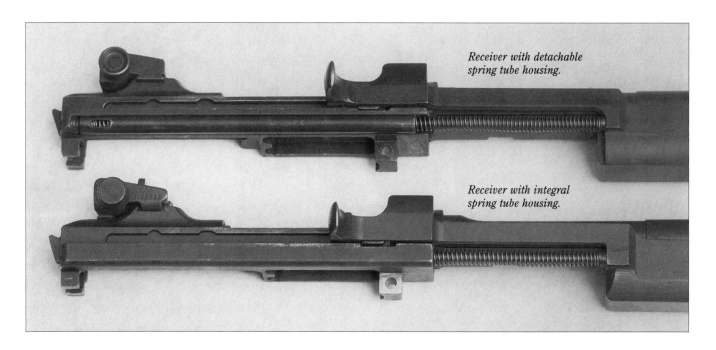

Receiver with detachable spring tube housing.

Receiver with integral spring tube housing.

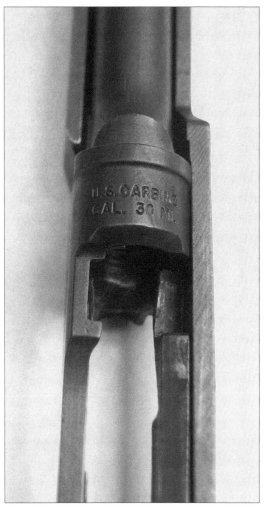

M1 carbine receiver markings. This same marking format was used on M1A1 carbines as well.

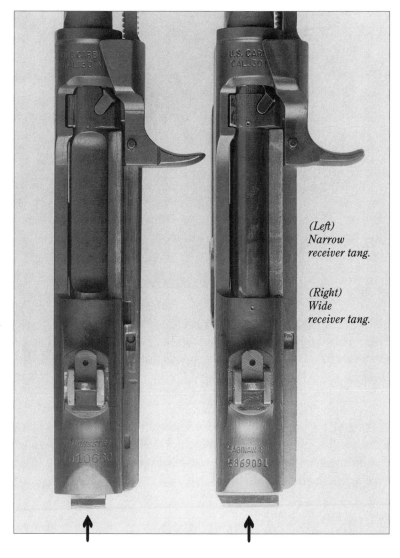

(Left) Narrow receiver tang.

(Right) Wide receiver tang.

minor differences such as the configuration of the operating slide guide way (rounded or square) and the construction details of the rear portion of the receiver. The major types of receivers (detachable or integral spring tube housing) used by each prime contractor will be discussed in a later section of this book.

One of the interesting aspects of carbine collecting was the practice of transferring receivers originally made by one contractor to another contractor for assembly into new production carbines. Some of these receivers were manufactured by one contractor for another specifically under contract. Others were not originally made with the intention of transferring, although this may have subsequently been done. The receivers made specifically under contract were normally stamped with the standard receiver markings of the prime contractor that ordered the receiver and marked with code letters to denote the actual manufacturer of the receiver. The receivers that

were not initially manufactured under contract for another company, but which were subsequently transferred, usually have the original maker's name buffed out or partially defaced with a line. The name or a code letter to denote the identity of the firm that ultimately used the receiver to assemble the carbine was generally stamped on the receiver. The specific firms that used these transferred receivers and details regarding them will be presented in the sections that follow on each prime contractor. Carbines made with transferred receivers are interesting collectibles and illustrate how many different variations of the weapon exist.

Trigger Housing

There are two distinct types of carbine trigger housing, which are characterized by the method of construction. The most common type is the so-called "milled" housing, which was machined from a solid piece of steel.

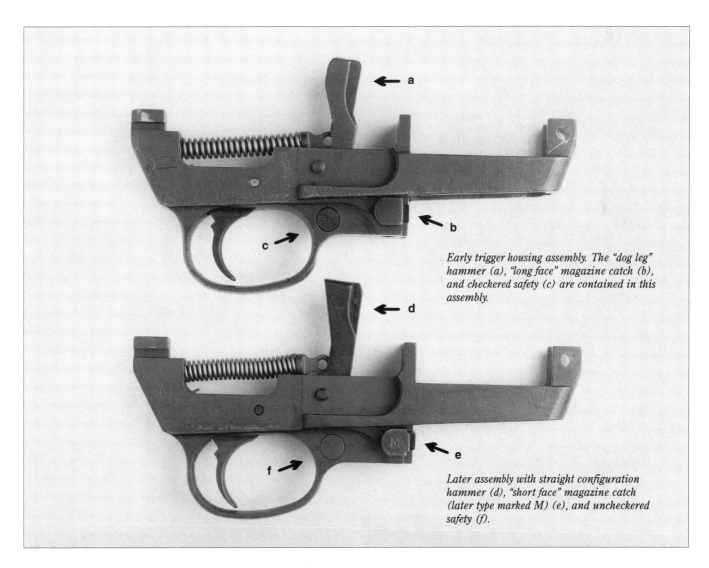

Early trigger housing assembly. The "dog leg" hammer (a), "long face" magazine catch (b), and checkered safety (c) are contained in this assembly.

Later assembly with straight configuration hammer (d), "short face" magazine catch (later type marked M) (e), and unchecked safety (f).

Some manufacturers utilized a trigger housing constructed from stamped pieces of metal welded together and brazed into a solid unit. Only a few contractors utilized the brazed trigger housings.

The brazed triggerguards will normally have very similar features, but there are a number of differences found in the milled triggerguards. For example, some milled triggerguards will feature magazine guide slots that run the entire length of the rear of the magazine

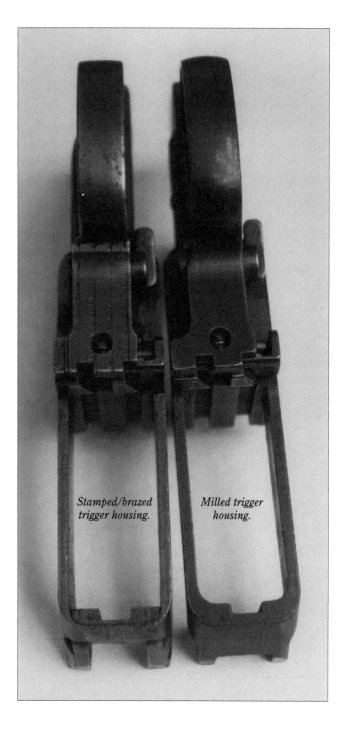

Stamped/brazed trigger housing.   *Milled trigger housing.*

well, while others are only notched high enough to allow the magazine to properly seat. Other differences include the presence of a hole in the triggerguard to allow lubrication of the magazine catch spring (found only on late production carbines), variances in the width of the rear magazine well and changes in the configuration of the bevel of the front and rear lugs. Specific information regarding what type of trigger housings (milled or stamped) were utilized by the various prime contractors will be discussed later.

When the selective fire M2 carbine was adopted, a special trigger housing was developed for this variant. The M2 trigger housing will be discussed subsequently.

Safety

The original design of the carbine's safety proved to be unsatisfactory. As originally designed, the safety and magazine catch both utilized "push buttons." There are four basic variants of carbine safeties. The first pattern (a.k.a. "Type 1") is very early production and is characterized by checkering on both sides. The second variant (a.k.a. "Type 2") was essentially identical but had the checkering eliminated to speed production. This type of safety remained in use well into 1943. There were some problems encountered with positive locking of the safety and the third pattern ("Type 3") safety was adopted to reduce this problem. The primary difference between this improved pattern and the second variant was a change in the configuration of the plunger recess to provide for more secure locking action.

However, all three types of the "push button" safeties

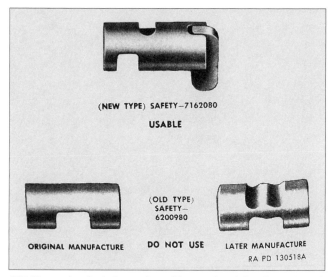

(NEW TYPE) SAFETY—7162080

USABLE

ORIGINAL MANUFACTURE   (OLD TYPE) SAFETY— 6200980   LATER MANUFACTURE

DO NOT USE

RA PD 130518A

TM illustration depicting early and late push safeties (bottom) and the latest variant rotary safety (top).

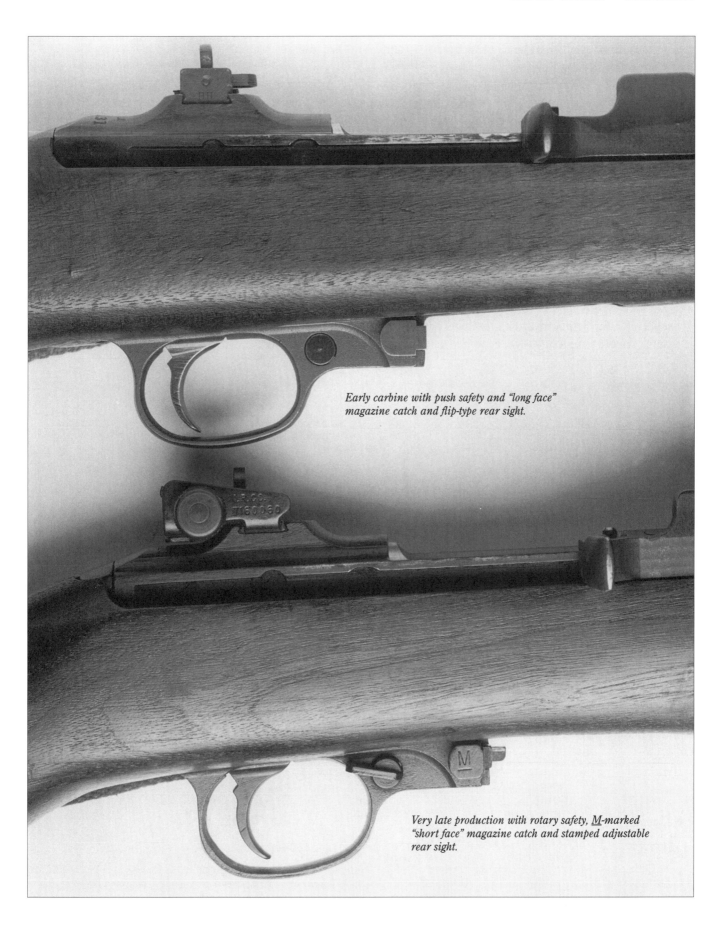

Early carbine with push safety and "long face" magazine catch and flip-type rear sight.

Very late production with rotary safety, M-marked "short face" magazine catch and stamped adjustable rear sight.

shared a common problem. The fact that the safety and magazine catch operated in a similar manner and were in close proximity to each other soon caused some problems. If one wished to disengage the safety, it was rather easy to accidentally release the magazine instead. Obviously, this could have embarrassing, if not disastrous, consequences in combat situations. While the potential problem didn't adversely affect the carbine's performance, it was deemed serious enough to warrant a "fix." A rotary safety was developed which eliminated this problem, but the new design did not get into production until extremely late. The rotary safety was retrofitted to all carbines during the extensive postwar rebuild programs. It should be noted that not all safeties were marked with contractor code markings. The section covering the details of each prime contractor will give specific information regarding the types of safeties and approximate time frames that each was used.

Trigger

There were two basic types of carbine triggers, which have been termed as "Type 1" and "Type 2" by collectors today. As with most such terms, these were not official government designations. The "Type 1" trigger and "Type 2" triggers differ slightly in the angle of the pedestal and the dimensions between the pedestal and the trigger pin hole. These differences are very subtle and require close observation or measurement to ascertain the variances. Only a few firms such as Winchester, Rock-Ola and Quality Hardware are known to have used any substantial number of "Type 1" triggers.

The markings are an important feature to observe to be certain that they are properly coded. Both blued and parkerized triggers may be encountered. Triggers made by casting and without markings are post-WWII items and should not be found on supposedly original, unaltered carbines.

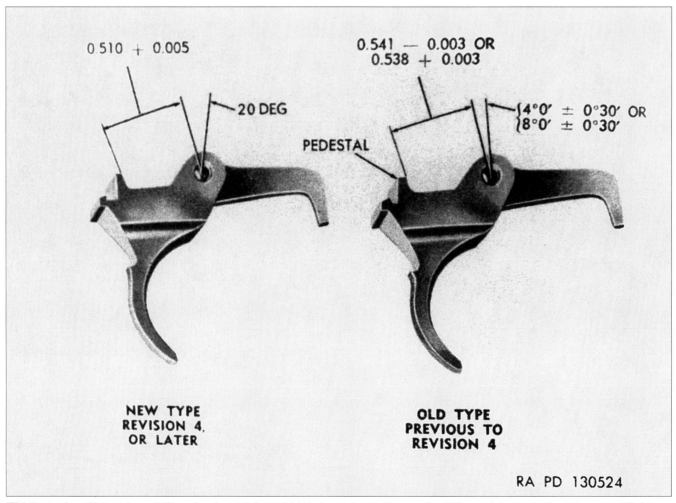

TM illustration of later trigger (left) and early style trigger (right). As can be readily seen, the difference between the two types are subtle in nature and can be hard to discern without very close examination.

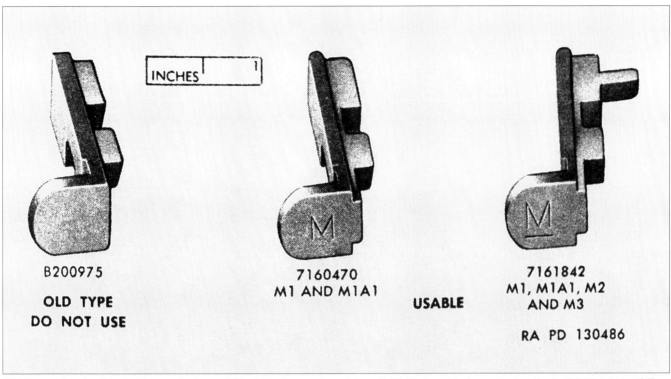

TM illustration showing the three major types of "short face" magazine catches: (Left) First variety (unmarked on face), (Middle) Later "M" marked type, (Right) Final variant (marked M) with lug on right side to support the extra weight of the 30-round magazine.

Magazine Catch

Although the basic design of the magazine catch, unlike the safety, was not changed, there were several variations of this part. There is some inconsistency in today's collector designations for the various types of magazine catches. As is normally the case, such designations as "Type 1," "Type 2," etc. are strictly present day collector shorthand and never were official terms. While other reference sources may designate the various magazine catches by other designations, for the purposes of this book, the following terms will be used:

Type 1: The first pattern magazine catch, which had a longer "face" than later versions and is logically referred to as a "long face" catch by many collectors. The earliest magazine catches of this type were serrated.

Type 2: This refers to "long face" magazine catches that had the serrations deleted.

Type 3: Eventually, the profile of the "face" changed to a less elongated profile or "short face" magazine catch.. Later "Type 3" magazine catches were stamped with a "M" on the face. The major difference between the "M" marked catches and the earlier type is a thinner "rail" profile.

Type 4: When the 30-round magazine was adopted, a small projection was added to the magazine catch to help support the magazine's greater weight. These are typically marked "M" on the face.

As can be seen, there are variations to be found within these categories. Some writers identify these as "Type 2A," etc. Again, such designations are strictly a means by which to identify and categorize particular variations.

Rear Sight

The carbine's rear sight came under some criticism due to its limited elevation settings of only 100 or 300 yards with no incremental adjustments possible. The lack of a windage adjustment was also seen as detrimental to the weapon's accuracy potential. The sight was probably sufficient for the carbine's intended purpose as a replacement for the pistol, but the utilization of the weapon in much the same role as a rifle made an improved rear sight desirable. A sight fully adjustable for windage and elevation was developed. Two variations of this sight, characterized by their method of construction (stamped or milled), were produced. These sights utilized the standard receiver dovetail base used by the original type of sights, and their replacement to the later variety was quite easy. The early non-

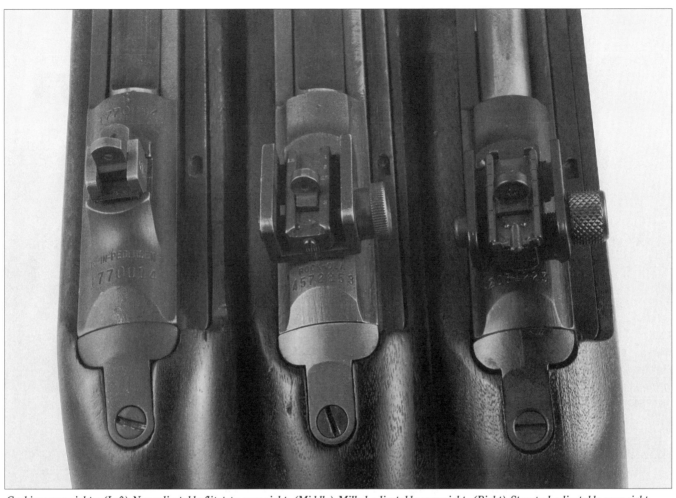

Carbine rear sights: (Left) Non-adjustable flip type rear sight, (Middle) Milled adjustable rear sight, (Right) Stamped adjustable rear sight.

Rear view of adjustable sights. (Left) Milled type, (Right) Stamped type.

adjustable sights are often called "L-type" for "flip" sights to distinguish them from the later adjustable variety. Not all makers changed to adjustable sights before the end of their production contracts. The specific types of sights used by each prime contractor are discussed later.

Front Sight

There were two basic types of carbine front sights, milled and stamped, characterized by their method of construction. Front sights made by some contractors can further be identified by certain machining differences. These include the so-called "thumb nail" front sights (so named because of the indention behind the sight blade caused by the method of routing the sight assembly during manufacture). The configuration of the front sight "key way" can also vary in sights made by different contractors. More information on the specific types and configuration of front sights is presented in the section covering the details of each prime contractor's carbines.

Operating Slide

There are six distinct types of carbine operating slides identified chiefly by the shape of the cam, the configuration of the "arm" joint, the profile of the rear of the box and the type of cam cut. These types are designated as:

E158. "Early" cam, intermediate size arm joint, rounded cut at rear of box, straight cam cut. Also referred to by some collectors as the "Type 1" slide.

E169. Same as E158 except the box cut is only partially rounded and the cam cut has a "heart shape" angle profile. Introduced circa early 1943. Not used by all makers. ("Type 2").

E279. Same as E169 except narrow arm joint and straight cut at rear of box. Appears to have come into use circa mid- to late 1943. Again, not used by all contractors. ("Type 3").

E379. Same as E279 but wide arm joint. This operating slide seems to have been introduced in very late 1943 or early 1944. Some are believed to have been subsequently modified to M2 configuration during postwar overhauls. ("Type 4").

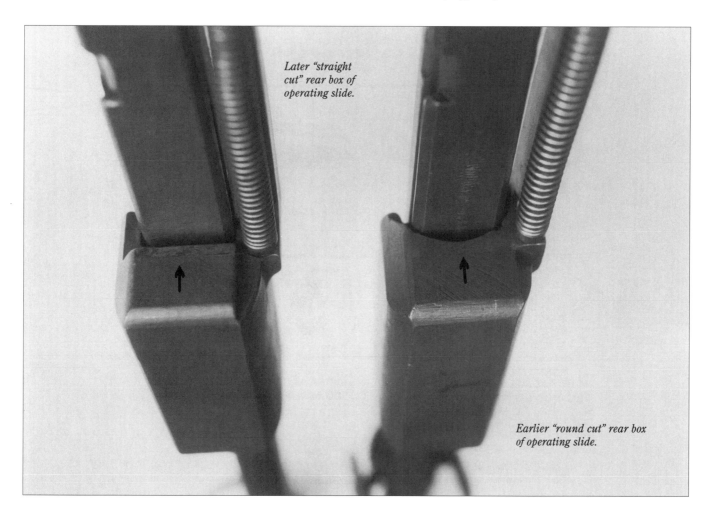

Later "straight cut" rear box of operating slide.

Earlier "round cut" rear box of operating slide.

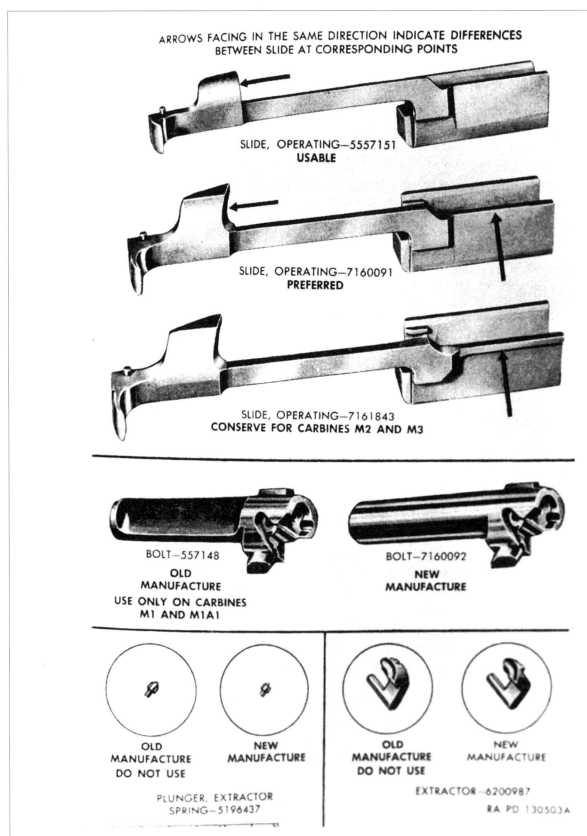

ARROWS FACING IN THE SAME DIRECTION INDICATE DIFFERENCES
BETWEEN SLIDE AT CORRESPONDING POINTS

SLIDE, OPERATING—5557151
USABLE

SLIDE, OPERATING—7160091
PREFERRED

SLIDE, OPERATING—7161843
CONSERVE FOR CARBINES M2 AND M3

BOLT—557148
**OLD
MANUFACTURE
USE ONLY ON CARBINES
M1 AND M1A1**

BOLT—7160092
**NEW
MANUFACTURE**

OLD
MANUFACTURE
DO NOT USE

NEW
MANUFACTURE

OLD
MANUFACTURE
DO NOT USE

NEW
MANUFACTURE

PLUNGER, EXTRACTOR
SPRING—5196437

EXTRACTOR—6200987

RA PD 130503A

*Illustration from U.S. Army Technical Manual (TM 9-1276) depicting the features of the
early and late operating slides, flat and round top bolts and extractors.*

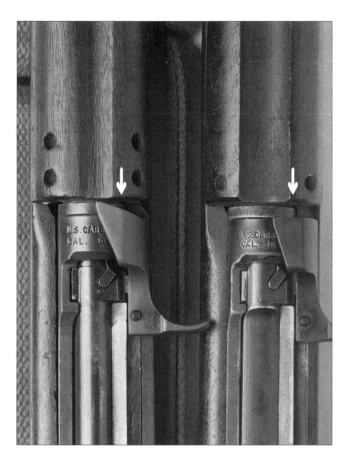

L379. Same as E379 but late cam. Came into use circa early 1944. Some examples will be found marked "7160091". It is believed that this slide was used only by Inland and Winchester carbines. ("Type 5").

L479. Same as L379 but arm joint has prominent ridges at back and top. This was the type of operating slide used on factory M2 carbines by Winchester and Inland. A number of these slides were marked "7161843". Many of these slides were used for postwar rebuilds and/or conversion from M1 to M2 specifications. ("Type 6").

The "Type 1" through "Type 6" designations are purely collector shorthand and were not the official nomenclature. Some collectors may refer to the various slides as "Type A," "Type B," etc.

Operating slides were typically stamped with the initials of the prime contractor and/or subcontractor. In addition to making sure a slide is properly coded, the

(Left) Top portion of later operating slide. (Right) Top portion of earlier pattern. This photo also clearly shows the narrow sighting groove on the four-rivet handguard at left and the wide sighting on the earlier two-rivet handguard at right, as well as the round top and flat top bolts.

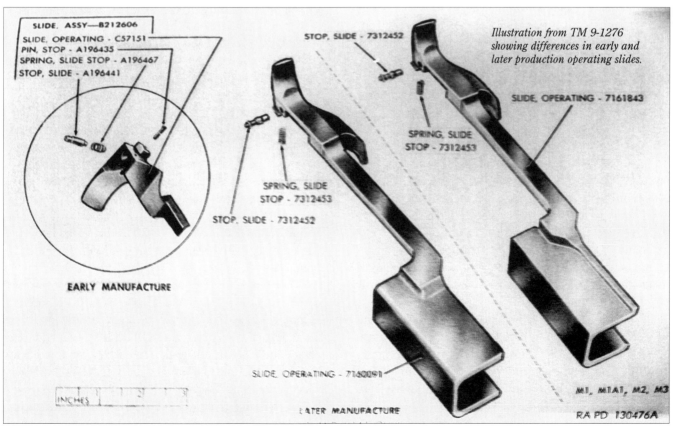

Illustration from TM 9-1276 showing differences in early and later production operating slides.

type should match the vintage of the carbine. For example, a L379 ("Type 5") slide would not be found on a supposedly original early 1943 vintage carbine. Information pertaining to the proper type of operating slide is presented in the section covering each prime contractor.

Bolt

There are two basic types of carbine bolts to consider: the "flat top" bolt and the type with a rounded top. This change was done primarily as a measure to reduce manufacturing time. Some people believe that the round bolt was adopted concurrently with the M2 carbine, but this was not the case. Several manufacturers began to incorporate round bolts into their M1 carbines well before the adoption of the M2. It is true, however, that the round bolt was used with the M2 carbine and probably provided slightly better operation than the flat top bolt for fully automatic firing. The round top bolt will also have a small "lube hole" on the bottom. Some later production flat bolts will have locking lugs with a pointier profile than the typical rounded shape lug found on the early and mid-production bolts. A very early carbine shouldn't have a bolt with a pointed shaped lug even if it is properly coded.

As originally manufactured, all carbine bolts, flat top and round, were blued. As these items were subjected to overhaul, many were parkerized. One of the hallmarks of an original WWII carbine is the presence of a blued bolt. A carbine that may appear otherwise correct but with a parkerized bolt should be examined very carefully as the odds are high that it has had some degree of restoration work performed on it.

Barrel

There were two basic types of carbine barrels. The so-called "Type 1" was used by Winchester and a few other contractors. This type of barrel is characterized by an integral gas cylinder. The "Type 2" barrel, which was used by the majority of contractors, utilized a separate gas cylinder that was swaged on. Extremely early Inland carbines had gas cylinders that were held in place by a metal pin. This very scarce variant was only in use for a short period of time.

In addition to the type of gas cylinder attachment (integral or swaged on), carbine barrels are also characterized by what was officially designated as the "spacer" but which is typically referred to by collectors today as a long or short "skirt" at the rear portion of the barrel. The early "long skirts" encircled almost ⅔ of the bolt (when in closed position). It was eventually determined

that the barrels with the long spacers were sometimes damaged in this area and a barrel with a smaller spacer ("short skirt") was developed. Some of the earlier barrels have been observed with the long spacers cut down to short spacer size in order to salvage barrels that had been damaged in this area. The various contractors changed from long spacer to short spacer barrels at different times but by the middle of 1944 the short skirt variety was in use exclusively.

All carbine barrels were stamped with the identification of the contractor and many were also marked with the Ordnance Department's "flaming bomb" insignia. Some, but not all, were also marked with the date of production. Some carbine prime contractors made their own barrels, and others utilized barrels obtained from either a subcontractor or another prime contractor. Buffalo Arms Corporation and Marlin Firearms Company were subcontractors that produced carbine barrels during WWII. Early Buffalo Arms barrels were marked "BA" while later barrels were marked "Buffalo Arms". The company stamped their carbine barrels with the date of production. Marlin stamped their barrels with just the name of the company (i.e., "Marlin"). Two different size Marlin markings have been observed. After World War II, Springfield Armory manufactured a number of carbine barrels for replacement purposes. The "SA" barrels would be properly found on an overhauled carbine but would not be correct for an "as issued" WWII example. Specific marking details are given in the sections detailing each prime contractor.

Barrel Band

Later in World War II, the need for a bayonet attachment for the carbine was voiced. Although the wisdom of equipping a weapon such as the M1 carbine with a bayonet can be debated, the using services nevertheless wished to have this feature added. A barrel band with an integral bayonet lug was developed as the "T4." A modified M3 trench knife was adopted as the "Bayonet-Knife, M4" for use with carbines equipped with the new T4 band. The M4 bayonet is discussed later.

There are actually three distinct types of barrel bands found on carbines. These have been dubbed "Type 1," "Type 2" and "Type 3" by collectors today. Such designations are strictly collector "shorthand" and are not official designations. The original type of barrel band, and the most commonly used on WWII carbines, was the so-called "Type 1." This type is characterized by a narrow band that was retained by the band spring. This band did not always properly secure the barrel to

Typical markings on carbine barrel made by Buffalo Arms. This example was made in September 1943. The marking is unusual in that the year "1943" is fully marked rather than the last two digits ("43") as was normally done. The rough machining marks are visible in this photo. Note also the manner of staking the front sight.

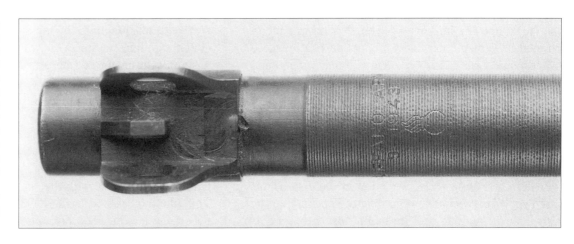

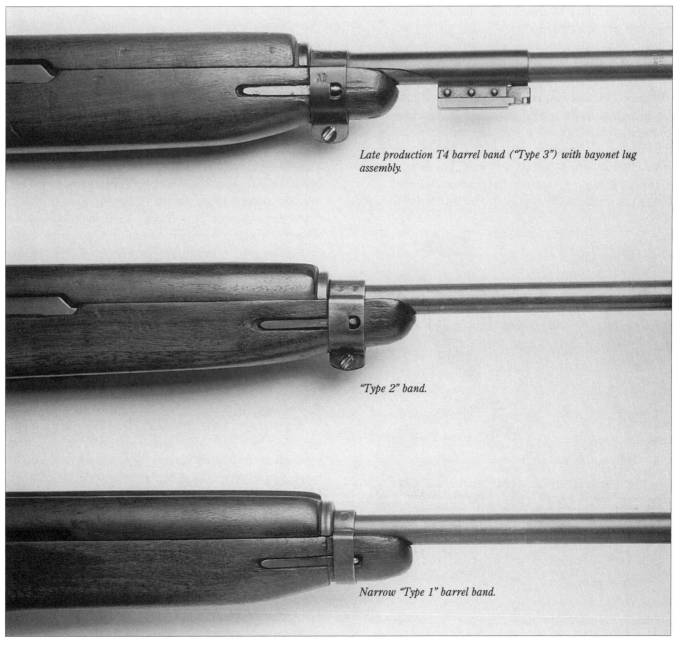

Late production T4 barrel band ("Type 3") with bayonet lug assembly.

"Type 2" band.

Narrow "Type 1" barrel band.

the stock, and the improved "Type 2" band was incorporated later in the carbine's production run by some prime contractors. This type had a much wider band that better secured the barrel. Relatively few "Type 2" bands were used. The T4 ("Type 3") band was similar to the "Type 2" but had the added feature of the attached bayonet lug. Only Inland and Winchester used the "Type 3" band in production carbines, although it was retrofitted to earlier carbines during postwar overhaul.

There are some variances found in the dimensions on "Type 1" barrel bands regarding the opening on the swivel for the sling to pass through. Most early production carbines had a narrower opening than later swivels but specific data is uncertain. Some swivels were stamped with code markings.

Hammer

There were four basic types of hammers utilized on carbines. The first two early variants have been termed by collectors as "dog leg" hammers to describe their configuration compared to the later varieties. The first type of dog leg hammer can be identified by a vertical slot milled into the top of the hammer. The second style ("Type 2") dog leg hammer has a flat area milled into the top rather than the slot. A sub-variant of the second

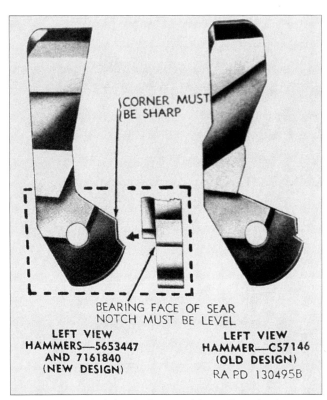

TM illustration depicting the later straight configuration hammer (left) and the Earlier "dog leg" hammer (right).

style with machining to the left side has been noted but not enough information is known to give further details. A significant change occurred with the introduction of the so-called "Type 3" hammer, which has a straighter contour than the earlier dog leg hammers. This change was presumably done to increase the force of the hammer without increasing the trigger pull. These hammers began to show up in production carbines in the fall of 1943. The fourth basic type of carbine hammer is the type adopted for use with the selective fire M2 carbine. This hammer can be easily identified by the relief cut necessary for the M2's disconnector. Specific information on the early and later hammers is presented subsequently.

Sear

The primary difference is in the presence of a hole in the center of the top area of the sear. The hole is present in the later variants but is not found in the earlier sears. These have been called "Type 1" sears (no hole in the rear center area) or "Type 2" sears (with a hole or grinding mark in this area). The sear utilized with the M2 carbine was different in configuration than the M1 carbine sears. The M2 sear could be used with the M1 carbine, but the reverse was not true. Sears were normally marked with contractor codes, so it is important to observe this part to be certain that it is properly coded.

Sear Spring

There were two basic types of sear springs characterized by the configuration of the ends. "Type 1" sear spring had straight ends whereas "Type 2" had tapered ends. The sear springs were not stamped with any code markings. Blued and unfinished springs have been observed.

Extractor

Early carbine extractors (a.k.a. "Type 1") can be identified by a V-shaped notch which was eliminated as production continued. Some of the early "V notch" extractors were modified to the later style by grinding off a portion ("Type 2"). As production continued, new extractors of the later pattern were put into production ("Type 3"). Most extractors were originally blued, though a few case hardened extractors have been noted. When carbines were overhauled, it was common practice to parkerize many originally blued parts, including extractors. Therefore, a carbine that is purported to be 100 percent original and unaltered but which has a parkerized extractor is suspect. It may be the only part

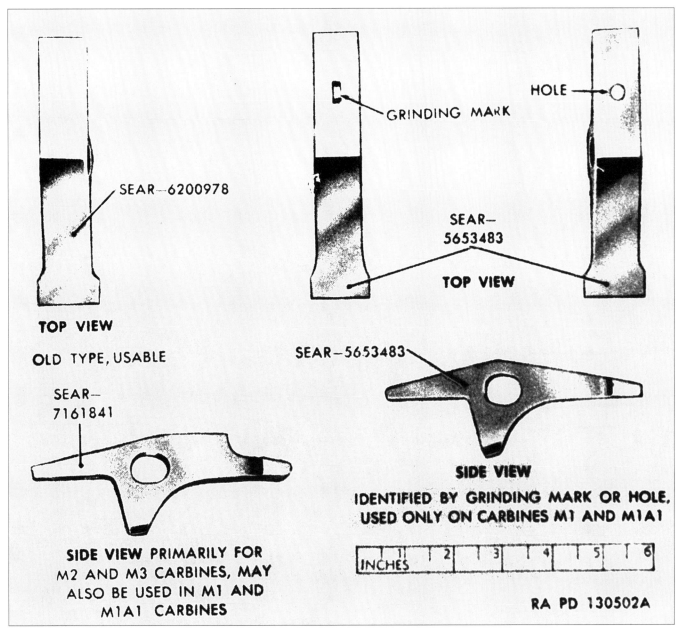

SEAR—6200978

TOP VIEW

OLD TYPE, USABLE

SEAR—7161841

SIDE VIEW PRIMARILY FOR M2 AND M3 CARBINES, MAY ALSO BE USED IN M1 AND M1A1 CARBINES

HOLE

GRINDING MARK

SEAR—5653483

TOP VIEW

SEAR—5653483

SIDE VIEW

IDENTIFIED BY GRINDING MARK OR HOLE, USED ONLY ON CARBINES M1 AND M1A1

INCHES 1 2 3 4 5 6

RA PD 130502A

TM illustration showing early sear with no hole and late type with hole.

that has been changed but any alteration raises the odds that the piece in question has undergone at least some other form of restoration. A seemingly unimportant feature such as an extractor can sometimes provide valuable clues to the authenticity of a particular carbine.

Extractor Plunger

There were two types of extractor plungers, which differed in their configuration on the front profile. "Type 1" extractors had a rounded or sharp pointed end. "Type 2" was similar but had a portion of the front tip ground

away to reduce the tendency of the plunger to become disengaged from the bolt. Some contractors modified "Type 1" plungers into "Type 2" configuration. Extractor plungers were not stamped with code markings. Original extractor plungers were blued. Parkerized or other finishes indicate a non-original part.

Firing Pin

There are three distinct types of carbine firing pins. The first pattern ("Type 1") can be identified by the flat profile on the area that came into contact with the ham-

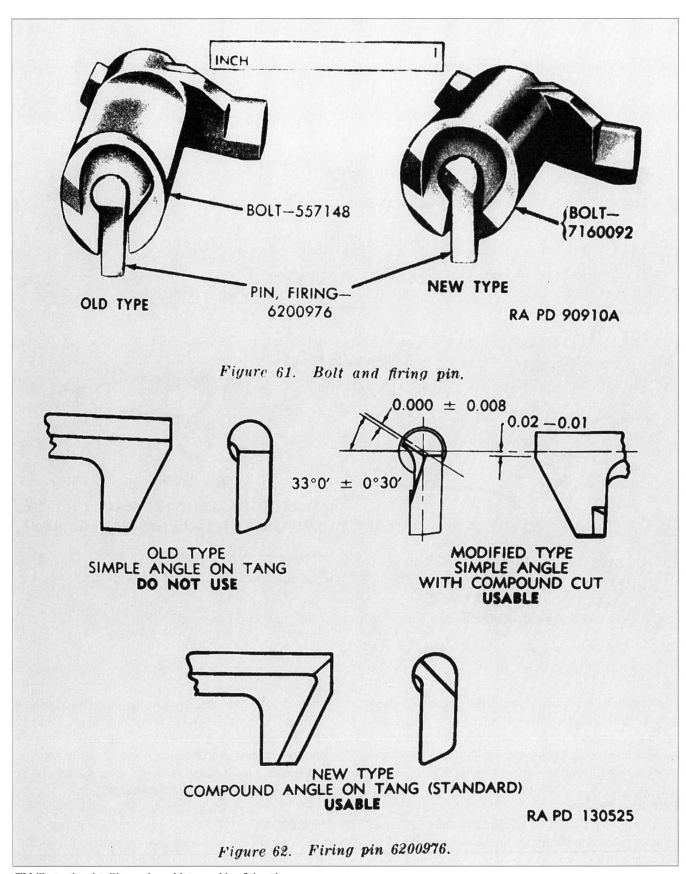

INCH

BOLT—557148

{BOLT—7160092

PIN, FIRING—6200976

OLD TYPE

NEW TYPE

RA PD 90910A

Figure 61. Bolt and firing pin.

OLD TYPE
SIMPLE ANGLE ON TANG
DO NOT USE

0.000 ± 0.008

$0.02 - 0.01$

$33°0' \pm 0°30'$

MODIFIED TYPE
SIMPLE ANGLE
WITH COMPOUND CUT
USABLE

NEW TYPE
COMPOUND ANGLE ON TANG (STANDARD)
USABLE

RA PD 130525

Figure 62. Firing pin 6200976.

TM illustration detailing early and later carbine firing pins.

mer. A second type, adopted in the latter part of 1943, provided for greater clearance between the firing pin and hammer by relieving part of the left side of the firing pin. Initially, these second-type firing pins were made by modifying the original pattern. The modified firing pins are referred to by some collectors today as the "Type 2." In the spring of 1944, this modification was incorporated into new production firing pins along with a change in the angle of the left portion. The newly made improved firing pins are generally designated as the "Type 3." As is the case with most other parts, firing pins were normally marked with the initials of the prime contractor and/or the subcontractor. Some early firing pins were unmarked.

Buttplates

The buttplate is frequently all but ignored when evaluating the correctness of a particular carbine. There is often only a cursory glance to determine if the general condition of the buttplate matches the rest of the weapon. Actually, some original carbines in excellent condition may be found with somewhat worn buttplates due to the practice of placing the butt on the ground. Since the carbine's buttplate was made of thin stamped metal, it wouldn't take much to deform or scratch the item. On the other hand, a well-used carbine with a pristine buttplate is very suspect.

In addition to observing the general condition, it should be noted that there were rather subtle but discernible differences found in the buttplates used by some prime contractors. The differences are primarily in the pattern of checkering and the sharpness of the "diamonds" or "dimples." Most contractors did not stamp their buttplates with code markings, and this lack of markings makes positive identification often difficult. An incorrect buttplate is a relatively minor flaw that can probably be corrected rather easily. One handy tip to remember: remove the buttplate and observe the impressions made into the wood covered by the plate. If the pattern impressed into the wood is not the same as the pattern found on the buttplate, you can be sure that the buttplate has been replaced. While this may not mean anything other than that the buttplate has been replaced, *any* changes increase the probability that the piece has had other "restoration" work done on it.

Recoil Plate and Recoil Plate Screw

Three basic types of recoil plates exist. "Type 1" was used only on very early production carbines and did not allow the receiver to seat securely in the stock. In early to mid-1942, the contour of the recoil plate was changed to provide better seating ("Type 2"). By mid-1943, the contour was again changed by milling out more of the area where the receiver tang seated into the recoil plate ("Type 3"). This further secured the receiver to the stock and provided for better accuracy since the receiver was less likely to shift as the weapon recoiled. Most recoil plates were coded, so this item should be removed from the stock and examined whenever possible prior to consummating a purchase.

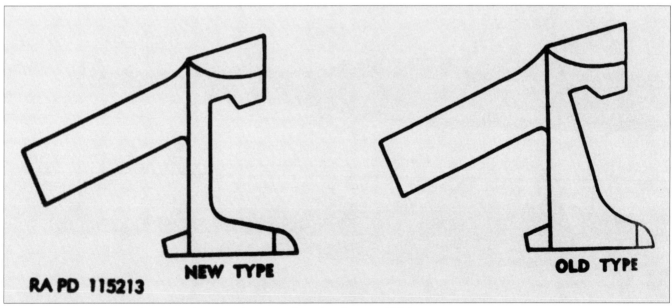

RA PD 115213   NEW TYPE   OLD TYPE

TM illustration showing configuration of later recoil plate (left) and earlier type (right).

Two basic styles of recoil plate screws will be found. The first type was threaded only on the bottom portion that fit into the recoil plate. The second type was completely threaded for the entire length of the screw. The partially threaded type is, by far, the most commonly encountered. It is likely that the fully threaded screw was not used during WWII by any prime contractor and was installed as a postwar replacement part during overhaul. Any supposedly all original carbine with a fully threaded recoil plate screw should be looked at very closely.

Stock and Handguard

The configuration of the stock also changed as carbine production continued. The section of wood covering the operating slide was rather thin and could easily become cracked or otherwise damaged. It was eventually determined that the weakness could be eliminated by enlarging this area on new production stocks. As the older stocks were overhauled, the high wood section was generally removed to prevent future damage. Collectors have designated the early, unmodified stocks as "high wood" and the later type as "low wood." Again, such terms are strictly unofficial collector designations but are useful in identifying the type of stock in question.

Another difference between early and later production stocks is the configuration of the oiler recess. From the beginning of production until sometime in early 1943 (depending on contractor), the top and bottom of the oiler recess were flared. The original purpose of this recess configuration was to accommodate an oiler, which

was intended for use with the carbine but was not adopted. The standard oiler was used instead, however, the tooling for the stock recess cutout was not changed for some time. Eventually, an oval-shaped oiler recess was incorporated and used for the duration of production. Collectors today have dubbed the early type of stock as the "I-cut" (in recognition of the shape of the recess) and "oval cut" for the later variety. Most manufacturers used the "I-cut" stocks and changed to oval type as production continued. Specific information on the stocks used by each prime contractor is presented later.

On stocks manufactured by (or for) some prime contractors, there may be rather subtle differences in the configuration. The most noteworthy of these is discussed individually later in this book.

The initials of the subcontractor that produced the stock and the prime contractor were normally stamped inside of the sling recess on the left side of the stock. Occasionally, other markings such as a "flaming bomb", etc. will also be found. Many early to mid-production carbines will have stocks with the initials of the prime contractor (and some also with head of the contractor's ordnance district) stamped in a cartouche on the right side. Except for some early Inlands, virtually all stocks were also stamped with the "crossed cannons" Ordnance Department escutcheon on the right side. This marking was sometimes lightly stamped and can be easily obscured by wear and refinishing. Stocks with the proper markings are quite desirable and some fakes may be encountered.

One sometimes overlooked stock component is the

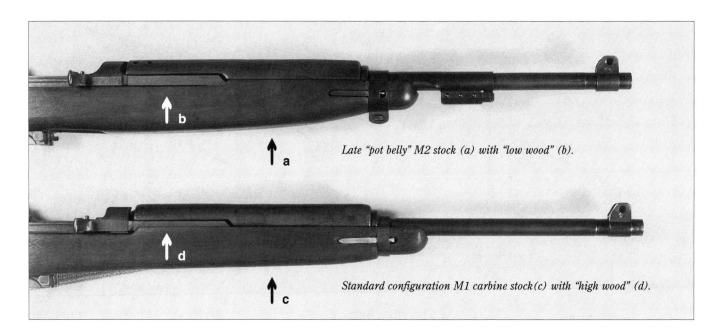

Late "pot belly" M2 stock (a) with "low wood" (b).

Standard configuration M1 carbine stock (c) with "high wood" (d).

escutcheon into which the recoil plate screw fastens. The original type of stock escutcheon had a short spline which was replaced by an escutcheon with a longer spline circa 1944. Since removal of the escutcheon is extremely difficult (without ruining the stock), this feature is rarely a problem when considering the originality of a carbine stock.

There were two basic variations of carbine handguards. They are characterized by the number of rivets. Early handguards utilized two rivets while the later variety had four. There was also some variance in the configuration and depth of the channel on top of the handguard in the early two-rivet models. More information on the specific details follows in the discussion of each prime contractor.

Some parts such as the ejector spring, ejector plunger spring, gas piston, operating slide spring, operating slide spring guide were relatively unchanged throughout the carbine's production run. Such parts will not normally be discussed in this book since they are not terribly significant when evaluating the originality of a particular carbine as compared to many of the other parts. A number of the other components of the carbine including pins and some springs will be given only cursory mention due the relative lack of importance as compared to most other parts. This is not to imply that there were not any differences found in such items since there often were. For example, the original type of hammer spring had 22 coils but some later variants had 26 coils. Likewise, there were differences in the configuration of some trigger springs, trigger housing retaining pins, magazine catch and safety plunger assemblies, ejectors operating slide stop, operating slide spring housing hammer pin and hammer spring plunger (among others). Realistically speaking, someone probably isn't going to disassemble a carbine at a gun show and count the number of coils in the hammer spring. This doesn't mean that such parts should be totally ignored but, rather, that there are more significant components to evaluate. However, some of these normally less consequential parts may be discussed if they play a significant part in determining if a carbine may or may not be original.

It should not be inferred that the above components were the only ones changed during the carbine's production run. However, the above enumerated parts are perhaps the most significant, and the absence or presence of specific parts can easily help determine if a carbine remains in its original factory configuration or has been altered. Many of the above changes were done late

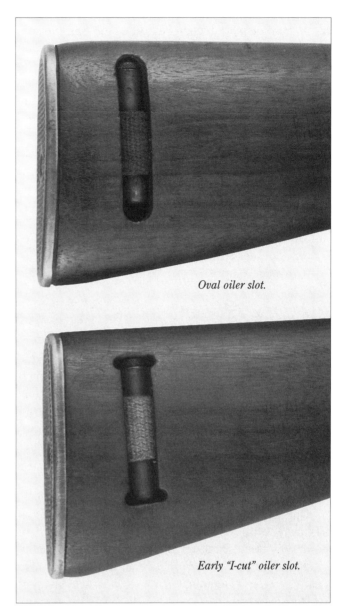

Oval oiler slot.

Early "I-cut" oiler slot.

"Crossed cannons" escutcheon found on virtually all original WWII M1 carbine stocks.

in the carbine's production run. After the war, the vast majority of carbines in inventory were overhauled, and the improved components were installed as part of the rebuild procedure. Therefore, most of the carbines seen today have these later features. Carbines remaining in their original WWII factory configuration are quite desirable and will normally bring substantial premiums over the typical arsenal rebuilt carbines. The desirability of unaltered carbines has resulted in many instances of collectors attempting to restore overhauled weapons to the original factory configuration. Early parts such as "Type 1" barrel bands, "L-type" flip sights, flat top blued bolts and high wood stocks are all eagerly sought after by collectors for restoration purposes.

As stated, a properly restored carbine is a desirable collector's item, but it is not as valuable or sought after as an all original example. Unfortunately, the problem of restored carbines being passed off as originals is rather widespread. As is the case with Garands, a person can restore a carbine with no larceny in mind and can disclose this information to a subsequent purchaser. However, if the weapon should change hands again, the new seller may not disclose the fact that the weapon has been restored to the new buyer in order to bring a higher price. It is not uncommon for a seller to claim that the carbine he is trying to dispose of was carried ashore by his grandfather at Normandy or was brought back from Iwo Jima by an marine in his duffel bag. The old collector's adage is always apropos: "Don't buy the story, buy the gun."

➤ ➤ ➤ ➤ Accessories and Accouterments ◄ ◄ ◄ ◄ ◄

There were many fascinating accessories and related items produced for the carbine that can add much interest and color to a collection. Finding collectible accessories can be almost as rewarding as turning up new carbines. Many of these are well covered in the two *War Baby* books by Larry L. Ruth, which are recommended for beginning and advanced collectors.

Ammunition

One often overlooked but quite interesting item associated with the carbine is ammunition. There were numerous plants involved in producing carbine ammunition during and after World War II. Perhaps the most desirable types of ammunition are the 50-round boxes of cartridges as produced from 1941 to 1945. Ball, dummy (for training), tracer (M16 and M27) and grenade launching ammunition (M6) was produced in 50-round cartons by several contractors including Winchester Repeating Arms Co., Western Cartridge Co., Lake City Ordnance Plant, Kings Mills Ordnance Plant and Evansville Ordnance Plant (steel case cartridges). Especially desirable are the sealed metal cans (often called "spam cans" by collectors) containing sixteen 50-round boxes (800 rounds total). M6 grenade launching cartridges were packed in either 50-round or 6-round cartons. Late in the war, ten round chargers ("stripper clips") in web bandoleers were produced for the 30-round magazines. The nomenclature of the ammunition and name of the contractor were stenciled on the outside of the bandoleer. Any type of "GI" carbine ammunition remaining in its factory boxing is an excellent addition to a collection and should be obtained whenever possible if priced reasonably. At one time, surplus GI carbine ammunition rivaled .22 rimfire for plinking fodder but such ammunition is now quite expensive as well as desirable collector material.

Magazines

Another sometimes neglected carbine related accessory is the magazine. While still quite common, prices have started to rise significantly due in large measure to recent federal restrictions on high capacity rifle magazines. The 15-round magazines were made under subcontract and were generally marked with the initials of the prime contractor and subcontractor. Many collectors desire to have magazines coded with the initials of the prime contractor that made the carbine into which a magazine is placed. This is a nice touch, but in actual service such a match would have been strictly a matter of coincidence. Magazines made by some of the prime contractors, most notably Irwin-Pedersen can be somewhat difficult to locate. There were several minor variations found in 15-round carbine magazines that pertain primarily to the configuration of the floor plate. The two basic configurations were a flat bottom plate and an indented bottom plate.

Late in WWII, a 30-round magazine was developed mainly for the selective fire M2 carbine. By the time of this magazine's mass production, the only prime contractors still in operation were Inland and Winchester. Many of the 30-round magazines were only marked with the name of the maker and not the prime contractor.

(Below, left) 15-round magazine with flat floor plate.

(Below, right) 15-round magazine with indented floor plate.

30-round magazine.

15-round magazine.

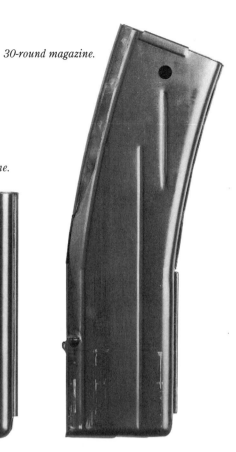

*Grouping of various carbine ammunition including ball, dummy, M16 tracer, M27 tracer and M6 grenade launching.
At center is a sealed metal can of 800 ball cartridges.*

Typical magazine code marking. This example was made for Irwin-Pedersen.

Thirty-round magazines were also put back into production after World War II. An improved follower was used in the 30-round magazines.

As originally made, all GI carbine magazines were blued. Some parkerized examples may be encountered but these have been refinished. Interestingly, many carbine magazines were overhauled by ordnance depots . The overhaul process for carbine magazines often included parkerizing and installation of the improved follower. Parkerized carbine magazines would be properly found on postwar carbines as few, if any, are believed to have been issued during WWII. Ten round chargers to assist in loading the extended capacity 30-round magazines were issued.

Magazine Pouches

Not all carbine accessories are expensive or elusive items. One common, but quite interesting, accessory is the pouch issued to carry magazines. There are several distinct variants that were produced by numerous manufacturers. The first pattern pouch was constructed of canvas material and designed to carry two 15-round carbine magazines in separate pockets and had a cover flap secured by a "lift the dot" fastener. Most examples were made of a khaki colored material and stamped with "US" in black ink on the outside of the cover flap and with the identity of the maker and the year of production inside. "1942" and "1943" dates have been observed. This pouch is characterized by a wide belt loop with a snap inside to enable it to be secured to the corresponding snap on a standard pistol belt. It was soon discovered that the wide belt loop could fit on the carbine's buttstock. This practice quickly became very popular among combat soldiers of WWII, although the pouch was not designed for this use. Collectors today should note that the snap inside the belt loop can mar the stock.

The second variant carbine magazine pouch was similar in most respects to the first version but had two narrow belt loops rather than the single wide loop. This precluded the pouch from being installed on the stock. The second pattern pouch was the most widely produced type and huge numbers were made from circa 1943 until the end of the war. The pouch was put back into production several times after WWII, and examples dated well into the late 1950s (and later) may be observed. In addition to being able to carry two 15-round carbine magazines, these pouches could be utilized to carry two 8-round Garand clips instead. Early examples of this pouch were made of khaki colored web material, often with contrasting piping. Later variants were made of darker olive green material. As with the first pattern, the cover flap was stamped "US" on the outside with the name of the maker and year of production inside.

An interesting and little-known type of carbine magazine pouch is the so-called "paratrooper pouch" or "rigger made" pouch. These pouches were fabricated by Army Air Corps personnel for issue to airborne troops early in WWII. The Air Corps was responsible for much of the equipment of the paratroopers early in the war. The need to carry more ammunition on the pistol belt than was permitted by the standard two pocket carbine magazine pouch resulted in the procurement of this item. This pouch's official Air Corps nomenclature was "Holder-Rifle Clip (Short)." The "rigger made" pouches were designed to carry four 15-round carbine magazines

WWII carbine magazine pouches: (left) scarce "rigger made" pouch for airborne troops. (middle) first pattern pouch with single wide belt loop and snap fastener. This is the type that could be attached to the stock. (Bottom) Later pattern with two narrow belt loops. This pattern was made during WWII and was also saw postwar production.

U.S. Army mortar 60mm team. Note the M1 carbine (with stock pouch attached) carried by the soldier at right center.

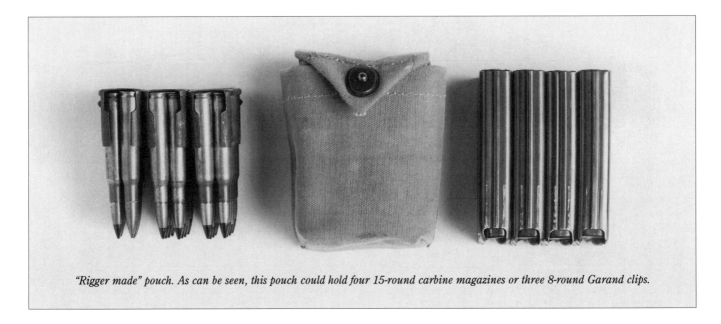

"Rigger made" pouch. As can be seen, this pouch could hold four 15-round carbine magazines or three 8-round Garand clips.

in about the same space on the belt as the standard two pocket variety. This was accomplished by having the magazines lie perpendicular to the body rather than parallel as on the standard pouches, thus twice as many magazines could be carried on the belt. These pouches could also carry three 8-round Garand clips in place of the four carbine magazines. The "rigger made" pouches were generally constructed on khaki material with a single "lift the dot" fastener and a wide belt loop on back. Slightly later variants made of somewhat darker green material have been observed. The only markings typically found on the pouches is the Air Corps" stock number ("42B15006") stamped in black ink on back of the belt loop.

As compared to the standard carbine magazine pouches, the "rigger made" pouches exhibited rather crude workmanship but were entirely serviceable items. Although almost unheard of today, these pouches were widely issued to paratroopers early in the war. One of the first uses of this item was during the Sicily campaign. A similar (and much rarer) pouch was also made to carry 20-round Thompson submachine gun magazines. The "rigger made" pouches are certainly the hardest to find and generally the most expensive variety of carbine magazine pouches.

With the adoption of the 30-round magazine, a pouch was required to carry these extended capacity magazines. One was adopted that held two 30-round magazines with sufficient space to carry extra 10-round chargers. Several minor variations of this pouch exist, but relatively few of these pouches were procured during WWII. Most will be found with postwar (1950s or later)

dates. Some collectors assume that these pouches were designed to carry four 30-round magazines. While some 4-round capacity pouches have been reported, most were designed to carry only two magazines plus extra chargers. Attempting to force four magazines in these pouches is generally unsuccessful and has caused more than one beginning collector to scratch his head in frustration after having been told that these pouches should hold four magazines. The World War II dated pouches of this type are rather scarce and usually more expensive than the more common post-WWII variety.

Collecting carbine magazine pouches is a good way to assemble an interesting array of reasonably priced carbine ancillary items. Due to the large number of pouches in circulation and the rather modest prices, fakes have not been a problem. The cost required to produce a bogus pouch would not be worthwhile given the current low market price. Other than the "rigger made" pouches and, to a lesser extent, the WWII dated 30-round pouches, carbine magazine pouches are usually easy to obtain at reasonable prices.

Carrying Cases

In order to transport and protect the carbine, a canvas carrying case was issued. Very early examples were made of khaki colored material while slightly later versions were constructed of darker olive green canvas. The case had a zipper opening with leather tabs on both ends and an adjustable web shoulder sling. The outside was stamped with a "US" in black ink and the maker's name and year of production were marked inside. Such carrying cases were also produced in the postwar era.

Few of these carrying cases were utilized in the field.

A special padded canvas carrying case for the folding stock M1A1 carbine was produced and issued to airborne troops armed with this weapon. This case was attached to the paratrooper's pistol belt, and the bottom end secured to the leg with an adjustable strap. The M1A1 carbine (with the stock folded) was inserted into the case. The idea was to have the carbine instantly available when the paratrooper completed his descent. The inside of the case was padded to protect the carbine. Early examples were made of khaki colored canvas material and subsequent variants were made of darker olive green material. The case was secured by a cover flap with a "lift the dot" fastener. The outside of the flap was marked "US", and the name of the maker and year of production were stamped inside. These pouches are highly desirable items and some fakes have been reported.

Another interesting, if slightly bizarre, belt scabbard was manufactured for the M1 carbine. This case attached to the pistol belt and was intended to hold the standard full stock carbine in much the same manner as

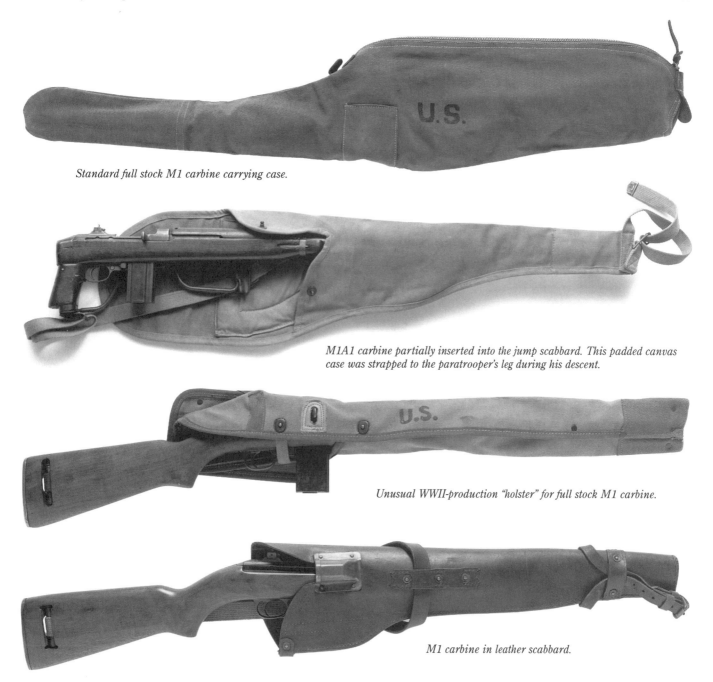

Standard full stock M1 carbine carrying case.

M1A1 carbine partially inserted into the jump scabbard. This padded canvas case was strapped to the paratrooper's leg during his descent.

Unusual WWII-production "holster" for full stock M1 carbine.

M1 carbine in leather scabbard.

a pistol. Apparently the fact that the carbine was originally intended to replace the pistol led to the misguided procurement of this item. Fairly large numbers were made but, mercifully, few (if any) were actually issued. While not extremely common today, most examples are found in excellent to new condition due to the fact that they weren't used to any great extent. The item is not pictured in any of the standard manuals for the carbine, but a line drawing of this scabbard attached to a pistol belt (along with an unknown type of magazine pouch) has been reproduced in at least one early WWII Quartermaster publication. Although not an item of widespread issue, the full stock belt scabbard nevertheless is an interesting addition to a carbine collection.

A fairly common but very popular carrying case for the carbine is the leather scabbard. This item is somewhat similar to the leather scabbard made for the M1 Garand rifle but differs in size and configuration. While originally intended for use with the horse cavalry, it was not used prior to such units being disbanded (or "dehorsed"). The scabbard had two metal snap hooks which allowed it to be attached to jeeps and other vehicles. The case was marked with the name of the maker

and year of production. Many of these cases are missing the attachment straps and/or metal buckles which detracts somewhat from their collector value. In decent condition, these are quite desirable items and are very popular with many collectors.

Slings and Oilers

A sometimes overlooked but very important carbine accessory is the sling. Since the carbine is actually incomplete without its sling and oiler, these items should be obtained whenever possible. While carbine slings are still very common today, the vast majority seen are of the post-World War II variety. Obviously, these would not be correct for display on a WWII vintage weapon. Reproduction and fake carbine slings abound on the market today, and the demand for original WWII vintage slings continues to be strong.

There are several features to look for when attempting to identify an original Second World War vintage carbine sling. The most important aspect is the configuration of the metal tab on the end of the sling. The WWII slings had a "C"-shaped (sometimes called "horseshoe") shaped metal tab. The post-WWII carbine slings utilized

A group of airborne troops inspecting a crashed glider. The trooper in the center has an M1A1 carbine slung over his shoulder.　　(Credit: U.S. Army)

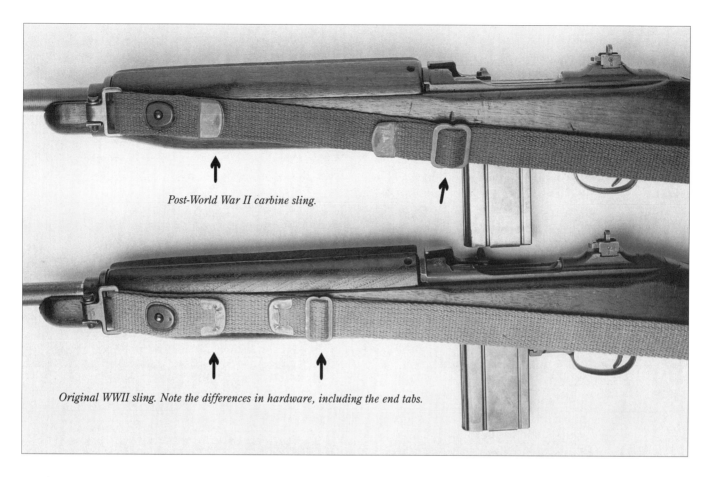

Post-World War II carbine sling.

Original WWII sling. Note the differences in hardware, including the end tabs.

a solid metal tab. This is a key point of identification between WWII and post-WWII slings. It has been reported that some of the solid tab slings were made very late in World War II, but this has not been adequately confirmed. Some of the better fakes will have the Second World War pattern "C shaped" tabs.

As is the case with most canvas or web goods, the early WWII carbine slings were made of a khaki colored material. This was changed to a darker olive green as the war progressed. Some, but by no means all, of the original carbine slings were marked (typically inside of the area enclosed by the snap fastener) with the date of production and/or the name or initials of the maker. Again, most fake slings will have this feature as well. There are subtle differences in the thickness and weave pattern of the original slings and many of the present day reproductions. If possible, a sling offered for sale and purported to be original should be compared closely to a known authentic carbine sling. Many attractive khaki carbine slings in new condition with bold date and manufacturer markings are around and most of these are fakes. A carbine sling in new condition could well be an original but any such item should be examined very closely. A well-worn original sling with no markings is

infinitely preferable to a new condition fake with pristine markings.

Original WWII carbine slings are surprisingly hard to find today and are highly sought after by collectors. The post-WWII slings are extremely common and inexpensive. These slings would be properly found only on carbines remaining in service after 1945, including any of the post-WWII rebuilds. Some slings for the Reising submachine gun have surfaced on the market over the past few years. Reising slings are very similar to carbine slings but have several important differences. These include a shorter length, different spacing of the snap fastener and, interestingly, a solid metal end tab as used on the post-WWII carbine slings. Many of the Reising slings are also marked "USMC" and stamped with the name of the maker and date of production ("Boyt" and "1943" are the most commonly seen). Some purveyors of militaria have offered Reising SMG slings for sale as "rare Marine Corps carbine slings." These slings are incorrect for use on carbines.

Oilers are often overlooked by some collectors. There is actually not a great deal of hard data available on oilers. The vast majority of the carbine oilers produced during WWII were manufactured by International Silver

Company. This subcontractor was assigned the code letter "I" for use on oilers. This should not be confused with the "I" code assigned to Inland. It appears that perhaps two other firms also made carbine oilers as some marked with "SW" and "BK" codes will be found. Both parkerized and blued oilers will be found. Early oilers had leather gaskets between the screw top and the body of the oiler, but this was soon changed to rubber.

Most of the oilers originally produced by International Silver for the carbine prime contractors were marked with the subcontractor code ("I") along with the prime contractor code. The following oiler codes have been observed:

> "II" — Inland
> "IW" — Winchester
> "IR" — Rock-Ola
> "IN" — National Postal Meter
> "IU" — Underwood
> "IQ" — Quality Hardware
> "ISP" — Standard Products

As production continued, the practice of stamping prime contractor codes ceased and just the initials of the subcontractor that actually manufactured the part was stamped on the oilers (i.e., "IS" for International Silver). Some prime contractors such as IBM and Saginaw Steering Gear (Saginaw plant) apparently used only the "IS" oilers. Many unmarked oilers may be found, but these are presumably post-WWII items.

Actually, a collector shouldn't get too hung up on the presence on a "incorrect" oiler. The absence of a "properly" coded oiler is not a major problem in an otherwise correct carbine. Since the time period when the "IS" coded oilers came into use exclusively is not known, there may be some question as to what constitutes the correct oiler. Generally speaking, the earlier the vintage of a carbine, the higher the odds it had a coded oiler, the two above exceptions notwithstanding. Properly coded oilers are not generally hard to find unless, of course, you need one! If an oiler marked with a prime contractor's code can be found at a reasonable price, buy it and tuck it away even if you don't need the item at the time. Such items can be good trading material.

The proper sling is also very important. An incorrect (post-WWII or commercial production) sling stands out like the proverbial sore thumb on an otherwise 100 percent correct carbine. It is actually preferable not to have a sling on a carbine at all than to put on the wrong type. As stated, caution should be exercised when contemplating the purchase of a carbine sling that appears in new or near new condition. It may be a collector's gem, but it could also be bogus.

M4 Bayonet

As discussed, the perceived need for a bayonet spurred the development and standardization of the "M4 Bayonet-Knife." Several prototype designs were tested prior to the decision to adopt a slightly modified version of the issue M3 trench knife with a modified guard

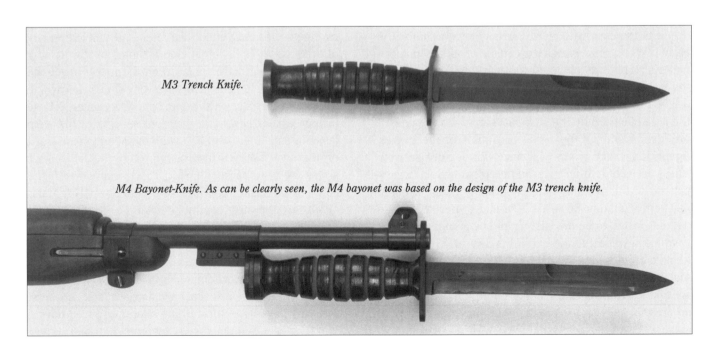

M3 Trench Knife.

M4 Bayonet-Knife. As can be clearly seen, the M4 bayonet was based on the design of the M3 trench knife.

which incorporated a barrel ring and a locking mechanism on the pommel. The original design was designated as the "T6," and improved variants were subsequently tested as the "T8" and "T8E1." In January 1944, the Infantry Board recommended adoption of the "T8E1." The recommendation was quickly approved, and the "M4 Bayonet-Knife" was standardized in April 1944. With the adoption of the M4, the M3 trench knife was officially replaced by the new bayonet. Since the M4 bayonet was essentially a modified M3 trench knife, it could serve the same purposes, and there was no need to continue production of the knife. However, the M3 stayed into service through the war.

The M4 bayonet was issued with the M8 and M8A1 scabbards. The M8 had been adopted in July 1943 to replace the leather M6 scabbards for use with the M3 trench knife. The M8 had a plastic (composition) body and a web belt loop for use on the pistol belt. The M8A1 was identical except it was fitted with metal hooks which enabled it to be carried on the cartridge belt as well as the pistol belt.

Although production began in July 1944, manufacture of the M4 bayonet did not get fully underway until September. A total of 2,260,519 M4 bayonets was produced by the time production contracts were canceled in August 1945. Even though well over two million M4 bayonets were made during WWII, relatively few were issued since the bayo-

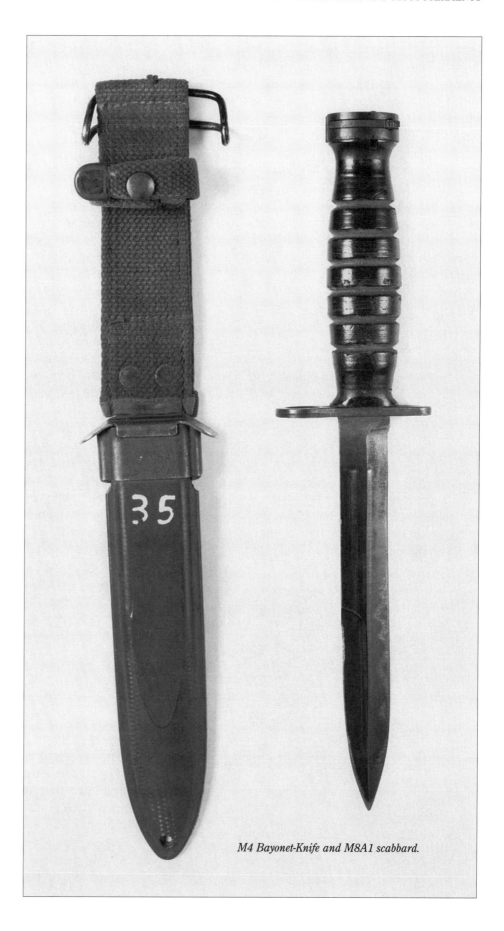

M4 Bayonet-Knife and M8A1 scabbard.

nets did not get into the hands of our troops overseas until the latter stages of the war. The M4 was issued to soldiers armed with the latest pattern carbines that had the T4 barrel band and was also issued to troops armed with weapons other than carbines. The M4 saw widespread issue for many years after World War II.

Even though the wisdom of fitting the carbine with a bayonet can be debated, the M4 bayonet was a popular item. As pointed out by an Ordnance Department document following the end of the war. "The Bayonet-Knife, M4…which could readily substitute for a pocket knife on occasion, in addition to its manifold uses as a bayonet or a trench knife…was the outstanding development of its field of World War II."

A number of firms produced the M4 bayonet during WWII. These companies were:

(1) Imperial
(2) Case
(3) American Cutlery Co.
(4) Camillus
(5) Utica
(6) Aerial
(7) Kinfolks, Inc.
(8) Pal Cutlery

The name of the maker was stamped on the guard, and an ordnance "flaming bomb" marking was commonly applied to the top of the hilt. As originally produced, the M4 bayonet, like the M3 trench knife, had a grooved

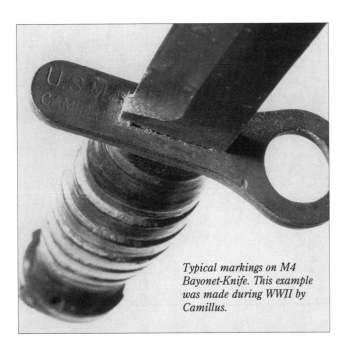

Typical markings on M4 Bayonet-Knife. This example was made during WWII by Camillus.

leather grip. The leather was prone to deterioration and often had to be replaced. Overhauled M4 bayonets with plastic, rubber or, occasionally, wooden grips may be encountered. These have obviously been modified from their original factory configuration and would be correct for display with an rebuilt carbine. During the Vietnam war era, the government procured a number of M4 bayonets which had plastic grips similar to those used on the M5, M6 and M7 bayonets. Some commercial production M4 bayonets will also be encountered from time to time. These typically exhibit somewhat cruder workmanship than the government issue items. The firm of Camillus has recently produced many reproduction M4 bayonets as well as M3 trench knives. The company was one of the original manufacturers of the M4 during the war. The newly made reproductions are well crafted but differ from the originals in minor respects. It is possible that one of these could be passed off as a mint original WWII Camillus bayonet or one could be artificially aged to resemble a fifty-year-old bayonet. Camillus M4 bayonets (and M3 trench knives) should be scrutinized very closely if purported to be original Second World War examples. On the other hand, there are many original Camillus bayonets available on the market today but a little more caution should be exercised when examining bayonets by this maker. The overhauled M4 bayonets are interesting collectibles but do not have the value of original, unaltered WWII bayonets.

M8 scabbards are relatively uncommon today and are sought after by collectors for use with M3 trench knives as well as M4 bayonets. The M8A1 scabbards are common and finding a nice example shouldn't be a problem. Later (and the most common) versions of the M8A1 scabbard have a metal reinforcing tab at the bottom where the thong hole is located.

Manuals

There were numerous field (FM) and technical (TM) manuals issued for the carbine. The hardest to find, as well as the most valuable, are original World War II vintage manuals in nice condition. The postwar carbines manuals (dated in the 1950s and later) are more commonly found but still make nice additions to a collection. It is interesting to note that manuals continued to be printed at least through the late 1970s, over thirty years after the carbine was out of production. The fact that the carbine was widely used in Vietnam and many Latin American nations (along with other allies) resulted in its service period being extended much longer than most other WWII-vintage U.S. small arms.

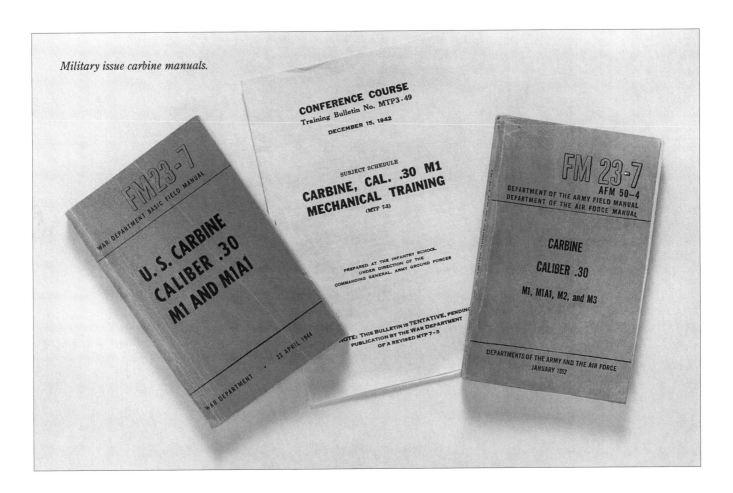

Military issue carbine manuals.

There are large numbers of commercially reprinted carbine manuals available today. While these are fine for obtaining information on detail stripping and etc., such items do not have any value as martial collectibles. The original GI carbine manuals often do not cost a great deal more than some of the reprints and will retain their value as the years go by. As is the case with many of the items discussed, one does not have to hit the lottery to assemble an interesting collection of auxiliary carbine items. The proper original manual accompanying a carbine is a nice and inexpensive touch.

M8 Grenade Launcher

As the carbine saw increasing combat use during WWII, the military determined that a grenade launcher would be of immense value. The fact that the Garand's M7 launcher rendered that weapon incapable of firing semiautomatically with the launcher attached added to te desirability of a grenade launcher for the carbine.

The carbine's gas system made the task of designing a suitable grenade launcher much easier than was the case with the Garand rifle. A launcher similar to the M1 launcher used with the M1903 rifle was developed for the carbine. This launcher clamped to the end of the barrel and fastened behind the front sight by a wing nut. Since venting excess gas was not necessary due to the design of the carbine's gas system, the weapon could be fired in the normal manner with the launcher in place.

The carbine grenade launcher was standardized as the "M8" on February 11, 1943. It was initially determined that 100,000 M8 launchers would be neded. In order to speed production and have some geographic dispersion, the Ordnance Department directed that half of this total be manufactured in the new York Ordnance District and half in the St. Louis Ordnance District. The Knapp-Monarch Company was granted the contract for the St. Louis District even though the firm was heavily burdened at the time with production of M1 and M2 grenade launchers (for the M1903 and M1917 rifles) and had just been awarded a contract for M7 launchers (for the M1 rifle). The New York District contracts were awarded to the Sun Ray Photo company and the Reliance Machine & Tool Company.

The first firm to get into production was Reliance which delivered its first batch of ten M8 launchers in July of 1943 to the Aberden Proving Ground for testing. The

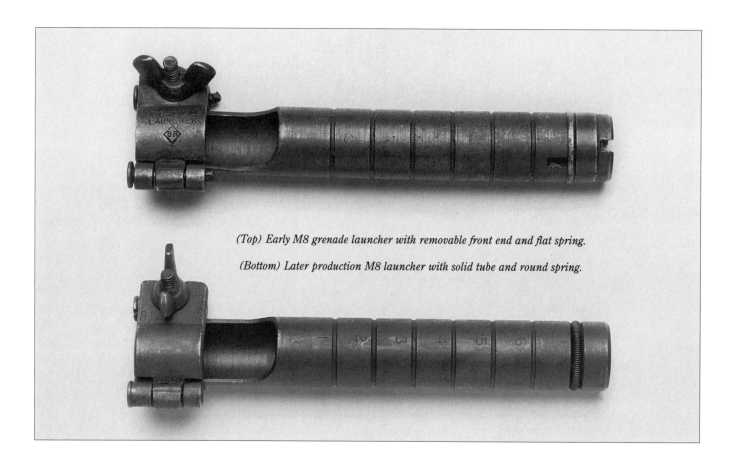

(Top) Early M8 grenade launcher with removable front end and flat spring.

(Bottom) Later production M8 launcher with solid tube and round spring.

ordnance tests revealed that the launchers were satisfactory, and the firm began full-scale production. Reliance delivered 1,520 M8 launchers to the government in August of 1943.

Sun Ray Photo did not complete its first batch of M8 launchers until October of the same year when the firm shipped 92 of the items. Knapp-Monarch also completed its first one hundred M8 launchers in October. The Ordnance Department had changed the drawings and specifications of the M8 launcher several times which resulted in initial production delays. However, by the end of 1943, all three firms were operating at peak capacity and turning out large numbers of M8 launchers.

By February of 1944, the number of M8 launchers produced was sufficient to warrant reductions in further deliveries. Sun Ray's and Reliance's contracts were not renewed after they manufactured their original allocation of M8 launchers. Knapp-Monarch remained in production until July of 1944 when its initial contract was completed. After the three firms ceased production, an unexpected increase in demand resulted in the need for new procurement of M8 launchers. In January of 1945, Knapp-Monarch resumed production of the item. The U.S. Cabinet Bed Company was also given a contract for the

production of 55,000 M8 grenade launchers. U.S. Cabinet Bed delivered its first launchers to the government in March of 1945. By April, the supply had again met the demand, and Knapp-Monarch's contract was cancelled although U.S. Cabinet Bed continued in production until the end of the war by which time it had produced 41,680 M8 launchers. The total production of M8 grenade launchers by all four firms was 387,165 which was almost four times the projected initial requirement. the M8 remained standard after World War II and no improved carbine grenade launchers were adopted to replace it.

There are two major variants of M8 launchers. The first type had a removable front section (similar to the early production M7 launchers) and a flat retaining spring. This first variant was made by Knapp-Monarch (18,904 produced), Sun Ray (25,000) and Reliance (60,108). This first variant represented just over 25 percent of the total production of M8 launchers.

The second variant had a solid tube without the removable front section and a coil spring rather than a flat retaining spring. All launchers were marked "M8 Grenade Launcher" along with the name and/or logo of the manufacturer. A large number of reproduction M8 launchers are on the market today. Virtually all of these

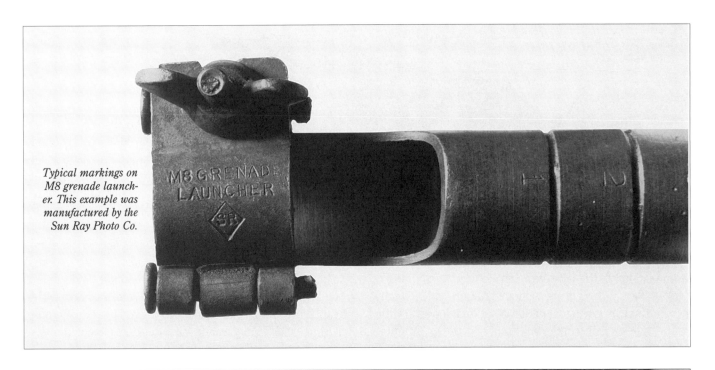

Typical markings on M8 grenade launcher. This example was manufactured by the Sun Ray Photo Co.

Marines on Okinawa, May 1945. The Marine in the center has an M1 carbine with an M8 grenade launcher attached (Credit: USMC)

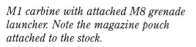

M1 carbine with attached M8 grenade launcher. Note the magazine pouch attached to the stock.

are of the second pattern. While normally well made, the reproduction launchers can easily be distinguished from the originals due to the lack of proper contractor markings. Only the above four firms produced M8 grenade launchers for the U.S. government and any examples seen with other types of markings are reproductions. Original "GI" M8 carbine grenade launchers are not rare but are often quite hard to find today. The early pattern is less commonly seen due to the smaller number made and will typically bring a premium over the second pattern. Both types are excellent additions to a collection. The various types of rifle grenades used with the M8 launcher are also interesting items to display. My book *U.S. Infantry Weapons of World War II* covers the various rifle grenades used with the M8 grenade launchers.

The use of the carbine to launch rifle grenades was not envisioned when the original specifications were compiled. However, the M8 launcher became quite popular during the war, and many vintage photographs depict carbines equipped with this item. The recoil generated when firing rifle grenades precluded use of the M1A1 carbine with the M8 launcher. The M1A1's stock could easily be damaged or broken if extended and placed on the ground to fire rifle grenades in the typical manner. Regulations stated that, if the M1A1 carbine had to be used to fire rifle grenades in an "emergency", the stock should be folded and the pistol grip area placed on the ground to absorb the recoil. Use of the M1A1 to fire rifle grenades was limited. However, large numbers of standard M1 carbines were utilized in this manner. It is interesting to note that a weapon weighing just over five pounds could stop a tank by means of armor-piercing rifle grenades. This capability further illustrated the versatility of the carbine. Original "GI" M8 grenade launchers are excellent investments and should continue to increase in value.

M3 Flash Hider

When the infrared night vision sights were fielded, the need for an instrument to help shield the muzzle flash was soon apparent. Several prototype flash hiders were tested and a design was eventually adopted at the "Hider, Flash, M3." The M3 was a funnel shaped flash hider that clamped to the carbine's barrel in much the same manner as the M8 grenade launcher. Few were apparently fielded in World War II although many were used during the Korean War (and later).

Two manufacturers, Underwood (marked "U") and Springfield Armory (marked "SA"), produced M3 flash hiders for the government. As in the case with the M8 grenade launchers, large numbers of commercialy made

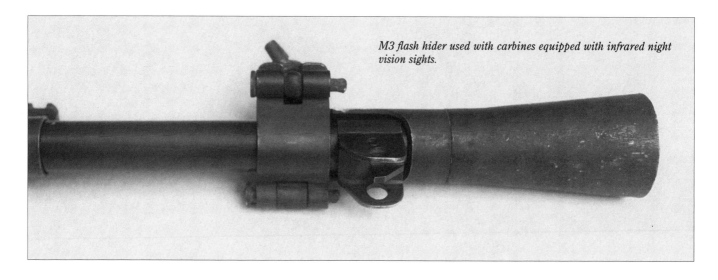

M3 flash hider used with carbines equipped with infrared night vision sights.

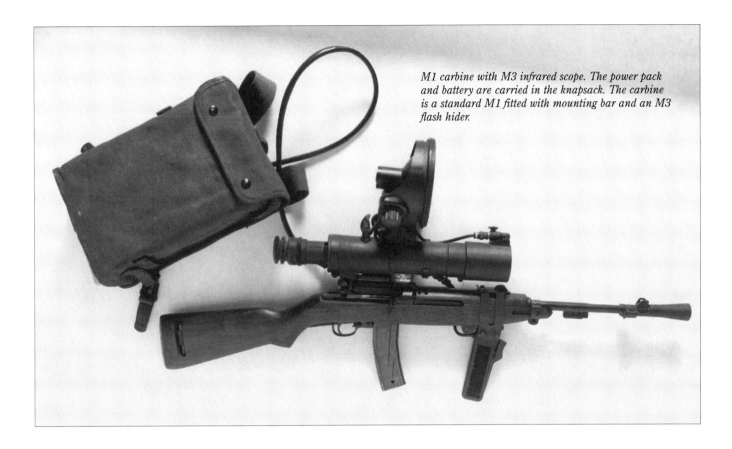

M1 carbine with M3 infrared scope. The power pack and battery are carried in the knapsack. The carbine is a standard M1 fitted with mounting bar and an M3 flash hider.

M3 flash hiders are on the market today. These can be distinguished from the originals by the lack of either the "U" or "SA" markings. Once fairly common, GI M3 flash hiders are getting to be rather difficult to find at attractive prices. These items would be properly found on any carbine fitted with an infrared night vision sight, particularly the post-WWII variants. Prices for the "U" and "SA" types seem to be comparable although most collectors would probably prefer the former. Either type would be a nice addition to a collection. Ancillary items such as grenade launchers and flash hiders can be the basis for impressive collections in their own right. Some collectors focus strictly on the firearms and overlook the equally interesting, and usually much less expensive, accessories and accouterments. Any original carbine accessory should be obtained if found in nice condition at reasonable prices.

Infrared Scopes

A quite interesting, although often rather expensive, accessory for the carbine is one of the various types of infrared night vision scopes. The original prototype scope as fielded in late WWII was standardized as the "M1." This was followed by development and adoption of the improved "M2" infrared scope. The M1 infrared

scopes and the later M2 variety were teamed with the T3 carbines in the closing days of fighting in the Pacific. As stated, though these rigs saw limited use, they proved to be valuable weapons. However, even this modicum of field use revealed several weaknesses with the early infrared units. The fact that a specially manufactured carbine was necessary for use with the infrared scopes also limited their widespread utilization by the military.

A mounting bar that could be attached to the standard carbine rear sight base and barrel was developed. Modifying an issue M1 carbine to accept this mounting bar required only removal of the rear sight, routing a hole in the handguard to accept the barrel mounting clamp and removing a small amount of wood from the inside of the stock to provide room for the barrel clamp. This procedure was much more practical than the procurement of specially manufactured carbines and caused the rapid demise of the T3 variant from service. The infrared lamp was mounted below the stock on the original T3 design. The lamp could become partially obscured by brush and other obstacles when the operator was firing from the prone or kneeling positions. Relocation of the lamp above the scope tube reduced this problem. The M2 infrared scopes still in inventory were modified by fastening the lamps to the top of the tubes. Both M1 and M2 scopes were altered in this manner. A number of modified and unmodified infrared scope/carbine rigs were issued during the Korean War. The infrared scopes were powered by means of a wet cell battery. The power pack and battery were carried in a canvas knapsack.

Battlefield experience revealed that the WWII vintage infrared units had limited effectiveness due to lack of range and durability. A vastly improved infrared telescope was developed and adopted in 1950 as the "Sniperscope, 20,000 Volts, M3." The M3 infrared scope was manufactured by two firms: American Optical and Capehart-Farnsworth. The first M3 scopes were ordered by the government from American Optical in August 1950. The reported amount acquired under this contract was 6,913 units. Capehart-Farnsworth received a subsequent order for M3 scopes. The number produced by Capehart-Farnsworth is not known but was undoubtedly less than the number produced by American Optical based on the number of surviving units encountered today. The M3 scopes made by each company were serially numbered in sequential order beginning with serial number "1".

The M3 infrared scope had much greater capabilities over the older units, including increased range, better optics and superior durability. However, the M3 was even bulkier and heavier than the previous infrared sights, and its use was generally limited to static, front line positions. The M3 infrared scope was attached on standard M1 carbine by means of the mounting bar attached to the rear sight base and clamped to the barrel. Active hostilities ended in Korea before large numbers of the M3 infrared scopes could be fielded. However, the M3 infrared scope remained in use throughout the 1950s and 1960s and some saw service in the early days of the Vietnam War as well.

As discussed previously, there were three basic types of infrared-equipped carbines: the T3 carbine (semiauto only), M1 carbine (semiauto) fitted with any model infrared scope by means of the mounting bar, and the M3 carbine (M2 selective fire carbine) fitted with any model infrared scope by means of the mounting bar. The M3 infrared scope is the infrared scope most often seen on the market today (by a wide margin) and the one typically used with the selective fire M3 carbines and the semi-automatic M1 carbines fitted with mounting bars.

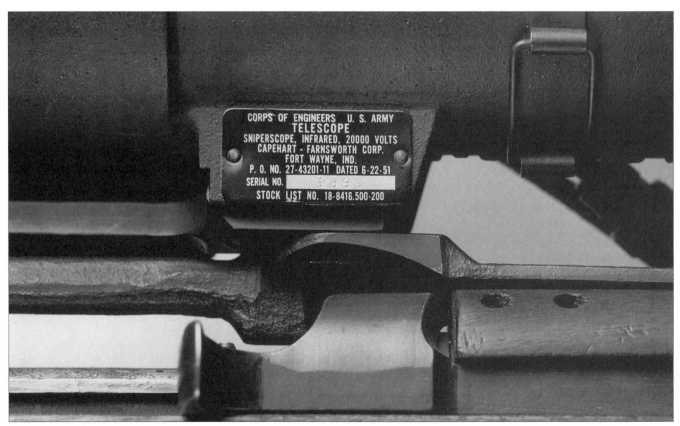

Close-up view of data plate on M3 infrared sight. This example was made by Capehart-Farnsworth Corp. and is dated June 22, 1951. American Optical also manufactured the M3 infrared sight.

Vietnam war era soldier sighting an M3 infrared night vision sight attached to an M1/ M2 carbine by means of a sight attachment bar. Note the M3 flash hider on the barrel.

The M3 infrared telescopes are still relatively easy to obtain today as many have been disposed of as surplus since the 1960s. Condition of the units range from brand new to totally inoperable. As originally issued, the M3 scope was shipped in a wooden packing chest complete with accessories and spare parts including tools. The chest was painted olive drab and boldly stenciled on the front in white paint:

U.S.
SNIPERSCOPE
INFRARED
SET NO. 1, 20000 VOLTS

A rubberized canvas knapsack was issued to carry the power pack and battery. Some of the power packs for the M3 scopes have been rebuilt because the more than 40-year-old original electronics have usually deteriorated beyond use. New motorcycle type batteries can be used since the original batteries are too old, and their utilization is not recommended. A number of M3 infrared scopes with refurbished electronics are fully capable of use today. The GI carbine mounting bars have always been rather tough to find. Some inoperable

units are used for display purposes but do not have nearly the value and desirability of operational scopes. Functional M1 and M2 infrared units are extremely hard to find and are much more valuable than comparable M3 sets. The most valuable and rarest of the infrared carbine rigs are the T3s fitted with WWII vintage infrared sights. Any original T3 with the proper infrared scope in

Wooden shipping and storage chest issued with M3 infrared sight.

223

place (functional or not) is a very desirable item. However any type of infrared night vision scope mounted on a carbine makes an impressive and colorful addition to a collection.

There were many other accessories and related items associated with the carbines including various ordnance tools and similar items. Some interesting collections of carbine related items have been assembled, and they further illustrate the almost endless approaches to this collecting genre.

Some General Considerations

Before the features of the carbines made by each prime contractor are examined in detail, some general information that pertains to virtually all GI carbines will be discussed. As we will soon see, there are many variances between some of the carbines made by each prime contractor and, indeed, often differences found in

carbines made by the same firm. However, there are several important features that are present in most original carbines. Any aspiring collector should be aware of these key features.

One important, but sometimes overlooked, feature is the type of finish found on original WWII carbines. It is well known that the standard type of metal finish employed by the United States on most military small arms during the Second World War was parkerizing. Actually, the term "parkerizing" was a proprietary trade name of a phosphate metal finish patented by the Parker Rust Proof Company soon after the turn of the century. However, the term has now come into the public domain, and the generally accepted generic term for phosphate finishes of this type is parkerizing.

Parkerizing is an ideal finish for military weapons as it is more durable than rust bluing and gives the weapon a dull, non-reflective appearance. There are many tints and textures of parkerized finishes which can often be

Marines in foxhole on Saipan, July 10, 1944. The Marine in the foreground is armed with an M1 Garand rifle with fixed M1 bayonet. The rest of the Marines are armed with M1 carbines. (Credit: U.S. Navy)

*Group of U.S. Marines during World War II. The Marine in the back row (center) is armed with a Winchester Model 12 trench gun (shotgun),
and the rest of the party is armed with M1 carbines.*
(Credit: National Archives)

quite confusing. The typical WWII-era parkerizing finish was a grayish color normally with a green tint. The exact tint varied widely depending on the type of weapon (carbine, Garand, machine gun, pistol, etc.) and manufacturer. Even weapons made by the same contractor can have variances in the parkerizing since the solution got weaker as more weapons were finished during the manufacturing process. In addition, the application of cosmoline or oil to a parkerized finish will normally impart a greenish hue.

Many commercial firms specialize in parkerizing today. The quality of this work runs from extremely good to quite shoddy. Most reparkerized weapons can be spotted by an experienced collector, but some reparkerizing jobs have even fooled experts. If a carbine having all parts finished in a uniform parkerized finish should be encountered, the weapon is not original no matter how good its appearance may be. During WWII,

most of the parts were not made by the prime contractor but were supplied by a vast network of many subcontractors that were generally hundreds or thousands of miles apart. Obviously, one would not expect several dozen parts made by as many different companies to have parkerized finishes that exactly match. An exact match in color and tint on all parts is a sure sign that a carbine has been refinished.

It is also sometimes forgotten that not all of the carbine's parts were parkerized. While the major components and many smaller parts of the carbine were parkerized, a number of parts on carbines were blued or, in some examples, left unfinished. This is discussed later in the book.

One area of concern for beginning, as well as more advanced, collectors is determining if a carbine remains in its original "as issued" WWII factory configuration, or if it has been overhauled and subsequently restored. While there is no substitute for a detailed examination

Marine "War Dog" handler taking a well-deserved rest on Iwo Jima with his M1 carbine close at hand. The carbine was developed for issue to troops whose duties made the use of standard service rifles impractical. (Credit: USMC)

by an experienced student of the subject, there are several things to look for that will normally identify a rebuilt carbine from one remaining in its original condition. One item that can be examined without even removing a carbine from a table at a gun show is the safety. The rotary safety was only used during WWII by Winchester and Inland at the very end of their production run. The "push button" safeties used on all other carbines during the war were replaced during postwar overhaul by the improved rotary safety. Therefore, except for extremely late production Inlands and Winchesters (which can be determined by a glance at the serial number), if a car-

bine today has a rotary safety, the odds are very high that the piece is a rebuild.

The odds are also overwhelming that the carbine in question has been rebuilt if it has an adjustable rear sight and T4 barrel band (with bayonet lug) since these updated components were also added during rebuild. Regulations called for the initials of the ordnance facility that performed the rebuild to be stamped on the stock. Such markings are definitive proof that the weapon has been overhauled. Of course, it is possible that such markings could be removed or that another stock has been put on the piece.

➤ ➤ ➤ ➤ ➤ ➤ ➤ ➤ ➤ Prime Contractors ◄ ◄ ◄ ◄ ◄ ◄ ◄ ◄ ◄

The carbines made by each prime contractor will be examined individually and data on the types of parts and proper markings for each will be presented. It should be stressed that most of this information is based on years of research and is generally accepted as correct by serious students of the subject. There can certainly be differing opinions on some of these points and on-going research may or may not clarify some of the "gray areas," but great effort is made to use such terms as "generally", "usually", "often" and similar phrases. One should be extremely careful when using the words "never" and "always." Any experienced carbine collector can tell you this is often skating on thin ice. Likewise, a carbine which gives every appearance of being totally original and untouched should not have any parts removed based on the data in this, or any other, book. On the other hand, there are many cases where parts are obviously incorrect, and the weapon can be improved (from a collecting viewpoint) by substitution of the correct part or parts. Anyone who claims to know everything there is to know about carbines (or anything else for that matter) should be avoided like the plague. A truly experienced collector and student of the subject can be of great assistance to a beginning collector, but most will readily admit that there are many areas which remain uncertain. This is probably truer in carbine collecting than almost any other field one can think of.

In any event, the following section will give a general idea of the proper type of parts and features found on the carbines made by each prime contractor. There will be many approximate serial number ranges given in the sections that follow. It cannot be stressed enough that all of these ranges are estimates and some variances on both sides of the serial number ranges may be expected. It is generally a mistake for a collector to rule out or rule

in the legitimacy of a carbine based solely on an arbitrary serial number range. Serial numbers well outside of the generally accepted ranges should be viewed with much caution. However, a few dozen or even a few hundred numbers off the estimated ranges should normally not be a cause for great concern regarding the originality of any U.S. military weapon, including (and especially) carbines.

WINCHESTER REPEATING ARMS COMPANY
Table #2

Assigned Serial Number Blocks
6–10
1,000,000–1,349,999
4,075,000–4,075,009
5,549,922–5,834,618
6,449,868–6,629,883
7,234,884–7,369,660
01701–07545*

*T3

Designated Code Letter
W

Winchester carbines have long been a favorite with many collectors due to the different variants available and the undeniable cachet of the company name. With only a couple of exceptions, standard Winchester carbines will normally bring somewhat more in the collector's market today than carbines produced by other prime contractors in comparable condition.

"Transition" Winchester M1 carbine with both early and later features. Note it has the "Type 2" wide barrel band (without bayonet) lug and "low wood" stock but still retains the non-adjustable rear sight.

As we have discussed, Winchester was the firm that developed the M1 carbine. The company was the second largest producer of the weapon and manufactured all of the standardized variants (M1, M2 and T3) except the M1A1. Winchester also made very small quantities of experimental models designated as the "M1E1A" and the "M1E1B." These had modified gas systems and were not approved for production. Winchester also produced a small number of experimental carbines incorporating the "Model 3" mechanism. This was a forerunner of the M2 selective fire mechanism. It is highly unlikely that any of the Winchester engineering prototypes will be encountered by collectors today. Anyone wishing to explore these topics in greater depth should consult the *War Baby* book.

Finish

It has been reported that very early production Winchester carbine receivers were finished in the company's "Du Lite" (similar to bluing) rather than parkerizing. This is probably not the case since the first production carbine, which appears to remain in its original unaltered condition, has a parkerized receiver. This makes the reports of "Du Lite" finished receivers doubtful. However, some Winchester barrels give every indication of utilizing this type of finish.

Receiver

Receivers made by Winchester were marked:

Winchester

Trademark

Serial #

There are three distinct variations of Winchester carbine receivers recognized by collectors today. The first variant utilized the detachable operating slide spring housing (or tube) with small projection or lug on the side. This projection was designed to fit into an "index hole" machined into the top of the receiver. This first type of receiver was used until just over the 1,050,000 serial number range, although a few with numbers a bit higher have been observed. It was discovered that the index hole milled into the receiver could weaken it in a critical area and some of these receivers developed cracks.

A second variant receiver was adopted that also used the detachable operating slide spring tube but eliminated the projection on the side and the corresponding index hole machined into the receiver. It is interesting to note that some of the first variant spring tubes were modified by grinding off the lug. This procedure enabled Winchester to use up its inventory of first variant housings after the index hole in the receiver was deleted. The "modified first variant" operating spring tubes are a little known sub-variant of the Winchester carbine. A rough estimate of the serial number range for the second type of receiver is 1,065,000 to 1,195,000. There was some overlap between the first and second types of receivers in this range.

The third, and by far the most widely used, Winchester carbine receiver variant was the type without the detachable operating slide spring housing. A hole drilled into the right side of the receiver replaced the detachable housing. Winchester changed its production tooling to incorporate this change sometime after the 1,195,000 serial number range and continued with this type of receiver until the end of production. Some collectors, particularly those specializing in Winchesters, wish to obtain a specimen of each type of receiver. Such an array of seemingly minor sub-variations is one of the reasons why carbines can be a surprisingly varied collecting theme.

Winchester was the largest user of receivers made by other firms. Over 50,000 receivers were sent to Winchester by Underwood after the latter company ceased carbine production. Winchester also received smaller numbers of receivers from firms that were not prime contractors such as Universal Winding, Singer and Intertype. If the receivers had not been heat treated, Winchester normally stamped them with standard company markings. If the receiver had already been heat treated, the original manufacturer's name (i.e., Underwood) was sometimes left intact and code letters such as "WWA" or "WA" were stamped on the receiver bevel to identify Winchester as the terminal user of the receiver. Other receivers had the original maker's name ground off and the Winchester marking stamped over it. These were also typically stamped with letter codes on the bevel as well. Letter code markings included "T", "WA", "WWA", "AW", "ABW" and perhaps others. Transferred receivers are interesting and collectible sub-variants and further illustrate how Winchester carbines can be an excellent collecting theme in their own right.

After adoption of the adjustable rear sight, the Winchester name and the serial number were moved further to the rear of the receiver so as not to be obscured by the larger sight. It is estimated that this change took place early in the next to last block of serial numbers (6,449,000–6,629,883).

Early production Winchester carbine receiver.

Later production Winchester receiver. Note the "W" code marking on the recoil plate.

Barrel

Winchester was one of the prime contractors that made its own barrels as well as supplying some to other contractors. There are two distinct marking variants found on Winchester carbine barrels. From the beginning of assembly line production until approximately serial number 1,030,000, the barrels were stamped with an ordnance "flaming bomb", "W.R.A." and the month and year of production. Barrel dates have been noted ranging from 10-42 to 2-43. A barrel with a date a month earlier or later is possible. The barrel dates on Winchester carbines generally track the serial numbers very well indicating that the barrels were manufactured and installed in close chronological proximity to receiver production. Carbines from other prime contractors may not show as close correlation since the barrels may have been supplied by another firm, hence a time lag between barrel production and date of assembly into a complete carbine.

Winchester carbine barrels also had a small "p" proof mark stamped between the company marking/date and the receiver. After approximately serial #1,030,000, the flaming bomb, company initials and date were deleted and a small "W" was stamped on top of the barrel instead about midway between the muzzle and receiver. The small "p" was retained as was the entwined "PW" Winchester corporate logo.

Early Winchester carbines with dated barrels are much in demand by collectors today and original examples will normally command a fairly substantial premium over later production Winchester carbines without dated barrels.

One characteristic often found in Winchester carbine barrels as compared to most other manufacturers is a very smooth finish. As stated previously, some early Winchester barrels appear to have been finished in the company's "Du Lite," and many later WRA barrels have what appears to be a blue-like finish (but it is not as pronounced as Du Lite). Most other contractors' barrels were dull parkerized and/or fairly roughly finished.

Front Sight

Winchester carbine front sights, unlike those of some contractors, were not coded but are characterized by a more rounded top than sights made for other contractors. Early and mid-production Winchester sights also typically have the section of the base behind the blade rounded out in a so-called "thumbnail" fashion. This was caused by the machine tool used to mill out this area. Other contractors' front sights may have similar "thumbnail" recessed areas, but it is often more prominent on the Winchester sights.

Barrel Band

Winchester carbines used the narrow "Type 1" band through approximately serial #5,550,000 when it was replaced by the wider "Type 2" band with no bayonet lug. The "Type 3" (T4) band came into use very late in production (approx. #6,475,000). This band was also used exclusively on Winchester M2 carbines. Winchester Barrel bands were unmarked except for some of the "Type 3" bands which were marked "C".

Trigger Housing

Winchester carbines utilized the milled type of trigger housing exclusively. After approximately serial number 5,650,000 (circa late 1944), the "lube hole" was incorporated. Winchester trigger housings were machined with partial notches to accept the magazine locking projections rather than the full length slots used by some other prime contractors. Some Winchester trigger housings with the top corner beveled may be found

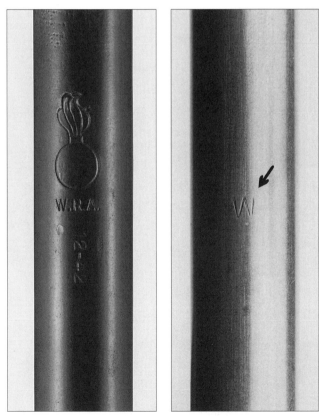

(Left) Early production Winchester barrel marked with date and "flaming bomb." (Right) Typically seen Winchester barrel marked with "W".

as well as some that have a square shape in this area.

When the M2 carbine was adopted and put into production, the trigger housing was changed to incorporate the features related to selective fire operation. Winchester, along with Inland, were the only two prime contractors to produce M2 trigger housings during WWII. However, large numbers of M1 trigger housings were modified to M2 specs after the war for use in the large scale overhaul programs of the postwar period.

Winchester triggers housings can normally be identified by a "W" stamped on the outside of the housing.

Trigger

Except for early production carbines below approximately serial #1,020,000, most Winchesters will be found with the so-called "Type 2" trigger. Winchester triggers were normally stamped "W", sometimes in an upside down position.

Safety

Early production Winchester safeties were checkered on both ends. The checkering was eliminated fairly early in production, around serial #1,075,000. Both the checkered and uncheckered first pattern safeties were unmarked. This pattern safety was utilized until approximately the serial number 1,300,000 when the improved push button safety with a more secure locking recess was adopted. Winchester safeties of this variety were generally marked "EW" or "SW".

The rotary safety came into use extremely late in production at approximately serial #6,600,000 and was utilized mainly in M2 carbines. The rotary safeties made by Winchester were generally marked "EW".

Magazine Catch

The magazine catch utilized on early production Winchester carbines was the so-called "long face" type with serrations ("Type 1"). This catch was used until somewhere around serial number 1,040,000 when the serrations were eliminated ("Type 2"). The later "Type 3" "short face" catch came into use after the serial #1,130,000 range. This catch was unmarked on the face until fairly late in production (circa serial #5,670,000) when an "M" was stamped on the catch. The M2 magazine catch (a.k.a. "Type 4") was introduced and used by Winchester in M1 carbines very late in the production run (around #6,500,000). However, some of the earlier "M" marked M1 catches also saw use through the end of production.

Sear

Winchester used a sear without the hole for most of its production run. The later type sear with the added hole began to be used somewhere between serial #5,640,000 and 5,670,000. Carbines below the lower range used the sear without the hole and carbines above the later range had sears with the hole. The carbines in between the two ranges can conceivably be found with either type. When the M2 carbine was adopted, the M2 type sear was also used to assemble some later production M1 carbines. Winchester sears were marked "W" and were either blued or left unfinished.

Sear Spring

Winchester used the non-tapered "Type 1" sear spring until approximately serial number 107000 when the tapered "Type 2" came into use.

Hammer

Early production Winchester carbines utilized the first variety "dog leg" hammer characterized by a slot milled into the face. This hammer was used at least through serial #1,100,000. The second type of "dog leg" hammer with the flat area instead of the milled slot was used for a fairly short period of time, estimated at between serial #1,108,000 and 1,170,000. After approximately serial #1,170,000, the straight configuration hammer came into use although overlap can be expected. The M2 hammer was used for all M2 carbines and some M1 carbines after its introduction. Winchester hammers were marked "W". A few in the 5,550,000 to 5,700,000 range were also marked with an additional "S" on the right side.

Bolt

As stated, all known original M1 carbines were originally assembled with blued bolts, although many were parkerized during the postwar overhauls. Winchester used the flat top type bolt until approximately serial #5,665,000. The round bolt came into use just after this number, although both flat and round top bolts were used concurrently until around serial number 5,700,000 when the round bolt was used exclusively. The round top bolt was used on all production M2 carbines as well. Very early Winchester bolts were unmarked but most were marked "W" on the right lug. Some early bolts marked with a "flaming bomb" on the lug have also been reported.

Extractor

The original early "V notch" extractor was used by Winchester until somewhere between serial number 1,035,000 and 1,040,000 when the later "flat notch" extractors came into use. Extractors were normally blued although some case-hardened types have been noted. Except for very early examples, Winchester extractors were marked "W".

Extractor Plunger

Winchester utilized the "Type 1" extractor plunger until approximately serial #1,030,000 when the improved "Type 2" came into use. Winchester modified some of the earlier extractors into the later configuration.

Firing Pin

The first pattern firing pin with the flat area at the rear was used until late in production, around serial #5,665,000. It is not believed that any of the so-called "Type 2" (modified first pattern) firing pins were used. The final type with a production clearance cut was used soon after the 5,665,000 serial number range. Again, except for very early examples, Winchester firing pins were stamped "W". Most were blued, but some unfinished firing pins may be encountered.

Operating Slide

It is estimated that the first variety E158 "round cut" operating slide ("Type 1") was used until circa serial #1,090,000 when the E279 ("Type 3") operating slide came into use. This slide remained in use until approximately serial number 1,235,000 when the E379 slide ("Type 4") was utilized. This slide remained in use for a rather long period of time until just after serial number 5,707,000 when the later ("Type 5") L379 slide came into use. These slides were marked "7160091" on the bottom and were unique to Winchester and Inland carbines. The L379 operating slide remained the type used until the introduction of the "Type 6" M2 slide marked "7161843" very late in production.

Winchester operating slides can easily be identified by the "W" marked in the bottom of the slide well.

Rear Sight

The "L-type" (flip) non-adjustable rear sight was used for most of Winchester's production until around serial #5,660,000 when the adjustable variety came into use. From this number until the 5,680,000 range both flip type and adjustable sights were used.

Early Winchester L-type sights (below circa serial #1,100,000) were marked with a small script "s". Afterward, the sights were stamped with a larger block type "S".

Winchester adjustable sights were originally of the stamped variety. Most were marked with an "H" enclosed in a shield and some were marked "I.R.C.O." The "H"-marked, stamped, adjustable rear sights continued to be the most common until circa serial #6,550,000 when a milled adjustable sight (same markings) was introduced.

Recoil Plate

The very early "Type 1" recoil plate was only used on prototype carbines by Winchester. The second pattern ("Type 2") came into use at the beginning of production (serial #1,000,000). The improved third pattern ("Type 3") was utilized somewhere between serial numbers 1,100,000 and 1,140,000. Winchester recoil plates are marked "W" on the outside, thus making identification quite easy since the plate doesn't have to be removed from the stock like with many makers.

Stock and Handguard

From the beginning of production until around the serial #1,040,000, Winchester carbine stocks were of the high wood, "I-cut" variety with a cartouche stamped on the right side consisting of "WRA/GHD" enclosed in a box with the "crossed cannons" escutcheon stamped next to it. This was followed by the same configuration stock (I-cut, high wood) but with the "W.R.A./G.H.D." cartouche not enclosed in a box. The oval oiler cut stock (still with high wood) came into use sometime after serial #1,100,000 with the same stock markings. Some of these stocks had a "W" stamped in the sling recess. The low wood stock began to be used fairly late in production (around serial #5,550,000). The use of the same stock markings (including some marked "W" in the sling recess) continued until very late in Winchester's production run (around serial #5,720,000). By this time, the "WRA/GHD" marking was deleted, and just the "crossed cannons" escutcheon was stamped on the right side and a "W" was stamped inside of the sling recess.

Markings aside, except for early production, Winchester carbine stocks are typically easy to identify, as many were made with a distinctive flat profile on the bottom of the forend rather than the noticeably rounded profile on stocks made by other contractors. Winchester M2 carbines rarely utilized the so-called "pot belly" stock.

Winchester handguards were normally stamped with a "W" on the bottom edge. Early Winchester handguards had a distinctive high profile in front. This was changed to a more typical profile as production continued. Except for very late production carbines (into the M2 range), Winchester handguards were of the two-rivet variety. As was the case with most contractors, there is almost always a very close match in color and texture of the wood between the handguard and the stock.

(Above, left) Stock cartouche on early production Winchester M1 carbine. This was similar to the "WRA/GHD" found on Winchester Garand stocks. (Above, right) Stock cartouche on later production Winchester carbine. Note the different format of the cartouche as compared to the cartouche applied to the earlier Winchester carbines.

Other Variants

T3

As stated previously, Winchester and Inland were to only two firms to produce the T3 carbine. The T3 as made by Winchester differed from the Inland version primarily in the configuration of the integral receiver mounting bracket. The WRA T3's mounting brackets were not connected with a bar as was the Inland variety. The government initially ordered 5,160 T3 carbines from Winchester, but only 1,108 were manufactured before the contract was terminated due to the end of WWII. The receiver was marked "U.S. Carbine Cal. .30 T3" under the right rear leg of the mounting bracket. The rear of the receiver was stamped with "Winchester" and the serial number. A special block of serial numbers was assigned to Winchester for T3 production. This block was "01701" to "07545."

Original T3 carbines are quite scarce today and make excellent additions to a carbine or martial arms collection. Most of the receivers were eventually destroyed ("demilled") by the government after WWII. Some of these torch-cut receivers were subsequently salvaged by welding. Some reproduction T3 stocks have also been fabricated over the past ten years or so since originals are all but impossible to find. Any T3 offered for sale should be examined very closely to verify that the receiver has not been welded and that the stock is original.

M2

The only other production variant of the carbine made by Winchester was the selective-fire M2. The receiver ring was stamped "U.S. Carbine, Cal. .30 M2". The majority of Winchester M2 carbines were originally marked "M1" on the receiver ring, but the "1" was over-stamped with a "2". Some Winchester M2 carbines were originally stamped "M2" but the over-stamped variety is more commonly seen. After WWII when many M1 carbines (including Winchesters) were converted to M2 specifications by the government, the "1" was also over-stamped with a "2". One must not assume that a Winchester M2

View of Winchester T3 receiver.
(Credit: Larry L. Ruth)

carbine with an over-stamped "1" is not original. The most important feature to observe is the serial number range. Winchester M2 carbines will fall into the 7,234,884–7,369,660 block of serial numbers. The first deliveries of M2 carbines were in March 1945, and the final delivery was in September of the same year. Winchester produced approximately 17,500 M2 carbines before cancellation of the contract. Winchester M2s are much harder to find than Inlands due to the much smaller number made.

The M2 stock can be identified by the cut-out area on the left side for the selector lever. While the "pot belly" stock was developed for use with the M2 carbines, most of the stocks used by Winchester with production M2 stocks appear to be standard M1-type stocks with the selector lever slot inletted into the left side. As is the case with the over-stamped "2," one must not necessarily assume that a Winchester M2 with a modified M1 stock has been overhauled or otherwise altered. It well could be original to the piece. By the time of M2 production by Winchester, the stock markings consisted of the "crossed cannons" escutcheon on the right side and a "W" stamped in the sling recess.

In addition to the selector lever, other special M2 parts included the selector lever spring, disconnector, disconnector lever assembly and the M2 trigger housing.

Original M2 carbines are surprisingly scarce today and are excellent investments if in collectible condition and reasonably priced. The M1 carbines that were overhauled to M2 specifications are interesting collectibles in their own right but do not command the prices of original production M2s. Of course, any selective fire weapon, including M2 carbines, must be properly registered with the ATF in order to be legally possessed. Some people do not realize that a M2 receiver with the selective-fire parts removed making it incapable of fully automatic operation is still considered a machine gun under federal statutes, and it is illegal to possess unless it has been previously registered. This is the infamous "Once a machine gun, always a machine gun" rule. It is not possible to now register automatic weapons that have not been previously registered. My book *U.S. Infantry Weapons of World War II* contains information on the laws pertaining to full automatic weapons.

Other Variants

There were several prototype and experimental models of the carbine produced by Winchester. These include the early "tool room" models, the "M1E1" vari-

ants (including the M1E1A and M1E1B) with modified gas systems, and the "No. 3 Mechanism" (forerunner of the selective fire M2 carbine). The company also contemplated manufacturing some commercial versions of the carbine after WWII, but except for three pilot models, none were produced. The probability of encountering any of these other variants is quite slim. Unlike many other prime contractors, Winchester apparently did not produce many specially finished carbines for presentation to company officials and other "VIPs" as gifts.

A few unmarked, rough appearing carbines have been observed which are purported to be Winchester "tool room" carbines. Without accompanying documentation, such weapons should be approached very warily since most bear high asking prices. Any carbine of Winchester make that appears to be non-standard should, likewise, be scrutinized very closely before any substantial sums are paid. Some inept restorations or otherwise bogus pieces are often offered for sale as rare "experimental" carbines.

As discussed, there are few distinct categorized variants of the standard M1 carbine. The early types with the detachable spring tube housings can certainly be classified as a distinct variant. In addition, some collectors wish to acquire an example of an early Winchester carbines (I-cut, high wood stock, flip sight, "Type 1" band, etc.), a "transition" carbine (oval cut, low wood stock, flip sight, "Type 2" band, etc.) and a late production version (adjustable rear sight, "Type 3" band, etc.). This is only one of several approaches to collecting Winchester carbines. An impressive collection of Winchester carbines can be assembled, if so desired, by acquiring each of the above in addition to some of the letter coded receivers and, perhaps, an original T3 and M2 carbine as well.

Winchester also produced large quantities of carbine ammunition for the government during WWII. Boxed WRA ammo makes a nice and relatively inexpensive supplement to a Winchester carbine when displayed in a collection.

Winchester carbines are certain to continue as one of the most desired of the prime contractors. Even though Winchester was the second largest producer of the carbine, the prices have always been higher than the available supply warrants. The undeniable glamour of the Winchester name certainly adds to the demand for carbines produced by the company. Many collectors who desire just one representative example of a carbine will select a Winchester.

INLAND MANUFACTURING
Division of General Motors
Table #3

Assigned Serial Number Blocks
1–5
11–30
31–99
XA3–XA50
0001–1700*
00001–00900*
000001–000500**
100–699,999
700,000–940,000***
940,001–999,999
2,912,520–3,152,519
3,152,520–3,212,519***
4,879,526–5,549,821
6,219,689–6,449,867
6,664,884–7,234,883
7,369,661–8,069,660

*T3
**T4
***Includes some Saginaw Steering Gear
Division subcontracted receivers

Designated Code Letter
I

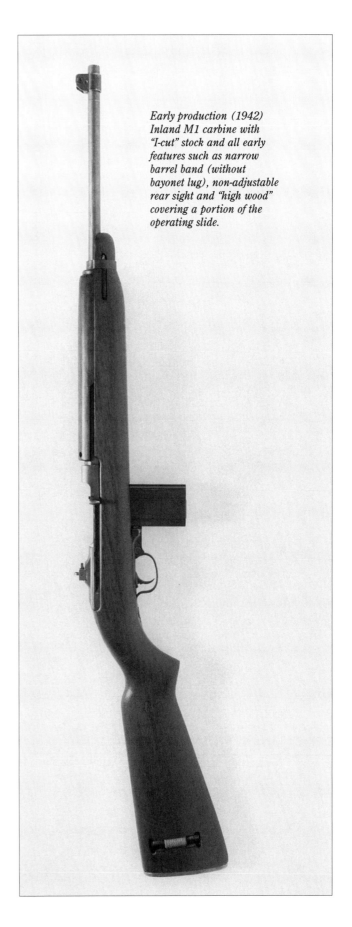

Early production (1942) Inland M1 carbine with "I-cut" stock and all early features such as narrow barrel band (without bayonet lug), non-adjustable rear sight and "high wood" covering a portion of the operating slide.

Inland was the largest producer of the carbine and greatly aided mass production of the weapon due to its expertise in manufacturing techniques. Today, Inland carbines are the most commonly found since the firm produced some 43 percent of the total. However, there are many interesting and valuable variants and sub-variants of the Inland carbine available to collectors.

Inland Manufacturing Division was a well established subsidiary of General Motors and possessed a talented engineering staff with expertise in mass production of automotive related items. Although the firm had no real prior experience with mass production of firearms, Inland played a vital role in the successful carbine production program by working out many of the "glitches" that were encountered when setting up the weapon for large scale manufacture. Even though Winchester designed the carbine, Inland's contribution to the carbine production program was no less impressive.

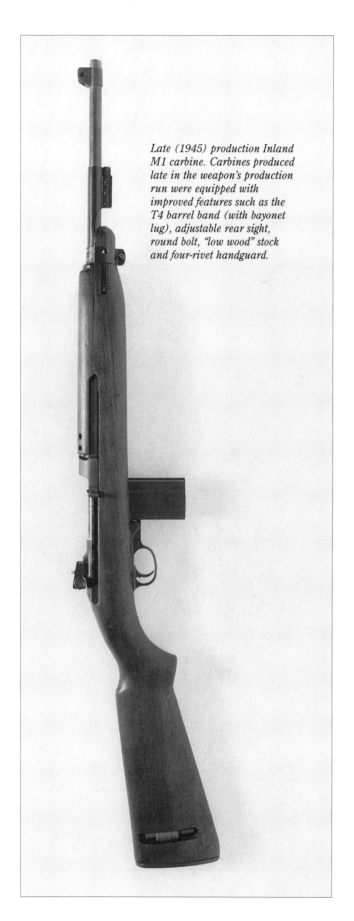

Late (1945) production Inland M1 carbine. Carbines produced late in the weapon's production run were equipped with improved features such as the T4 barrel band (with bayonet lug), adjustable rear sight, round bolt, "low wood" stock and four-rivet handguard.

Inland produced every standardized variant of the carbine including the M1, M1A1, T3 and M2. Like Winchester, Inland's carbine manufacturing program began with the first production version and continued until all contracts were canceled near the end of the war. The M1A1 variant which was only manufactured by Inland, will be discussed in this section. The M1A1 is one of the most popular variants of the carbine and many questionable pieces are around today so it is important that this weapon be examined at length.

Receiver

Inland receivers were marked behind the rear sight:

INLAND DIV.
Serial #

The majority of Inland receivers were the type with an integral spring tube housing. However, like Winchester, Inland manufactured some receivers with the detachable spring tube housing. Definitive information regarding these receivers is sketchy, and the actual number of receivers is not known. Most observed specimens seem to fall in the 300,000 to 600,000 serial number range. It has been speculated that the Inland receivers with the detachable spring tube housing were originally integral spring tube receivers which were damaged during production and converted to the detachable spring tube variety so they could be salvaged and used in subsequent production carbines. This theory is bolstered by the fact that Inland purchased some 10,000 spring tube housing assemblies from Rock-Ola in mid-1943. In any event, Inland receivers with the detachable spring tube housing represent a definite minority of production and are interesting and desirable collector variant.

Inland also made use of many receivers manufactured for the firm by its fellow General Motors subsidiary, Saginaw Steering Gear Division. The receivers made by Saginaw for Inland were marked "SI" (Saginaw-Inland) on the left side. These receivers were in the 700,000 to 709,000 serial number range. Receivers from a second run in the 700,000 to 940,000 serial number range were marked "SG" on the left side. There may be some overlap in the range between the "SI" and "SG" marked receivers. Some of the receivers in the latter range duplicated existing Inland serial numbers. These were marked with a "X" after the serial number and are generally referred to by collectors today as the Inland "X-suffix" receivers. Saginaw subsequently manufactured a number of receivers for Inland in the 3,152,520–3,212,519 serial number block. However, Saginaw-coded receivers with serial numbers outside of these two blocks have been observed. Some of the receivers made for Inland by Saginaw may be found with a wide tang at the rear which fits into the recoil plate.

Interestingly, although the company utilized many receivers made by Saginaw, Inland also supplied some receivers to other prime contractors such as National Postal Meter. This seemingly confusing shuffle of receivers between contractors illustrates the necessity for the Carbine Integration Committee during WWII. This ability to shift parts between contractors in order to alleviate production bottlenecks is a primary reason why such large numbers of carbines could be manufactured in such a relatively short period of time.

Inland Manufacturing Division receiver. This example is a fairly early production.

Barrel

Inland produced its own barrels and also supplied some to other contractors. Inland barrels utilized the swaged-on gas cylinder. The vast majority of Inland carbine barrels were stamped with the name of the maker (INLAND MFG. DIV. GENERAL MOTORS) and the month and year of production. Unlike other makers, Inland did not mark its barrels with the "flaming bomb" insignia.

Front Sight

Inland used the milled type of front sight exclusively during its production run. None of the stamped front sights have been observed

Inland barrel dated September 1942.

on Inland carbines. Some of the Inland front sights were stamped with code markings such as "RI", "II", "SI/3", "WI", "PI" and "L.I." and "N" while others were unmarked.

Barrel Band

Inland used the narrow "Type 1" barrel band until fairly late in production, around serial #5,000,000 when the wider "Type 2" band began to see use. Very early Inland barrel bands were unmarked. At approximately serial number 120,000 Inland increased the size of the opening of the sling swivel. At around this same time some, but not all, of the barrel bands and swivels were stamped with code markings, primarily "UI". Not all of the "Type 2" barrel bands were stamped with code markings, although many were. The "Type 3" band with bayonet lug came into use around serial #6,300,000 (circa late 1944). Most of these later barrel bands were marked with codes such as "KI", "AI", "UI", "JI" or "HI".

Trigger Housing

Inland utilized the milled type of trigger housing exclusively although several variants exist. Inland trigger housings had full length slots for the magazine rather than the notched type found on Winchesters. A "lube hole" was added in mid-1944. The M2 trigger housing was incorporated very late in production.

Inland trigger housings were typically stamped with the Inland logo. It is interesting to note that the shape of the logo was actually derived from the front profile of the company's production buildings at Dayton, Ohio.

Trigger

Except for very early production, Inland triggers utilized the "Type 2" trigger. Identification is easy as the triggers were stamped with code markings "RI", "RHI" and "FI". Both blued and parkerized triggers have been observed.

Safety

The checkered push-button safety was in use on Inland carbines from the beginning of production until approximately serial #200,000 when the checkering was deleted. The third type of safety with improved locking performance was introduced around serial #3,000,000. All three variants of Inland safeties were unmarked. The rotary type safety came into use quite late in the production run (circa serial #6,850,000) at about the time that the M2 carbine was introduced, although it was used on late production M1s as well. These safeties were stamped with code markings such as "HI" or "EI".

Magazine Catch

The first production Inland carbines were equipped with "Type 1" magazine catches characterized by vertical serrations and the "long face" profile. In early 1942, the serrations were eliminated ("Type 2" magazine catch). A very scarce variant safety used by Inland for a very short period of time was the serrated "short face" variety. These earlier catches were generally marked "WI" or "EI". The serrations were soon deleted, and the short face, unmarked (on the face) "Type 3" safety was used from circa mid-1943 until about a year later when the "M" marked variant came into use. This variant was found with various code markings including "WI", "SI", "HI" and "EI". The final variant ("Type 4") with the extra lug to support the weight of the 30-round magazine came into use concurrent with the introduction of the M2 carbine. These were usually marked "EI" or "HI". This catch was marked "M" on the face and was retrofitted to most carbines during rebuild.

Sear

The so-called "Type 1" sear (no hole in the top) was used until approximately serial number 3,100,000 when the "Type 2" (with hole) came into use. The M2 sear began to be used around serial number 6,850,000. The "Type 1" Inland sears were usually marked "BI" or "RI"; the "Type 2" were found with various code markings including "DI", "XI", "RI" and "BI". The M2 sears were marked either "HI" or "BI".

Sear Spring

Inland used the "Type 1" sear spring until somewhere between serial #80,000 and #100,000 when the tapered "Type 2" spring came into use.

Hammer

The earliest variant "dog leg" hammer (with vertical slot) was used from the beginning of production until the later "dog leg" style (machined flat area rather than slot) came into use around serial number 133,000. The earliest hammers were normally marked "GI" or "HI" and the second variety were marked "HI" or "NI".

The straight configuration hammer was introduced around serial #950,000. These hammers may be found with various code markings including the same type used with the "dog leg" hammers in addition to "WI" or "I-I" markings. The M2 hammer came into use with the introduction of the selective fire M2 carbine. These were generally marked "I-I". Most Inland hammers of all varieties were blued.

Bolt

The flat top bolt was used by Inland for the majority of its production run at least through approximately serial #5,000,000 when the round top bolt was introduced. Inland tested the round top bolt as early as the latter part of 1943, and it was standardized in mid-1944. Most of Inland's bolts were marked on the left locking lug either "OI" or "AI". A very few of the round top variety were marked "SI". As was the case with the other contractors, Inland's bolts were blued.

Extractor

The early "V notch" extractors were in use by Inland until approximately the 160,000 serial number range when the "flat notch" variety came into use. Most Inland extractors were marked "WI" although some very early types were unmarked.

Extractor Plunger

Inland used the "Type 1" extractor plunger until approximately serial number 160,000 when the improved "Type 2" came into use. Initially, Inland used modified "Type 1" extractors that were changed into "Type 2" configuration for a period of time. The modified extractors were used until approximately serial #230,000 when new production "Type 2" extractors began to be utilized.

Firing Pin

The first type of firing pin (flat rear profile) was in use by Inland until approximately the 3,100,000 serial number range when the second type came into use. The third variant firing pin began to be used by Inland around serial #4,900,000. Inland firing pins will be found with many types of code markings including "EI" (circled on early variants), "RI", "WI", "NI", "I-I" and "BI". It should be noted that the above serial number ranges are very rough estimates and much overlap will be found in original specimens.

Operating Slide

The earliest E158 slide ("Type 1") was used by Inland until around serial #100,000 when the second variety E169 slide ("Type 2") was introduced. The early slides of both types were normally marked "EI" (circled). Some of the later E169 slides were stamped "PI". The E279 slide ("Type 3") came into use around the 450,000 serial number range and were marked "PI". The E379 slide began to be used circa late 1943 (800,000 range) and remained in use for a relatively short period of time until the L379 slide ("Type 5") was introduced. These were normally marked "7160091" in addition to the Inland code marking ("PI"). The L479 ("Type 6") operating slide was used beginning in the 6,850,000 serial number block. These were generally marked "7161843" in addition to the "PI" code. This was the same type of slide used with the M2 carbine.

Rear Sight

Inland utilized the "L-type" flip sight exclusively until around serial number 5,000,000. The left side of the sight base was normally marked "s" though a very few may be found marked "WSI". The milled adjustable rear sight was introduced after the flip type , but some overlap may be found. The milled sights were typically marked either "PI" or "HI". The stamped adjustable rear sight began to be used by Inland around the 6,220,000 serial number range. These will be found marked either

"I.R. Co." or "JAO". Again, there may some overlap in the use of the milled and stamped adjustable rear sights.

Recoil Plate

The first pattern ("Type 1") recoil plate was used by Inland until approximately the 30,000 serial number range when the "Type 2" was incorporated into production carbines. The "Type 1" and some of the "Type 2" Inland recoil plates were unmarked. Inland was the only contractor to utilize the first pattern recoil plate in production carbines. As previously stated, Winchester used this pattern only on its prototype carbines. A number of the second type were marked either "WI" or "DI". The improved "Type 3" recoil plate came into use around the 530,000 serial number range. These can found with several types of code markings including "BI", "PI", "DI" and "WI".

Stock and Handguard

Inland stocks were of the high wood and "I-cut" variety from the beginning of production until approximately serial #400,000 when the oval oiler slot was instituted. Very early Inland carbines were *not* stamped with the "crossed cannons" Ordnance Department escutcheon on the right side of the stock as found on virtually all other carbine stocks. Rather, on these early Inland stocks, the "flaming bomb" bomb insignia was stamped inside of the sling recess on the left side along with the contractor code. A very early (and desirable) manufacturer's code marking is "LA". Beginning around serial #125,000, the "crossed cannons" stamp was applied to the right side. This marking is normally much larger on the Inland stocks than those of other contractors, a trait continued on subsequent Inland stocks. Both types of high wood Inland stocks ("I-cut" and oval slot) were marked with "OI" or "HI" in the sling recess.

The low wood variety stock came into use by Inland around serial #4,900,000. These were marked in the same manner as the earlier stocks including the same contractor codes in the sling recess and the large "crossed cannons" escutcheon on the right side.

With the adoption of the M2 carbine, the selector lever slot was added around serial #6,850,000. The late production "pot belly" M2 stock came into use by Inland very late in production, around serial #7,400,000. Both types of Inland M2 stocks were stamped in the sling recess with the same contractor codes as found on the earlier stocks.

The two-rivet type of handguard was used by Inland from the beginning of production until late 1944 when

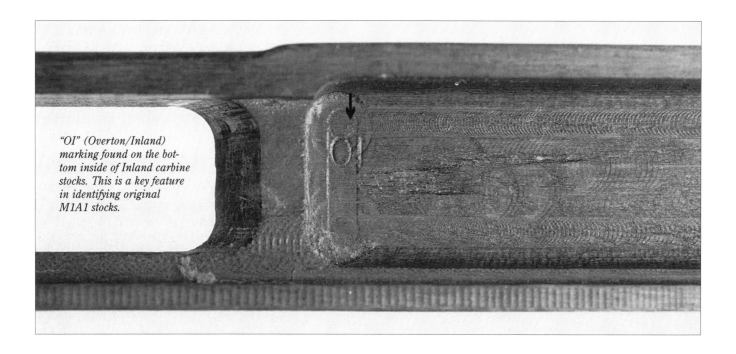

"OI" (Overton/Inland) marking found on the bottom inside of Inland carbine stocks. This is a key feature in identifying original M1A1 stocks.

the four-rivet type was introduced (around serial #6,220,000). The two-rivet Inland handguards had a wide groove on top until around the 500,000 serial number range when the groove was made narrower. This change was done to strengthen the handguard. Code markings (stamped on the bottom edge) include "OI" and "HI" which indicates production by the same firms that made the stocks.

Variants

M1A1 Carbine

One of the most interesting and sought after variants of the carbine is the M1A1 which was produced solely by Inland and designed for issue to airborne troops. The only difference between the M1A1 and M1 carbines is the stock with the folding metal butt assembly. Due to

Text continued on page 243

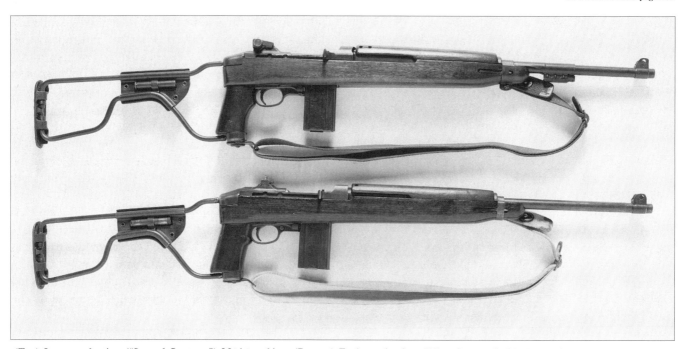

(Top) Later production ("Second Contract") M1A1 carbine. (Bottom) Early production ("First Contract") M1A1 carbine.

U.S. Army paratroopers sending a message via a homing pigeon. Note the M1A1 carbine (stock folded) resting on the pigeon cage. (Credit: U.S. Army)

17th Airborne Division paratroopers preparing for Operation Varsity, March 1945. The Tech. Sgt. on the left has an M1A1 carbine in the canvas scabbard strapped to his right leg. Note the two-pocket carbine magazine pouch on his belt next to the scabbard. (Credit: U.S. Army)

Text continued from page 240

the importance of this variant as a collectible item, it is covered here in some detail. It is vital to closely examine any purported original M1A1 offered for sale, as the overwhelming majority on the market today have reproduction ("fake") stocks or stock components. In addition, like the standard M1 carbine, most of the M1A1 carbines were overhauled after WWII and fitted with updated and/or refurbished parts. Therefore, not only must the originality of the piece be considered but also whether or not it has been rebuilt. As stated previously, rebuilt carbines are certainly legitimate collector items, but they are not as desirable or valuable as unaltered specimens remaining in their factory configuration.

There were two distinct production runs of the M1A1 carbine. Examples from each may be considered as different variants. The terms "first run" and "second run" are used as descriptive phrases and are not official terms. Inland delivered some 140,000 M1A1 carbines to the government during World War II. The numbers made in each production run are very close. Approximately 71,000 were made during the "first run," and the balance (approximately 69,000) were made during the "second run."

The first delivery of M1A1 carbines to the government was in October 1942. There are no known original M1A1 carbines with serial numbers below 42,000. The "first run" M1A1 carbines had serial numbers primarily in the 50,000 to 950,000 range and were manufactured through October 1943. These will be found with features consistent with standard Inland M1 carbines made during the same period including high wood stocks, flip rear sights, "Type 1" barrel bands, etc.

M1A1 carbines procured under the "second run" began to be manufactured in April of 1944 with the first deliveries in May. The weapons continued to be produced through December 1944. These M1A1 carbines will have features consistent with mid- to late 1944 Inland carbines such as low wood stocks, adjustable rear sights (in most cases) and "T4" barrel bands very late in the production run. Some of the second run M1A1 carbines may be found with high wood stocks, which was undoubtedly due to the sensible practice of using up parts on hand before changing over to newly manufactured parts. However, the low wood stocks are certainly

Airborne troops firing an M18 57mm recoilless rifle late in WWII. Note the M1A1 carbine (with stock folded) slung over the shoulder.
(Credit: Konrad F. Schreier, Jr.)

Photo of Army troops in Europe with a variety of infantry weapons. These include the M1A1 carbine (at far left), an M1 rifle with an attached M7 grenade launcher, a jeep-mounted M1919A4 .30 cal. machine gun and an M3 trench knife in an M6 sheath. (Credit: U.S. Army)

General Dwight Eisenhower and British Prime Minister Winston Churchill inspecting an American airborne mortar team prior to Operation Overlord. Note the M3 trench knife in a leather M6 sheath on the belt of the soldir at far left. He also has a folding stock M1A1 carbine slung over his shoulder. (Credit: National Archives)

the norm for the second run M1A1 carbines. Table #13 lists the approximate number of M1A1 carbines delivered monthly during the weapon's production run.

Many collectors want to know how to tell if the carbine in their M1A1 stock is original or if the action has been replaced. The short answer to this question is, "You can't tell." There are no known serial numbers to indicate which Inland carbines were originally procured under the M1A1 contracts. Therefore, there is no way to definitely ascertain if a specific carbine action is original to an M1A1 stock. If the action was manufactured by Inland, retains the original features proper for the vintage of the stock assembly and exhibits wear consistent with the stock, its originality cannot be determined one way or the other. Specific serial number data for M1A1 carbines would be invaluable to collectors today, but this information has not surfaced, if it still exists.

Since there are no distinguishing features for the M1A1 actions, the stock assembly is the key feature for determining the originality of a particular weapon. To begin with, the general condition of the action and the stock assembly must be considered. A pristine action in a well-used M1A1 stock assembly is a sure sign that something is amiss. There should be consistent wear found in both the action and the stock assembly.

The first component to consider is the wood portion of the stock assembly including the pistol grip. All original production M1A1 stocks were made of walnut. Some of the current reproductions are constructed of birch or other types of wood. These can immediately be dismissed as fakes. However, some excellent reproduction walnut M1A1 stocks may also be encountered. Among the first things to look for are the markings in the bottom of the stock, inside of the forearm. Original M1A1

U.S. paratroopers in France in 1944. Note the folding stock M1A1 carbines. The M1A1 carbine was the Army's only small arm of WWII designed for airborne use. Note also the M3 trench knife in a plastic M8 scabbard strapped to the leg of the trooper at the far left. (Credit: U.S. Army)

stocks were marked "OI" (Overton/Inland) in this area. The fakes are generally unmarked. Almost all of the original "first run" M1A1 stocks are stamped with a "circled P" proof mark on the stock. This marking is typically found at the rear of the stock by the recoil plate, although some were marked on the pistol grip instead. The "circle P" marking was deleted circa late 1943.

The next item to examine is the pistol grip. Earlier original M1A1 pistol grips are marked on the bottom with "OI" (Overton/Inland) and with a small "crossed cannons" escutcheon as well. Later grips may be marked "RI/3" on the bottom of the grip. It is likely that these were made by Royal Typewriters for Inland. It is known that Royal was the contractor that supplied the metal stock assemblies to Inland. These later grips normally have the "crossed cannons" marking moved from the bottom to the side and the size of the escutcheon enlarged. A grip without the "crossed cannons" marking is almost certainly either a fake or an unissued replacement grip. It is always possible that the original marking was obscured through refinishing, etc. so the grip

should be looked at very closely to determine if even a trace of the marking remains. It should be noted that there are two distinct configurations of the M1A1 pistol grips. The pistol grips used with the "first run" stocks have a slim profile. Most of the "second run" stocks have pistol grips that have a noticeably squarer profile. Some of the early second run stocks, however, used the earlier slim pistol grips. This was presumably done to use up components on hand.

After determining if the wooden portions of the stock are original, one should examine the stock for signs that it went through rebuild. When the earlier high wood stocks were rebuilt, they were cut down to low wood configuration. However, some M1A1 carbines have been observed with the high wood area modified to low wood configuration but with no other indications of arsenal overhaul. These are believed to have been field modified stocks altered to either relieve binding of the operating slide or to modify stocks that had become cracked in this area.

Regulations called for the overhauled stocks to be

stamped with the initials of the ordnance facility that performed the rebuild. These initials were typically stamped on the left side of the stock. (See Table #19 in the Garand section for a list of ordnance overhaul facilities). Most of the rebuilt stocks were also stamped with a "P" proof mark, usually on the grip. Unlike the original factory "circle P" markings, the rebuild proof stamp was in the form of a block letter "P", sometimes enclosed in a square box. An M1A1 stock with rebuild markings should not be teamed with an Inland carbine retaining its original WWII factory features. Rather, such a stock should contain a carbine with late/updated parts including adjustable rear sight, T4 barrel band, rotary safety, etc. It should be noted that any make of carbine was reinstalled in the M1A1 stock after rebuild so such weapons do not necessarily have to have Inland actions installed. A number of M1A1 wooden assemblies stamped "SA" on the pistol grip may be found. These were post-WWII replacement components made by Springfield Armory for rebuild. Again, such stocks would only be properly found on an arsenal overhauled carbine.

After evaluating the wooden components, the metal folding stock assembly must be examined in detail. This is vital because there are a number of original wood assemblies that have been fitted with bogus metal folding buttstocks. It is somewhat curious that more of the wooden components survived intact than the metal assemblies but that is the case. This is likely due to the fact that the folding metal stock assembly received the brunt of the stress and was relatively fragile as compared to even the standard wooden carbine stock. Improved, stronger folding stock units were tested by the military but were not standardized or put into production.

There are several key features to examine on the metal folding stocks. The leather cheek pad on the left side should be looked at very closely. The original pads were constructed of fairly thin leather. The leather pad was fastened to the metal frame by rivets. Both solid and tubular rivets have been observed. Some rivets were marked "7/4". It is possible that these were automobile brake shoe rivets made by Inland. The "first run" M1A1 stocks utilized brass rivets while many (or most) of the "second run" stocks had parkerized steel rivets. Many fake stocks will have either blued or black painted rivets. Close attention should be paid to the quality of the workmanship in this area. The original brass or steel rivets were flush with the surface of the leather pad and were often painted to approximately match the color of the leather Some of the original leather pads have dete-

riorated and have been replaced by homemade leather pads. A thick leather pad that appears too new for the stock assembly and/or sloppy workmanship such as poorly fitted rivets are indicative of a reworked stock

One very key feature to examine is the metal buttplate. Originals will have a number cast (not stamped) inside of the buttplate. This is the part's drawing number "B257614" followed by a circled asterisk-like marking and a one or two digit number. Numbers from "1" to "12" have been observed. This marking is often faint and may not be easy to read. Fake stocks will typically be unmarked, although some with deeply stamped markings on the inside of the buttplate are around.

The handguards used with the M1A1 stocks were standard types including markings. The "first run" M1A1s were fitted with two-rivet handguards and some of the "second run" carbines made in the latter part of production may have had four-rivet handguards.

As can be seen, there are a number of features to examine when determining the originality of an M1A1 stock. The number of reproduction stocks (wood, metal or both) cannot be overemphasized. Without question, the number of bogus stocks exceeds the number of originals by an extremely large margin. As is the case with standard M1 carbines, the rebuilt M1A1s are definitely collectible items but are not as desirable or valuable as the originals. Some may be found with the arsenal rebuild markings defaced so any sanded areas should be observed. However, the modification to low wood cannot be disguised. Therefore, the workmanship in this area should be minutely examined to determined if a stock is, in fact, an original low wood unit or was an earlier high wood stock that has been cut down.

In any event, original M1A1 carbines will certainly continue their steady rise in value and desirability as the years go by. The M1A1 is one of the most interesting and colorful variants of the carbine given its unique folding stock assembly and its association with the elite airborne units of World War II. The acquisition of a decent collectible specimen is likely to be a smart investment if the weapon is fairly priced. However, be very wary to any carbine of this type offered for sale. If the seller says its original but the factory "forgot" to stamp some markings or it's a "transition prototype piece" or whatever, keep your wallet in your pocket. When you have to start making excuses for a gun, it's almost always wise not to buy it, and certainly not at any sort of inflated price. You may miss a "gem" from time to time, but the odds are much higher that you will be spared the agony of finding out later that you bought a fake.

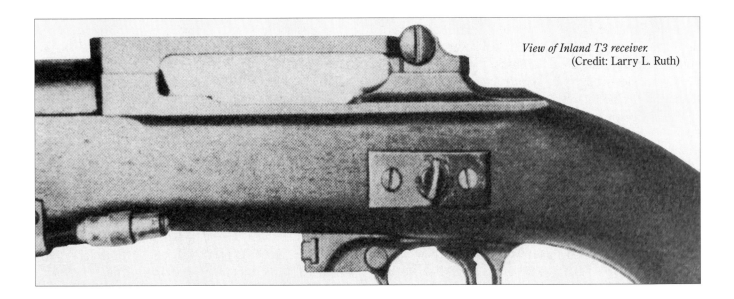

View of Inland T3 receiver.
(Credit: Larry L. Ruth)

T3 Carbine

Inland was the only other manufacturer of this scarce variant besides Winchester. The integral receiver mounting bracket for the infrared scope unit was constructed with a transverse bar in much the same manner as the Redfield "Junior" telescope mount. Inland T3 carbines were marked like the Winchester variant with the manufacturer's name and serial number stamped on the receiver ring in the normal manner and the "U.S. Carbine, Cal. .30 T3" stamped on the right side of the receiver under the scope mount. Inland used two blocks of serial numbers for T3 production:

0001–1700
00001–00900

The exact number of T3 carbines made by Inland is not known. Estimates run from just over 800 to as many as 1,700. Inland and Winchester T3 carbines appear to be about equally scarce today, and the value of either variant should be about the same if all other factors are equal. The same admonition mentioned for the Winchester T3 carbines with welded receivers and reproduction stocks applies equally to the Inland variant. The original M1 and M2 infrared scope units are exceedingly hard to find today, and a T3 carbine with the proper infrared unit mounted would be a great addition to any carbine or U.S. martial collection.

M2 Carbine

Inland made many more M2 carbines than did Winchester (approximately 202,000 compared to just 17,500). Since Inland made such a vast amount more of the M2 carbines, there are more differences found in these weapons than those made by Winchester. One significant difference is the fact that few, if any, Winchester's had the "2" in "M2" machine stamped on the receiver, whereas the majority of Inland's were machine stamped. Very early production Inland M2's had the "2" hand stamped, but by serial #7,003,000, the machine stamped markings are seen.

As was the case with Winchester, the Inland M2 carbines used later parts, including milled adjustable rear sights, round bolts, L479 slides, T4 barrel bands, four-rivet handguards and all other parts consistent with late production carbines. Some Inland M1 trigger housings were modified by the company to M2 configuration and used in production M2 carbines. Later production Inland M2 stocks were of the "pot belly" variety and marked in the sling recess with typical Inland code markings such as "HI" or "OI". As was the case with the standard components, the special M2 parts such as the selector lever, disconnector, etc. were stamped with Inland "I" code markings.

Many Inland M1 carbines were converted to M2 specifications after WWII. Such carbines will generally have the original "1" on the receiver ring over-stamped to "2". Since some of the original early Inland M2s may have had this same feature, close attention should be paid to the balance of the parts to be certain that all are Inland coded and correct for a M2 carbine. As was the case with most rebuilt carbines, the converted M1s typically contain a mixture of parts from various contractors and vintages. The original M2 carbines should contain all Inland parts of mid-1945 vintage.

Despite the paperwork involved, an original M2 carbine is a great addition to a collection if your state and municipality allows for the ownership of such weapons. My book *U.S. Infantry Weapons of World War II* contains a section that gives detailed information on the regulations regarding ownership and transfer or automatic weapons. This should be a handy reference for anyone unfamiliar with the laws pertaining to these guns.

Other Variants

In addition to the standardized models such as the M1, M1A1, T3 and M2, Inland produced several other variants that are of interest to a number of collectors. Some of these are quite rare and others are a bit more common, but all are distinct and interesting variants.

The "X Guns"

There are two types of Inland carbines that have either an "X" prefix or suffix to the serial number. As we discussed previously regarding Inland receivers, the "X suffix" carbines were those made by Saginaw under contract with serial numbers that duplicated some carbines previously made by Inland. There were approximately 10,000 to 11,000 receivers in this range. In addition to the "X suffix" on the serial numbers, these receivers were marked "SG" on the left side to denote production by Saginaw.

The so-called "X prefix" carbines were made by Inland for experimental purposes though many were subsequently given to VIPs, company executives and other dignitaries as presentation guns. The first batch were marked "X1", "X2", etc. up to "X100". A second letter was then added "XA1", "XA2", etc. until serial #100 was reached, then "XB1", "XB2", etc. was substituted. The only exception noted are the carbines in the "XB" prefix block which are numbered over 250. Otherwise, the letter prefix sequence changed after serial number "100" in each block. Prefixes as high as "XG" have been observed. Some of the "X prefix" guns were produced by Inland as cut-away models, and others were used for various engineering tests. The carbines made up as presentation pieces will frequently have features such as highly figured stocks and fancy metal finishes. Often a plaque identifying the recipient of the presentation carbine was affixed to the stock. It is believed that approximately 800 "X prefix" carbines were made by Inland, so the variant is scarce but not exceedingly rare. These weapons normally lack the "crossed cannons" cartouche on the stock which indicates acceptance into government service. They were the property of Inland and were not billed to Uncle Sam. Therefore, the company could do with them as it wished. Since none were issued to the armed forces and subjected to the rigors of service use, the survival rate is higher (percentage wise) than standard issue carbines. In any event, the "X guns" illustrate how many different variants of the Inland carbine there truly are.

T4 Carbine

In addition to the production T3 carbine, Inland also produced a few prototype "T series" carbines such as the "T4" (pre-production M2). These can be easily identified by the special serial numbers such as 000001 to 000500. The T4 carbines are covered by the National Firearms Act as automatic weapons and are unlikely to be encountered today at a gun show, garage sale or flea market.

As can be seen, a surprisingly large and varied collection of just Inland carbines can be assembled for a collection. Due to the relatively large numbers made, some collectors are not extremely interested in Inland carbines and prefer to concentrate on the less common makes. This can be a mistake since there are some very scarce and quite desirable Inland carbines around. Even a "plain vanilla" Inland M1 carbine retaining its original WWII factory features is a good acquisition for any collector.

UNDERWOOD-ELLIOTT-FISHER
Table #4

Assigned Serial Number Blocks
1,350,000–1,499,999
2,352,520–2,912,519
4,010,000–4,074,999
6,099,689–6,199,688

Designated Code Letter
U

While Winchester and Inland did a remarkable job in pioneering mass production of the carbine, a number of other commercial firms played a vital role in manufacturing the huge number of the weapons required by the government. Underwood was the first contractor after Winchester and Inland to get into carbine production. The company was a well established maker of typewriters and other office equipment. The trained and dedicated management team and work force eagerly accepted the challenge of converting from peacetime to wartime production and played a valuable role in producing the M1 carbine.

Underwood's first deliveries were in November 1942, but it was some time before the company got underway with can truly be called mass production. Underwood's engineering staff generated some useful ways to speed up the production of several components. As was the case with the prime contractors other than Winchester and Inland, Underwood produced only the M1 carbine and none of the standardized variants (M1A1, M2, etc.).

Receiver

Receivers were marked:

UNDERWOOD
Serial #

Early production models also had a "flaming bomb" insignia stamped on the receiver bevel.

Underwood used the integral spring housing receiver throughout production. Underwood receivers were of the narrow rear tang type. There are some interesting sub-variants of the Underwood receiver, which are char-

acterized by letter codes: "T", "W", "B" and "S". The codes represent subcontractors who manufactured these receivers for Underwood. The possible identities of some of these contractors are believed to be known, but, in the sake of not disseminating unverified material, this speculation will not be repeated. The coded Underwood receivers can be interesting and rewarding variants and, although not rare, are sought after by many carbine collectors.

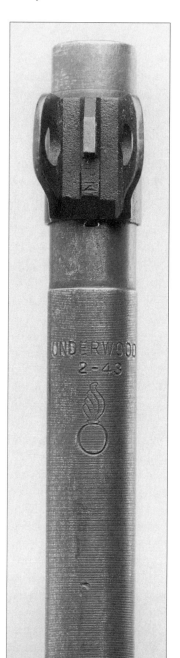

Barrel

Underwood manufactured its own barrels and also produced large numbers for other contractors. The barrels were marked with a large "flaming bomb" and the month and year the barrel was manufactured. Observed dates have ranged from "10-42" to "4-44". Underwood barrels were of the so-called "Type 1" style with integral gas cylinder.

Front Sight

The milled ("Type 1") front sight was used by Underwood from the inception of production until very early 1944 when the stamped type came into use. Fairly early milled Underwood sights were unmarked, but many of the later ones were stamped "U". The stamped sights were generally coded either "SI U" or "EU".

Underwood-Elliott-Fisher receiver. Note the "flaming bomb" stamped on the receiver bevel below the serial number.

Underwood barrel dated February 1943. Note the small staking mark behind the front sight and code markings behind the sight blade.

Barrel Band

Except for very late production carbines (in the 6,100,000 range), Underwood used the narrow "Type 1" barrel band. Neither the band or sling swivel were marked. No "Type 3" barrel bands were used by Underwood.

Trigger Housing

Underwood was instrumental in development of the stamped and brazed trigger housing. The company used the milled triggerguard from the beginning of production until the low 4,060,000 serial number range at which time the stamped/brazed housing came into use.

Milled and stamped/brazed Underwood trigger housings were marked with the company's "U" code letter and were also stamped with the "flaming bomb" insignia.

Trigger

Except for the possibility that some early "Type 1" triggers were utilized by Underwood, the carbines made by the firm were fitted with the more common "Type 2" trigger. These were normally stamped with Underwood code markings.

Safety

Underwood used the "Type 1" safety with checkering at the beginning of its production (#1,350,000) until approximately the 1,360,000 range when the unchecked "Type 2" safety came into use. There was a rather long period of time when the use of the Types 1 and 2 safeties overlapped. The "Type 2" safety continued to be used until fairly early in the second block of Underwood serial numbers, around #2,380,000, then the "Type 3" safety was introduced. The "Type 3" safety was used through the end of production. All Underwood safeties were unmarked. As was the case with all contractors except for Winchester and Inland, Underwood did not utilize any of the latest pattern rotary safeties.

Magazine Catch

Underwood did not utilize any of the "Type 1" serrated "long face" magazine catches. The company used the long face, "Type 2" magazine catch without serrations from the beginning of its production until short face "Type 3" came into use. It is reported that Underwood used a very small quantity of serrated "short face" magazine catches for a short period of time until the unserrated, "short face" began to be used exclusively. This latter catch was the type utilized through the end of production. Underwood magazine catches were typically stamped with code markings such as "U" or "AU".

Sear

The "no hole" sear was used by Underwood until late in production. The later sear with the hole came into use early in the last block of serial numbers (6,099,689–6,199,688). Both unmarked and marked sears were used by Underwood. The marked variety were typically stamped ".U."

Sear Spring

The "Type 1" sear spring with straight ends was used until the 2,352,520 block of numbers when the "Type 2" spring with tapered ends began to be used.

Hammer

The "Type 1," "dog leg" hammer (with vertical slot) was used by Underwood until the "Type 2" (angled slot) came into use just around serial #1,396,000. This hammer remained in use until the straight hammer ("Type 3") was introduced in the second block of serial numbers, around #2,380,000. Overlap between Types 2 and 3 hammers may be observed. Underwood hammers were typically marked with contractor codes such as ".U." or "WU".

Bolt

Underwood utilized the flat top bolt until the last serial number block (6,099,689–6,199,688) at which time the company began use of the round top variety. The exact time frame of the change to the round bolt is not known. Underwood bolts will be found with several types of codes including ".U.", "WU", "CU", "H.U." and "S.U."

Extractor

Underwood used the early "V"-notch extractor for a relatively short period of time, until approximately serial #1,358,000, after which the modified "V"-type came into use. The final variant (flat notch) extractor was used from the 1,360,000 range until the end of production. Most Underwood extractors were unmarked.

Extractor Plunger

Underwood used the first variant extractor plunger (cone shaped with sharp point) until around serial #1,358,000 when the modified plungers (flat area milled into the front) were used. The final variant plunger (factory made with the flat area) was used from around serial #1,440,000 until the end of production.

Firing Pin

The so-called "Type 1" firing pin was used until the 2,650,000 serial number block when the "Type 3" with clearance cut came into use. Use of the "Type 2" firing pin by Underwood is unclear. Firing pins will be found with various code markings including ".U.", "WU" and "DU". Some unmarked firing pins have also been observed in original Underwood carbines, although the majority are marked.

Operating Slide

The E169 ("Type 2") operating slide was used in the first two blocks of serial numbers and into the early 4,060,000 range when the E279 slide ("Type 3") began to be used. This slide was used until the 6,099,689–6,199,688 block of numbers when the later E379 operating slide ("Type 4") was utilized. Both the E279 and E379 operating slides were used concurrently by Underwood in the last block of serial numbers. Underwood operating slides were stamped with code markings including ".U.", ".O.U." and "WU".

Rear Sight

Underwood used the "L-type" flip sight exclusively and did not produce any carbines with adjustable sights. Underwood rear sights may be found with a variety of code markings including a large block "S" or small rounded "s" on the base as well as some ".U." markings on the leaf.

Recoil Plate

The "Type 2" recoil plate was used by Underwood in the first serial number block as well as the 4,010,000–4,074,999 block. Interestingly, none of the letter-coded Underwood receivers have been observed with the early recoil plate. The later pattern recoil plate ("Type 3") was used in the 2,370,000 serial number range (second block of numbers) as well as the final block. Underwood recoil plates were normally stamped with code markings such as ".U." or "AU".

Stock and Handguard

The high wood stock with the "I-cut" oiler slot was used from the beginning of production (serial #1,350,000) until approximately the low 1,400,000 range when the oval oiler slot was instituted. The low wood stock did not come into widespread use by Underwood until around the last block of serial numbers (#6,099,689), although some low wood stocks have been reported earlier. There was some overlap in the use of

high wood and low wood stocks by Underwood. Early stocks (mostly "I-cut") were stamped with a cartouche on the right side "UEF/GHD" next to the "crossed cannons" Ordnance escutcheon. Later stocks had the "crossed cannons" included in the cartouche "box". The code letters of the subcontractor who manufactured the stock were stamped in the sling recess, typically "RMC". Many Underwood carbines also had a "circle P" stamped on the bottom of the pistol grip.

The early variety handguard with the deep sighting groove was used throughout the first block of serial numbers. The more common type with the shallower groove was used shortly afterward and remained in use by Underwood until the end of production. All Underwood handguards were of the two-rivet type. Most were stamped "RMC" inside, but some later handguards may be found marked "Pedersen U".

Having produced almost 9 percent of all carbines made, Underwoods are not particularly scarce. They are, of course, harder to find than standard production Inlands or Winchesters due to the smaller numbers made. Even though the company did not make any "exotic" variants such as the M1A1 or T3, Underwood carbines are quite collectible. The various letter coded receivers are interesting and desirable sub-variants for those interested in specializing in Underwood carbines.

ROCK-OLA MANUFACTURING CORPORATION
Table #5

Assigned Serial Number Blocks
1,662,250–1,762,519
4,532,100–4,632,099
6,071,189–6,099,688
6,199,684–6,219,688

Designated Code Letter
R

The Rock-Ola company had an established and experienced management team and engineering staff. The firm also possessed an extensive woodworking department and produced large numbers of stocks and handguards for several other prime contractors. Unlike some prime contractors, Rock-Ola produced a large percentage of components in their own factory rather than subcontracting the parts to other firms. The company produced its own receivers, barrels, operating slides, bolts, trigger housings, firing pins, ejectors, gas cylinders and extractors along with stocks and handguards. The firm also deviated at times from the standard practice of marking parts with the assigned initials and stamped many parts "ROCK-OLA".

Receiver

Receivers were marked as follows:

ROCK-OLA
Serial Number

Rock-Ola was one of the firms that produced the detachable spring tube receiver. The company manufactured the "Type 1" detachable spring tube receiver until sometime midway into the first serial number block (circa #1,666,000). Around this point, Rock-Ola switched to the "Type 2" detachable spring tube receiver for a fairly short period of time. The integral spring tube housing receiver came into use by Rock-Ola around serial number 1,676,000. All subsequent serial number blocks were manufactured with the "Type 3" integral spring tube receiver.

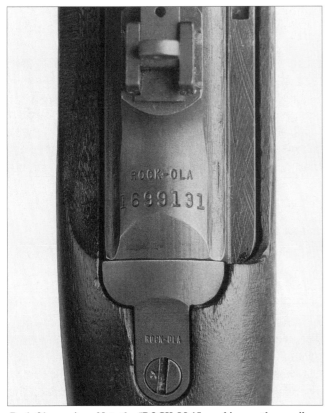

Rock-Ola receiver. Note the "ROCK-OLA" marking on the recoil plate. Rock-Ola stamped several parts with the full company name rather than its assigned contractor's code letter.

In early to mid-1943, Rock-Ola obtained some 2,000 receivers from Inland to expedite their delivery schedule. These receivers fall in the high 400,000 to low 500,000 serial number range and can identified by the Inland name which was lined out and "ROCK-OLA" stamped below. This is a scarce variant of the Rock-Ola carbine.

When Rock-Ola adopted the adjustable rear sight very late in its production (primarily the final block of serial numbers), the location of the receiver markings was moved to the rear so they would not be obscured by the larger sight.

Barrel

Rock-Ola made its own carbine barrels and also supplied many of them to other prime contractors. The barrels made by the firm were of the swaged-on gas cylinder type. Early Rock-Ola barrels were stamped with a "flaming bomb" by the gas cylinder but this stamping was deleted as production continued. A number of Rock-Ola barrels were also stamped with a letter or number code on the bottom. Since Rock-Ola did not acquire any barrels from subcontractors, the meaning of this code marking is not known.

The barrels were marked "ROCK-OLA" and were also stamped with the month and year of production until this practice ceased in mid-to late-1943 (in the latter part of the first serial number block). Rock-Ola barrels were of the long spacer ("skirt") type until sometime after mid-1943 when the short spacer barrels came into use.

Rock-Ola carbine barrel dated June 1943.

Front Sight

The milled front sight was used by Rock-Ola until somewhere midway into the 4,500,000 serial number range when the stamped/brazed front sight appeared. The early milled sights were normally marked "TR" and some marked "RP" may also be encountered. The later stamped/brazed front sights were typically uncoded.

Barrel Band

Rock-Ola used the "Type 1" barrel band from the beginning of production until sometime in the second block of serial numbers (circa #4,560,000) when the wider "Type 2" band came into use. However, Rock-Ola continued using the "Type 1" bands well after the introduction of the "Type 2" band. Most of the "Type 1" bands were marked "M-R". Many of the "Type 2" bands were unmarked. Rock-Ola did not use any of the later "Type 3" barrel bands.

Trigger Housing

Rock-Ola was one of the contractors that utilized both milled and stamped/brazed trigger housings. The firm utilized the milled housing exclusively until the mid-4,500,000 range when the stamped/brazed trigger housing was introduced. Early milled housings had a bevel on the front and rear, but later types had only the rear bevel. Rock-Ola trigger housing are very easy to identify as the company name was stamped on the right rear of the housing. Some of the milled Rock-Ola trigger housings will also be found stamped with the "flaming bomb" insignia.

Trigger

Rock-Ola utilized the "Type 1" trigger for most, if not all, of its production. It is uncertain if the firm ever changed to the "Type 2" trigger. As is the case with most parts, the triggers made by the company are easy to identify since they were stamped "ROCK-OLA" on the left side.

Safety

The "Type 1" (checkered) safety was used by Rock-Ola in the first block of serial numbers until just before serial #1,700,000. The uncheckered "Type 2" safety then came into use and remained until almost the end of the second serial number block (around #4,628,000). The "Type 3 " safety with the improved locking recess was utilized exclusively in the final two blocks of numbers in the six million + range. Rock-Ola safeties were unmarked.

Magazine Catch

Rock-Ola may have used the "Type 1" serrated (long face) magazine catch extremely early in production, but, if so, only a handful were utilized. The unserrated long face "Type 2" magazine catch was used until circa serial #1,680,000 when the short face "Type 3" catch was introduced. However, both Types 2 and 3 were used concurrently in some later production Rock-Ola carbines.

Rock-Ola magazine catches were normally stamped with code markings including "F R", "B R", and "A-R".

Sear

The "Type 1" sear (without hole) was used from the start of Rock-Ola production until early in the second block of serial numbers (approximately #4,540,000) when the "Type 2" sear was used. Early Rock-Ola sears were marked "R" (until around #1,680,000) when the part began to be marked "ROCK-OLA".

Sear Spring

The "Type 1" sear spring (straight ends) was used for a short period of time until around serial #1,670,000 when the "Type 2" (tapered ends) came into use.

Hammer

"Types 1 and 2," "dog leg" hammers were used by Rock-Ola from the beginning of production until late in the first block of serial numbers, estimated at sometime after #1,685,000, when the straight "Type 3" hammer was used. This type was used for the remaining Rock-Ola production run. The early hammers were marked "KR" while some of the later "dog leg" hammers had a "C" mark enclosed in a circle. The "Type 3" hammers can be found with a variety of code markings including "KR2", "LT-R" , "R/LTQ" and "B/R".

Bolt

The flat top bolt was used by Rock-Ola exclusively in the first block of serial numbers and into the early portion of the second block. The company began use of the round top bolt just after serial number 4,530,000. Interestingly, however, about 50,000 numbers later the flat top bolt was again in use by Rock-Ola and remained the predominant type of bolt used for the balance of the second serial number block. All known original Rock-Ola carbines in the last two serial number blocks (the six million range) were fitted with round top bolts. The flat top bolts were stamped "ROCK-OLA" on the face of either the left or right lug. The round top bolts were marked on the face of the left lug.

Extractor

Rock-Ola's use of the first pattern "V"-notch extractor, if any, was limited to a handful of carbines at the very beginning of production. Some modified ("Type 2") extractors were used for a short period of time until the "Type 3" extractors came into use for the rest of production. The Types 1 and 2 extractors were unmarked, and the "Type 3" extractors were normally marked "R".

Extractor Plunger

Rock-Ola's use of the early "Type 1" extractor plunger seems to have paralleled the limited use of the first pattern "V"-notch extractor. The vast majority of Rock-Ola extractor plungers were of the "Type 2" configuration.

Firing Pin

Rock-Ola utilized the first pattern ("Type 1") firing pin throughout its first block of assigned serial numbers. Early firing pins of this type were marked "R", although some stamped "ROCK-OLA" have also been seen. Rock-Ola's use of the so-called "Type 2" firing pin, if any, was very limited. The latest "Type 3" variant was used by the firm from the second serial number block until the end of production. As was often the case, some concurrent use of the "Type 1" and "Type 3" firing pins has been observed.

Operating Slide

The "Type 2" E169 slide was used from the start of production by Rock-Ola until sometime into the late 1,690,000 serial number range when the E279 slide ("Type 3") began to be used. The more common E379 ("Type 4") operating slide was used in most of the last three serial number blocks. However, use of the various types of slides continued throughout much of Rock-Ola's production. The early E169 slides were normally marked "ROCK OLA" inside of the box. This marking was later changed to the outside of the box. It has been reported that some E169 slides made by Inland were used by Rock-Ola and an "R" was stamped next to the original Inland code markings.

Rear Sight

Rock-Ola utilized the original flip sight until late in its production run when both the milled and stamped adjustable sights were used. The "L-type" flip sights were generally marked with codes (such as "RR", "BR" and "A-R" on the rear sight base. Some of the sight leaves were also coded and others were unmarked. The

milled rear was used fairly late in production. The time period of the change from the flip sight to the adjustable sight is not known. Some have speculated that it occurred as early as the latter part of the second serial number block, around #4,600,000. It appears, however, that the use of adjustable rear sights was primarily later in the last two serial number block (the six million range).

The milled adjustable rear sights were made by the Hemphill Company and were marked with an "H" enclosed in a shield. The stamped adjustable rear sights came into use a bit after the milled variety and were marked "I.R. Co." As stated, Rock-Ola relocated receiver markings when the adjustable rear sights came into use.

Rock-Ola used a rather unusual method of staking their flip sights. The company lightly staked all four corners of the sight when it was originally installed. The adjustable sights typically had one or two deeper staking marks applied to the rear. Since the time period of the change in rear sights is still rather unclear, the pattern of staking marks should be closely examined to determine what type of rear sight was originally fitted. If the four shallow staking marks are present, the carbine originally had a flip sight, regardless of the type that may be currently installed. On the other hand, one or two deep staking punch marks at the rear is a sure sign that an adjustable sight was on the weapon at one time. Some "restorers" may attempt to peen over the deep staking marks, therefore the rear sight dovetail area should be closely examined.

Recoil Plate

The "Type 2" recoil plate was used up through the 1,680,000 serial number range when the improved "Type 3" came into use. Most were stamped "ROCK-OLA" on the top but some late types have been observed which were marked "S G" with a smaller "R" stamped between the letters. These were apparently acquired by Rock-Ola from Saginaw Steering Gear. However, the recoil plate marked "ROCK-OLA" is by far the most commonly encountered.

Stock and Handguard

As stated previously, Rock-Ola made all of its own stocks and handguards and produced large numbers for other prime contractors. The firm utilized the early pattern "I-cut," high wood stock from the beginning of production until around serial #1,690,000 when the oval cut (high wood) stock came into use. The oval cut (low wood) stock began to come into use in the late 6,090,000 serial number range. Curiously, some Rock-Ola carbines that appear to be totally original as late as the 6,200,000 serial number range have been observed with "I-cut" stocks. The reason for this apparent anomaly is not known, but possibly it was due to the use of early stocks which were made in excess of the company's needs at the time. As additional contracts were granted to the company, the older pattern stocks still in inventory were utilized on new production carbines so that no unused parts would be on hand after production ceased.

Rock-Ola stocks were stamped with the initials "RMC" enclosed in a cartouche next to the "crossed cannons" escutcheon. The company's initials were also stamped inside of the sling recess. The stocks made for other contractors were also stamped "RMC" in the recess and had the code letter of the contractor stamped next to it. For example, the stocks Rock-Ola made for Quality Hardware Machine Corporation were stamped "Q-RMC" in this location.

Rock-Ola used the two-rivet type of handguard exclusively. As was the case with some other contractors, the early handguards had a deep sighting groove in top which was later changed to a shallower groove. "RMC" was stamped on the bottom edge of Rock-Ola's handguards. A few may also be found marked with the "flaming bomb" insignia in this location.

Other Variants

Although Rock-Ola only manufactured the standard M1 carbine for the government, the company did produce a number of special "presentation" pieces. As was the case with other contractors, the presentation carbines given to company officials and other "VIPs" were paid for by Rock-Ola and were not government issue weapons. Most of the Rock-Ola presentation carbines had a "EX" prefix to the serial number. Original examples noted have been in the 6,095,000 serial number range. These carbines typically had finely polished, blued finishes and modified stocks lacking the sling recess cutout. A few carbines of this type with a "EXP" marking and no serial number on the receive have also been observed. These were likely experimental engineering receivers that were subsequently used to assemble presentation pieces. It is reported that some sixty Rock-Ola carbines with "EXP" prefixes were produced in 1945 and that the majority of these were also accompanied by custom-made wooden cases. Most of the cases had an engraved plate inside the lid to identify the recipient of the carbine. The presentation carbines were fitted with late vintage Rock-Ola marked parts. While not military issue weapons, original presentation carbines are desirable collector items.

Since Rock-Ola made less than 4 percent of the total carbines produced, this is obviously one of the harder to find prime contractors. Rock-Ola carbines are certainly not rare, but examples can be a bit tough to turn up. As can be seen, with four distinct receiver variations (two detachable spring tube types, the integral type and the relatively few made by Inland) and the several serial number blocks, there are a number of Rock-Ola variants available to collectors. Any original, unmodified Rock-Ola carbine in decent condition is a great collectible and is certain to continue a steady appreciation in value and desirability.

QUALITY HARDWARE MACHINE CORPORATION
Table #6

Assigned Serial Number Blocks
1,550,000–1,562,519
1,562,520–1,662,519
1,675,040–1,907,519
1,907,520–1,937,519
4,432,100–4,532,099*
4,632,100–4,879,525

UN-Quality receivers made by Union Switch & Signal

Designated Code Letter
Q

As was the case with most prime contractors, Quality Hardware Machine Corporation had no experience in manufacturing firearms prior to their carbine contract. The firm had a talented engineering staff and accepted many military related contracts during the early days of WWII.

Quality Hardware Machine Corporation carbines may be found with several unusual features relating primarily with the use of subcontracted parts. While all prime contractors utilized subcontractors for many of their components, Quality HMC carried this practice further than any other. The company only manufactured the receiver (along with the spring tube) and procured all remaining parts from other firms. As stated previously, Quality HMC even purchased a number of receivers from a subcontractor, so it is possible to encounter a carbine assembled by Quality HMC but which contains no parts made by the company. The carbines made with receivers manufactured by Union Switch & Signal for Quality HMC (marked "UN-QUALITY") are desirable and significant weapons (from a collecting viewpoint) and are considered a separate and distinct variation of the carbine by some collectors. This variant will be discussed concurrently with the standard receivers produced by Quality Hardware Machine Corporation.

In addition, QHMC carbines are unique because many will contain parts marked with other contractors' codes. For example, with few exceptions, a carbine made by one prime contractor will not contain parts marked with another prime contractor's code. Therefore, when "incorrectly" coded parts are present, it is normally assumed that the parts have been switched and that the carbine is not all original. This assumption cannot always be made when evaluating a Quality HMC carbine. The company frequently made use of various parts marked with other prime contractor codes. This was, by no means, always the case, but it happened with enough frequency to make positive confirmation that all parts are correct rather difficult. A collector is cautioned not to "restore" a Quality HMC carbine just because it contains what may appear to be incorrect parts.

Receiver

Receivers manufactured by Quality Hardware were marked:

QUALITY H.M.C.
Serial #

The receivers made under subcontract by Union Switch & Signal were marked:

UN-QUALITY
Serial #

The receivers made by Quality HMC were of the detachable spring tube housing variety. When production first began, the company used the so-called "Type 1" detachable spring tube housing receiver. Only a handful, perhaps as few as 100, of the receivers of this type were manufactured by Quality HMC before the firms changed to the "Type 2" detachable spring tube housing receiver. Unlike most other contractors who

Quality Hardware Machine Corporation receiver.

used the detachable spring tube housing receiver, Quality Hardware used the detachable variety until it ceased production and did not switch to the integral housing receiver later.

The UN-Quality receivers, on the other hand, were all of the integral spring tube housing variety. It is estimated that no more than 35,000 UN-Quality receivers were manufactured and that most numbers in the latter portion of the serial number block were not used.

Barrel

As stated, Quality Hardware Machine Corporation did not manufacture any barrels and instead used barrels from several firms. Most early Quality HMC carbines were fitted with Rock-Ola barrels, but some Inland and Underwood barrels were also used. As production continued, the company utilized barrels purchased from Buffalo Arms in addition to those acquired from Rock-Ola, Inland, Underwood, IBM, and a relatively small quantity from Winchester. There was little pattern to the use by Quality HMC of any particular make of barrel. The company apparently procured barrels from any available source as production demands dictated. A variety of undated and dated barrels, as well as long and short spacer ("skirt") barrels will be encountered.

UN-Quality receivers were normally teamed with Underwood barrels, although a fair number of Winchester and Inland barrels were also used in the latter part of the serial number range of this receiver variant.

As can be seen, ascertaining if a particular barrel is correct for a Quality or UN-Quality receiver can be difficult. The other prime contractors discussed up to this point all made their own barrels. Therefore if, for example, a Winchester receiver was encountered with a Inland barrel, it can be assumed that the carbine in question is an assembly of parts or a rebuild. This determination cannot be as easily made in regards to Quality HMC carbines, since so many different makes of barrels could be correct.

Front Sight

Quality HMC used the milled type of front sight for most of its production run until the fourth block of serial numbers. The stamped/brazed front sight came into use in the 1,900,000 serial number range. However, there was little consistency from this point until the low to mid-4,600,000 serial number range as both milled and stamped front sights were used. After this range, the stamped sights predominate until the end of production. There will be a number of different code markings found on Quality HMC front sights including "QJ", "JQ" "PO-Q" and "N". A number of the front sights were unmarked.

The UN-Quality carbines were fitted with either stamped or brazed front sights though the latter are more commonly encountered. Again, a variety of code markings may be seen including "J-Q", "PO-Q" and "N". The front sight is one of the parts used by Quality HMC that may be marked with other contractors' codes markings such as "PO-B" (IBM) and "EU" (Underwood), which have been seen on verified original UN-Quality carbines. Some of these have also been reported on Quality HMC carbines.

Barrel Band

Quality HMC utilized the "Type 1" barrel band for its entire production run. Any use of the wider "Type 2" band has not been confirmed. The company ceased manufacture prior to the incorporation of the "Type 3" barrel band in production carbines. Some "Type 3" barrel bands marked "Q" (maker unknown) may be observed from time to time but these are post-WWII

Typical prime contractor and subcontractor markings inside of sling recess. This example was made for Quality Hardware by Rock-Ola.

replacement items and were not used by the company during WWII. Many of the bands were unmarked but some with code markings will be seen. The same is true for the swivels, both unmarked and marked types will be seen. Code markings include "QU", "UI/QU" and "Q-TK". Some bands and/or swivels with other contractors' code markings may also be seen including "UI" and "M-R".

UN-Quality carbines used the "Type 1" barrel band for the majority of the production run but some "Type 2" bands did come into use around the mid-4,400,000 serial number range. Overlap between the two types of barrel bands will be found. Code markings on the "Type 1" band and/or swivel include "UI", "MR" and "KV-B" (all non-Quality HMC contractor codes) as well as unmarked types. The "Type 2" bands appear to have been unmarked. As can be seen, another anomaly of the UN-Quality carbine is the use of non-"Q" coded barrel bands and/or swivels.

Trigger Housing

Quality Hardware Machine Corp. used the milled trigger housing for its entire production run. The company's trigger housings had the full length magazine guide slots. Several different bevel and no bevel configurations will be encountered. The most commonly seen code markings are "NL-Q" or "Q-NL". Interestingly, some stamped/brazed trigger housings marked "Q-TX" have been seen. Though none are thought to have been used by Quality HMC for production carbines, the use of this housing by Quality HMC cannot be absolutely ruled out.

The UN-Quality carbines used both the "no bevel," milled trigger housing with the same code markings as utilized by Quality HMC. It does appear that some original UN-Quality carbines were equipped with the stamped/brazed, "Q-TX"-coded trigger housing, but the serial number range is not known.

Trigger

Quality HMC used the "Type 1" trigger early in production but changed to the "Type 2" in the first block of serial numbers. Early production triggers were marked "Q-LT", and the marking was slightly changed to "LT-Q" for the balance of production. This latter marking was the same type used with the UN-Quality carbines as well.

Safety

QHMC likely used the checkered "Type 1" safety extremely early in its production but details are uncertain. The company soon changed to the uncheckered "Type 2" safety and continued its use until the fifth block of serial numbers (circa #4,430,000) when the improved "Type 3" safety was used. UN-Quality carbines used the "Type 3" safety exclusively. Various code markings will be found for Quality HMC safeties including "Q-NL". Unmarked safeties were also used and so were some stamped with non-QHMC markings such as "EPB" (IBM code).

Magazine Catch

Quality HMC utilized the "short face" ("Type 3") unserrated magazine catch for all of its production carbines including UN-Quality carbines as well. Code markings include "LT-Q", "EP-Q" and "TQ".

Sear

The "Type 1" sear (without hole) was used until about midway through the last block of serial numbers when the later type sear (with hole) was used. The exact time of the change is not known, but it likely occurred somewhere between #4,670,000 and #4,780,000. Quality Hardware Machine Corporation coded sears ("GE-Q") were used as well as some sears stamped with other contractor codes "BOB" (IBM). UN-Quality carbines all appear to have used the later type sear (with hole) marked "GE-Q".

Sear Spring

The "Type 1" sear spring (straight ends) was used at the beginning of production, but the "Type 2" sear spring came into use early in the second serial number block (circa #1,565,000).

Hammer

The first type "dog leg" hammer was used by Quality HMC from the start of production until sometime in the latter part of the first serial number block. The second type "dog leg" hammer began to be used around the low 1,560,000 serial number range. The later straight configuration hammer was used after circa serial #1,900,000 (either extremely late in the third block of numbers or very early in the fourth block). This later pattern hammer was the type used with all UN-Quality carbines. The early "Type 1" hammers were typically marked "Q-LT", and the later hammers were marked "LT-Q". Many of the straight hammers were unfinished (i.e., not blued).

Bolt

Quality HMC made use of the flat top bolt for the vast majority of its carbines. The company did use some round top bolts very late in its production run, around serial #4,800,000. The flat top and round top bolts were typically marked "EMQ" although a few "UN Q" flat top bolts have been reported.

UN-Quality carbines were equipped with flat top bolts until around #4,438,000 when both types began to be used concurrently. The round bolt was used exclusively just prior to circa serial #4,460,000 and continued until production of this variant ceased. Both varieties of bolts were marked "EM-Q".

Extractor

Quality HMC used the "Type 3" flat notch extractor throughout production including in the UN-Quality carbines. Several different code markings will be seen including "W-Q", "IQ", "Q" and "ST/Q".

Extractor Plunger

The company made use of the "Type 2" extractor plunger exclusively. This type of plunger was always used in conjunction with the later types of extractors. No code markings were used due to the small size of the part.

Firing Pin

The early "Type 1" firing pin was used until the last block of numbers when the "Type 3" came into use. Some of the earlier firing pins were used very late in production, but the "Type 3" predominated in the last block. No "Type 2" firing pins have been noted in Quality HMC carbines. Most Quality HMC firing pins were marked "NL-Q", but other codes such as "BQ" have been observed. Original "UN-Quality carbines will be found with Types 1, 2 and 3 firing pins. Most were coded "NL-Q".

Operating Slide

The E169 ("Type 2") operating slide was used by Quality HMC until about #1,675,000 when the E279 ("Type 3") slide began to see use. The E379 ("Type 4") slide was used concurrently with the "Type 3" from around the 1,920,000 until the 4,490,000 serial number range when the later type was used exclusively. The most common code marking was "DA-Q" though some "UN-Q" slides may be found.

These serial number ranges are rough estimates, and more overlap could be encountered. UN-Quality carbines appear to have utilized the "Type 3" (E279) slide exclusively. These were normally marked "DA-Q".

Rear Sight

The non-adjustable flip sight was used by Quality Hardware for virtually all of its production run. It is probable that the company used a few adjustable rear sights at the very end of its production run, circa serial #4,700,000. No UN-Quality carbines are believed to have used adjustable sights. Most Quality HMC flip type rear sights were marked "GE-Q", but some were marked "B-Q". UN-Quality carbines used this same type of rear sight. Interestingly, some rear sights with a block "S" stamped on the base (as found on Standard Products and Winchester sights) have been noted on original Quality Hardware carbines.

Recoil Plate

The "Type 2" recoil plate was used by Quality HMC from the start of production until around serial #1,900,000 (or perhaps a bit earlier) when the latest pattern ("Type 3") recoil plate was used. Most recoil plates were marked "RO-Q", but some "Q-RO" markings have been observed. UN-Quality recoil plates were all believed to have been marked "RO-Q".

Stock and Handguard

Quality HMC used the "I-cut," high wood stock until somewhere prior to serial #1,900,000 when the oval slot (high wood) was used. It is has not been absolutely confirmed that Quality HMC used any low wood stocks. If

so, these only came into use late in the last serial number block. It does appear, however, that some original low wood stocks were used with later production UN-Quality carbines.

Rock-Ola manufactured the stocks utilized by Quality HMC and UN-Quality carbines. The typical "crossed cannons" escutcheon was stamped on the right side in the normal location. Several different sizes of "crossed cannons" may be observed. Code markings were stamped in the sling recess. "Q-RMC" and "QRMC" code markings have been noted for both Quality HMC and UN-Quality carbines. As was the case with other parts used by the company, some stocks were not stamped with the prime contractor code letter and will be found marked "RMC" in the sling recess. One should not automatically assume that a stock marked in this manner should only be on a Rock-Ola rather than on a Quality Hardware carbine. It may well be original.

Quality HMC used both the deep and shallow groove two-rivet handguards. Some were marked "QRMC" or "HQ", but many were stamped "RMC" without any Quality Hardware code letters. Most original UN-Quality carbines were of the shallow groove variety and stamped "Q-RMC". No Quality HMC or UN-Quality carbines were fitted with four-rivet handguards.

Other Variants

The only recognized collector variant beyond the production Quality HMC and UN-Quality carbines are the presentation carbines made by the company. As was the case with most other prime contractors, Quality Hardware made up a few finely finished carbines. These were undoubtedly intended as gifts to company officials, VIPs, etc. Quality Hardware reportedly made only 25 presentation carbines and just a couple of examples have surfaced. These are in a special serial number range with a "Q-EX" prefix and numbered, presumably, from "1" to "25". The few examined lack any sort of proof or government inspection stamps and have finely finished wood and metal. An original presentation Quality Hardware Corporation carbine would be a real find and a valuable collector's piece.

As can be seen, Quality HMC and UN-Quality carbines can pose problems for even experienced collectors. The lack of Quality HMC prime contractor code letters on many parts can be confusing and may raise questions as to the originality of a weapon. Unquestionably, some original Quality Hardware carbines have been improperly "restored" when a collector discovered some parts stamped with code letters indicating other prime contractors. The tendency in cases such as this is to remove the "incorrect" parts and substitute those with "Q" code letters. Normally, this practice is acceptable, but in the case of Quality Hardware carbines, an original piece can easily be devalued. The best advice when dealing with a seemingly original Quality HMC carbine is to leave it alone even if contains some "incorrectly" coded parts. If the questionable parts appear to match the rest of the weapon regarding finish wear, etc., don't mess with it. If an irresistible urge strikes to replace any "incorrect" parts with "Q" marked parts, at least put the "wrong" parts in a safe place and don't sell or trade them. If you subsequently discovered that you "restored" an unaltered piece, you can always replace the original parts, and the carbine will be back in its factory configuration.

With just under 6 percent of the total produced, Quality Hardware carbines are not rare. However, for some reason, they seem to be a bit harder to turn up than the percentage suggests. The UN-Quality carbines are much harder to find with only some 35,000 (or less) manufactured. Some UN-Quality carbines may go unrecognized today if they have been fitted with adjustable sights since the name would be mostly obscured. The letters "UN" are visible and one might easily infer that he was looking at a much more common Underwood carbine rather than the scarce UN-Quality. If the carbine has a 4,4000,00 or 4,500,000 range serial number, it is a UN-Quality and not an Underwood.

A number of questions regarding Quality HMC carbines are still unanswered and research continues. QHMC carbines are very interesting, if occasionally frustrating, carbines and original examples continue to appreciate in price and desirability.

National Postal Meter was one of the myriad civilian firms with little or no experience in manufacturing war material, especially firearms, prior to the Second World War. The company was one of two financial backers of the "Rochester Defense Corporation" which was formed in December of 1941. This entity was organized for defense-related work. Rochester Defense Corp. received its first carbine contract in April of 1942, but the parent company, National Postal Meter, officially became the prime contractor instead. In April 1944, just prior to the cancellation of its carbine contract, National Postal Meter changed its name to Commercial Controls Corporation. National Postal Meter apparently received a great deal of assistance from Inland in setting up its production program as a number of parts will be found with Inland code markings in some early vintage NPM carbines.

Receiver

Receivers were marked:

NATIONAL
POSTAL METER
Serial #

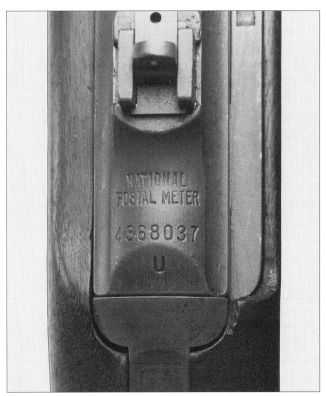

National Postal Meter receiver. This example was manufactured by Union Switch and Signal under subcontract for NPM as evidenced by the "U" marking below the serial number.

NATIONAL POSTAL METER Table #7
Assigned Serial Number Blocks
1,450,000–1,549,999
1,937,520–1,982,519
4,075,010–4,079,999
4,080,000–4,425,099
4,425,100–4,432,099
Designated Code Letter
N

National Postal Meter utilized receivers with the integral spring housing and did not produce any with detachable housings. As was the case with Quality Hardware, National Postal Meter acquired a quantity from Union Switch & Signal. These had standard NPM receiver markings but also had a "U" stamped below the serial number. The "U"-coded National Postal Meter receivers are more commonly encountered than the UN-Quality receivers. It is estimated that perhaps as many as 60,000 receivers were acquired from US&S. These fall into roughly the 4,325,000 to 4,425,000 serial number range.

National Postal Meter also acquired some receivers from other prime contractors. These can be identified by the original maker's name which was marked through with a line and the letter "N" stamped below. National Postal Meter procured receivers from Inland, Underwood and IBM. The IBM receivers noted with the lined out name and the added "N" marking were originally manufactured under subcontract by Auto Ordnance. The receivers transferred to National Postal Meter are not particularly rare but can be somewhat elusive.

Barrel

National Postal Meter did not manufacture any barrels and used those made by several firms. The first three serial number blocks utilized primarily Underwood barrels along with some made by Marlin and a few by Rock-Ola. As production continued, National Postal Meter used some IBM and Buffalo Arms barrels along with Underwood and Marlin barrels.

The Underwood, Rock-Ola and Buffalo Arms barrels were typically stamped with the date (month and year) that the barrel was made. IBM barrels were not generally dated after the end of 1943, and Marlin-made barrels were not dated at all. Barrel dates normally tracked assembly dates fairly closely, but some variance will be encountered. A National Postal Meter carbine that has a barrel other than one of the barrels the makers listed above is very likely an incorrect assembly of parts.

Front Sight

The milled front sight was used by the company until fairly late in production, likely into the fourth serial number block (circa #4,100,000) when use of the stamped/brazed sight began. Codes include "N", "NN" on the milled front sights, and "SN" on the stamped variety.

Barrel Band

It appears that all National Postal Meter carbines utilized the "Type 1" barrel band exclusively. No wider "Type 2" barrel bands have been encountered on original NPM carbines. Early "Type 1" bands were unmarked, but later bands were stamped "U". No band marked with an "N" code have been observed. However, most sling swivels used by National Postal Meter were stamped "UN".

Trigger Housing

National Postal Meter used the milled type trigger housing throughout production and did not make use of any stamped/brazed housings. One of the interesting features found on NPM trigger housings was a one or two digit number stamped next to the "N" code marking. Numbers as low as "1" and as high as "23" have been observed. These are presumably a revision number as there is some correlation between the date the receiver was made and the number on the trigger housing. However, there is not enough hard data available to determine with certainty the precise relationship.

Trigger

National Postal Meter may have used a very small quantity of the "Type 1" triggers early in production, but the improved "Type 2" will be found in virtually all original examples. The triggers were coded "SN". Some triggers marked "N" next to a trident shaped logo have been seen in rebuilds, but none are believed to have been used by National Postal Meter for production carbines.

Safety

The first pattern safety used by National Postal Meter was the so-called "Type 2" safety without checkering. There is no evidence that the company utilized any checkered safeties. The improved "Type 3" safety came into use by NPM around the beginning of the third block of serial numbers (circa #4,075,010). Most safeties of both types were marked "IN", although some marked "SN" were used later in production. Some collectors are unsure whether the "IN" marked safety is correct for an Inland carbine or National Postal Meter. Based on the observation of known original specimens, this safety is proper for National Postal Meter carbines.

Magazine Catch

All known original National Postal Meter carbines were equipped with the short face "Type 3" magazine. Early production versions were coded "MN", and later catches were coded "SN". None of the later "Type 3" catches marked "M" on the face have been observed on original National Postal Meter carbines.

Sear

The "Type 1" sear (no hole) was used by NPM from the start of production until sometime in the fourth block of serial numbers (circa #4,150,000) when the "Type 2" came into use. The most common code marking found on the earlier production sears was "LN" though some were unmarked. As production continued, other code markings were seen including "SW-N" and "BN". Sears coded for other prime contractors were also used by National Postal Meter including sears made for Inland and IBM.

Sear Spring

The "Type 1" (straight ends) sear spring was used on very early NPM carbines, but the "Type 2" (tapered ends) began to be used about midway through the second serial number block (around serial #1,960,000).

Hammer

The first pattern ("Type 1") "dog leg" hammer was used very early in production, but the "Type 2," "dog leg" hammer began to see use circa serial #1,453,000. The straight configuration "Type 3" hammer was used by NPM beginning in the third block of serial numbers (circa #1,960,000). A number of hammers made for Inland ("HI" coded) with an added "N" marking have been observed. Other code markings used by National Postal Meter include "HN" and "N".

Bolt

National Postal Meter used only the flat top bolt. These were normally marked on the left lug with an "N" code and a one or two digit number such as "9", "11" or "14". Some bolts marked with a "UN" code have also been seen. Interestingly, some purported original National Postal Meter carbines in the 4,400,000 range have been observed with round bolts made by Inland (marked "AI"). If original, this would indicate that NPM procured some standard Inland round bolts late in the company's production run. This would be yet another example of close cooperation between National Postal Meter and Inland.

Extractor

NPM used the "Type 3" extractor (flat notch) exclusively. These were marked "N" or "IN".

Extractor Plunger

The "Type 2" extractor plunger (with flat area machined on one side of the cone) was used by National Postal Meter throughout production.

Firing Pin

The early "Type 1" firing pin was used by NPM from the start of production until around serial #4,140,000 when the "Type 3" (manufactured with the clearance cut at the rear) was used. It is not believed that National Postal Meter utilized any modified "Type 2" firing pins. Code markings include "WN", "NN" and "DN".

Operating Slide

The E169 ("Type 2") slide with partially rounded rear box cut was used by NPM until very late in the first serial number block (circa #1,540,000) when the company began using the E279 ("Type 3") operating slide with the straight cut at the rear of the box. This slide stayed in use until early in the fourth serial number block (around #4,100,000) when the E379 ("Type 4") slide with the wide arm joint was used. This slide remained in use by NPM until the cessation of production. Slides were marked "N" or "UN" with a one or two digit number. As was the case with trigger housings, the meaning of the number has not been positively determined.

Rear Sight

National Postal Meter used only the non-adjustable flip rear sight. Various markings will be found on the rear sight base and leaf. The earliest were generally marked "RN" on both the base and leaf. A relatively few sights having bases stamped with a large block "S", signifying production by Lyman, were used as production continued. Later codes included "TN" on the base and/or leaf. No original production National Postal Meter carbines were assembled with either type of adjustable rear sight.

Recoil Plate

The "Type 2" recoil plate was replaced fairly early in production, around serial #1,540,000 by the improved "Type 3." Some "Type 2" recoil plates were marked "LN", but uncoded recoil plates of this type may also be encountered. "Type 3" recoil plates were normally marked "PN" or "LN".

Stock and Handguard

The early pattern "I-cut" stock with high wood in front of the operating slide was used by NPM until the

Stock cartouche on National Postal Meter carbine. "FJA" represents the initials of Col. Frank J. Atwood, head of NPM's Ordnance District. Note the faint "crossed cannons" escutcheon next to the cartouche.

1,490,000 serial number range (or perhaps a bit later) when the oval cut (high wood) stock came into use. It is not believed that any original NPM stocks were of the low wood variety. If so, any such use would have been limited to very late in the company's production run.

Some very early stocks were marked "OI" or "LA" in the sling recess, which indicated that they were acquired from Inland. Later stocks were stamped "TN" or "Trimble/TN" in the sling recess indicating production by the Trimble Nursery Company. National Postal Meter stamped a cartouche on the right side of their stocks consisting of "NPM/FJA" next to the "crossed cannons" escutcheon. "FJA" represents the initials of Col. Frank J. Atwood, head of National Postal Meter's Ordnance District.

Some early handguards were marked "OI" indicating production by Inland, but most handguards used by the company were stamped "TN". National Postal Meter handguards were of the deep groove variety until late in 1943 when the shallow groove was instituted. All handguards were of the two-rivet type.

Other Variants

A very rare and sometimes overlooked variant are the carbines marked "Commercial Controls". In April 1944, about a week prior to the cancellation of its carbine contract, National Postal Meter changed its corporate name to Commercial Controls Corporation. Although the firm was essentially out of the carbine manufacturing business, some 239 unfinished receivers still on hand were stamped "Commercial Controls" and serially numbered in the range 0001–0239. These were assembled into complete carbines by the company using a variety of leftover early and late NPM parts. In reality, the newly named Commercial Controls Corp. did not actually manufacture any carbine parts and used components (including the unfinished receivers) remaining on hand after National Postal Meter ceased production to assemble the few carbines. The ultimate disposition of the 239 Commercial Controls carbines is not known, although some were probably used as presentation pieces. Obviously, an original example would be a very rare and valuable item. It should be noted that some fakes have been observed over the years so one should proceed very carefully if such a carbine is offered for sale. The area of the receiver where the maker's name and serial number were stamped should be especially scrutinized. The fakes normally have the original markings buffed out and the bogus markings stamped in their place.

No original presentation (except for possibly a few of the Commercial Controls marked examples) or other types of non-standard NPM carbines have been reported. Some pre-production "tool room" examples have been observed. The few known examples have unmarked receivers that are believed to have been made by Inland along with many Inland coded parts. Barrels were normally Underwood and some "N" marked parts. Positive identification should be obtained before any substantial sum is paid for a supposedly original NPM tool room carbine.

There are a number of interesting variants of National Postal Meter carbines including the "U" coded receivers and the receivers made for other prime contractors, which were transferred to NPM, and the rare Commercial Controls variant. The fact that the company often used parts made for other contractors and that bore their code markings can be confusing to some beginning collectors. Just because an otherwise original appearing National Postal Meter carbine contains one or more parts with seemingly improper codes should not necessarily mean the piece is not correct. It would be a shame to replace original parts with incorrect parts even if the latter are marked with "N" codes. As mentioned previously, even if any seemingly incorrect parts are removed, they should be put away so that the piece can be restored if an error is later discovered.

National Postal Meter carbines are not particularly scarce, but the "U"-coded receivers may be a bit tough to locate. The company made some 6.8 percent of the total production so a good example can usually be found with a little searching. As is the case with all original GI carbines, any original example of a National Postal Meter should be obtained whenever found at a reasonable price.

STANDARD PRODUCTS
Table #8

Assigned Serial Number Blocks
1,982,520–2,352,519

Designated Code Letter
S

Unlike the prime contractors discussed previously, Standard Products was only assigned one block of serial numbers even though it produced slightly more carbines than did Rock-Ola, which was assigned four separate serial number blocks. Standard Products produced four components of the carbine: the receiver, bolt, operating slide and trigger housing.

Receiver

Receivers were marked:

STD. PRO.
Serial #

Standard Products utilized the integral spring tube housing receiver exclusively and did not use any detachable housing receivers. Standard Products used very few receivers made by other contractors. It appears that approximately one hundred receivers were acquired by the firm from Underwood in late 1943. Such receivers reportedly had the Underwood name defaced with a line and stamped below, "STD. PRO" and a serial number in the SP range. If original, such a carbine would be a scarce item.

Barrel

Standard Products carbines are most often found with Underwood barrels. However the company also used some Buffalo Arms and Marlin barrels. A few Inland and IBM barrels have also been reported, but such usage, if any, would have been limited.

Front Sight

Standard Products used the milled front sight exclusively. These sights were marked either "N" or "SN". The "N" code marking on this sight does not indicate that it was made for National Postal Meter but instead represented the initials of the subcontractor, Niedner Company, who manufactured the sight. Niedner made many carbine front sights for a number of prime contractors.

Barrel Band

Standard Products used the "Type 1" barrel band for the majority of its carbines but did change to the wider "Type 2" band around serial #2,175,000. None of the Standard Products bands were stamped with codes. The company did not use the "Type 3" barrel band as production ceased prior to their introduction of this band.

Trigger Housing

The milled trigger housing was used by SP for most of its production run. The company changed to the stamped/brazed housing fairly late in production, around

Standard Products receiver.

serial #2,100,000. The Standard Products trigger housings were stamped with code a letter (i.e., "S") along with a one or two digit number. Numbers ranging from 5 to as high as 25 have been noted. Some of the late stamped/brazed trigger housings will be found marked "ST" or "BE-B" on original SP carbines. The "BE-B" markings on Standard Product trigger housings are yet another example of a seemingly incorrect code that is, in fact, believed to be proper.

Trigger

Standard Products utilized the later "Type 2" trigger exclusively. Code markings at the beginning of production were "S-HR", "S IR" or "SA", while later production triggers were generally marked "S-C".

Safety

The uncheckered "Type 2" safety was used by SP until around serial #2,030,000 when the improved "Type 3" safety was introduced. The "Type 2" safeties were generally unmarked as were some of the "Type 3" safeties. However, many of the latter variety were stamped with codes such as "SW" or "S-MB".

Magazine Catch

The "short face," unserrated "Type 3" magazine catch was used throughout production by Standard Products. Most were stamped "SW".

Sear

Standard Products used the original pattern "Type 1" sear until around serial #2,130,000 when the company switched to the "Type 2". Code markings included "SD", "SW" and "SDP".

Sear Spring

Little, if any use, was made of the "Type 1" sear spring. The "Type 2" spring was used throughout Standard Products' production run.

Hammer

No early first pattern "dog leg" hammers are believed to have been used by Standard Products. The "Type 2" dog leg was utilized until approximately serial number 2,040,000 when the straight configuration hammer came into use. The dog leg hammers may be found with one of several types of code markings including "SW", "KR" and "HI". Note that the last two were not Standard Products codes. The later straight hammers were typically marked "SS", "SW" or "SHTE".

Bolt

Standard Products used the flat top variety bolt. As was the case with SP trigger housings and operating slides, bolts were normally stamped with a "S" code letter and a one or two digit number. Numbers ranging from "2" to as high as "53" have been observed. Most bolts were marked on the right lug, but later production bolts were stamped with code letters/numbers on the left lug. The bolt numbers tend to track production closely. For example, early production SP carbines will have lower bolt numbers than later production weapons. There is not enough data to pin down the precise serial number ranges when bolt numbers changed.

Extractor

The "Type 3" extractor (manufactured with flat notch) was used in all Standard Products carbines. Code markings include "S WI" and "SW".

Extractor Plunger

The "Type 2" extractor plunger was fitted to all original Standard Products carbines. As was the case with other contractors, Standard Products extractor plungers were blued.

Firing Pin

The "Type 1" firing pin was used from the start of production until the improved "Type 3" was introduced around serial #2,140,000. It is possible that some of the modified "Type 2" firing pins were used by Standard Products for a brief period of time prior to adoption of the later type. Firing pins may be found with code markings, which include "HS", "WS" and "SDP".

Operating Slide

The first variety operating slide used by Standard Products was the E279 ("Type 3"). These were normally stamped with an "S" inside of the bottom of the box. SP changed to the E379 ("Type 4") around serial number 2,040,000. This slide was used for the balance of production. Later E379 slides were stamped with an "S" enclosed in a circle. In addition to the "S" or "circled S" code markings, Standard Products slides were marked with a number code as well.

Rear Sight

Standard Products used the non-adjustable flip rear sight from the start of production to just past serial #2,200,000 range when the milled adjustable sight started to be used. Most of the early sights were marked with a block letter "S" on the left side of the base. The leaves were not coded. The milled adjustable rear sights used by SP were coded with an "H" enclosed in a shield-shaped logo. No stamped adjustable rear sights have been noted.

Recoil Plate

The "Type 2" recoil plate was utilized from the onset of Standard Products' contract until around serial #2,010,000 when the improved "Type 3" began to appear. Standard Products' "Type 2" recoil plates were marked "SW", and the later variety were normally coded "SW" or "SWI".

Buttplate

Standard Products was one of the few prime contractors to have utilized buttplates stamped with code markings. Some buttplates used by the company were marked "S-S3".

Stock and Handguard

Early Standard Products carbines were manufactured with the "I-cut", high wood stocks. However, use of this early pattern stock by SP was short-lived, and it was replaced by the oval cut, high wood stock very early in production, likely around serial #1,985,000. The high wood stock continued in use until just before serial #2,090,000 when the low wood stock began to see production. Standard Products stocks were normally stamped with the "crossed cannons" escutcheon on the right side and subcontractor codes in the sling recess. These codes were "SJ" or "S-HB".

The two-rivet handguard with the deep groove was used until around serial #1,990,000 when the two-rivet shallow groove variety made its appearance. No four-rivet handguards were used. Code markings were "S-HB" for most handguards, but some of the later production handguards were coded "SJ".

Other Variants

The standard M1 carbine was the only type manufactured by Standard Products and no special variants were produced. There is some evidence that the company did turn out a few presentation pieces since a small number of carbines marked "STD. PRO." on the receiver but lacking serial numbers have been observed. Such pieces typically have deluxe grade wood, and some are reported with highly polished and blued finishes. All components were marked with normal Standard Products codes. Little is known about these presenta-

tion Standard Products carbines. The lack of a serial number is the key feature. Any example offered for sale should be closely examined to be certain that it was originally manufactured without a serial number rather than a receiver with a buffed out number.

The various parts stamped with numbers as well as letter codes are an interesting feature of Standard Products carbines. With just 4 percent of the total production, Standard Product carbines can sometimes be a bit difficult to find in comparison to some of the other prime contractors.

INTERNATIONAL BUSINESS MACHINES (IBM)
Table #9

Assigned Serial Number Block
3,651,520–4,009,999

Designated Code Letter
B

To most non-collectors, IBM is probably the most recognized of the corporate entities that produced carbines during World War II. The company was the last to receive a carbine production contract. And in addition to producing carbines, IBM manufactured large numbers of M1918A2 Browning Automatic Rifles (BARs) and a quantity of M7 rifle grenade launchers along with many other types of war material.

Receiver

Receivers manufactured by International Business Machines were marked:

I.B.M. CORP
Serial #

Extremely early receivers (probably just the first couple of hundred or less) were marked, in irregularly spaced, deeply stamped letters, "I.B.M." (without "Corp."). These letters were much larger and very crudely applied compared to those found on subsequent production IBM carbines.

IBM also procured a quantity of receivers manufactured by Auto-Ordnance Corporation. These receivers were marked the same as those made by IBM but were stamped "AO" below the serial numbers.

International Business Machines receiver.

IBM barrel dated October 1943. IBM barrels were also marked with the Ordnance "flaming bomb" insignia.

All receivers used by IBM were of the integral spring housing variety. Receivers made by IBM were of the narrow tang type while the receivers procured from Auto-Ordnance were of the wide tang variety.

Barrel

IBM made their own barrels and supplied many to other prime contractors. The barrels were stamped with "I.B.M. CORP." and the "flaming bomb" insignia. IBM barrels were marked with the month and year of production up through "12-43" at which time dates were eliminated. As was the case with the receivers, very early production barrels were stamped with crude "I.B.M." markings and year "43". This was soon changed to the better aligned markings used subsequently. IBM barrels were made with the integral gas cylinder.

Front Sight

The milled front sight (marked "N") was used by IBM very early in production, but the company soon changed to the stamped/brazed sight just after serial #3,650,000. The stamped/brazed front sight was used from this point until the end of production. Markings were either "PO B" and "SI-B".

Barrel Band

IBM used the "Type 1" barrel band from the start of production until around the low 3,890,000 serial number range at which time the wider "Type 2" band began to be used. Most "Type 1" IBM barrel bands were not marked, but the sling swivel was coded ("KV-B" being the most commonly encountered code). The "Type 2" bands were typically unmarked. No "Type 3" bands were used by IBM.

Trigger Housing

IBM was one of the few contractors to use the stamped/brazed trigger housing exclusively. It has been reported that a handful of extremely early production IBM carbines may have been equipped with milled trigger housings that were originally made for National

Typical code marking on front sight of an IBM carbine.

Postal Meter in order to get production underway. However, any such use was very short-lived and IBM utilized the stamped/brazed trigger housings in all of their regular production carbines. The most common code marking was "BE-B".

Trigger

The "Type 2" trigger was used for all IBM carbines. Most early triggers were coded "TB", but later triggers will be found with various codes including, "PDB", "PMB" and "SKB". Occasionally, a trigger with other contractors' codes may be found in what appear to be completely original carbines. "SN" (National Postal Meter) and "HR" (Rock-Ola) have been observed. These, however, are in the minority, and the overwhelming majority of IBM triggers will be found with the company's code markings.

Safety

IBM used the "Type 3" safety for all of its carbines. Except for a very few unmarked safeties used in extremely early production, the safeties were marked "EPB". Some were marked on the face of the safety and others had the markings stamped inside.

Magazine Catch

The "Type 3" magazine catch (not marked "M" on the face) was used by IBM for all production carbines. The catches were typically coded either "PRB" or "EPB".

Sear

The "Type 1" sear (no hole) was used by IBM throughout production. However, some of the later sears (with hole) have been reported in the "AO" coded receivers just above serial number 3,890,000. Code markings used on IBM sears include "SW-B", "G.B.", "BOB" and "SG-B".

Sear Spring

The "Type 2" sear spring with straight ends was used for all IBM carbines.

Hammer

No variety of the dog leg hammer was used in any IBM carbines. The straight configuration hammers used by IBM were typically coded "AMB", "GMB" or "WMB". Both case hardened and blued hammers may be encountered.

Bolt

The flat top bolt was utilized by IBM from the start of the company's production run until sometime after the 3,780,000 serial number range when the round top bolt began to be used. This serial range is a rough approximation and some overlap will definitely be found. By serial number 3,875,000 (approximately) the round top bolt was used almost exclusively by IBM. Flat top bolts were initially coded "AOB" (made by Auto Ordnance), but "SB" coded bolts have also been observed. IBM used a few flat top bolts acquired from Inland (coded "S.I.") just prior to the change to the round top bolt. IBM round top bolts were typically coded "AOB" or "EM-B". Most bolts were stamped with codes on the right lug.

Extractor

The "Type 3" extractor (manufactured with the flat notch) was used by IBM in all production carbines. Code markings were normally either "IB" or "W-B".

Extractor Plunger

The "Type 2" extractor plunger (with flat area machined on the side) was the type used in all IBM carbines.

Firing Pin

The first pattern firing pin was used by IBM at the beginning of production until the early 3,800,000 serial number range when the second type began to be utilized. The third pattern firing pin came into use around the mid-3,850,000 serial number range. All three types of firing pins were utilized by IBM on a more-or-less random basis until the cessation of production. A variety of different code markings may be found on IBM firing pins including "BTB", "BR-B", "BEB", "OBB", "SVB" and "WB".

Operating Slide

The first variety of operating slide used by IBM was the E279 ("Type 3"). The E379 ("Type 4") appears to have been first used with "AO" coded receivers in the low 3,890,000 serial number range and with standard IBM receivers slightly later. As was often the case, both types of operating slides were used concurrently to some extent until the end of production. Most IBM operating slides were manufactured under subcontract by Auto Ordnance (coded "AOB"). Many IBM slides were also stamped with letter codes other than the contractor/subcontractor marking. Some slides were procured from Inland in late 1943. There will be some inconsistency found among slides in IBM carbines so making a lot of hard and fast assumptions is not advised.

Rear Sight

IBM used the non-adjustable flip rear sight until around the low 3,890,000 serial number range when the firm began to install the stamped adjustable variety. A few milled adjustable rear sights were also reportedly used by IBM, but this has not been positively confirmed. There was a substantial period of overlap during which the flip sights and adjustable sights were used

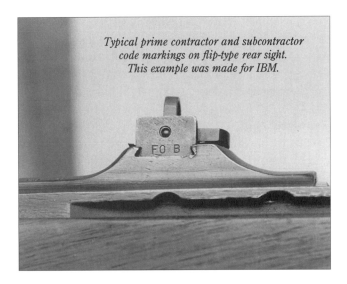

Typical prime contractor and subcontractor code markings on flip-type rear sight. This example was made for IBM.

concurrently. In fact, IBM apparently made use of a fair number of the early flip sights rather late in production and long after the adjustable sight began to be used. Therefore, a properly coded flip-type sight can theoretically be found in any vintage IBM carbine, but the adjustable variety should not be encountered prior to the low 3,890,000 serial number range. Early sights were typically marked "INB" which was followed by sights marked "FO B". Some marked "W-B" have also been observed. The stamped adjustable sights were marked "I.R. Co."

Recoil Plate

All original IBM carbines are known to have been fitted with the later "Type 3" recoil plate. Most were marked "PR-B", but a few coded "BB" have been reported.

Stock and Handguard

The early "I-cut," high wood stock was the original pattern used by IBM from the beginning until the low 3,700,000 serial number range at which time the oval cut, high wood stock began to see use. The low wood modification began to be used around serial number 3,890,000. The "AO"-coded receivers were fitted with

oval slot stocks, either high or low wood. Most, if not all, early "I-cut" IBM stocks were manufactured by Rock-Ola and were marked "RMC B" in the sling recess. Various code markings may be found on the later stocks including "BR-B", "JL-B", "SC-B" and a very few marked "LW-B". As was the case with other prime contractors, IBM stocks were stamped with a "crossed cannons" escutcheon on the right side.

The early production "I-cut," high wood stocks were teamed with handguards having the deep sighting groove marked "RMC". The shallow groove handguard was introduced fairly early in production, and both types were used concurrently for a rather long period of time. Various code markings on the later type of handguards include "LW-B", "SCB", "BR-B" and "JL-B". No four-rivet handguards were used by IBM.

Other Variants

IBM produced a small number of presentation carbines, estimated at half a dozen or perhaps a few more. Such carbines were finished in bluing rather than parkerizing. All parts were standard IBM components. The handful of apparently original specimens were fitted with metal plagues on the stock to identify the recipient. Since the IBM presentation did not have special serial numbers, the possibility always exists that a bogus example of this type could be produced with little effort.

The "AO" coded receivers are desirable variants of IBM carbines, and many collectors hope to obtain original examples. Such carbines are not rare but can be tough to find. A number of experienced carbine collectors have commented that IBM carbines seem to be found in original, unaltered condition more than any other make. The reason(s) for this apparent anomaly are unknown, but this does appear to be the case. In any event, with some 5.7 percent of the total production, IBM carbines are not particularly difficult to find. Barrel and receiver markings on many IBM carbines are somewhat indistinct, and the company apparently had some difficulty stamping these components. One former employee commented that the dies used to stamp markings on barrels were very powerful and care had to be taken not to impress the markings too deeply. This perhaps explains why a number of IBM barrels have weak and indistinct markings.

Given the fame of the IBM name today, many noncollectors are a bit surprised that a well known computer maker produced large number of carbines during WWII. An IBM carbine is an excellent example of how

America's civilian firms were able to shift to wartime industries in a brief period of time and turn out vast quantities of weaponry.

Saginaw Steering Gear
Division of General Motors
Tables #10 and #12

One of the more interesting carbine prime contractors was Saginaw Steering Gear. Like the prolific contractor, Inland, Saginaw was a subsidiary of the General Motors Corporation. Saginaw Steering Gear Division is noteworthy among carbine makers as it operated two separate plants in two different cities. In order to clarify a potentially confusing story, production at the "main" plant in Saginaw, Michigan, will be discussed first. The second plant in Grand Rapids, Michigan, was taken over by Saginaw Steering Gear after the failure of the Irwin-Pedersen Company to fulfill their carbine production contract. The Irwin-Pedersen carbines and those subsequently made by Saginaw at the Grand Rapids plant will be discussed together as they are inexorably linked.

SAGINAW STEERING GEAR — SAGINAW PLANT
Table #10

Although Saginaw Steering Gear was a long-time producer of automotive items, the company began plans for production of weaponry in the late 1930s. Even before Pearl Harbor, Saginaw had constructed a large plant for the purpose of manufacturing machine guns for the United States government. During the war, the company produced M1919A4 and M1919A6 .30 caliber, air-cooled machine guns along with many other types of war material. Saginaw received its carbine production contract in February 1943, and the first carbine was completed in April.

Assigned Serial Number Blocks
3,250,020–3,651,519
5,834,619–6,071,188

Designated Code Letters
SG

Receiver

Receivers were marked:

Saginaw S.G.
Serial #

All Saginaw receivers were of the integral spring housing variety. The receivers are also characterized by the wide rear tang though a few narrow tang receivers with "SG" code markings have been reported. The narrow tang receivers were used from the start of production until approximately serial number 3,288,000 when the wide tang came into use. Both narrow and wide tang receivers were used concurrently for a period of time, until just after serial number 3,375,000 when the wide tang was used exclusively.

Saginaw Steering Gear receiver produced at the company's main plant in Saginaw, Michigan. Note the "SG" code on the recoil plate.

Barrel

Saginaw manufactured its own barrels. These were marked:

SAGINAW S.G. DIV.
GENERAL MOTORS

The barrels were not dated or marked with the "flaming bomb" insignia and were of the swaged-on gas cylin-

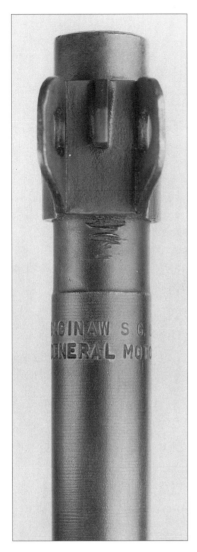

Carbine barrel made by the Saginaw Steering Gear Division at its main plant in Saginaw, Michigan. Note the crude staking marks behind the front sight.

der type. Early production barrels utilized the "short skirt," but later production barrels were of the "long skirt" variety. Unlike some other prime contractors who made their own barrels, Saginaw was not a large supplier of barrels to other carbine manufacturers.

Front Sight

The milled front sight was used by Saginaw for most of their carbines. The firm may have changed to the stamped/brazed front sight (marked "SG" or "PD") later in its production run. If so, use of this type of sight was limited. The milled sights were unmarked.

Barrel Band

Saginaw used the "Type 1" barrel band for most its production carbines. A few "Type 2" bands appear to have been used in the later 5,860,000 serial number range. Both types have been observed on late production carbines. Saginaw barrel bands were unmarked.

Trigger Housing

The milled trigger housing (without beveled rear corners) was used by Saginaw from the beginning until the end of production. No stamped/brazed trigger housings were utilized by the company. The trigger housings were stamped with the "SG" code marking on the right side. Some of the code markings were stamped in an inverted position.

Trigger

Saginaw exclusively used the "Type 2" triggers. These can generally be identified by the "SG" marking, however, a few unmarked triggers were used by Saginaw.

Safety

Saginaw made use of the "Type 2" safety from the start of production until sometime before the 3,340,000 serial number range when the improved "Type 3" came into use. Most safties were marked "SG", although some unmarked examples may be observed.

Magazine Catch

The "Type 3" (short face, unserrated) catch with unmarked face (i.e., no "M") was used by Saginaw until the second serial number block. At this time the later variant "M"-marked, "Type 3" catches were used. As was often the case, some overlap may be observed. Code markings included "SG", "W-SG", "E-SG" and "ISG".

Sear

Saginaw apparently used the early type of unmarked sear (without the hole) for most, if not all, of its production.

Sear Spring

The "Type 2" sear spring (with tapered ends) was used by Saginaw throughout its production run.

Hammer

It appears that the straight configuration hammer was used by Saginaw throughout production. A few were unmarked, but most were marked "SG".

Bolt

The flat top bolt was the first type used by Saginaw until early in the second serial number block when the round bolt came into use. Saginaw bolts were marked "SG" on the left lug.

Extractor

The "Type 3" extractor (flat notch) was used in all Saginaw carbines. These were typically coded "SG" or "WSG".

Extractor Plunger

The "Type 2" extractor plunger, with the flat area machined on one side of the cone, was used.

Firing Pin

The "Type 1" firing pin was used from the start of Saginaw's production and for most of the first serial number block. "Type 2" and "Type 3" firing pins were used in some later production Saginaw carbines, generally in the second serial number block. The majority of firing pins were marked "SG", but some unmarked ones are also believed to have been used.

Operating Slide

The E279 ("Type 3") slide was the first variant utilized by Saginaw. None of the earlier "round box"-type slides are believed to have be used by the company. The E379 slide came into use by Saginaw sometime around serial number 3,475,000, however, some overlap between the two types may be encountered. Saginaw operating slides were marked "SG" on the bottom.

Rear Sight

The flip-type, non-adjustable rear sight was used by Saginaw for virtually all of its carbines. Early sights of this type were stamped with a block "S" on the base, and others had a small rounded "S". Some milled adjustable rear sights may have been used extremely late in production — around the 6,060,000 serial number range. Any such use of adjustable rear sights by Saginaw would have been very limited.

Recoil Plate

The latest pattern "Type 3" recoil plate was used by all Saginaw carbines except for perhaps the very earliest production models. Many of the recoil plates made by the firm are easy to identify without removing the action from the stock because they are stamped "SG" on the top surface.

Stock and Handguards

Saginaw used the "high wood," oval cut stock from the beginning of production until around serial number 3,550,000 when the low wood stock came into use. Both types (low and high wood) were used concurrently through the end of production. It has been reported that the firm used some "I-cut" stocks *very* early in production, which were acquired from other sources primarily Inland (marked "OI") and Rock-Ola (marked "RMC"). Saginaw stocks were typically stamped "RSG" in the sling recess. The stocks were stamped with a "SG" cartouche and a "crossed cannons" escutcheon on the right side.

Handguards with the wide sighting groove were used by Saginaw early in production until sometime in the first serial number block at which time the narrow groove variety was used. Saginaw handguards were marked "RSG" on the bottom edge. All are believed to be of the two-rivet type.

Other Variants

Saginaw fabricated a few presentation carbines apparently near the termination of production. Too few original examples are known to make any solid conclusions. Generally, the receivers were unmarked but fitted with "SG"-coded parts. Various vintages of parts have been noted, which was likely due to the use of leftover parts still on hand. Unlike some contractors that produced finely blued presentation carbines with fancy wood, the Saginaw presentation carbines were usually finished in standard parkerizing. The stock and handguards were of the issue configuration but some were reportedly made from higher than standard grade wood. Some of the presentation carbines (perhaps those made at the Grand Rapids plant) were also equipped with wooden display stands. As is always the case, one should proceed very cautiously when contemplating the purchase of a supposedly original presentation carbine.

For some inexplicable reason, Saginaw carbines seem to be much harder to find today than the production totals would suggest. This is not to state that the weapons are rare, but many collectors have discovered that carbines made by other firms with far smaller production totals seem to turn up more often than do Saginaw carbines. Any original Saginaw carbine in collectible condition is a great find.

IRWIN-PEDERSEN ARMS COMPANY
Table #11

Assigned Serial Number Block
1,762,520–1,875,039
3,212,520–3,250,019*

*Block assigned to Saginaw — Grand Rapids Plant

Designated Code Letter
IP

In general, the World War II carbine production program was an unqualified success with over six million manufactured in just over four years. While every contractor experienced varying degrees of difficulty in getting their carbine production program underway, one firm was unable to deliver any acceptable carbines to the government. Like many fledging arms producers during the early days of WWII, the Irwin-Pedersen Company was formed in hopes of cashing in on the lucrative government contracts of the period. The company was a joint venture between the famous arms designer, John D. Pedersen and an established Grand Rapids, Michigan, manufacturer of furniture, the Irwin Brothers. Mr. Pedersen brought his firearms engineering expertise (along with his well-known name) to the firm and the Irwin Brothers who possessed the necessary manufacturing equipment and plant. In March 1942, the newly organized Irwin-Pedersen Arms Company signed a contract with the government for the production of M1 carbines. Delivery was to begin by October of the same year. A revision of the contract the following month increased the number of carbines to be manufactured by Irwin-Pedersen to 112,520. The company was to produce all parts of the carbine except the barrel (and gas cylinder).

As soon as the company began to tool up for carbine production, many problems were encountered. The Irwin Brothers were apparently competent furniture makers, but they did not possess the expertise necessary to produce such items as firearms which required machine work to exacting tolerances. John Pedersen was undeniably a talented firearms designer, but his talents did not lie in managing a manufacturing plant.

The company struggled to complete a number of finished M1 carbines, but none were able to pass inspection. The situation was so critical that the government eventually canceled the Irwin-Pedersen contract due to unsatisfactory performance and negotiated with Saginaw Steering Gear Division of General Motors to take over the failed operation. Saginaw assumed operation of the Grand Rapids plant as a separate arms making facility. The company used the satisfactory Irwin-Pedersen parts on hand, including many receivers, to assemble carbines that met the government's specifications. A number of the receivers were marked with the Irwin-Pedersen name but were not serially numbered. Saginaw stamped these receivers with serial numbers from their assigned block. Therefore, there will be two separate serial number ranges found on Irwin-Pedersen marked receivers. It appears that some receivers in the second serial number block were actually assembled into complete carbines prior to all of the serial numbers

in the first block being used.

Irwin-Pedersen had trouble with many aspects of carbine production including the heat treatment of key parts. Many of the early carbines shipped from the plant after Saginaw took over contained all, or virtually all, I-P parts. It has been estimated that no more than 4,000 Irwin-Pedersen carbines were assembled and ready for inspection prior to Saginaw assuming operation of the Grand Rapids plant. This section will give details on the carbines built by Irwin-Pedersen prior to the cancellation of their contract, and those completed by Saginaw using Irwin-Pedersen marked receivers.

Receiver
Receivers were marked:

IRWIN-PEDERSEN
Serial #

All Irwin-Pedersen receivers were of the integral housing type. One difference between I-P receivers and those made by other contractors was the presence of a "locator" hole on the left rear of the receiver. The hole secured the receiver to the manufacturing tooling during production.

Irwin-Pedersen receiver.

Barrel

The vast majority of Irwin-Pedersen carbines were fitted with Underwood barrels, however, some Rock-Ola barrels were used in later assembled I-P receivers.

Front Sight

The milled "Type 1" front sight was used on all Irwin-Pedersen carbines. Codes were either "N" (Nieder) or "IPN".

Barrel Band

Irwin-Pedersen carbines were all fitted with the "Type 1" barrel band. Some bands were unmarked, but many were stamped "UP".

Trigger Housing

The milled trigger housing was used exclusively by Irwin-Pedersen. These are easy to identify as they were marked "IP".

Trigger

Irwin-Pedersen carbines were equipped with the "Type 1" trigger. Most were marked "IP", although some unmarked examples have been noted.

Safety

The so-called "Type 2" safety (first pattern, uncheckedered) was utilized by Irwin-Pedersen. These were marked on the face with code markings. Most were marked "IP-W" although some marked "IP-A" may also be encountered.

Magazine Catch

Irwin-Pedersen exclusively used the "Type 3" magazine catch with "short face" and no serrations. None of the later catches of this type with the "M" marked face were utilized. Irwin-Pedersen magazine catch code markings include "IP-B", "IP-W", "P-IP" and "E-IP".

Sear

All Irwin-Pedersen sears were of the "Type 1" (no hole) variety. These were marked either "IP-SW" or "SW-IP".

Sear Spring

The company used the "Type 1" sear spring with straight ends.

Hammer

All of the hammers made by Irwin-Pedersen prior to cancellation of their contract are believed to have been the early pattern "Type 1," dog leg hammer. These were marked "IP". Soon after operations were assumed by Saginaw, the "Type 2" hammer came into use.

Bolt

All bolts used by Irwin-Pedersen were the flat top type and marked "IP". As was the case with all contractors, the bolts were originally blued.

Extractor

Irwin-Pedersen extractors were of the "Type 3" (flat notch) variety. These were marked "IP-W".

Extractor Plunger

The extractor plunger with the flat area machined on one side of the cone ("Type 2") was used by I-P throughout its brief production run.

Firing Pin

The "Type 1" firing pin was the only variant utilized by Irwin-Pedersen. Firing pins were marked "IP".

Operating Slide

Some very early production Irwin-Pedersen carbines may have used the "Type 2," E169 slide (with partially rounded rear), but the vast majority utilized the "Type 3," E279 slide. The slides were marked "IP".

Rear Sight

All Irwin-Pedersen carbines were originally equipped with the non-adjustable, flip rear sight. The left side of the base was stamped with a small script "s", and the right side of the base was stamped with either "RP" or "B-IP". Some of the leaves were unmarked, while others were marked with the same code letters stamped on the base.

Recoil Plate

The "Type 2" recoil plate was used for most of Irwin-Pedersen's production, but the improved "Type 3" came into use before the company ceased operation. The earliest type was marked "IP-W", but most of the later variety were marked "W:P".

Buttplate

Irwin-Pedersen buttplates were marked on the outside edge either "IP-PM" or "PM-IP".

View of buttplate markings on Irwin-Pedersen carbines. Most contractors did not stamp their buttplates with code markings.

Stock and Handguard

The first pattern, "I-cut," high wood stock was used by Irwin-Pedersen from the beginning of production. However, the oval slot, high wood stock apparently came into use just prior to the takeover by Saginaw. Irwin-Pedersen stocks were normally marked "IR-IP" in the sling recess, although some other code markings, such as "RMC", have been reported on supposedly original examples. The right side of the stock was stamped "IP" in a cartouche. This marking is very uncommon, and some carbines containing 100 percent Irwin-Pedersen marked parts may be found stamped with an "SG" cartouche in this location. This would seem to indicate that such carbines were completed and on hand when Saginaw assumed operation of the Grand Rapids plant. The carbines were then inspected under Saginaw's auspices and stamped with the firm's cartouche prior to delivery to the government.

Irwin-Pedersen handguards were all of the wide sighting groove type with two-rivets. These were normally marked "IR-IP" on the bottom edge.

Irwin-Pedersen carbines are very popular with collectors and many on the market today will exhibit varying degrees of restoration work. One common mistake made by some collectors when restoring an Irwin-Pedersen carbine is to replace every part with an "IP" marked part. While this might be proper for very early production, the bulk of the carbines assembled using Irwin-Pedersen receivers used a mixture of "IP" and "S'G'" parts, as will be subsequently discuss. Generally speaking, the earlier the serial number, the greater the preponderance of "IP"-marked parts. Irwin-Pedersen carbines in 3.2 million serial number range will typically contain only a comparative few "IP" marked parts.

The acquisition of an Irwin-Pedersen carbine is a great find for any collector. While these carbines are far

from common, they are not as rare as some collectors believe. They are certainly worth a premium over any other standard production carbine in comparable condition. The magnitude of the premium is primarily based on how badly a collector desires an example. A good rule of thumb is that an Irwin-Pedersen is probably worth from 50 percent to 75 percent over most other prime contractors. This, of course, assumes comparable condition and degree of originality. As is the case with all makers, a totally original unaltered Irwin-Pedersen in collectible condition is a great find.

SAGINAW STEERING GEAR DIVISION — GRAND RAPIDS PLANT
Table #12

Assigned Serial Number Blocks
3,212,520–3,250,019

Designated Code Letters
S'G'

Receiver

Receivers were marked:

SAGINAW S'G'
Serial #

In order to verbally differentiate the carbines made by the Saginaw plant with those made at Grand Rapids, the latter are normally referred to as "S prime — G prime" carbines.

As stated previously, some of the 3.2 million serial number range receivers were apparently used to assembly carbines before all of the receivers in the Irwin-Pedersen range (1,762,520–1,875,039) were utilized. Also, some receivers stamped with the Saginaw S'G' name have been noted with serial numbers from the Irwin-Pedersen block. Therefore, it would appear that Saginaw marked some of their newly made receivers with serial numbers from the I-P range.

Saginaw-Grand Rapids receivers were all of the integral spring housing type. The Irwin-Pedersen receivers were of the "round ear" variety, but this was changed around the 1,830,000 serial number range to the "square ear" shape by Saginaw. It appears that at least some, if not all, receivers in the 1,800,000 range were actually assembled *after* the 3,212,520–3,250,019 range.

Saginaw-Grand Rapids receiver. Note the prime (') marking after the letters S and G.

Barrel

Saginaw S'G' carbines were fitted primarily with Underwood early in production and primarily Underwood and Buffalo Arms later in production. Some Rock-Ola, Inland and Saginaw barrels have been reported but the extent of usage by these makers is not known.

Front Sight

The milled "Type 1" front sight was used on the S'G' carbines. Most were marked "N", "S'G'" or "N-S'G'".

Barrel Band

The Saginaw-Grand Rapids carbines were manufactured with the "Type 1" barrel band. Unmarked bands may be encountered, but the most commonly seen marking is "KV-S'G'".

Trigger Housing

All S'G' carbines utilized the milled trigger housing having square corners at rear. These trigger housings were marked "S'G'".

Trigger

The "Type 2" trigger was used by Saginaw-Grand Rapids. Many of the early carbines assembled by the firm used "IP" marked triggers, but later examples were

stamped "S'G'". Some unmarked triggers have also been reported.

Safety

The "Type 1" safety was carried over from the Irwin-Pedersen carbines and continued in use on the S'G' carbines early into the 3.2 million serial number block when the improved "Type 3" safety was used. All of the "Type 1" safeties used on the S'G' carbines are believed to have been carried over from Irwin-Pedersen production and marked either "IP-A" or "IP-W". The "Type 2" safeties were typically marked either "S'G'" or "E-S'G'".

Magazine Catch

The "short face," unserrated magazine catch was used in all Saginaw-Grand Rapids carbines. Markings included "S'G'", "E-S'G'" or "W-S'G'".

Sear

The no-hole "Type 1" sear was used exclusively on the S'G' carbines. Some were unmarked, but most were marked "SW-S'G'".

Sear Spring

The "Type 1" sear spring with straight ends was used on S'G' prime carbines until sometime in the 3.2 million serial number block when the "Type 2" sear spring with tapered ends was used.

Hammer

Interestingly, S'G' carbines may be found with three types of M1 carbine hammers. Early production versions were fitted with "Type 1" dog leg hammers made by Irwin-Pedersen (marked "IP"). Slightly later, the "Type 2" dog leg came into use by Saginaw (marked "S'G'"). The straight configuration "Type 3" hammer began to see use in the 3.2 million serial number block. These were marked in the same manner as the "Type 2" hammers.

Bolt

The Saginaw-Grand Rapids carbines used flat top bolts. A number of "IP"-marked bolts which on hand were used until the supply was exhausted. New bolts were marked "S'G'".

Extractor

All S'G' carbines used the later type, flat notch "Type 3" extractor. Irwin-Pedersen extractors, marked "IP-W" were used in the carbines assembled after Saginaw assumed operations. Later extractors of this type were marked "S'G'", "W/S'G'" or "I-S'G'".

Extractor Plunger

All extractor plungers were of the second variety.

Firing Pin

Saginaw utilized the "Type 1" firing pin for all of the carbines assembled by the company. As was the case with many other parts, the serviceable "IP" firing pins on hand were used first, and then the "S'G'"marked firing pins were utilized.

Operating Slide

The first variant operating slide used by Saginaw-Grand Rapids was the E279 ("Type 3") with the straight cut at the rear of the box. The company apparently used some E379 ("Type 4") slides before the end of production. Some of the slides used in early production Saginaw carbines were marked "IP", but many of the later E279 and all of the E379 slides were marked "S'G'".

Rear Sight

All Saginaw-Grand Rapids carbines were equipped with the non-adjustable flip sights. The left side of the base was normally marked "s" and the right side "RG-S'G'", B-S'G'" or "W-S'G'". The leaves were often marked in the same manner, although some were unmarked. No adjustable rear sights were used on any S'G' carbines.

Recoil Plate

It is believed that all Saginaw-Grand Rapids carbines were fitted with the improved "Type 3" recoil plates. Some of the early recoil plates were marked "WP" but most were stamped "W-S'G'".

Buttplate

Buttplates used by Saginaw-Grand Rapids were marked "PM-S'G'" on the outside edge.

Stock and Handguard

All known original carbines were fitted with oval slot, high wood stocks. These were stamped with a "S'G'" cartouche on the right side next to the "crossed cannons" Ordnance escutcheon. The sling swivel recess was marked "IR IP" or "RSG" though some without markings in this area have been reported. No low wood stocks are believed to have been used on S'G' carbines.

Handguards were of the shallow groove, two-rivet variety. Early versions were stamped "IR-IP" on the bottom edge while later handguards were marked "RSG" in this area.

Making definitive statements regarding which parts are or are not correct for a Saginaw-Grand Rapids carbine should be avoided. There are still many gaps in the available data regarding when certain parts and/or code markings changed. In most cases, the carbines assembled soon after Saginaw assumed operations at the failed Irwin-Pedersen plant will have many "IP"-marked parts. As Saginaw continued production, these parts were either used up or, if unsatisfactory, were scrapped.

Stock cartouche on carbines made by Saginaw Steering Gear Division plant in Grand Rapids, Michigan. The difference between the cartouche of the Grand Rapids plant and the main plant in Saginaw are the "prime" (') marks after each letter. Many carbines assembled with Irwin-Pedersen receivers will be found with this cartouche although most other parts may be marked "IP". The S'G' initials were vertically aligned rather than horizontally aligned as on other contractors.

Newly procured parts were marked "S'G'" since they were acquired under Saginaw's contract. However, a sprinkling of "IP"-marked parts may be found throughout Saginaw's production run at the Grand Rapids plant.

Some collectors consider the Saginaw S'G' carbines as an entirely different variation from those made at the main Saginaw plant, and this logic is hard to argue with. The carbines made at the Grand Rapids plant had more differences than similarities compared to those produced at the Saginaw plant. As can readily be seen, the S'G' and the Irwin-Pedersen carbines should probably be grouped together since it is difficult to discuss one without discussing the other. The fact that the majority of Irwin-Pedersen carbines had at least some S'G'-marked parts and all of the Saginaw Grand Rapids carbines had some "IP"-marked parts makes these two makers inexorably linked. While Irwin-Pedersen must certainly be classified as one of the ten carbine prime contractors, Saginaw-Grand Rapids carbines are most definitely a major variant.

All of the serial number ranges pertaining to changes in parts and markings for all of the contractors are almost always rough approximations based on the observation of specimens believed to remain in their original configuration. Making unqualified conclusions based on serial number range information contained in this, or any other book, must be tempered with the realization that these are approximations. Variances will invariably occur and should be expected. Saying "always" or "never" regarding any U.S. martial weapon is asking for trouble and doubly so with the M1 carbine. The fact that over six million of the weapon were manufactured in less than four years by ten prime contractors and scores of subcontractors makes wrapping up every variant in a nice neat package, regarding correct parts and markings, all but impossible. There was a lot of "behind the scenes" acquisition of parts by one contractor from another that have not been preserved in any official records existing today. Therefore, a part that may seem totally incorrect may actually be original to the piece. As stated previously, any carbine that appears untouched since it left the factory but which contains one or two small seemingly "incorrect" parts should be left alone. If a collector is overwhelmed with a desire to replace the part with a "properly" coded one, the removed part should be saved. If, in the future, new information regarding what is and is not correct should come to light, the originality of the piece can be restored. This practice would be a true restoration in every sense of the word.

➤ ➤ ➤ ➤ ➤ Commercial Production Carbines ◄ ◄ ◄ ◄ ◄

Although over six million carbines were manufactured during World War II, the demand for the weapon by civilian arms enthusiasts was surprisingly high following the war. Winchester fabricated a couple of sporting versions of the carbine for potential commercial production after the war but abandoned the project before any were manufactured. The company probably missed a good bet when it backed away from a sporting carbine, but the fact that the company had previously sold manufacturing rights to the government may have played a part in this decision.

The appeal of the M1 carbine to civilian shooters is easy to understand given the weapon's light weight, mild recoil and attractive lines. However, from the end of WWII until the early 1960s, "GI" carbines were rather hard to find. Very few had been sold by the government, and the relatively small number that were unofficially "liberated" from Uncle Sam's inventory did not even begin to meet the demand. There were few collectors of the weapon in those days for obvious reasons, but many ex-servicemen and arms fanciers desired an M1 carbine. There were mountains of surplus parts available but no receivers. It didn't take long for some enterprising firms to produce ersatz carbine receivers and assemble commercial copies of the weapon using the readily available "GI" parts. Most of the receivers were investment castings. These were not as strong as the government contract receivers, but most were adequate for their intended purposes. A number of firms in the late 1950s and early 1960s turned out commercial versions of the carbine using the newly made receivers and the surplus parts. Some of these were almost "dead ringers" for the WWII government issue carbine and others were unmistakably civilian weapons easily distinguishable from the GI carbines. The most commonly encountered commercial production carbines included:

Alpine
Bullseye
Federal Ordnance
Global Arms
Howa (Japan)
Iver Johnson
Millsville Ordnance
National Ordnance
Plainfield
Rock Island Armory, Inc. (commercial firm)
Santa Fe
Springfield Armory, Inc. (commercial firm)
Universal Firearms

Since some of these commercial carbines are close copies of the GI weapons and may contain a number of martially marked parts, some beginning collectors may acquire such arms with the impression that they are purchasing original government issue carbines. Carbines made by any firm other than the original ten prime contractors are not genuine GI carbines. While commercial copies may be great shooters, they have no value as martial collectibles. For more information on civilian manufactured carbines, one should consult the excellent book *War Baby Comes Home*.

➤ ➤ ➤ ➤ ➤ ➤ ➤ ➤ ➤ M1 Carbine Tables ◄ ◄ ◄ ◄ ◄ ◄ ◄ ◄ ◄

TABLE #1

Original Characteristics for Lightweight Semiautomatic Rifle as a possible replacement for the cal. 45 pistol and submachine gun.
Author's note: These were the War Department's original specifications for the "Light Rifle."

1. The War Department desires to secure a satisfactory developed lightweight semi-automatic shoulder rifle. The general requirements of such an arms are as follows:
   a. Weight — not to exceed 5 pounds, including sling.
   b. Range — effective up to 300 yards.
   c. To be carried by a sling or some comparable carrying device.
2. The rifle must be adapted to function with a cartridge of caliber .30, of the Winchester self-loading type with case similar to that of the Winchester Self-Loading Cartridge, Caliber .32. The weight of the bullet will be from 100 to 110 grains, and the cartridge case shall be of the rimless type. The powder charge should be sufficient to impart a muzzle velocity of approximately 2,000 feet per second to the bullet which shall be of the full gilding, metal-jacketed type.
3. Competitive tests will be held beginning February 1, 1941. No delays will be granted. The War Department may receive and subject to preliminary examination and test such rifles that may be submitted prior to competitive trials. Weapons must be submitted by February 1, 1941.
4. Persons having semi-automatic rifles which they desire to submit for competitive test should address the application for such tests to the Chief of Ordnance, U.S. Army, Washington, D.C.
5. For guidance in perfecting a design of this type, the following information in regard to its characteristics is furnished.
   a. The rifle must be simple, strong and compact. Weights should be well balanced and so placed that the essential strength is given to components requiring it. Ease of manufacture should be a guiding factor in preparing a design.
   b. The mechanism must be well protected from the entrance of sand, rain, or dirt, and should not be liable to derangements due to accidents, long wear and tear, exposure to dampness, sand, etc.
   c. Components of the mechanism should be the fewest possible, consistent with ease of manufacture and proper functioning of the weapon. Parts requiring constant cleaning or which may require replacement should be designed with a view to ease of dismounting by the use of not more than one small tool, preferably the cartridge.
   d. The rifle must be designed with a box magazine which may be fed from clips or chargers. Magazines with capacities of 5, 10, and 50 rounds should be supplied.
   e. The breech mechanism must be designed as to preclude the possibility of injury to the firer due to premature unlocking. The firing mechanism should be designed that the firing pin is controlled by the trigger and sear direct; that is, the bolt mechanism should move forward to the locking or firing position with the firing pin under the control of the trigger and sear mechanism, so that the cartridge is not ignited until the trigger is pulled to release the firing pin. The bolt, or block, should remain open when the last cartridge in the magazine has been fired. It should be possible to insert a new magazine with the bolt in either open or closed position.
   f. The trigger pull, measured at the middle point of the bow of the trigger, should not be less than 3 nor more than 5 pounds.
   g. An efficient safety or locking device must be provided, permitting the rifle to be carried cocked and with the cartridge in the chamber without danger. The rifle should remain cocked and ready for firing when the safety device is unlocked.
   h. The weight of the rifle, with sling, should not exceed 5 pounds.
   i. The rifle must be designed as to give good balance and be adapted for shoulder firing.
   j. The rifle is to be of self-loading type, capable of being fired either semi-automatically; that is, one shot for each pull of the trigger, or it shall be possible by the operation of a selector to fire the weapon fully automatically. Selector change shall be made only with a special tool.
   k. The accuracy of the rifle shall be reasonably comparable with that of the present service shoulder rifle at a range of 300 yards.
   l. The stock should be designed, if practicable, as to allow ventilation of the gun without charring or overheating.
   m. The rifle should be capable of being used as a hand-functioning arm in case the self-loading feature is disabled.
   n. The use of special high-grade material, high specialized heat treatment, or special-grade machine work or finish in general should not be required.
   o. The use of special oil or grease or any other material not readily obtainable in the field should not be necessary for the proper functioning of the piece.
   p. The use of special tools for adjustment or dismounting or assembling should be reduced to the minimum.
   q. Sights should be firmly fixed as to avoid the possibility of variation in position due to constant firing or rough handling.
   r. The rear sight should not be less than 2-1/2 and not more than 6 inches from the eye when using the weapon in prone position. It should be of a simple aperture type having two range adjustments only. Windage adjustment is not required.

TABLE #2
Winchester Repeating Arms Company
New Haven, Connecticut

Assigned Serial Number Blocks:
6–10
1,000,000–1,349,999
4,075,000–4,075,009
5,549,922–5,834,618
6,449,868–6,629,883
7,234,884–7,369,660

Number of carbines produced: 828,059
Percentage of total production: 13.5 percent
Types manufactured: M1, T3 and M2. (1,108 T3 and approximately 17,500 M2).
Receiver marking: Winchester
Barrels: Winchester manufactured their own barrels. Early versions marked "W.R.A." and the month and year of production. Later versions marked "W". Both types had the intertwined Winchester "WP" logo.
Assigned Code Letter: W
Number of components made: 15
Average cost to government: $37.75

TABLE #3
Inland Manufacturing
Division of General Motors
Dayton, Ohio

Assigned Serial Number Blocks:
1–5
11–30
31–99
XA3–XA50
100–699,999
700,000–940,000
940,001–999,999
2,912,520–3,152,519
3,152,520–3,212,519
4,879,526–5,549,821
6,219,689–6,449,867
6,664,884–7,234,883
7,369,661–8,069,660

Number of carbines produced: 2,632,097
Percentage of total production: 43 percent
Types manufactured: M1, M1A1, T3, M2
Receiver marking: INLAND DIV.
Barrels: Inland manufactured their own barrels. Markings were: "INLAND MFG. DIV. OF GENERAL MOTORS". Most Inland barrels were dated.
Assigned code letter: I
Number of components made: 5
Average cost to government: $39.60

TABLE #4
Underwood-Elliott-Fisher
Hartford, Connecticut

Assigned Serial Number Blocks:
1,350,000–1,499,999
2,352,520–2,912,519
4,010,000–4,074,999
6,099,689–6,199,688

Number of carbines produced: 545,616
Percentage of total production: 8.9 percent
Receiver marking: UNDERWOOD
Barrels: Underwood made their own barrels. Markings were "UNDERWOOD". Barrels were normally dated.
Assigned code letter: U
Number of components made: 7
Average cost to government: $47.82

TABLE #5
Rock-Ola Manufacturing Corporation
Chicago, Illinois

Assigned Serial Number Blocks:
1,662,250–1,762,519
4,532,100–4,632,099
6,071,189–6,099,688
6,199,684–6,219,688

Number of carbines produced: 228,500
Percentage of total production: 3.7 percent
Receiver markings: ROCK OLA
Barrels: Rock-Ola made their own barrels. Markings were "ROCK-OLA". Some were dated.
Assigned code letter: R
Number of components made: 11
Average cost to government: $58.00

TABLE #6
Quality Hardware Machine Corporation
Chicago, Illinois

Assigned Serial Number Blocks:
1,550,000–1,562,519
1,562,520–1,662,519
1,675,040–1,907,519
1,907,520–1,937,519
4,432,100–4,532,099*
4,632,100–4,879,525

Serial range of "UN-Quality" receivers made under subcontract by Union Switch & Signal

TABLE #6 continued on next page

TABLE #6 continued from page 281

Number of carbines produced: 359,666
Percentage of total production: 5.9 percent
Receiver marking: QUALITY HMC or UN-QUALITY
(subcontracted receivers)
Barrels: Mostly Rock-Ola, but other makers may be found
including Inland, Buffalo Arms, Underwood, IBM and
Winchester.
Assigned code letter: Q
Number of components made: 1 (receiver)
Average cost to government: $45.52

TABLE #7
National Postal Meter
Rochester, New York

Assigned Serial Number Blocks:
1,450,000–1,549,999
1,937,520–1,982,519
4,075,010–4,079,999
4,080,000–4,425,099
4,425,100–4,432,099

Number of carbine produced: 413,017
Percentage of total production: 6.8 percent
Receiver marking: NATIONAL POSTAL METER
Barrels: Primarily Underwood, but other makes, such as
Marlin, Rock-Ola, Buffalo Arms and IBM, may be
encountered.
Assigned code letter: N
Number of components made: 4
Average cost to government: $69.43

TABLE #8
Standard Products
Port Clinton, Ohio

Assigned Serial Number Block:
1,982,520–2,352,519

Number of carbines produced: 247,100
Percentage of total production: 4 percent
Receiver marking: STD. PRO.
Barrels: Mainly Underwood, but some Buffalo Arms or
Marlin barrels were used.
Assigned code letter: S
Number of components made: 4
Average cost to government: $53.79

TABLE #9
International Business Machines (IBM)
Poughkeepsie, New York

Assigned Serial Number Block:
3,651,520–4,009,999

Number of carbines produced: 346,500
Percentage of total production: 5.7 percent
Receiver marking: IBM
Barrels: IBM made their own barrels marked "IBM".
Some were dated.
Assigned code letter: B
Number of components made: 4
Average cost to government: $42.39

TABLE #10
Saginaw Steering Gear Division of General Motors
Saginaw, Michigan plant

Assigned Serial Number Blocks:
3,250,020–3,651,519
5,834,619–6,071,188

Number of carbines produced: 517,212 (Combined pro-
duction of Saginaw and Grand Rapids plants)
Percentage of total production: 8.5 percent (Combined
Saginaw and Grand Rapids plants)
Receiver marking: SAGINAW S.G.
Barrels: Saginaw made their own barrels marked
"SAGINAW S.G. DIV. GENERAL MOTORS"
Assigned code letters: SG
Number of components made: 15
Average cost to government: $38.00

TABLE #11
Irwin-Pedersen Arms Company
Grand Rapids, Michigan

Assigned Serial Number Block:
1,762,520–1,875,039

Number of carbines produced: Estimated at less than
4,000
Percentage of total production: Less than 1/10 of 1 percent
Receiver marking: IRWIN-PEDERSEN
Barrels: The vast majority used Underwood barrels,
although a few Rock-Ola barrels are reported to have been
used near the end of Irwin-Pedersen's limited production.
Assigned code letters: IP
Number of components made: Reportedly all but the barrel.
Average cost to government: N/A

TABLE #12
Saginaw Steering Gear
Division of General Motors
Grand Rapids, Michigan Plant

Assigned Serial Number Blocks:
1,762,520–1,875,039*
3,212,520–3,250,019

*Irwin-Pedersen serial number block assumed by Saginaw

Number of carbines produced: See Table #10
Percentage of total production: See Table #10
Receiver marking: SAGINAW S'G'
Barrels: Primarily Underwood, but some Buffalo Arms barrels were also used. Very limited numbers of Rock-Ola, Inland and Saginaw barrels also reportedly used.
Assigned code letters: S'G'
Number of components made: N/A
Average cost to government: N/A

TABLE #13
Estimated Deliveries of M1A1 Carbines
(By Month and Year)

	1942	1943	1944
January	N/A	9,800	N/A
February	N/A	N/A	N/A
March	N/A	9,400	N/A
April	N/A	12,900	N/A
May	N/A	17,100	10,000
June	N/A	3,300	10,000
July	N/A	6,300	2,700
August	N/A	4,700	5,000
September	N/A	1,800	6,000
October	N/A	1,200	10,000
November	3,200	N/A	13,200
December	3,000	N/A	13,200

Note: All M1A1 carbines were manufactured by Inland

TABLE #14
Inland "E" Series

These carbines represented various changes to the standard M1 (or M1A1) carbine developed by Inland to improve performance, ease of manufacture or to test prototype designs.

M1E2. The M1E2 had a receiver modified to accommodate an adjustment rear sight intended to replace the non-adjustable "L-type" flip sight. However, rather than modify the standard receiver, it was decided to develop an adjustable rear sight that could be used with the existing receiver. This eliminated any further consideration of the M1E2.

M1E3. Featuring a four link pantograph folding stock developed by the Murray Company, the M1E3 was intended to be an improvement over the M1A1 carbine. The M1E3 stock folded underneath the carbine rather than to the side as with the M1A1. And though, it offered a bit more strength than the M1A1, the M1E3 was not considered sufficiently better to warrant standardization.

M1E4. This was another attempt to develop a stronger folding stock. The M1E4 featured a sliding metal stock similar to that used on the M3 submachine gun. This variant was also not sufficiently improved over the M1A1 to warrant adoption.

M1E5. The M1E5 was developed to test the suitability of cast "Arma" steel for some carbine components. Testing revealed that Arma steel was not suitable for use in critical parts such as the receiver but could be used in some small parts.

M1E6. This weapon was fitted with a 24" barrel to test properties of various powder formulations for carbine cartridges. Most of this testing was done by the Frankford Arsenal.

M1E7. The M1E7 was developed as a potential lightweight sniping weapon. Telescope mounts similar to those used on the M1903A4 rifle were brazed on a carbine receiver. The standard Weaver M73B1 (330C) telescope was tested with the M1E7. Some functioning problems were experienced during testing. The carbine's lack of long range accuracy and power made a sniping rifle of this type a weapon of marginal value and the concept was not developed further. The M1E7 did serve as the basis for the T3 carbine used with infrared night vision sights. Some infrared scope mounting bars with a Weaver scope have been fitted to standard M1 carbines in an attempt to create a "rare sniper" carbine. Such assemblies of parts have no place in a carbine collection.

Note: Original "E" series carbines are quite rare and are very unlikely to be offered for sale.
Any purported originals of this type should be examined very closely.

Bibliography

Books

Brophy, Lt. Col. William S., *Arsenal of Freedom: The Springfield Armory, 1890–1948*, Andrew Mowbray Inc., Publishers, Lincoln, RI, 1991.

Canfield, Bruce N., *A Collector's Guide to the M1 Garand and M1 Carbine*, Andrew Mowbray Inc., Publishers, Lincoln, RI, 1988.

Canfield, Bruce N., *A Collector's Guide to Winchester in the Service*, Andrew Mowbray Inc., Publishers, Lincoln, RI, 1991.

Canfield, Bruce N., *U.S. Infantry Weapons of World War II*, Andrew Mowbray Inc., Publishers, Lincoln, RI, 1994.

Duff, Scott A., *The M1 Garand: World War I*, Scott A. Duff, Export, PA, 1993.

Duff, Scott A., *The M1 Garand: Post World War II*, Scott A. Duff, Export, PA, 1989.

Dunlap, Roy F., *Ordnance Went Up Front*, R&R Books, Livonia, NY, 1993.

Gebler, Robert F., *Philadelphia Ordnance District in World War II*, Westbrook Publishing Co., Philadelphia, PA, 1949.

George, Lt. Col. John, *Shots Fired in Anger*, NRA Publications, Washington, D.C., 1981.

Hardin, Albert N., Jr., *The American Bayonet 1776–1964*, Albert N. Hardin, Jr., Pennsauken, NJ, 1964.

Hatcher, Maj. Gen. Julian S., *The Book of the Garand*, Infantry Journal Press, Washington, D.C., 1948.

Johnson, George B. and Hans Bert Lockhoven, *International Armament — Vol. II*, International Small Arms Publishing Company, Cologne, Germany, 1965.

Johnson, Melvin M., Jr., *Rifles and Machine Guns*, William Morrow and Co., New York, NY, 1944.

Marshall, S.L.A., *Battlefield Analysis of Infantry Weapons (Korean War)*, Desert Publications, Cornville, AZ, 1984.

Mayo, Lida, *The Ordnance Department: On Beachhead and Battlefront*, Office of Chief of Military History, Washington, D.C., 1968.

Mueller, Chester, *The New York Ordnance District in World War II*, The New York Post Army Ordnance Association, New York, NY, 1947.

Perrett, Geoffrey, *There's a War to Be Won*, Random House, New York, NY, 1991.

Reisch, Craig, *U.S. M1 Carbines — Wartime Production*, North Cape Publications, Tustin, CA, 1994.

Pyle, Billy, *Ordnance Tools, Accessories & Appendages of the M1 Rifle*, G.S. Publications, Houston, TX, 1988.

Rosenquist, R.G., Col. Martin J. Sexton and Robert A. Buerlein, *Our Kind of War — Illustrated Saga of the U.S. Marine Raiders of World War II*, The American Historical Foundation, Richmond, VA, 1990.

Ruth, Larry L., *War Baby!*, Collector Grade Publications, Toronto, Canada, 1992.

Ruth, Larry L., *War Baby Comes Home*, Collector Grade Publications, Toronto, Canada, 1993.

Smith, Joseph E., *Small Arms of the World*, Stackpole Books, Harrisburg, PA, 1969.

Stevens, R. Blake, *U.S. Rifle M14 — From John Garand to the M21*, Collector Grade Publications, Inc., Toronto, Canada, 1991.

Thomson, Harry C. and Lida Mayo, *The Ordnance Department: Procurement and Supply*, Office of the Chief of Military History, Washington, D.C., 1960.

Wahl, Paul, *Carbine Handbook*, Arco Publishing Co., New York, NY, 1969.

Weeks, John, *Infantry Weapons, Ballentine's Illustrated History of the Violent Century*, Book No. 25, Ballentine Books, New York, NY, 1971.

Articles

Canfield, Bruce N., "The M1 Garand Sniper Rifles," *Man at Arms*, Volume 18, Number 6, November/December 1996.

Canfield, Bruce N, "The Army's Light Rifle," *American Rifleman*, February 1996.

Canfield, Bruce N., "The Unknown M1 Garand," *American Rifleman*, January 1994.

Canfield, Bruce N., "Maybe It's Not Just a Rebuild," *Garand Collectors Association Newsletter*, Volume 10, Number 2, Spring, 1996.

Pyle, Billy, "The Gas Trap M1 Rifles," *Guns Illustrated — 1997*, 1997.

Seijas, Robert, "Cornbinder!," *Garand Collectors Association Newsletter*, Volume 1, Number 1, Winter, 1986.

Seijas, Robert, "IHC Stock Numbers — A Theory," *Garand Collectors Association Newsletter*, Volume 6, Number 4, 1992.

Government Technical Manuals, Field Manuals and Technical Bulletins

FM 23-7, "U.S. Carbine, Caliber .30, M1 and M1A1," War Department, 1944.

FM 2307 and AFM 50-4, "Carbine, Caliber .30, M1, M1A1, M2 and M3," Departments of the Army and the Air Force, 1952.

FM 23-5, "U.S. Rifle, Caliber .30, M1," War Department, 1940.

TM 9-1276 and TO 39A-5AD-2, "Cal. .30 Carbines M1, M1A1, M2, and M3," Department of the Army and the Air Force, February 1953.

Conference Course Training Bulletin No. MTP3-49, "Carbine, Cal. .30 M1, Mechanical Training," December 15, 1942.

TB 9-1276-1, "Carbines, Cal. .30, M1 and M1A1, Misconception of Certain Features," War Department Technical Bulletin, January 15, 1945.

TM 9-2200, "Small Arms Material and Associated Equipment," Department of the Army, April 1949.

TM 9-1005-222-12, "Operator and Organizational Maintenance Manual Including Repair Parts and Special Tools List for Rifle, Caliber .30 M1, Rifle Caliber .30, M1C (Sniper's) and Rifle, Caliber .30, M1D (Sniper's)," Department of the Army Technical Manual, 1969.

Official Government Publications, Documents, Reports, Memos, etc.

"The New Semiautomatic Rifle — Development and Present Status of the U.S. Rifle, Cal. .30, M1," Army Ordnance, Vol. XIX, No. 111, Nov.–Dec. 1938.

Report on... "the status of pamphlets, drawings, etc. of the new Army rifle, caliber .30, M1," Army Ordnance, Vol. XIX, No. 113, March/April 1939.

"Report on manufacturing and distribution of M1 rifle," Army Ordnance, Vol. XX, No. 119, March/April 1940.

"Report on Infantry Board Tests of M1 rifle," Army Ordnance, Vol. XX, No. 120, May/June 1940.

"The Military Armament Program," Army Ordnance, July/August 1940.

"The Garand Rifle," Army Ordnance, Vol. XXI, No. 121, July/August 1940.

"Ordnance Production Contracts — Fiscal Year 1940," Army Ordnance, Vol. XXI, No. 122, September/October 1940.

"Report on M1 Rifle Production" by Winchester Repeating Arms Company, Army Ordnance, Vol. XXI, No. 125, March/April 1941.

"The Soldier and the M1 Rifle" by Lt. Howard L. Bagley, Army Ordnance, September/October 1942.

Ordnance Department, Project Supporting Paper Relating to Bayonets, Knives and Scabbards, 1917 — August 1945, Declassified September 27, 1958.

Ordnance Department Project Supporting Paper Relating to Grenade Launchers, 1917 — August 1945, dated January 15, 1947.

MIL-R-3285, dated September 9, 1950. Military Specifications for Rifles, U.S. Caliber .30, M1 and M1C.

Ordnance Department document dated August 7, 1957, regarding testing of rifle telescopes.

Various Springfield Armory Engineering Services documents dated September 7, 1945, pertaining to .30 Caliber carbines, M1, M1A1, M2 regarding:

Gas system modifications

Developments facilitating and reducing manufacturing costs for front sight and trigger housing

Functioning reliability tests using ammunition of varied powder characteristics

Field Service Carbine tools

Garand "Model B" and "Model D" Automatic and Semiautomatic carbines

Important design improvements for M1 and M1A1 carbines including operating slide, adjustable rear sight, ejector, grip (M1A1), Handguard assembly, hammer, hammer spring. Safety, Carbine Caliber .30 T4E1, Folding pantograph stock, T23 flash hider, M8 grenade launcher, magazine chargers, firing pin, stock, magazine follower, combination front sight and compensator and selective fire conversion unit

Ordnance Corps Expenditure Order Number 1868-1, dated December 10, 1951, signed by Col. James L. Guion regarding conversion of M1 rifles into M1D and M1C sniper rifles.

Ordnance Corps Memorandum dated September 13, 1951, regarding acquisition of commercial Lyman telescopes.

Chief of Ordnance Memorandum dated January 6, 1953. Subject: New Flash Hider for U.S. Rifle Cal. .30, M1C and M1D.

Ordnance Corps Memorandum dated June 11, 1954. Subject: Parkerizing of M1 Rifle Parts.

Chief of Ordnance Memorandum dated August 8, 1945. Subject: Pad, Cheek, D7312621, for Rifle, Cal. .30, M1C.

Ordnance Department Memorandum dated February 12, 1951. Subject: Sniper's Rifles, M1C and M1D Production.

Ordnance Department Memorandum dated February 21, 1951. Subject: Engineering Change Orders Pertaining to Rifle, U.S., Cal. .30, M1D.

Ordnance Corps Memorandum dated February 16, 1953. Subject: Comparison of U.S. Rifles, Cal. .30, M1C and M1D.

Springfield Armory Expenditure Order Number 1916, dated April 12, 1951, regarding conversion of M1 Rifles into M1D Rifles.

U.S. Army Air Forces, Illustrated Catalog — Clothing, Parachutes, Equipment and Supplies, dated September 30, 1943.

Chief of Ordnance Memorandum dated September 28, 1952, regarding allocation of M1C and M1D sniper rifles.

Letter dated March 5, 1941, from Commandant, U.S. Marine Corps to Chief of Ordnance regarding USMC adoption of M1 rifle.

Index

A

B

M

N

O

T

U

V

W

X

ABOUT THE AUTHOR

The author, Bruce N. Canfield, is an internationally recognized authority on post-Civil War U.S. military weapons. As an advanced collector of U.S. military weapons, he is a contributing editor for two of the most respected arms magazines in the country, *Man at Arms* and *American Rifleman,* and is a member of the *Man at Arms'* "Panel of Experts" and the *American Rifleman's* "Dope Bag" column. In addition, he has published over fifty articles in several national magazines including, *American Rifleman, Man at Arms*, and *The Gun Report*. He has acted as a consultant for the Arts & Entertainment (A&E) television network's highly acclaimed program, *Story of the Gun*, and he is a member of the Garand Collectors Association Board of Directors and a former Technical Advisor to the M1 Carbine Collectors Association.

In addition to contributing to numerous books by other authors, Bruce Canfield has published six books of his own on U.S. military weaponry: *A Collector's Guide to the M1 Garand and M1 Carbine, A Collector's Guide to the '03 Springfield, A Collector's Guide to Winchester in the Service, A Collector's Guide to U.S. Combat Shotguns, U.S. Infantry Weapons of World War II*, and *Bruce N. Canfield's Complete Guide to the M1 Garand and M1 Carbine*. He is currently busy working on a new book, due to be published in 1999, entitled *U.S. Infantry Weapons of World War I*.

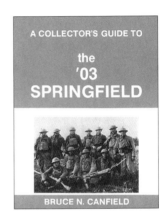
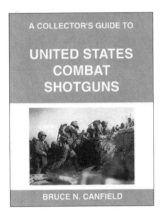
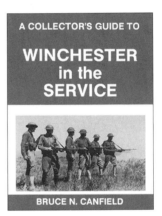